PAGE
50
ON THE
ROAD

YOUR COMPLETE DESTINATION GUIDE
In-depth reviews, detailed listings
and insider tips

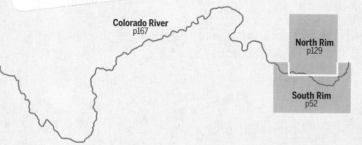

Colorado River
p167

North Rim
p129

South Rim
p52

PAGE
214
SURVIVAL
GUIDE

VITAL PRACTICAL INFORMATION TO
HELP YOU HAVE A SMOOTH TRIP

THIS EDITION WRITTEN AND RESEARCHED BY

Wendy Yanagihara & Jennifer Denniston

welcome to the Grand Canyon

Sublime Vistas

Although the Grand Canyon is infinitely more than the sum of its iconic views, they *are* truly sublime. We've all seen images of the canyon in print and on-screen, but there is nothing like arriving at the rim and taking it all in – the immensity, the depth, the atmosphere and the light. Views from both rims are equally beautiful, although South Rim overlooks are probably more dramatic and definitely greater in number. While there are far fewer overlooks on the North Rim, one of the most iconic Grand Canyon views is from the north side of the canyon; another is from the highest point on either rim. Wherever the overlook, it's worth finding a spot in the early morning or late afternoon – not necessarily sunrise or sunset – to sit quietly and watch the light and shadow work their magic on the canyon features.

Hiking an Inverted Mountain

Hiking into the canyon is one of the highlights of a Grand Canyon visit. Even a short roam below the rim serves up stunning views at nearly every turn of the trail, showing glimpses now and then of the Colorado River, which carved the curvaceous gorge. Descend deeper and get a closer look at the canyon's rock layers, a beautiful and mind-boggling record of geologic time on a seemingly incomprehensible scale. On the

The Grand Canyon warrants any hyperbolic language it inspires. Its vastness and staggering beauty are amazing, astounding and awesome – and its many-layered splendor isn't mere metaphor.

(left) The Grand Canyon from Toroweap (p138)
(below) An overnight hiker looks out over the canyon

more recent human timeline, it's fascinating to think that one's footfalls follow the paths originally established by ancient Native Americans who lived in and near the canyon. Hiking into the gorge presents the rare chance to climb an inverted mountain, making every return trip an ascent – always a good thing to remember as you traipse down a trail.

Rocks, Tracks & Pictographs

Even non-geologists will get to wondering about the hows and whys of the Grand Canyon while staring at its fins, its buttes and the multicolored rock layers of the canyon walls. Luckily for laypeople with burning questions, the South Rim has answers, primarily at Yavapai Geology Museum, the Trail of Time installation and geology talks given by the park's knowledgeable rangers. If rock talk doesn't inspire you, daily ranger-led fossil walks explore marine fossils embedded in stone just off the busy Rim Trail. For a more DIY experience, hike down the Hermit Trail to look for fossilized marine creatures, animal tracks and ferns. And for the intriguing human touch on canyon walls, you can find pictographs along the Bright Angel Trail.

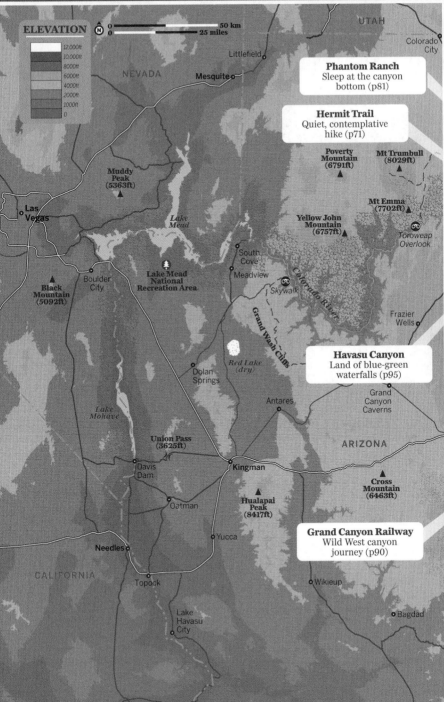

ELEVATION

12,000ft
10,000ft
8000ft
6000ft
4000ft
2000ft
1000ft
0

0 — 50 km
0 — 25 miles

Phantom Ranch
Sleep at the canyon
bottom (p81)

Hermit Trail
Quiet, contemplative
hike (p71)

Havasu Canyon
Land of blue-green
waterfalls (p95)

Grand Canyon Railway
Wild West canyon
journey (p90)

UTAH
Colorado City
Littlefield
NEVADA
Mesquite
Muddy Peak (5363ft)
Poverty Mountain (6791ft)
Mt Trumbull (8029ft)
Mt Emma (7702ft)
Toroweap Overlook
Yellow John Mountain (6757ft)
Las Vegas
Lake Mead
South Cove
Meadview
Skywalk
Colorado River
Frazier Wells
Black Mountain (5092ft)
Boulder City
Lake Mead National Recreation Area
Grand Wash Cliffs
Red Lake (dry)
Grand Canyon Caverns
Dolan Springs
Antares
Lake Mohave
ARIZONA
Union Pass (3625ft)
Davis Dam
Kingman
Cross Mountain (6463ft)
Oatman
Hualapai Peak (8417ft)
Yucca
Needles
Wikieup
CALIFORNIA
Topock
Lake Havasu City
Bagdad

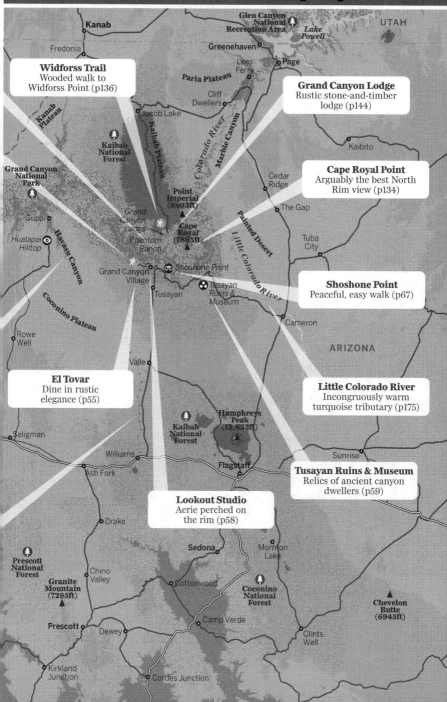

Widforss Trail
Wooded walk to
Widforss Point (p136)

Grand Canyon Lodge
Rustic stone-and-timber
lodge (p144)

Cape Royal Point
Arguably the best North
Rim view (p134)

Shoshone Point
Peaceful, easy walk (p67)

Little Colorado River
Incongruously warm
turquoise tributary (p175)

El Tovar
Dine in rustic
elegance (p55)

Tusayan Ruins & Museum
Relics of ancient canyon
dwellers (p59)

Lookout Studio
Aerie perched on
the rim (p58)

Kanab
Fredonia
Glen Canyon National Recreation Area
Lake Powell
UTAH
Greenehaven
Lees Ferry
Page
Paria Plateau
Cliff Dwellers
Jacob Lake
Kaibab National Forest
Kanab Plateau
Kaibab Plateau
Colorado River
Marble Canyon
Kaibito
Grand Canyon National Park
Cedar Ridge
The Gap
Point Imperial (8803ft)
Grand Canyon Lodge
Cape Royal (7865ft)
Painted Desert
Tuba City
Supai
Phantom Ranch
Little Colorado River
Havasu Canyon
Hualapai Hilltop
Grand Canyon Village
Shoshone Point
Tusayan
Tusayan Ruins & Museum
Cameron
Coconino Plateau
ARIZONA
Rowe Well
Valle
Seligman
Kaibab National Forest
Humphreys Peak (12,633ft)
Sunrise
Williams
Flagstaff
Ash Fork
Drake
Sedona
Mormon Lake
Prescott National Forest
Granite Mountain (7295ft)
Chino Valley
Cottonwood
Coconino National Forest
Chevelon Butte (6945ft)
Prescott
Dewey
Camp Verde
Clints Well
Kirkland Junction
Cordes Junction

20 TOP EXPERIENCES

South Rim Overlooks

1 The canyon doesn't have a photographic bad side, but it has to be said that the views from the South Rim (p59) are stunners. Each has its individual beauty, with some unique angle that sets it apart from the rest – a dizzyingly sheer drop, a view of river rapids or a felicitous arrangement of jagged temples and buttes. Sunrises and sunsets are particularly sublime, with the changing light creating depth and painting the features in unbelievably rich hues of vermilion and purple.

Mather Point (p64)

DAN BARBA/PHOTO LIBRARY ©

Hiking Rim to Rim

2 To really comprehend the scale of the Grand Canyon, there's no better way than hiking rim to rim. You can link a number of trails, but a good option is the classic corridor route, descending the North Kaibab (p141) and ascending the Bright Angel (p73). Distinct passage through all of the canyon's life zones means constant change in scenery and terrain. After a night at the bottom of the canyon, hikers cross the river and ascend the Bright Angel to the South Rim. A popular alternative is to descend the South Kaibab and ascend the North Kaibab (p72). Shoshone Point (p67)

ROBERTO GEROMETTA/LONELY PLANET IMAGES ©

Grand Canyon Lodge

3 Perched on the canyon rim, this stone-and-timber granddaddy of national-park lodges (p144) promises a high-country retreat like nothing else in the Grand Canyon. Completed in 1928, the original structure burned to the ground in 1932. It was rebuilt in 1937, and in the early days staff greeted guests with a welcome song and sang farewell as they left. Today, folks who find their way here discover that same sense of camaraderie, and it's easy to while away the days at a North Rim pace.

Havasu Canyon

4 The people of the blue-green waters, as the Havasupai call themselves, take their name from the otherworldly turquoise-colored waterfalls and creek that run through the canyon. Due to limestone deposits on the creekbed, the water appears sky-blue, a gorgeous contrast to the deep red of the canyon floor and the two sandstone spires watching over the Havasupai. The only ways into and out of Havasu Canyon (p94) are by foot, horse or helicopter, but those that make the trek are richly rewarded by the magic of this place, epitomized by spots such as Havasu Falls (below).

Widforss Trail

5 This gentle North Rim hike rises and dips along the plateau, veering towards a side canyon and meandering 5 miles to Widforss Point (p136). It's a mild, gentle amble, with canyon views whispering rather than screaming from the edges, plenty of shade, and room for children to play among wildflowers. A picnic table at the end makes a lovely spot for lunch, and at the overlook you can sit on a stone jutting over the Grand Canyon, dangling your feet above the rocky outcrop below, listening to the silence.

Phantom Ranch

6 After descending to the bottom of the canyon, it's a delight to ramble down a flat trail shaded by towering cottonwoods with leaves fluttering in the breeze. As the trail winds past a Puebloan kiva, a mule corral and a few scattered cabins, it leads to the Phantom Ranch canteen (p81), where you can relax with a cold lemonade, your feet up and your pack off. This lovely stone lodge, designed by Mary Colter and built in 1922, continues to be the only developed facility in the inner canyon.

Hermit Trail

8 The name seems apropos, even today, as you are unlikely to encounter many hikers and backpackers on the Hermit Trail (p71). It feels beautifully remote, and through the solitude you can feel a connection to Louis 'The Hermit' Boucher as you descend the cobblestones lining the trail. Day hikers can connect with the Dripping Springs Trail to reach a green little oasis where water seeps down from a small overhang festooned with maidenhair fern; here you can imagine the quiet life of the prospector who made the spot his home.

Cape Royal Point

7 A pleasant paved drive through woods with teasing canyon views leads to the trailhead for this most spectacular of North Rim overlooks. It's an easy 4-mile walk to Cape Royal Point (p134), along a paved trail with signs pointing out facts about the flora and fauna of the area. The walk is suitable for folks of all ages and capabilities. Once at the point, the expansive view includes the Colorado River below, Flagstaff's San Francisco Peaks in the distance and stunning canyon landmarks in both directions.

Grand Canyon Railway

9 Things start out with a bang at the Wild West shootout in Williams, and then the 'sheriff' boards the train to make sure everything's in its place. Is it hokey? Maybe a little. Interesting and informative? Sure. Fun? Absolutely. Riding the rails to the South Rim (see the boxed text p226) takes a bit longer than if you were to drive, but you leave traffic behind to watch the landscape rolling by and cattle and mule deer bounding away from the tracks, and then disembark relaxed and ready to explore the canyon.

Rafting the Colorado River

10 Considered the trip of a lifetime by many river enthusiasts, rafting the Colorado (p167) is a wild ride down a storied river, through burly rapids, past a stratified record of geologic time and up secretive side canyons – all within the wilderness at the bottom of the Big Ditch. Though riding the river is the initial attraction, the profound appeals of the trip reveal themselves each day and night in the quiet stretches on smooth water, the musicality of ripples and birdsong and the vast solitude of this awesome place.

Lookout Studio

11 Perched on the South Rim, Lookout Studio (p58) has stone walls that harmonize so well with their environment that a squint could turn it into a rocky outcropping. Another of Mary Colter's masterful designs, this little structure was originally a photo studio but is now a gift shop and one of the historic buildings at Grand Canyon Village. Browse the wares and have a peek from the balcony, or wander down to the terraces below and admire the billion-dollar view.

EDDIE BRADY/LONELY PLANET IMAGES ©

HOLGER LEUE/LONELY PLANET IMAGES ©

Mule Rides

12 There's something classically Grand Canyon about riding a mule into the canyon, the rhythmic lope and powdery clop of hooves picking their way down the trail. While less strenuous than hiking the canyon, mule rides (p37) are a physically active experience that require a sense of adventure. Ranging from short rimside rides on the South Rim to day trips from the North Rim and rim-to-river descents for overnights at Phantom Ranch, mule riders travel in style, like early canyon tourists.

Grandview Trail

13 Not as fancifully named as the Bright Angel, the Grandview (p70) nonetheless speaks for itself. Developed by prospector Pete Berry, whose crumbling stone cabin still sits on Horseshoe Mesa, this rugged trail is a South Rim favorite with fantastic views. The steep trail descends quickly, with switchbacks of cobblestone. After crossing a couple of narrow saddles to Horseshoe Mesa, you'll find open mine shafts speaking silently of the canyon's past. Pace yourself on the hike out, taking time to take in the grand views.

Flagstaff

14 Flagstaff (p98) is (give or take): one part granola, one part wild game, one part craft brew, one part espresso, one part mountain man, one part medicine woman. But unscientific formulas aside, the sum of Flagstaff is fun stuff. It's a university town with a Route 66 flavor, where railway history contributes as much to the town's zeitgeist as its haunted hotels and its New Year's pinecone drop. Social pursuits range from mountain biking and Nordic skiing to cocktail sipping and tapas tasting. Come for the canyon and stay for Flag.

Tusayan Ruins & Museum

15 Abandoned cliff dwellings, granaries caching sustenance in sheer cliff walls, kivas for long-forgotten rituals – all elicit more questions than explanations about the cultures who left these remnants behind. From afar, these ancient people might seem more abstract concept than relatable groups of individuals with common beliefs and the drive to survive. The Tusayan Ruins and Museum (p59) offer a bit of connective tissue, in the form of intricately handwrought split-twig figurines, perhaps meant to summon successful hunts.

Dinner at El Tovar

16 No one goes to the Grand Canyon for an epicurean adventure, but the finest dining on the South Rim is more than fine. Part of the El Tovar (p83) dinner experience is sitting in this grande dame on the rim, absorbing a little of its bygone glamour and rustic architectural elegance. Partaking of a meal and a glass of wine in these environs feels especially decadent after you've lugged a 40lb pack out of the canyon or if you've just spent the afternoon shooting shadows of clouds over canyon temples.

Kaibab National Forest

17 Spreading for miles across the Kaibab Plateau and towering over the vast desert expanses of the seemingly endless Arizona Strip, the Kaibab National Forest (North Rim; p147) hugs the Grand Canyon to the north and offers the traveler gentle respite from searing summer heat. Lush meadows are home to deer and buffalo, hiking trails wind through the aspen and ponderosa pine forests, and remote canyon overlooks lure curious travelers. You can camp anywhere for free, but after the first major snowfall the 44-mile road through the Kaibab to the North Rim closes.

The Watchtower

18 At the very eastern edge of the South Rim, the Watchtower (p59) could almost pass as a Native American ruin, but it's an amalgamation of Mary Colter's imagination and myriad Native American elements. This circular tower encases a spiral stairway that winds five stories to the top floor, with walls featuring a Hopi mural and graphic symbols from various Native American tribes. From its many windows on all sides, you can see rim, river and sky, all seemingly endless from this advantageous viewpoint.

RADIUS IMAGES/CORBIS ©

Best Friends Animal Sanctuary

19 Angel Canyon, where dozens of old Westerns were shot, is now home to the US' biggest no-kill animal shelter (p151). Nestled in over 30,000 acres of spectacular red-rock landscape sit seven idyllic sanctuaries for lost, sick and abandoned animals rescued from natural and human disasters around the world. At any given time, about 1700 animals call this canyon home. Free tours are given daily and volunteers are always welcome.

STEPHEN STUDD/GETTY IMAGES ©

Shoshone Point

20 For a leisurely walk away from the South Rim circus, hiking through the ponderosa to Shoshone Point (p67) does the trick. The soundtrack to this mostly flat 1-mile hike is that of pine needles crunching underfoot and birdsong trilling overhead, lacy shadows providing cover from the sun. Upon reaching the rim, you'll trace the edge for a short while before seeing the finger on which a monolith stands sentry. Shoshone Point, or the picnic area at the end of the trail, is perfect for a peaceful lunch.

need to know

Entrance Fees

» $25 per car, $12 per person on foot, bicycle or motorcycle; entrance fee valid at both rims for a total of seven days

Number of Visitors

» 4.5 million (2010)

When to Go

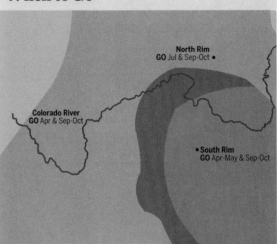

North Rim
GO Jul & Sep-Oct ●

Colorado River
GO Apr & Sep-Oct

● **South Rim**
GO Apr-May & Sep-Oct

Warm to Hot Summers, Mild Winters
Warm to Hot Summers, Cold Winters
Dry Climate
Desert, Dry Climate

High Season
(May–Oct)

» The peak of summer is the hottest and busiest season.

» Accommodations in gateway towns up significantly and sell out further in advance.

Shoulder
(Mar–Apr & Sep–Oct)

» Less crowds mean a more relaxed experience.

» Spring and fall bring cooler temps and wild colors.

» Note: the North Rim opens mid-May and closes mid-October.

Low Season
(Nov–Feb)

» The stream of South Rim visitors slows to a trickle.

» Fresh snowfalls promise dramatic, snow-frosted temples, pyramids and buttes.

» North Rim is closed and inaccessible by vehicle.

Your Daily Budget

Budget less than
$50

» Camping inside and outside the park $10-25

» Self-caterers can get groceries and cheap eats in the park, but gateway cities have better selection and prices

» South Rim shuttle, day hikes and spectacular scenery: free

Midrange
$50-150

» Two-star motel or hotel double $90-125

» Two can eat well at local cafes for $25

Top end over
$150

» B&Bs and three-star hotels $150+

» Sample the best of local culinary hot spots for $50+

Year Founded

» 1908 as a national monument; in 1919 it became the country's 17th national park

Money

» Sole ATM in the park is at Market Plaza on the South Rim; credit/debit cards accepted everywhere

Cell Phones

» Cell-phone coverage available around Grand Canyon Village on the South Rim but unavailable elsewhere in the park

Driving

» Paved roads on both rims; free shuttle buses minimize vehicle traffic at the South Rim, running along three routes with stops at several parking lots

Websites

» **National Park Service** (www.nps.gov/grca) Current weather conditions, events and planning tips.

» **Lonely Planet** (www.lonelyplanet.com) Destination information, hotel bookings, traveler forums and more.

» **Xanterra Parks & Resorts** (www.grandcanyonlodges.com) South Rim concessionaire, booking accommodations, mule trips and Grand Canyon Railway tickets.

» **Grand Canyon Association** (www.grandcanyon.org) Best online bookstore for the park; includes other useful links.

Exchange Rates

Australia	A$1	$1.07
Canada	C$1	$1.02
China	Y10	$1.57
Euro zone	€1	$1.43
Japan	¥100	$1.30
Mexico	MXN10	$0.81
New Zealand	NZ$1	$0.85
UK	£1	$1.62

For current exchange rates see www.xe.com.

Important Numbers

For long-distance and toll-free calls, dial 1 followed by three-digit area code and seven-digit local number.

Grand Canyon National Park	✆928-638-7888
North Rim Visitor Center	✆928-638-7864
Grand Canyon North Rim	✆928-638-2612
Grand Canyon South Rim	✆928-638-2631
Xanterra	✆888-297-2757

Opening Dates

» **South Rim**
Open year-round, 24 hours a day.

» **North Rim**
All lodging, facilities and visitor services are closed between mid-October and mid-May. Winter visitors may only enter the park on foot, skis or snowshoes. Backcountry permits must be obtained for winter camping.

Park Policies & Regulations

» Bicycles are allowed only on roads open to other vehicles, and on the Greenway Trail on the South Rim.

» This is extremely dry country, and the slightest spark may cause a devastating wildfire. Open fires are prohibited in the park except at established campgrounds on the rim.

» Dogs are permitted on developed rim trails and in the campgrounds but must be leashed at all times. Pets are not allowed in park lodges or below the rim, except for certified service dogs (only after checking in at the Backcountry Information Center).

» Weapons of any kind, including guns and bows, are prohibited on park grounds.

» It's illegal to feed wildlife in the park, including jump-in-your-lap squirrels and forward ravens. This is not only for your safety (squirrels can carry bubonic plague!), but also for the well-being of the animals.

if you like...

Hiking

You've picked a world-class venue for hiking. Not only is the inverted-mountain dynamic of the Grand Canyon its own fascinating beast, but it also offers something for everyone – from forested rimside walks to challenging backcountry expeditions in the gorge's desert climate.

South Rim Even a short hike down any South Rim trail will magnify the canyon's scale, and it also allows for a more intimate experience of it – discover ancient pictographs, fossilized lizard tracks and the differing textures, angles and colors of canyon strata (p65)

North Rim Fewer visitors means more peace among the pines and beauteous trails of the higher-altitude North Rim. Those in the know come to this side of the canyon for contemplative, scenic walks along the rim and rugged hikes below (p135)

Sedona Surrounded by a truly spectacular red-rock landscape, the hiking here feels almost mystical...or maybe that's the effect of all of Sedona's vortexes (p110)

Dramatic Views

If you're not here to hike, then you've come for canyon views. You can't really go wrong anywhere, but early-morning and late-afternoon light add depth, color, dimension and drama to the existing majesty.

Moran Point Named for the painter whose depiction helped secure national-park status; one of the South Rim's most sublime sunrises (p65)

Mohave Point Another great South Rim viewpoint for sunrise or sunset, where you can also see the river and hear Hermit Rapid (p63)

Bright Angel Point A brief walk along a fin on the North Rim brings you to a point surrounded by vast views (p136)

Cape Royal Point Arguably the best view of the canyon on the North Rim, where you can look down onto the Colorado River below (p134)

Toroweap If you can endure the long, rough road and the belly-crawl to the sheer cliff, you'll be rewarded with iconic views of river and canyon (boxed text p138)

Native American Culture

Both the largest Native American reservation and the most remote (the Navajo and Havasupai, respectively) exist within and around the Grand Canyon. The rich culture of various local tribes is alive and well, with a visible presence in the region.

Hopi Reservation One of the oldest continuously occupied villages on the entire continent sits on a sacred mesa on the Hopi Reservation, one of the most private Native American communities in the country (boxed text p163)

Navajo Reservation The largest reservation in the US contains some of the most dramatic natural landscapes in the region (boxed text p163)

Havasupai Reservation Has the most remote village in the continental US, but more distinctive for being home to the ethereal blue-green waters after which the people are named. You can hike, ride a horse or helicopter down to the village of Supai (p94)

RALPH HOPKINS/LONELY PLANET IMAGES ©

» Toroweap (p138)

Scenic Drives

Driving is by far the easiest way to get around the region, which is generous with its beauty. The ever-changing landscape goes from bizarre red-rock formations to ponderosa forest to high desert – and the grandest canyon.

North Rim Driving to the North Rim is a treat unto itself, first through the tall ponderosa of Kaibab National Forest, then following the contours of alpine meadows and aspen groves (p129)

Desert View Drive Coming in through the east entrance to drive along the South Rim introduces the canyon gradually and elegantly (p64)

Oak Creek Canyon Dropping from Flagstaff to Sedona through Oak Creek Canyon is an ongoing revelation, ending with surreal Sedona (p110)

Route 66 Though the landscape here can't compare to its neighboring natural wonders, these backroads evoke nostalgia in spades, with lots of little delights along the way (boxed text p99)

Water

Especially precious in the dry climate of the Southwest, the waterways of the Grand Canyon region offer some of the most unique experiences in the world – rafting the Colorado River being the most obvious but not the only one.

Rafting the Colorado The trip of a lifetime can occasionally happen last-minute if someone cancels their spot (p167)

Hualapai River Runners Motorized day trips on the Colorado are a great way to get on the river (p168)

Colorado River Discovery Motorized or row trips on the smooth water of the Colorado, from Glen Canyon Dam to Lees Ferry (p161)

Kayak Lake Powell Explore the peaceful hidden side canyons of Lake Powell using your own paddle power (p161)

Havasu Canyon Secreted within the Havasupai Reservation, these famous blue-green waterfalls are a 10-mile hike into the most remote village in the continental US (p94)

Art

As you'd expect in a place of great beauty, artists find inspiration here and often take root. Grand Canyon National Park hosts several artistic celebrations and residencies, as do nearby communities like Sedona and Flagstaff.

Kolb Studio The adventurous brothers Kolb established a photo studio on the rim, taking their cameras on river expeditions and exploring the canyon with obsessive zeal (p56)

Flagstaff First Friday ArtWalk Lively First Fridays throughout the year, with live music, open galleries and extended shop hours in Flagstaff's historic downtown (p98)

Grand Canyon Music Festival Live music of varying genres livens up the cultural scene at the South Rim (p24)

Grand Canyon Celebration of Art Includes a plein-air painting festival with a timed 'quick draw' event (p24)

Sedona International Film Festival Celebrate the moving picture in picture-perfect red-rock country (p23)

If you like... caverns, tour the cool chambers of Grand Canyon Caverns (boxed text p99), 220 ft underground. If you *really* like caverns, you can even sleep down there for $700 a night.

Architecture

'National Park Rustic' style was born at the Grand Canyon, when Mary Colter designed the park's buildings to blend harmoniously with the indigenous landscape, incorporating local materials and elements of Native American design.

Hermits Rest This cozy stone resthouse with its gigantic fireplace is something of a tribute to its hermit namesake (p61)

Lookout Studio Perched on the edge of the rim with a terraced path below; looking out gives the impression of floating over the canyon (p58)

Hopi House Inspired by and modeled after Hopi pueblo dwellings, this lovely structure was mostly built by Hopi workers (p55)

Watchtower At the eastern end of the park, this circular structure affords views from all sides (p64)

Phantom Ranch Canteen Down at the bottom of the canyon, this stone canteen is still the center of inner-canyon civilization (p84)

Cycling

What cooler way to meander around the canyon rim than by bike? Sorry, mountain bikers: bombing down Grand Canyon trails is strictly verboten. But beyond the park, excellent mountain biking awaits in Sedona.

Rainbow Rim Trail Winding along the North Rim, this 18-mile single track weaves in and out of meadow and forest with five scenic viewpoints along the way (p149)

Sedona Slickrock and single track amid red-rock monuments, fins and spires; stop into a bike shop in Flagstaff or Sedona to get trail info and a map before setting out (p110)

Greenway Trail Renting a bike at Bright Angel Bicycles on the South Rim is a fantastic, easy and relaxing way to get around and beat the crowds (p225)

Flagstaff There's great mountain biking in Flagstaff; check out woodsy Mt Elden for a start (p101)

Wildlife

Wild things you might spot around the Grand Canyon include the endangered California condor, elk, mule deer, bighorn sheep and tassel-eared Abert's squirrels and possibly even a Grand Canyon pink rattlesnake.

El Tovar lawn In the early morning or early evening, elk will sometimes lope over to nibble on the grass at this South Rim lodge (p86)

Rim Trail As you roam along the rim to admire the view, take a moment here and there to peer over the edge; condors can often be seen hanging out on flat ledges below if you don't see any soaring on thermals (p66)

Bearizona While not exactly a wild environment, this 'wildlife park' in Williams offers the chance to see native North American animals in a quasi free-range setting – timber wolves, black bears and bison are among the creatures you will encounter...from the safety of your car (p91)

month by month

February

According to some, this is the best time of year to visit – an empty South Rim (North Rim is still closed for winter), with snow often frosting the canyon features.

 Flagstaff Winterfest

Held throughout February, this Flagstaff festival celebrating all things winter features alpine and Nordic skiing, sled-dog races, concerts, food, skiing, a parade through historic downtown, art exhibits, theater, lectures, live music – oh, and skiing.

 **Sedona International Film Festival**

Founded in 1994, the Sedona International Film Festival (p116) is hosted by silver-screen veteran Sedona, whose red-rock backdrop has starred in numerous films. Takes place from late February to early March.

June

Summer is in full swing, with temperatures rising and crowds descending on the South Rim. That's a fact of Grand Canyon life. So drink it up, with a twist of culture, too.

Hopi Festival of Arts & Culture

At Flagstaff's Museum of Northern Arizona (p98), this festival features Hopi art, dance and food. Arts and cultural demonstrations include nature walks with a traditional healer, storytelling and basket weaving.

Star Party

Annual Star Parties illuminate the week following summer solstice. Organized by local astronomy clubs, the North Rim Star Party is hosted on the Grand Canyon Lodge veranda; on the South Rim, find the party at Grand Canyon Visitor Center.

July

One of the best months to visit the North Rim. Be cautious hiking slot canyons during this time, as monsoons can bring flash floods. Searing inner-canyon temps, lightning storms and holiday fireworks keep things exciting.

Fourth of July

Show up at the North Rim for the Fourth and prepare for some old-fashioned fun: water fights, a fire-engine parade and barbecue. Fire danger precludes fireworks, but you may get to enjoy Mother Nature's version instead.

 Flagstaff Fourth

Marking both the Fourth of July and the founding of Flagstaff, festivities include a parade, concerts, rodeo and fireworks. If July's first Friday falls on this weekend, the Flagstaff First Friday ArtWalk (www.flagstaffart walk.com) is also on.

August

Summer temperatures are still at their peak, as are South Rim crowds, both of which are bearable if you have a game plan. Or head to the North Rim for less of both.

⭐ Navajo Festival of Arts & Culture

Another Native American cultural festival at the Museum of Northern Arizona (p98) in Flagstaff, this early-August event features weaving demonstrations, talks on lore, ethnobotany and the Navajo language.

⭐ Heritage Days

Established by the Kaibab Paiute, this cultural festival celebrates several local Native American tribes, showcasing their music, art and cultural traditions. This North Rim festival takes place in mid-August.

September

Autumn arrives, bringing with it a respite from oppressive heat and the crush of crowds. September leaves room to breathe, listen and look – at the canyon and at the art it inspires.

⭐ Grand Canyon Music Festival

Chamber music, Native American flutes and other tunes enhance the aural dimensions of the South Rim in late August and early September; for more see www.grandcanyonmu sicfest.org.

⭐ Grand Canyon Celebration of Art

Plein-air painters (who paint outside, on location) do their thing at the South Rim as they engage with visitors. Though the events organized by the Grand Canyon Association happen in September, the art exhibition (www.grandcanyon .org/celebration.asp) extends through November.

October

Though North Rim services close mid-month, the earlier half of October is a fantastic time to visit. Art lovers should take note of the Sedona arts festivals.

⭐ Celebraciónes de la Gente

Held at the same time of year as Día de los Muertos (Day of the Dead) at the Museum of Northern Arizona in Flagstaff, this late-October festival celebrates the town's Latino heritage.

⭐ Sedona Plein Air Festival

Open-air painters from all over the country and the world are invited to visit Sedona's spectacular natural setting in late October to paint and show off their works (www.sedonaplein-airfestival.com). Paint-offs and art sales are accompanied by wine and food events.

⭐ Sedona Arts Festival

This arts fest (www.sedona artsfestival.org) in early October has been rated one of the country's top art festivals, showcasing fine arts and crafts, cuisine and entertainment. Includes a kids' zone featuring arts and crafts.

December

Grand Canyon might not be the first place you associate with the holidays, but the region's elevation makes it a winter wonderland. The South Rim and surrounds feel festive but relaxed.

⭐ Festival of Lights

Thousands of luminaria light up Tlaquepaque in Sedona in mid-December, accompanied by hot cider, a visit from Santa and other holiday festivities. Live music is a Sedona-style mix: from traditional carolers to wandering mariachis.

🏃 Polar Express

In Williams, the Grand Canyon Railway (www.thetrain.com) makes its magical trips to the 'North Pole.' Kids sip hot cocoa, nibble cookies, hear stories and best of all: meet Santa. Reserve very early; Polar Express trains begin running in November and into January.

itineraries

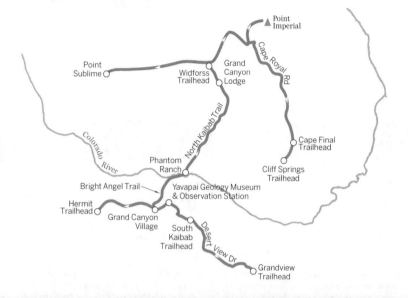

Totally immerse yourself in canyon splendor by starting at the North Rim, driving **Cape Royal Rd** and to **Point Imperial**, and venturing out to **Point Sublime**. Acclimatize yourself to the elevation with hikes to **Widforss Point, Cape Final** and **Cliff Springs**, and savor the silence, attend a ranger talk and stargaze on evening strolls. Relax on the **Grand Canyon Lodge** veranda to contemplate the rim-to-rim hike you're on the verge of undertaking. Hike down the **North Kaibab Trail**, spend a night or two by the river at **Phantom Ranch**, and then take two days to hike up the **Bright Angel Trail**. Reward yourself with a hearty dinner at **El Tovar**, and poke around **Hopi House**, **Lookout Studio** and **Kolb Studio** in **Grand Canyon Village**. Meander the rim along the **Trail of Time** to **Yavapai Geology Museum & Observation Station** and spend a few days hiking the **Hermit Trail**, **South Kaibab Trail** and **Grandview Trail** before catching a shuttle back to the North Rim.

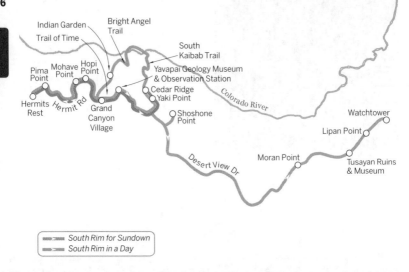

Indian Garden
Trail of Time
Bright Angel Trail
South Kaibab Trail
Yavapai Geology Museum & Observation Station
Pima Point
Mohave Point
Hopi Point
Hermits Rest
Hermit Rd
Grand Canyon Village
Cedar Ridge
Yaki Point
Shoshone Point
Colorado River
Watchtower
Lipan Point
Desert View Dr
Moran Point
Tusayan Ruins & Museum

South Rim for Sundown
South Rim in a Day

Half-Day
South Rim for Sundown

Admire the classic park architecture of **El Tovar** over lunch in the dining room before popping into **Hopi House** to compare its Native American style. Then stroll west along the **Rim Trail**, stopping to admire the view from the rim and from **Lookout Studio**. Stop into **Kolb Studio** before descending far enough down the **Bright Angel Trail** to look at the **rock art** above the trail, and to marvel at the canyon's scale from below the rim. Hike back up the trail and hop the shuttle to **Yavapai Geology Museum & Observation Station** for a Grand Canyon geology lesson. If you have time, stroll back toward the west along the Rim Trail to follow the **Trail of Time** and take in the ever-changing view. At the end of the afternoon, get an early start along **Hermit Rd** for sunset at **Pima, Mohave** or **Hopi Points**. Or, take the shuttle to **Yaki Point**, wander away from the parking lot and find a quiet spot from which to enjoy the changing light across the canyon.

One Day
South Rim in a Day

Catch a shuttle to the South Kaibab trailhead for the 8am ranger-led **Cedar Ridge hike**; remember to bring plenty of water. On your ascent, shuttle to **Yavapai Geology Museum & Observation Station** before heading back to Grand Canyon Village. Refuel with an early lunch at **El Tovar**, and meander along the **Rim Trail** to check out the **Trail of Time**. Along the rim, look for **condors** on ledges below and admire the green of **Indian Garden** in contrast with the red stone. See if any art exhibits are showing at the **Kolb Studio** gallery, then board the **Hermit Rd** shuttle to hop on and off at viewpoints as you please. Relax at **Hermits Rest** at the end of the line. Back at the village, take the **Desert View Dr**. Stop for spectacular sunset views at **Moran Point** and **Lipan Point**, and detour into tiny **Tusayan Ruins & Museum** for a glimpse into the lives of ancient canyon dwellers. Don't depart without climbing to the top of the **Watchtower**.

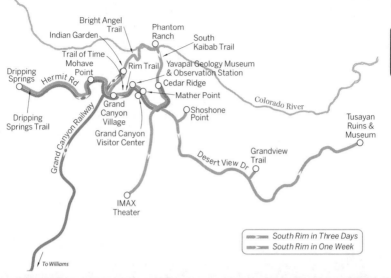

South Rim in Three Days
South Rim in One Week

Three Days
South Rim in Three Days

Board the **Grand Canyon Railway train** in Williams after the Wild West shoot-out. Stretch your legs and check out the views from one of the **Lookout Studio terraces**. Find inspiration at **Kolb Studio** and shoot the canyon from your own angle, then hop the **Hermit Rd** shuttle and explore the scenic **viewpoints**, taking in a sunset on your inbound trip. Stroll along the **Rim Trail**, follow the **Trail of Time** and hike down the **Bright Angel Trail** to One-and-a-Half or Three-Mile Resthouses. Sip a cocktail as you wait for a table at the **Arizona Room**, or bring a flashlight and attend an **evening ranger talk** at Shrine of the Ages. Spend the night in a cozy **Bright Angel cabin**, just steps from the rim. Take the **ranger-led hike** to Cedar Ridge on the South Kaibab Trail. Stop by the **bookstore** at Grand Canyon Visitor Center to find field guides and maps, or to **rent a bike**. Make a point of lunching at **El Tovar** before catching your train back to Williams.

One Week
South Rim in One Week

Wake for sunrise at **Mohave Point** or **Mather Point**, or save them for sunset. Take it slow on **Desert View Dr**, stopping for photos and bringing a picnic for the amble to peaceful **Shoshone Point**. See the Mary Colter architecture and historic spots around Grand Canyon Village with walks along the **Rim Trail**, and don't forget to look for **condors**. Attend a few **ranger walks** and **evening talks**, and learn about the canyon's geology and human history at **Yavapai Geology Museum & Observation Station** and **Tusayan Ruins & Museum**. Have a pizza dinner and see the **IMAX movie** in Tusayan. Spend a night by the river at **Phantom Ranch** and camp at **Indian Garden** on a backcountry hike down the **South Kaibab Trail** and up the **Bright Angel Trail**. Get away from it all on the **Dripping Springs Trail** and visit the ruins of a miner's cabin down the **Grandview Trail**. Enjoy a glass of wine on the patio at the **Arizona Room**, and have the requisite lunch or dinner at **El Tovar**.

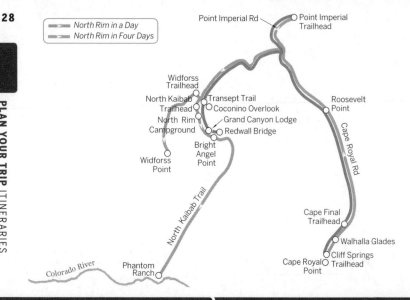

North Rim in a Day
North Rim in Four Days

Point Imperial Rd
Point Imperial Trailhead
Widforss Trailhead
North Kaibab Trailhead
Transept Trail
Coconino Overlook
North Rim Campground
Grand Canyon Lodge
Redwall Bridge
Bright Angel Point
Widforss Point
Roosevelt Point
Cape Royal Rd
North Kaibab Trail
Cape Final Trailhead
Walhalla Glades
Cliff Springs
Cape Royal Point
Cape Royal Trailhead
Colorado River
Phantom Ranch

One Day
North Rim in a Day

For a day at the North Rim, plan on spending two nights at the **Grand Canyon Lodge** or the **North Rim Campground**. Wake up with the sun and hike (or ride a mule) into the canyon on the **North Kaibab Trail**. Pause at **Coconino Overlook** and relax at **Redwall Bridge**, 2.6 miles below the rim, before tackling the haul back out of the canyon in time for lunch. Take your tray from **Deli in the Pines** to the **lodge's sun porch** and kick back in the Adirondack chairs, soaking in the view. Once you've refueled from the inner-canyon trek, head out to **Cape Royal Rd**. Pull over for a rimside stroll at **Roosevelt Point** and a scramble to **Cliff Springs**, check out ancient Puebloan ruins at **Walhalla Glades** and, at the road's end, walk out to **Angel's Window** and **Cape Royal Point**. On the drive back detour a few miles to **Point Imperial** before returning to the lodge. Grab a beer from the **Rough Rider Saloon**, amble out to **Bright Angel Point** and watch the sun settle over the canyon. After dinner at the lodge, take in an evening **ranger talk** and collapse into bed.

Four Days
North Rim in Four Days

Grand Canyon's North Rim transports even the most wearied spirits from harried lives of emails and deadlines into a slower time. Here, it's easy to find a quiet place to be alone with the canyon, and with four days you can settle into a groove that returns folks to the real world feeling just a little bit less weary and a little more inspired. Spend one day taking in sights along **Cape Royal and Point Imperial Drives**, another hiking through meadow and woods to **Widforss Point**, a third hiking the **North Kaibab** into the canyon and a fourth hiking **Cliff Springs** and **Cape Final**. Stroll out to **Bright Angel Point** and spend an evening walking the **Transept Trail**, perhaps catching the sunset over the side canyon, have a dinner or two in the historic **Grand Canyon Lodge** and take in BBQ and cowboy singing at the **Grand Canyon Cookout Experience**. Pepper in **ranger talks** on stargazing and condors, cocktails at the **Rough Rider Saloon**, long stretches relaxing on the lodge's **rimside sun porch** and picnic lunches among the aspen, and you'll have experienced some of the best the Grand Canyon has to offer.

Activities

Hike Classifications

The park service classifies canyon terrain into the following specific zones:

Corridor zone Heavily trafficked zone that includes well-maintained trails such as the South Kaibab, North Kaibab and Bright Angel. Wide and well marked, sometimes with water available, these trails are regularly patrolled by National Park Service (NPS) personnel and provide hiking and mule access to the inner canyon.

Threshold zone More rugged, less-traveled trails, with little or no water.

Primitive zone Little-used, unmaintained paths. Best suited to experienced canyon hikers who are comfortable with route-finding.

Wild zone Self-explanatory – don't expect to find trails in these zones.

Encompassing more than 1.2 million acres, the Grand Canyon is a world unto itself. To truly arrive at a deeper comprehension of the canyon, you need to get down and dirty on the trails or onto the river. Conveniently, there are many ways to experience the canyon, catering to all sorts of interests and skill levels. Whether it's by boot or hoof, paddle or motor, delving into the gorge will enormously enhance your intimacy with the canyon.

Hiking

The best way to appreciate the staggeringly magnificent Grand Canyon landscapes is to hike right into them. Hiking is the most popular and accessible activity within the park, the beauty of it being that it's open to everyone, year-round. Hikes range from paved trails that the mobility-challenged and children can navigate to primitive, unmaintained treks that will challenge backcountry experts.

All hikes listed in this book, both day excursions and backcountry forays, follow established and well-marked trails. The majority lie within the corridor and threshold zones, generally regarded as the safest areas to hike within the canyon; a section or two of the overnight treks may pass through a primitive zone.

As you follow the footfalls of ancient people along the same trails they traced into the canyon, you'll gaze up at rocky spires, spy condors wheeling above and bighorn sheep

PLAN YOUR TRIP ACTIVITIES

NAME	START LOCATION	DESCRIPTION
Bright Angel Trail		
To Mile-and-a-Half Resthouse	Bright Angel Trailhead	Short, rewarding hike that passes through two tunnels along the Grand Canyon's most popular trail
To Three-Mile Resthouse	Bright Angel Trailhead	Following Bright Angel Fault, this trail zigzags to a shaded resthouse with inner-canyon views
To Indian Garden	Bright Angel Trailhead	The grueling switchbacks of Jacob's Ladder lead to the leafy bliss of Indian Garden
Plateau Point Trail	Bright Angel Trailhead	Not recommended for summer day hikes, this trail leads to the edge of Tonto Plateau
Grandview Trail		
To Coconino Saddle	Grandview Trailhead	This steep, rocky challenge winds up at a shady spot with phenomenal views
To Horseshoe Mesa	Grandview Trailhead	Stay on the steep and narrow on this, one of the park's most exposed hikes
Hermit Trail		
Rim Trail	Hermit Trailhead	Popular paved and dirt point-to-point trail winds along the South Rim, connecting South Rim overlooks
To Santa Maria Spring	Hermit Trailhead	Beautiful and serene day hike along a steep wilderness trail to small, lovely cliffside spring
Dripping Springs Trail	Hermit Trailhead	Peaceful and challenging hike to Louis 'The Hermit' Boucher's favorite hangout
To Hermit Creek	Hermit Trailhead	Hard but beautiful hike to a sublime, cliffside camping spot near a creek
South Kaibab Trail		
To Cedar Ridge	South Kaibab Trailhead	Short, steep, scenic hike on the only corridor trail that descends along a ridge crest
To Skeleton Point	South Kaibab Trailhead	Panoramic views down the ridgeline and a challenging day-hike destination (best not attempted in summer)
To Phantom Ranch	South Kaibab Trailhead	Tough but rewarding hike to this cool oasis on the Colorado River
South Kaibab to North Kaibab	South Kaibab Trailhead	The park's classic rim-to-rim hike; can also be started from the North Rim
Other Hikes		
Shoshone Point	Shoshone Point Trailhead	Cool, shady walk to one of the South Rim's most spectacular viewpoints
Tonto Trail	South Kaibab Trailhead	Long, tough day hike offering a splendid look at the inner canyon, covering several trails

Wildlife Watching	Public Transportation to Trailhead	Great for Families	Waterfall	Restrooms

foraging below, all the while listening to the crunch of canyon dust beneath your feet and smelling wild sage on the breeze.

Unique Environment

Hiking at Grand Canyon is markedly different from hiking elsewhere. The sheer terrain is uniquely challenging, made even more so by the environment and climate. Many trails begin with sharp descents, which translate into equally steep ascents at the end of a hike, when you're most exhausted. Add the effects of altitude, hefty elevation changes and the desert environment, and you've got a set of circumstances that require heightened awareness and preparation. The key to

DIFFICULTY	DURATION	ROUND-TRIP DISTANCE	ELEVATION CHANGE	FEATURES	FACILITIES	PAGE
moderate	2-3hr	3 miles	1131ft			p67
moderate-difficult	4-5hr	6 miles	2112ft			p68
moderate-difficult	5-7hr	9.2 miles	3060ft			p68
difficult	8-10hr	12.2 miles	3120ft			p68
moderate-difficult	1-2hr	1.5 miles	1600ft			p70
difficult	4-6hr	6 miles	2699ft			p70
easy-moderate	varies	12 miles (one way)	200ft			p66
moderate-difficult	2-4hr	5 miles	1680ft			p71
moderate-difficult	3-5hr	7 miles	1700ft			p71
difficult	2 days	15.6 miles	3660ft			p76
moderate	1-2hr	3 miles	1140ft			p69
moderate-difficult	3-5hr	6 miles	2040ft			p69
difficult	3 days	18.6 miles	4714ft			p75
difficult	3 days	20.9 miles	5770ft			boxed text p72
easy	40min	2 miles	50ft			p67
very difficult	7-9hr	13.1 miles (one way)	3260ft			p72

Drinking Water · Backcountry Campsite · Views · Ranger Station · Wheelchair Access

enjoying the Grand Canyon on foot is to take proper precautions, honestly assess and respect your limitations and select hikes that best match your ability. Please refer to our comprehensive hiking chart and detailed trail descriptions for suggestions.

Promising snow-dusted buttes and crisp blue days, winter hiking is spectacular, though only the South Rim remains open. Trails are often icy in the early morning – to safeguard against glissading into the canyon, outfit yourself with a pair of crampons, available at Canyon Village Marketplace (p83). You can still hike into the canyon from the North Rim after the first major snowfall, but you'll have to purchase a

PLAN YOUR TRIP ACTIVITIES

NAME	START LOCATION	DESCRIPTION
Bright Angel Point	Grand Canyon Lodge	Short, easy paved hike to a narrow peninsula with canyon views on three sides
Cape Final	Cape Royal Rd	Flat, easy tramp along the Kaibab Plateau to a nice overlook
Cliff Springs	Cape Royal Rd	Perfect for kids, this short trail passes ancient ruins and ends at a verdant spring
Ken Patrick Trail	North Kaibab Trailhead parking lot	Point-to-point wooded trail opening up to spectacular views at Point Imperial
Point Imperial	Point Imperial	Short rim trail with views of the eastern canyon
Transept Trail	Grand Canyon Lodge	Enjoyable amble along a path rimming the canyon, connecting Grand Canyon Lodge with the campground
Uncle Jim Trail	North Kaibab Trailhead parking lot	A loop atop the Kaibab Plateau, with views of Roaring Springs Canyon
Widforss Trail	signed turnoff 2.7 miles north of Grand Canyon Lodge	Lovely forested walk with some of the finest canyon views on the North Rim
North Kaibab Trail		
To Coconino Overlook	North Kaibab Trailhead	Views of Roaring Springs and Bright Angel Canyon at the end of this short hike
To Supai Tunnel	North Kaibab Trailhead	Steep, spectacular hike to red sandstone tunnel with sweeping views of the inner canyon chutes
To Cottonwood Campground	North Kaibab Trailhead	Last 2 miles of this trail traces Bright Angel Creek to the campground
To Redwall Bridge	North Kaibab Trailhead	Challenging descent along switchbacks leads to Redwall Bridge, which crosses Roaring Springs Canyon
To Roaring Springs	North Kaibab Trailhead	A favorite for strong hikers, featuring pools in a green oasis on the otherwise hot trail
Clear Creek Trail	North Kaibab, 0.3 miles north of Phantom Ranch	Off the North Kaibab, the most popular inner canyon hike on the Colorado's north side
Bridle Trail	Grand Canyon Lodge	Flat, utilitarian trail provides access between lodge, campground and North Kaibab trailhead

 Wildlife Watching   View   Great for Families   Waterfall   Restrooms

backcountry permit and then ski or snowshoe 44 miles to the rim first.

Difficulty Level

From first timers to veteran hikers, everyone will find suitable trails within the park. Most trails are also out-and-backs that cover the same stretch in both directions, making it easy to tailor a hike to your abilities. Rangers cite average hiking speed as 2mph going down and 1mph climbing up, an important consideration when selecting a trail and distance. On your first hike or two, observe how long each mile takes (both out and back).

The hikes in this book are organized into four difficulty levels. Remember that a single trail can have several difficulty ratings, depending on which segment you plan to hike.

» Easy Less than 2 miles over fairly even, possibly paved terrain, with no significant elevation gain or loss.

» Moderate Some elevation change (500ft to 1000ft) and longer or more exposed than those rated 'easy.' Generally fine for all ability levels.

DIFFICULTY	DURATION	ROUND-TRIP DISTANCE	ELEVATION CHANGE	FEATURES	FACILITIES	PAGE
easy	30min	0.5 mile	150ft			p136
easy	2hr	4 miles	150ft			p137
easy-moderate	1hr	1 mile	600ft			p136
moderate-difficult	6-7hr (one way)	10 miles (one way)	800ft			p140
easy	2hr	4 miles	100ft			p139
easy	1½hr	3 miles	200ft			p138
easy-moderate	3hr	5 miles	600ft			p140
moderate	6hr	10 miles	350ft			p136
easy-moderate	1hr	1.5 miles	800ft			p141
moderate-difficult	3-4hr	4 miles	1410ft			p139
difficult	4½hr (one way)	6.8 miles (one way)	4170ft			p141
difficult	4-5hr	5.2 miles	2150ft			p141
difficult	7-8hr	9.4 miles	3050ft			p141
moderate-difficult	10hr	16.8 miles	1500ft			p139
easy	40min (one way)	1.2 miles (one way)	25ft			p140

Drinking Water   Ranger Station   Backcountry Campsite   Grocery Store nearby   Snack Shop

» **Difficult** Significant elevation change and longer mileage. Require more hiking experience.

» **Very Difficult** Tough hikes, involving the greatest exposure and mileage, as well as substantial elevation change (2500ft to 4000ft). Better left to the fittest, most experienced hikers.

Day Hikes

Generally speaking, the only truly easy hikes in the Grand Canyon are those above or close to the rims, along with a handful of fairly flat trails like Uncle Jim (p140) or short jaunts such as Cliff Springs (p136). Another option is to hike short segments of more challenging trails. Anyone venturing below the rim should know that it's a place of extremes. Even on short hikes, preparation is key: whether you're hiking half a mile on the Rim Trail or six on the Bright Angel, always carry plenty of water. Also wear a wide-brimmed hat, sunglasses and sunscreen.

Perennial favorites include the well-maintained corridor trails – Bright Angel (p67), South Kaibab (p69) and North Kaibab (p141). Though they may feel like superhighways in summer, plan on hiking at least one of these magnificent trails, if only for a short distance.

One lovely, rewarding, less trafficked day hike on the South Rim is the Dripping Springs Trail (p71), while almost any trail on the North Rim will yield solitude on a day hike.

Overnight Hikes

If you like challenging terrain, gape-worthy scenery and absolute serenity, plan an overnight hike into the canyon. There's simply no substitute for experiencing the Grand Canyon in the heart of its vast backcountry. While the elevation change can be daunting and the distances long, backcountry hiking is far more accessible than people tend to think.

Provided you train and prepare, plan an appropriate route and itinerary and take your time, virtually anyone with basic camping and hiking skills and a thirst for adventure can experience the wonders of the inner gorge. Ideally, you should put together a hiking itinerary that is within the capabilities of every member of your group. You'll need a backcountry permit to stay overnight anywhere within the canyon (see below).

Favorites include the well-traveled Bright Angel Trail (p73), the sublime backcountry escape of Hermit Trail (p76) and the legendary Kaibab rim-to-rim hike (boxed text p72), a 21-mile classic journey across the canyon.

Before setting out on any backcountry excursion, check trail conditions and water availability at one of the backcountry offices or call park headquarters at ☏928-638-7888. If you're at all nervous about tackling the backcountry alone, or feel you might need

some guidance, consider taking a group outing (see p36). Perks include camaraderie and helpful instruction.

Permit Information

Overnight backpacking at Grand Canyon National Park requires a backcountry permit, as does camping in undeveloped areas on the rim, such as along the Ken Patrick Trail. The only exceptions are hikers or mule riders with reservations at Phantom Ranch or Havasu Canyon.

Control of camper numbers is very tight, and demand for permits often far exceeds available slots. Due to overcrowding and environmental concerns, rangers limit the number of people per night at each of the park's backcountry campgrounds. If you're caught camping in the backcountry without a permit, expect a hefty fine and possible court appearance.

Submit permit requests to the **Backcountry Information Center** (☏928-638-7875; fax 928-638-2125; www.nps.gov/grca/planyourvisit/backcountry-permit.htm; GCNP, PO Box 129, Grand Canyon, AZ 86023). The website has the Backcountry Permit request form and detailed application instructions. Allow three weeks for the permit to be mailed to you. Permits cost $10, plus an additional $5 per person per night; the nonrefundable fee is payable by check or credit card.

If you plan on backcountry camping in the canyon at least three separate times in a given year, the $25 Frequent Hiker membership waives the $10 permit fee for all trips following the first one. On your backcountry permit application, simply check the box for membership and include payment with your application.

THE ARIZONA TRAIL

Established in 1988, the Arizona Trail started out as the vision of Flagstaff schoolteacher Dale Shewalter as he was hiking in the Santa Rita Mountains. Stretching the length of Arizona from Mexico to Utah, the completed trail will cover 800 continuous miles over Arizona's diverse landscapes, even passing through Grand Canyon National Park on its way. Connecting many pre-existing trail systems, the AZ Trail was already 96% complete at the time of research.

Many sections of the AZ Trail make excellent day hikes. On the North Rim, a lovely section of the trail (p149) runs through Kaibab National Forest (North Rim). The trail roughly parallels the highway leading into the North Entrance of Grand Canyon National Park, where, about 10 miles in, it then connects with the North Kaibab Trail.

Beyond the South Rim, the AZ Trail meanders through the Flagstaff area, with a forested section alongside beautiful Walnut Canyon (p109).

Find more information and current news on the trail at www.aztrail.org.

DON'T HORSE AROUND WITH MULES

Day hikers are bound to encounter mules, which always have the right of way. If you're hiking when a mule train approaches, stand quietly on the inner side of the trail, turn your pack away from the animals (lest one bumps your pack and knocks you off balance) and listen for directions from the guide. Be especially careful if you're hiking with kids.

Once a permit is granted, itinerary changes are not allowed, except for emergencies. You can list three alternative dates and routes, which can markedly increase your chances of securing a permit. Applications are accepted in person or by mail or fax beginning the first day of the month, four months prior to the planned trip; for instance, if you'd like to hike the Bright Angel in June, you can apply as early as February 1.

If you're denied a permit, there's still hope! Provided you can be flexible about where and when you hike, show up in person at the Backcountry Information Center on either rim. Add your name to the waiting list by submitting a written request for a permit for the following day. Waits can take from a day to a week (with longer waits on the South Rim), and you must show up in person by 8am every morning to maintain your position on the waiting list. Though requests are accepted in person only, you can get an idea of how long the wait is by calling the Backcountry Information Center.

Responsible Backcountry Use

To help preserve the ecology and beauty of Grand Canyon National Park, strive to make as minimal a footprint as possible when enjoying the backcountry. For more information on low-impact backpacking, learn the seven principles of the Leave No Trace ethic (www.lnt.org; click the Programs link) and live them.

Trash

» Pack out all waste, including food scraps and biodegradable items like orange peels.

» Don't bury trash; not only will it take years to decompose, but it's detrimental to the health of the animals that will likely dig it up.

Human Waste

» Where there are no toilets, bury solid human waste in a cathole (about 6in deep and at least 200ft from trails, campsites or water sources). Cover the waste with soil and a rock. In snow, dig down to the soil.

» To further minimize your impact, consider bringing along a 'poop tube' (see www.fastq.com/~jrschroeder/poop.htm for a great DIY version) and dispose of your waste at a local sewage treatment plant or RV dump station after your trek.

» Urinate 200ft from water, preferably on sand or rock, but not in catholes or with waste you are packing out.

» When camping along the Colorado River, the sheer volume of water makes washing up and peeing in the river an acceptable option. However, this applies only to the Colorado and not to the creeks and rivers flowing into it.

Washing

» For personal washing, use biodegradable soap and toothpaste with a water container; disperse waste water at least 200ft away from any water source, scattering it widely to allow the soil to filter it fully.

» When washing dishes and utensils, use sand or snow rather than detergent.

Erosion

» Hillsides and mountain slopes, especially at high altitudes, are prone to erosion. Stick to existing trails and avoid shortcuts.

» Where a well-used trail passes through a mud patch, walk through the mud so as not to widen the trail.

» Avoid removing or trampling the plant life that keeps topsoils in place.

Fires & Low-Impact Cooking

» Open fires are prohibited in Grand Canyon National Park except at established campgrounds on the rim.

» Where fires are allowed, keep them in established fire rings or grills. Never leave fires unattended; extinguish them thoroughly with water.

ng wood; instead, purchase
e Marketplace (p83) or the
re (p146).

nt kerosene, alcohol or
ng those powered by
isters.

ood that doesn't require
e weight in your pack by
not bringing a stove at all.

Wildlife Conservation

» It is illegal to feed wildlife, as this can lead to unbalanced populations, diseases and animals becoming dependent on handouts.

» Discourage the presence of wildlife by wrapping up and packing out all food scraps (and watch those ravens – they're brave, clever and opportunistic!).

» Keep all food and fragrant items (soap, deodorant, toothpaste etc) in your pack and hang it from a tree overnight to keep critters at bay.

Hiking Outfitters & Groups

Group outings are a terrific way for first-time hikers to enjoy safe and social hiking. Even if you're an experienced hiker, group hikes offer opportunities to learn about the canyon in the company of like-minded adventurers. The highly respected Grand Canyon Field Institute (p216) offers many naturalist-led hikes and backpacking trips for all skill levels. These fairly priced, expertly guided expeditions generally last three to nine days.

For short guided hikes, you can't beat the free and justly popular ranger-led hikes, offered year-round on the South Rim and from June to October on the North Rim. Check *The Guide* for listings. The guided Cedar Ridge Hike (p79), departing daily at 8am from the South Kaibab Trailhead, is a fantastic introduction to this classic South Rim trail. Bring water, snacks and appropriate clothing.

Many local outfitters offer a range of guided hiking excursions in the park. Trips, prices, dates and styles vary widely, so definitely peruse a few before making your choice. In any case, you're best off reserving a spot at least five months in advance. Pick up a full list of accredited backcountry guide services at the park's visitor centers or on the NPS website (www.nps.gov/grca/planyourvisit /guided-hikes.htm).

The following list is just a sampling of outfitters.

Discovery Treks (☎888-256-8731; www. discoverytreks.com) Offers a wide selection of guided trips, from one-day hikes on the Grandview Trail to five-day backpacking excursions on the North Rim.

Four Season Guides (☎877-272-5032, 928-525-1552; www.fsguides.com) Straight outta Flagstaff, offering guided multiday backcountry trips, including the rim-to-rim and Havasu Canyon.

Just Roughin' It Adventure Co (☎877-399-2477, 480-857-2477; www.justroughinit.com) Catering to hikers of all levels looking to challenge themselves, have fun and leave a minimal impact.

Pygmy Guides (☎877-279-4697, 928-707-0215; www.pygmyguides.com) Excellent outfit guiding

---

COOL TRAILS FOR A HOT DAY

Looking for a reprieve from the scorching sun? Take on one of the following trails (see the hiking charts for full hike descriptions). Tip: the less exposed, higher altitude North Rim is the better choice when trees and shade are priorities.

» **Cliff Springs** (p136) Short and sweet, this trail starts out as a sunny downhill, then cools with each step as it dips beneath overhangs, hugs a sandstone wall and ends at a misty, fern-fringed oasis.

» **Shoshone Point** (p67) An almost entirely shaded ramble through a patch of South Rim pine forest, this trail ends at a gorgeous, secluded overlook.

» **Transept Trail** (p138) Wending along the rim of its namesake canyon, this trail offers a nice mix of sun and shade, open and hidden overlooks and refreshing breezes from below.

» **Widforss Trail** (p136) If you're after a longer cool hike, this is the star. The trail ribbons through aspen groves, swings by several views and offers a soothing mix of sun and shade, with a nice picnic spot at the turnaround.

everything from day hikes to rim-to-rim. Attempts to accommodate special-needs travelers as much as possible.

Rubicon Outdoors (☑800-903-6987; www. rubiconoutdoors.com) Consummate professionals and minimal-impact wilderness adventurers run trips from day hikes to the five-day Hermit Trail trip.

Wildland Trekking (☑800-715-4453, 970-903-3719; www.wildlandtrekking.com) Regularly offered hiking or backpacking tours are guided by experts – or design your own adventure.

Mule Rides

Riding a mule down into the canyon is a time-honored park tradition. Mule trains have been making their way down the Bright Angel and other trails into the canyon for over a century, taking delighted tourists below the rim and ferrying supplies in and out of the canyon. Traveling the trails on the backs of these mellow, sure-footed creatures is the classic way to get below the rim and makes for a memorable trip.

Mule trains – up to 10 animals per group – are only permitted on the corridor trails, the Uncle Jim Trail and the first mile of the Ken Patrick Trail. Just because you're not doing the walking doesn't mean it's effortless. If you don't ride regularly, you should expect to be rather saddle-sore once you dismount – don't plan any ambitious hikes for the day after. Those scared of heights or big animals – gentle and cute though they may be – are best off exploring the canyon by other means.

Rides down to Phantom Ranch are offered year-round from the South Rim. On the South Rim, it's possible to do overnight mule trips with one or two nights spent at Phantom Ranch, giving you the chance to explore the inner canyon before trekking back up to the rim. Overnight trips are not offered from the North Rim, due to the lengthy distance to Phantom Ranch.

River Rafting

Rafting the Colorado ranks among the top outdoor adventures for many, not only for its thrill factor but also for its romance. It's a geological journey through time, an adrenaline rush, secluded wilderness getaway and riparian paradise all rolled into one phenomenal ride.

Rafting season begins in mid-April and runs into September for motorized boats and November for oared vessels. Though the park carefully regulates the number of rafts on the Colorado, visitors have several options. For those short on time, there are half- and full-day rafting trips, though not necessarily on sections within the Grand Canyon. Most rafters join a commercial outing (see p172) with one of many accredited outfitters for trips lasting from three to 21 days. Each year a few hundred private rafting excursions (p169) are allowed on the river as well.

Road & Mountain Biking

Not exactly known as a cyclist's park, the Grand Canyon nonetheless has some very nice stretches for two-wheeling. Bikes are not allowed on any hiking trails (except the Greenway Trail) within the park, but they are welcome on all roads open to automobile traffic. The best riding on the South Rim is along Desert View Dr and Hermit Rd, both leading to successive scenic overlooks. The biking is much better on the North Rim, where you'll find both long hauls and short spins.

See p225 for more information on specific bike rides and where to rent bikes.

A reliable outfitter offering guided bike trips is **Backroads** (☑800-462-2848; www.back roads.com). A six-day hiking/biking/inn adventure to Bryce, Zion and Grand Canyon National Parks costs around $2500 per person.

Horseback Riding

Horseback riding is offered outside the park, mostly in the lovely and cool Kaibab National Forest.

At the North Rim, try Allen's Trail Rides (p150). On the South Rim, near Tusayan, Apache Stables (p88) offers trail rides along the piney trails of the Kaibab and campfire rides (BYO hot dogs and s'mores).

On the Havasupai Reservation (p94), you can travel by horseback from Hualapai Hilltop to the campground at Supai ($187/94 round-trip/one way), or take a tour from the lodge to the waterfalls ($60).

Rock Climbing

Rock climbing is allowed anywhere in the Grand Canyon, except above established trails (for obvious reasons). While Arizona is rife with climbing areas, climbing in the canyon is not extremely popular, nor very visible. Climbers who plan to hike into the canyon and camp will need a backcountry permit.

Stop by Vertical Relief Rock Climbing (p102) in Flagstaff to hit up the employees there for info on climbing throughout the region. It also sells guidebooks and gear.

Stewart M Green's *Rock Climbing Arizona* (Falcon, 1999) is a comprehensive guide to prime Arizona climbing areas and includes topo maps and detailed route information. An updated *Grand Canyon Summit Select II* by Aaron and Pernell Tomasi (Pseudalpine, 2011) features more than 100 routes in the canyon.

Helicopter & Airplane Tours

While it's a less direct experience than hiking, flying over the Grand Canyon does offer an incredible perspective – especially for visitors with limited mobility – and air tours are understandably popular. Close to 100,000 flights take almost a million passengers above the canyon each year.

Canyon flyovers are controversial, however, as flights can be tricky; they involve high-altitude takeoffs, sudden wind shifts, unpredictable air currents and few level landing areas should an emergency arise. There have been some 60 crashes over the past half-century. Stiff regulations now govern all flights crossing the canyon, to limit noise and promote safety. More than 75% of park airspace is seasonally off-limits to planes, and flying below the rim is prohibited in all but the West Rim area.

At the time of research, the NPS had published a draft proposal to reduce the number of flights, restrict flight areas in the park and require noise-reduction technology for aircraft flying over the canyon.

Air tours operate out of Grand Canyon National Park Airport in Tusayan, and from Las Vegas (see p122), Phoenix and the Hualapai Reservation (Grand Canyon West; see

---

BEST BIKE RIDES IN THE PARK

Though not the park for hard-core cyclists, the Grand Canyon nonetheless offers up some great rides. Stretch out your trail-tested or mule-sore legs on one of these scenic routes. Distances listed are for one-way travel.

» **Desert View Dr** (22 miles) You'll have to concentrate to keep your eyes from wandering off the road to the stunning canyon views. This hot ride is best tackled at sunrise or in the late afternoon.

» **Grand Canyon Lodge to Point Imperial** (8 miles) A winding, shady ride through pine forests and thickets of aspen and bright-orange Indian paintbrush. Ends at a picnic spot on the rim with a spectacular view.

» **Hermit Rd** (10 miles) This relatively traffic-free ride offers a series of breathtaking overlooks. Cold drinks and ice-cream bars await at Hermits Rest.

» **Point Imperial to Cape Royal** (15 miles) Long and winding with lots of small rolling hills, this delightful pedal along a forest-fringed road eventually opens up to sage-dusted terrain and big views. Don't veer off the road when you first glimpse magical Angels Window.

RIM TO RIVER

Experienced hikers and fit newcomers alike are often tempted to hike from the rim to the river and back in a single day, an outing that involves close to 9000ft of elevation change. But no matter how early you start, how many previous miles you've logged or how many energy bars you eat, it's just a bad idea – and rangers, numerous posted signs and this book will discourage you from attempting this stunt. A particularly poignant sign is the one featuring the photo and story of super-fit, 24-year-old marathoner Margaret Bradley, who died of dehydration on her run into the canyon.

While it's possible for strong, well-prepared hikers to accomplish this haul from the South Rim in the cooler air of spring and fall, attempting to do so in the summer heat is downright foolish. It makes no difference if you're a fit 25-year-old or a 65-year-old trail veteran. Annually, about 300 hikers require rescue from the canyon (at their own expense), around 80% of which are due to heat-related causes. Still not convinced? Read the gripping *Over the Edge: Death in Grand Canyon*, by Michael Ghiglieri and Thomas Myers, which details the many ways in which people have died at the Grand Canyon.

p96). Pick up a partial list of operators at the visitor centers.

Airplane tours tend to cost less than helicopter trips, and cover more distance; in addition to the Grand Canyon, they fly over Marble Canyon and Lake Powell. Helicopter trips sometimes include a descent into the western canyon and can be combined with a motorized rafting excursion on the Colorado River.

Cross-Country Skiing & Snowshoeing

North Rim

In winter, the North Rim and environs receive an average of 150in of snow annually, offering miles of snow-covered forest roads and a patchwork of wide meadows for those willing to make the trek. There are no designated trails, so you can ski or snowshoe virtually anywhere, opening up limitless options for backcountry exploration.

The park road officially closes from mid-October to mid-May, and visitors must ski or snowshoe the 44 miles to the rim.

South Rim

The South Rim boasts a few cross-country loops within the Kaibab National Forest, 0.3 miles north of Grandview Lookout Tower.

You can rent skis in Flagstaff, where you'll find several more cross-country circuits, as well as downhill facilities. The popular Flagstaff Nordic Center (p102) has lovely groomed trails for cross-country skiing, unless you prefer to explore the surrounding national forest trails for free.

Travel with Children

Best Activities for Kids

Ranger Programs

Stargazing talks around the fire, activity books and kid-friendly lectures intrigue kids of all ages.

Rafting

White-water trips through the canyon, perfect for older kids and teens, and calm-water floats along the Colorado River from Glen Canyon Dam to Lees Ferry for all ages.

Hiking

Scrambles through desert scrub, rambles through aspen and meadows and overnight expeditions down to the Colorado River; the Grand Canyon offers plenty of fantastic hiking opportunities for young children and teenagers alike.

Mule Rides

Treks to the canyon bottom are offered from the South Rim only; half-day rides from the North Rim gives a taste of the canyon interior and follow a less precipitous trail. Children must be 10, but the North Rim offers a rimside option for kids as young as seven.

Parents, many remembering their own childhood vacation to the desert Southwest, pack the sunscreen and camera, hiking boots and sun hats, and drag their children to the Grand Canyon. Perhaps the kids were pushing for Disney, or maybe they argued for staying home and hanging out with friends. It is, after all, nothing more than a big hole. But there's a reason why generation after generation of families flock to this quintessential national park. Here, everything from lazy days along dusty trails, searching for fossils and picnicking on the rim to white-water adventures down the Colorado and the classic canyon mule ride make for memories that imprint not only into photos but into the spirit. Maybe it's the air and the silence, maybe it's the history and the wildlife, maybe it's the geology. Or perhaps it's nothing more than the sheer size of the canyon, which makes even small people realize how very big the world is. Whatever it is, children don't easily forget their family trip to the Grand Canyon. It remains *the* iconic American destination, amplified in the imagination by cowboy movies and advertisements, and powerfully symbolic of American ideals of freedom, self-reliance and the transformative power of the Western landscape. With a little planning and a lot of patience and flexibility, a trip to this region could go down as one of your best family vacations.

BEFORE YOU GO

It's possible to cruise into the South Rim, check out the museums and hike the trails on a whim, but for the following activities you'll need to make some advanced reservations.

☐ White-water rafting trips on the Colorado River through the Grand Canyon (p167)

☐ Family trips with the Grand Canyon Field Institute (www .grandcanyon.org/fieldinstitute)

☐ Grand Canyon Summer Camp for high-school students (www.nps.gov/grca/forkids/camp)

☐ Overnight stays at Phantom Ranch or park campgrounds (www.nps.gov/grca)

☐ Accommodations at Grand Canyon Lodge (www.foreverlodging.com)

☐ Grand Canyon Railway (www.thetrain.com)

☐ Mule treks into the canyon (www.nps.gov/grca)

☐ Museum of Arizona discovery programs and tours (www.musnaz.org)

☐ Volunteering at Best Friends Animal Sanctuary (www.bestfriends.org) and spending a night with a borrowed cat, dog or pot-bellied pig

Grand Canyon for Kids

Long drives, precarious canyon overlooks, crowded shuttles and stifling summer heat can be a challenge. The rewards, however, rest in the most mundane of activities – a sunset picnic at Cape Royal, playing in the grassy area behind El Tovar, watching the condors over the canyon. And the canyon's geology, human history and wildlife, accessible in concrete ways at every turn, make the park the world's largest classroom – kids learn without even trying. While the South Rim has more sights, museums and a broader variety of ranger-led interpretive programs designed for children, the chaos and crowds can be intimidating and exhausting. The intimacy of the North Rim attracts families looking for a quieter vacation.

Most tours to the Grand Canyon offer children's discounts. The child-friendly icon (🏃) in this book indicates sights, restaurants and hotels that are particularly accommodating to children.

Ranger Programs

In the **Junior Ranger Program**, geared towards children aged four to 14, children pick up an activity book from the visitor center on either rim, complete three pages and attend a ranger program. Upon completion, a ranger solemnly swears them in as junior rangers and the child receives a junior ranger certificate and a badge. While the whole thing sounds rather hokey, a leisurely afternoon completing the project just might be the highlight of your six-year-old's visit. The **Discovery Pack Program** (ages nine to 14) begins with a 90-minute ranger talk, after which children check out

binoculars, a magnifying lens, field guides and other naturalist tools. Children must complete parts of the activity book and return the material by 4pm to become junior rangers. Rangers use hands-on activities to teach children about the park's ecology and wildlife at **Way Cool Stuff for Kids** and **Kids Rock**.

Check *The Guide* (a National Park Service newspaper available on both rims) for current programs, times and locations. You can download a seasonal schedule of ranger programs from the For Kids link on the park's website (www.nps.gov/grca). National monuments surrounding the park offer Junior Ranger and kid-friendly ranger programs as well.

Hiking

Both rims offer opportunities for kids to get dirty and dusty on the trails, but each offer a distinct experience. With miles of rimside rambles and several opportunities to descend into the canyon, hiking on the South Rim is particularly suited for older kids. The constant danger of the rim and rocky interior precipices can be nerve-wracking for parents of little ones. On the North Rim, the grassy meadows, shaded trails and elevation offer relief from the summer sun, and it's almost guaranteed that you'll see mule deer and wild turkeys. The paved Rim Trail on the South Rim is suitable for strollers, but if you plan on more extensive hiking, consider a front carrier for infants or a backpack carrier for toddlers. You can rent a jogging stroller at the bike rental in the gas station on the North Rim.

Children's Highlights

Family Hikes

Rim Trail Popular path to sights and overlooks on South Rim.

Shoshone Point Easy, wide, wooded dirt road to quiet overlook.

Bright Angel At the first tunnel, check out the pictographs.

Widforss Trail Gentle hike through woods to canyon rim.

Cape Final Jutting canyon view rewards mild hike.

Children 11 & Under

IMAX Grand Canyon Amazing aerial canyon footage.

Junior Ranger Activity books and hands-on fun.

Grand Canyon Cookout Experience Cowboy tunes and barbecue on North Rim.

Trail of Time Three-mile geologic timeline.

Cape Royal Dr Picnic at Greenland Lake and stroll out to Cape Royal Point.

The Watchtower Children love climbing the spiral staircase and taking in the view at this Mary Colter classic on the South Rim.

Tweens & Teens

Raft the Colorado Ride the rapids through the canyon.

Mule Trek Ride a mule from the South Rim to the canyon bottom.

Grand Canyon Summer Camp Overnight adventures with a park ranger.

Rim-to-Rim Huff it down one side and out the other.

Planning

While any trip should allow plenty of time for serendipitous discoveries, anything more than a day trip requires some advance planning. If possible, try to come to the park during the fall, after the summer crowds of school-aged children ebbs and the gripping desert heat softens, but before that teasing hint of winter becomes a full-fledged snowstorm. It's the best time to be here, but remember, the North Rim closes October 15.

Accommodations

Reservations are accepted up to a year in advance, and the cancellation policy is generous, so reserve a room as soon as you can. If you travel with lots of gear, you might prefer to stay at the **Yavapai Lodge** or **Maswik Lodge** on the South Rim, as you can park right outside your door. **Bright Angel Lodge** offers two-room cabins, and **El Tovar** has several suites. On the North Rim, Grand Canyon Lodge's **Pioneer Cabins** sport two rooms and sleep six. Children under 16 stay free at all Grand Canyon lodgings, but there is a $10-per-day charge for cribs and cots. Most accommodations outside the park do not charge extra for children under 12, and many have suites and pools. In Flagstaff, **Inn at Little America** borders acres of national

PARK & POKE FROM THE SOUTH TO NORTH RIM

Sometimes the best times are had by simply parking the car and poking around – no charge, no destination, no agenda. Break up the four-hour drive around the canyon from the South to North Rim with a few park and pokes.
Little Colorado Gorge (Hwy 64, east of South Rim's East Gate) Peruse Navajo crafts and take in the view.
Cameron Trading Post (Cameron) Shady green gardens and tourist trinkets.
Balanced Rocks (Lees Ferry) Scramble and hide among giant boulders.
Historic Lees Ferry (Lees Ferry) Picnic in the apricot orchard at Lonely Dell Ranch.
Jacob Lake Inn (Jacob Lake) Grab a milkshake for the last leg to the North Rim.

You can't avoid long stretches in the car, particularly if you're headed to the North Rim, but the right frame of mind and some smart packing can minimize backseat whining.

☐ Try not to squeeze too much in. Endless hours in the car rushing from overlook to overlook, sight to sight, can result in grumpy, tired kids and frustrated parents. After a while, canyon views start to look alike, and the trip becomes a blur.

☐ Stop often and stay flexible.

☐ Remember sunshades for the window, and a football, soccer ball or Frisbee – any grassy area or meadow is a potential playing field.

☐ Surprise the kids with a Grand Canyon trip bag filled with canyon books, a special treat, a car-friendly toy and game.

☐ Bring a journal, an enlarged Xeroxed map and colored pencils for each child. Kids can follow along on their map as you drive, drawing pictures of what they see and do, and record the trip in their journal. Note: crayons melt. – do not bring them on summer road-trips.

☐ Pack favorite CDs, or more conveniently an iPod and car speaker connector. Books on CD from your local library can help pass the hours as well.

forest, has a grass-surrounded outdoor pool and offers spacious rooms.

Dining

While 'family-friendly restaurant' evokes images of pizza buffets and play areas at McDonald's, even the fanciest restaurants in and around the park welcome families and most provide children's menus. Both rims offer cafeterias and plenty of picnic spots. There's a full grocery store on the South Rim, but because there is only a limited general store on the North Rim consider bringing a cooler and stocking it in Page or Kanab. Note that not all rooms in the park have refrigerators, but you can buy ice on both rims.

Safety

It's easy to forget, as you're waiting in line for a shuttle or walking a rim trail with hundreds of other folk, that this is a wilderness. In most areas, there are no guardrails along the rim, and even where there are, there is room for a small child to slide through. Children and adults alike have plummeted to their deaths engaging in the most mundane activities in the most populated parts of the park. Secure toddlers in backpacks, always clutch young children's hands, and absolutely do not allow anyone to run and scramble along the rim. Hikes into the canyon can be treacherous – consider carefully before bringing children under 10 years old.

Arizona law requires that children five years old and younger sit in a car seat except on public transportation. Most car rental agencies rent rear-facing car seats (for infants under one year old), forward-facing seats and boosters for about $10 per day, but you must reserve these in advance. Clarify the correct type of seat when you make the reservation, as each is suitable only for specified ages and weight.

Note that the North Rim is isolated and the closest medical facilities are 1½ hours away in Kanab. See the Health & Safety chapter for other safety issues, including dehydration, altitude sickness, snakes and scorpions.

Beyond the Park

Families with children of all ages could spend several days, even weeks, exploring the mountains and desert surrounding Grand Canyon National Park. Remember, however, that distances are long, particularly in and around the North Rim. Try to factor in a couple of lazy days, and never underestimate the value of simply hanging out at a playground, pool or park.

Around the South Rim

Flagstaff With excellent parks, outdoor family movies, and a pedestrian-friendly downtown, this mountain college town is an exceptionally kid-friendly base for the region.

Slide Rock State Park Splash around in Oak Creek just outside Sedona.

Walnut Canyon National Monument Explore ancient Puebloan cliff dwellings.

Sunset Crater National Monument Hike through the striking black basalt of a lava flow.

WHAT TO PACK

You'll be able to find just about anything you could need on the South Rim, but options on the North Rim are limited to the general store and a gift shop.

☐ **Children's paracetemol and ibuprofen** You'll be glad you packed these when your child wakes up with a fever of 102°F at 3am.

☐ **Fleece** Even in the summer, desert nights can be chilly and the North Rim can be downright bitter.

☐ **Rain jacket** Yes, it's the desert, but summer monsoons bring torrential rains and passing showers are common.

☐ **Water sandals** You'll want to splash in creeks without worrying about sharp rocks and desert pricklies.

☐ **Hiking shoes** Bring something sturdy that ties and covers the toes, and socks.

☐ **Sunscreen and bug repellent** Even in the winter, the sun sears and mosquitoes and ticks pester from March through October.

☐ **Water bottles** Altitude sickness and dehydration bring headaches, nausea and worse.

☐ **Sun hat** A must in the summer.

☐ **Beach towels** For exploring creeks and reservoirs surrounding the park, and perfect for picnics.

Around the North Rim

North Kaibab National Forest Gentle trails and meadows.

Kanab Small and quiet red-rock Utah town with kitschy Western fun.

Coral Sand Dunes State Park Kids love sliding down the soft pink sand.

Best Friends Animal Sanctuary Visit critters in the nation's largest no-kill animal shelter.

Lake Powell Houseboat or kayak on the cold clear waters of this massive desert reservoir.

Travel with Pets

Best Spots for Dogs

Kaibab National Forest (North)

With miles of trails and dirt roads, no leash laws and plenty of big meadows, the national forest that borders Grand Canyon National Park to the north is dog heaven. Even in summer the high elevation and thick shade of the Kaibab Plateau keep them cool.

Kanab

Down the road from the nation's largest no-kill animal shelter, this tiny Utah town an hour-and-a-half drive from the North Rim is particularly dog-friendly. Just about every hotel takes dogs, and most restaurants and shops have water bowls and dog treats.

Flagstaff

A college town with a soft spot for four-legged friends; you'll find lots of hotels that accept dogs and a couple of dog parks.

While it's certainly possible to enjoy a trip to the Grand Canyon with your pet, summer heat and park restrictions can be challenging. A little advanced planning will go a long way to making the trip smoother and happier for both you and your four-legged friend.

Rules & Regulations

Dogs and cats are allowed at rim campgrounds and throughout the park's developed areas, but cannot go below the rim, ride the shuttles or enter any hotels, stores or restaurants on either rim, and they must be leashed at all times. It is illegal to leave a dog tied up alone at a campground, and you must clean up after your dog. Official service animals are welcome throughout the park, but you must register at the backcountry office before taking them below the rim.

Health & Safety

The environment can be harsh on pets, and mountain lions, rattlesnakes, scorpions and other critters are prevalent in the region. Prepare for weather extremes. In the summer, do not leave them in the car or RV unattended at any time. Think twice before taking pets on desert hikes in the summer, as it's excruciatingly hot and the sand burns tender paws, and always bring a portable water bowl. The only complete pet-supply shop in the region is Flagstaff's **Petsmart** (928-213-1737; 1121 S Plaza Way; 9am-9pm Mon-Sat, to 7pm Sun).

Remember that dogs, like humans, need to be in good shape before taking off on

VETERINARIANS

Canyon Pet Hospital (928-774-5197; www.canyonpet.com; 12 S Mikes Pike, Flagstaff; 8am-8pm Mon-Fri, 9am-6pm Sat, noon-4pm Sun) Call 928-266-5762 for after-hours emergencies.

Aspen Veterinary Clinic (928 526 2423; 7861 N US Hwy 89, Flagstaff; 8:15am-5:30pm Mon-Fri, 8am-noon Sat) Messages direct you to emergency contacts after hours.

Kanab Veterinary Hospital (435-644-2400; 484 S 100 East) 1½ hour drive from North Rim.

Page Animal Hospital (928-645-2816; www.pageanimalhospital.com; 87 S 7th Ave) Only service between South and North Rims.

extended hikes, and are susceptible to altitude sickness and dehydration.

Dog-friendly Trails
In the Park

The only trails that allow dogs are the South Rim's paved Rim Trail and the North Rim's Bridle Trail.

Beyond the Park

See Renee Guillory's recommended *Best Hikes with Dogs: Arizona* for a full listing of dog-friendly trails.

Kaibab National Forest Just outside the park's North Rim gate; all the trails and dirt roads allow dogs and they are not required to be leashed.

Paria Canyon Dogs are welcomed off-leash on this five-day wilderness hike, but you must pay $5 per day and pick up special dog-doo bags at the Paria Contact Station.

Havasupai Reservation Leashed dogs can go below the canyon rim along the trails in Havasu Canyon.

Buffalo Park An open mesa outside Flagstaff with a lovely 2-mile gravel loop trail. Leashed dogs only.

Dog-friendly Accommodations

No hotels in Grand Canyon National Park allow dogs, though they are welcome at the campgrounds. However, several motels just outside Grand Canyon National Park, including the historic **Hotel Monte Vista** in Flagstaff, the **Grand Hotel** in Tusayan, several chain motels in Page, the **Kaibab Lodge** just outside the entrance to the North Rim, and most hotels in Kanab, UT, accept dogs and cats. You may be restricted to a smoking room or have to pay a small fee or deposit. Look for the paw-print

symbol in Sleeping listings for pet-friendly accommodations.

Kennels

Proof of vaccination is required for all kennels. Note that there is a kennel on the South Rim, but none on or even within a couple of hours of the North Rim.

South Rim Kennel (928-638-0534; overnight dog/cat $22/13, day boarding dog/cat $16/12; 7:30am-5pm) Convenient for one or two days, but not recommended for extended stays. There are no large play areas for the dogs, and individual walks are limited to one five-minute walk per day. Rates include meals.

Canyon Pet Resort (928-214-9324; www.canyonpetresort.com; ste 300, 1802 W Kristy Lane, Flagstaff; per day dog $17-28, cat $10; 7:30am-6pm Mon-Fri, 8am-6pm Sat, 4-6pm Sun) Offers luxury suites and doggie day camp, with camp counselors, kiddy pools, shade and dog-runs. Ask about Tender Loving Care Packages.

Canyon Pet Hospital (928-774-5197; www.canyonpet.com; 12 S Mikes Pike, Flagstaff; overnight dog standard/luxury $19/36, cat per day $15; 8am-8pm Mon-Fri, 9am-6pm Sat, noon-4pm Sun) Boarding and grooming. Rates include meals. VIP packages, with extra play time, walks and treats, are an additional $10 per day.

Doggy Dude Ranch (435-772-105; www.doggyduderanch.com; Hwy 9 btwn Rockville & Springdale; overnight/day boarding $26/20; 8am-6pm Mon-Sat, 9am-5pm Sun) Five miles outside of Zion National Park and three hours from the North Rim, this dog ranch offers quality day care and specializes in extended stays.

Sleepover Rover (866-817-0500; www.sleepoverrover.com; per night $40-50) Host families in Phoenix and Las Vegas dog-sit cage-free in their home. All hosts have dog-safe yards, are home full time, and have been personally approved by the company's founder and owner.

Horse Trails & Equestrian Facilities
In the Park

Horses and pack animals are allowed in the park, including below the rim, and there are corrals on both rims. Access www.nps .gov/grca/planyourvisit/backcountry.htm for updated regulations and contact the backcountry office at either rim for the required overnight permit.

Beyond the Park

The **Kaibab National Forest** that borders the North Rim offers excellent riding opportunities with all trails open to horses and miles of dirt roads. Ranchers who run cattle in the Kaibab have a permit to use corrals within the forest, and while they welcome riders passing through you need to call or stop by the Kaibab Plateau Visitor Center in Jacob Lake for locations and current information.

In the **Coconino National Forest** just outside of Flagstaff, **Little Elden Springs Horse Camp** (☑877-444-6777; day/night $9/20; ☺May-Oct) is a campground designated only for people with horses. It offers 15 horse-friendly campsites with hitching posts but no corrals. From here, riders can access more than 100 miles of equestrian trails, ranging from easy to the challenging Heart Trail. To get to Little Elden, head 5 miles northeast of Flagstaff on Hwy 89. Turn west on FR 556 and drive 2 miles to FR 556A. Turn right to the campground. As of June 2011, this campground was closed due to a fire; call for updated conditions.

In Flagstaff, board your horse at **MCS Stables** (☑928-774-5835; www.mcsstables.com; 5835 S Hwy Alt 89, Flagstaff; per night $22). You're welcome to camp on-site at no extra charge. The closest facility to the North Rim is **Paria Canyon Guest Ranch** (☑928-660-2674; www. pariacampground.com; Hwy 89), 30 miles west of Page, about a two-hour drive from the park.

regions at a glance

The vast majority of visitors to the Grand Canyon wind up at the South Rim, which is the park's most developed area. Its navigability and accessibility make it the logical choice to see a lot in a limited time.

Those in the know make tracks for the quieter experience of the North Rim. It takes some effort to get there, and you won't find many services even during its open season. But if all you're looking for is canyon beauty and you don't mind remoteness, this is the rim for you.

River trips require plenty of advance planning, though you'll find a few options for day trips.

South Rim

Views ✓✓✓
Hiking ✓✓✓
Activities ✓✓

Stunning Views
Truly awe-inspiring upon first look, the iconic South Rim views are astoundingly gorgeous. Take time to settle down at a viewpoint, sometime toward the beginning or end of a day, and simply watch the light transform the canyon features.

Hiking Shoes
Simply put, hiking is the best way to experience the canyon. Hiking even a short way below the rim gives new perspective on this immense, intense place. Fantastic hikes for every fitness level are accessible from Grand Canyon Village, or a shuttle ride away.

To-Dos
Grand Canyon Village is where the action is: condor-spotting, ranger talks day and night, art exhibitions, historic architecture, museums, bookstore, souvenir shops, train depot, cafes, mule rides along the rim, bicycles to rent and shuttles to ride.

p52

North Rim

Hiking ✓✓✓
Views ✓✓✓
Peace ✓✓✓

Hiker's Paradise

From the easy, quarter-mile walk to Bright Angel Point to wilderness expeditions for experienced backcountry route-finders, the North Rim has trails suiting every hiker – all of which are un-marred by the nonexistent masses.

Canyon & Beyond

With names like Point Im-perial and Point Sublime, you know these views are marvelous. You need go no further than the Grand Can-yon Lodge veranda to enjoy them, but you can also take far-flung adventures to dis-cover more.

Rest & Relaxation

Not the R&R of a luxury resort, but the kind that comes from ditching crowds, cars and commerce. North Rim charms are composed of endless quiet places, a beer in an Adiron-dack chair, breeze rustling aspen leaves and changing light over the canyon.

p129

Colorado River

Rafting ✓✓✓
Wilderness ✓✓✓
Hiking ✓✓✓

White water, Smooth Water

With over 160 major rapids tumbling along 277 river miles at the bottom of the Grand Canyon, it's not an exaggeration to say that rafting the Colorado is the ride of a lifetime. Still, sections of smooth water allow for ample meditative moments.

Wildness & Serenity

In the wilderness at the can-yon bottom, your chances of seeing bighorn sheep, pink rattlesnakes or canyon wrens are pretty good, and you'll pass your nights un-der a dark, starry sky and the white noise of the river.

Side Hikes

Floating down the river al-lows access to side canyons, tributaries and grottos that are extremely difficult to reach or inaccessible from the rim. Sidling up slot canyons and standing under waterfalls are some of the best rewards of a river trip.

p167

Look out for these icons:

 Our author's recommendation

 A green or sustainable option

 No payment required

On the Road

South Rim

Best Hikes

» Rim to rim (p72)

» Grandview Trail to Horse-shoe Mesa (p70)

» Hermit Trail to Santa Maria Spring (p71)

» South Kaibab Trail to Cedar Ridge (p69)

» Shoshone Point (p67)

Best Places to Stay

» El Tovar (p81)

» Bright Angel Lodge (p81)

» Desert View Campground (p80)

» Inn at 410 (p103)

» L'Auberge de Sedona (p114)

Why Go?

Step up to a South Rim overlook, and as the maw dramatically opens out before you – breeze carrying a soaring California condor along with high-desert hints of piñon and sage – you can expect to feel very small.

Taking in the grandeur from the rim is as far as most visitors go. But ranging below the rim brings the sheer immensity and splendor of the gorge into perspective; even hiking down a short way reveals fossils embedded in sandstone and rock art left by ancient Native Americans. Hiking up exposes the canyon's scale in a new, sweat-sheened light.

Desert wildflowers bloom out of rock in the springtime, autumn leaves light up the landscape in the fall, and the canyon's spires and temples are breathtaking when frosted with snow. All the while, light and shadow creep across the canyon, constantly recreating the landscape before you – a beautiful reminder to be here now.

When to Go
South Rim

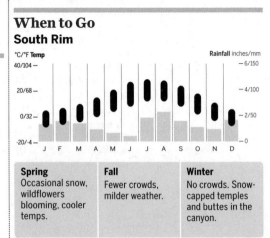

	Spring	Fall	Winter
	Occasional snow, wildflowers blooming, cooler temps.	Fewer crowds, milder weather.	No crowds. Snow-capped temples and buttes in the canyon.

Entrances

The South Rim has two park entrances: the South Entrance, 80 miles north of Flagstaff on Hwy 180, and the East Entrance on Hwy 64, 32 miles west of Cameron.

Unlike the Spanish explorers led by García López de Cárdenas in 1540, when you arrive at the South Rim you'll have some idea of the awesome views awaiting you. What you might not expect are long lines at the South Entrance, with waits of 30 minutes or more in the summer. Most visitors enter here, heading a few miles thereafter to Grand Canyon Village.

If possible, enter the park through the East Entrance, which is only 10 miles further from Flagstaff than the South Entrance. At this entrance you'll find a campground, a gas station and the Desert View service hub, which offers a snack bar, small information center, general store, gift shop and the Watchtower (p59). As you drive the 25 rim-hugging miles to Grand Canyon Village, your first glimpses of the canyon will be more dramatic and much less hectic.

PLANNING TIP

53

Consult *The Guide* or the kiosk at Desert View Information Center for sunrise and sunset times. It's worth showing up early to stake out a prime location.

Fast Facts

» Miles of rim trails: 12

» Highest elevation: 7420ft

» Elevation change: 4420ft

Reservations

» Make in-park accommodation reservations as early as possible if visiting the South Rim during high season. Hikers wishing to stay at Phantom Ranch can book as early as 13 months ahead; the same timeframe applies for mule-ride reservations.

Resources

» Xanterra (www.grand canyonlodges.com) is the primary in-park concessionaire, booking South Rim and Phantom Ranch lodgings and mule trips.

DON'T MISS

As in life, the best things at the South Rim are free – like **sunrise** or **sunset** at a viewpoint along Desert View Dr, or a stop at **Mohave Point** to listen for the mighty **Hermit Rapid** below. Get inspired at **Kolb Studio**, shore up your geology knowledge at **Yavapai Geology Museum** and marvel at the canyon's human history at **Tusayan Ruins**.

Only slightly more expensive are prickly-pear margaritas on the porch swing at **El Tovar**, or an ice-cream cone from **Bright Angel Fountain** to enjoy on a walk along the **Rim Trail**. Or rent a bike at **Bright Angel Bicycles** for a spin along the rim.

When You Arrive

» The $25-per-vehicle park entrance fee permits unlimited visits to both rims within seven days of purchase. Those entering by bicycle, motorcycle or on foot pay $12.

» Upon entry, you'll receive a map and a copy of *The Guide*, a National Park Service (NPS) newspaper with current park news, and information on ranger programs, hikes, accommodations and park services.

» Make your first stop at Grand Canyon Visitor Center to get your bearings, walk out to Mather Point and then carry on with your day.

SOUTH RIM

The park's South Rim comprises four distinct sections: Grand Canyon Village, Hermit Rd, Desert View Dr and the below-the-rim backcountry.

You'll find most services in and around Grand Canyon Village, where lodges, restaurants, two of the three developed campgrounds, the backcountry office, visitor center, clinic, bank, grocery store, shuttles and other services almost comprise a full-fledged town.

Hermit Rd (p61) follows the rim from the village 8 miles west to Hermits Rest, offering seven viewpoints along the way.

Desert View Dr (p64) spans 25 miles from Grand Canyon Village through Desert View to the East Entrance, passing several excellent viewpoints, picnic areas and the Tusayan Ruins and Museum.

The Rim Trail (p66) starts at Hermits Rest, passes Kolb Studio, the lodges, Yavapai Observation Station and Mather Point in the village, and stretches east to Yaki Point. About 6½ miles of it is paved, from Powell Point through the village east to South Kaibab Trailhead. Access to the backcountry is by foot or mule along established trails.

MAJOR ROADS

Hwy 180 runs north to the South Entrance from Tusayan (2 miles), Valle (22 miles) and Flagstaff (80 miles). From Williams (30 miles west of Flagstaff on I-40), Hwy 64 heads north to Valle, where it connects with Hwy 180 to the park.

Hwy 89 runs from Flagstaff 44 miles north to Cameron, where Hwy 64 heads west to the park's East Entrance. It is 25 miles from the East Entrance to Grand Canyon Village.

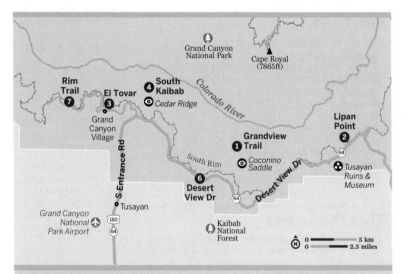

South Rim Highlights

❶ Feel the burn on the steep **Grandview Trail** (p70) and experience the blessing of rugged solitude

❷ Watch the changing shadow and light of another spectacular sunrise at **Lipan Point** (p65)

❸ Reward yourself après-hike with a deservedly decadent dinner at **El Tovar** (p55)

❹ Soak up stories and natural history on a morning ranger-led hike down the **South Kaibab** (p69)

❺ Linger under the stars for an evening **ranger talk** along the rim (p79)

❻ Take in the smells of sage, juniper and piñon at the spectacular overlooks along **Desert View Dr** (p64)

❼ Follow the Trail of Time along the **Rim Trail** (p66) for an accessible, close-up look at canyon geology

Back in the day, before digital photography or even one-hour processing existed, the Kolb brothers were shooting souvenir photos of mule-riding Grand Canyon visitors as they began their descent down the Bright Angel Trail. In true American entrepreneurial fashion, they'd then sell finished prints to the tourists returning to the rim at the end of the day. This was in the early 1900s, before there was even running water on the South Rim. So how did they process the prints?

After snapping photos from their studio window, which strategically overlooked a bend in the trail, one of the brothers would then run 4.6 miles down to the waters of Indian Garden with the negatives, print the photos in their lab there and then run (or perhaps hike briskly) back up the Bright Angel to meet delighted visitors with their print.

Park Policies & Regulations

Have a look at p19 for general information on park policies and regulations on both rims.

SIGHTS

While you'll obviously want to marvel at the main attraction, the South Rim is also the site of notable buildings and museums that offer some fascinating and enriching historical perspective on your canyon experience. Many of the historic buildings on the South Rim were designed by visionary architect Mary Colter (boxed text p191), painstakingly researched and designed to complement the landscape and reflect the local culture.

Consider purchasing the self-guided *Walking Tour of Grand Canyon Village Historical District* brochure ($1) at park bookstores. Hours listed here are for the summer season; unless otherwise noted, hours vary seasonally.

Grand Canyon Village

TOP CHOICE El Tovar HISTORIC BUILDING
(Map p60) With its unusual spires and darkwood beams rising behind the Rim Trail, elegant El Tovar remains a grande dame of national-park lodges. El Tovar was built in 1905 for the Atchison, Topeka & Santa Fe Railway and designed by architect Charles Whittlesey as a blend between a Swiss chalet and the more rustic style that would come to define national-park lodges in the 1920s. Spacious rooms (many with sleigh beds and rim overlooks), a dining room with panoramic views, and wide, inviting porches with rocking chairs offered visitors a comfortable and elegant place to relax after a long journey to the park.

Today the public spaces look much as they did when the lodge opened, though many of the rooms are smaller, and it remains the most luxurious lodge (p81) on the South Rim. Moose and elk trophy heads, reproduction Remington bronzes and Craftsman-style furniture lend the interior a classic Western feel. A gift shop and restaurant adjoin the lobby, and the helpful concierge can book bus tours and answer questions. The lodge sits about 100 yards from the rim, and though it's thronged with tourists by day, the scene mellows in the evening. The back porch, a sweet spot to relax with a drink, looks out over a small lawn, one of the park's few grassy areas and a great place for small children to play. If the back porch is full, take your drink to the side porch – it's closer to the Rim Trail but has a delightful bench swing that's the perfect perch after a long hike.

Hopi House HISTORIC BUILDING
(Map p60; ⊘8am-8pm) Another beautiful stone building designed by Mary Colter for Fred Harvey, Hopi House was built largely by Hopi Indians and was finished a few weeks before the completion of El Tovar in 1905. It was modeled after the pueblos at Old Oraibi, a Hopi settlement on the Third Mesa in eastern Arizona that vies with Acoma, New Mexico, for the title of longest continually inhabited village in the US. The interior does resemble an ancient pueblo, featuring adobe walls and concrete walls made to look like dirt, corner fireplaces and a timbered ceiling. Exterior ladders and interior staircases connect each story. In the park's early days, Hopi Indians lived here, sold crafts and entertained travelers with nightly dances. Today, it's a wonderful place to shop

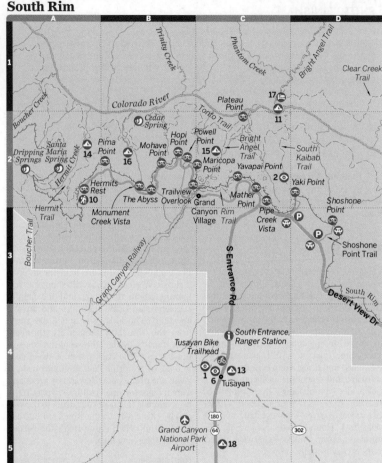

for high-quality Native American jewelry, basketwork, pottery and other crafts.

Kolb Studio   HISTORIC BUILDING
(Map p60; ⊙8am-7pm) Photographer brothers Ellsworth and Emery Kolb first came to the Grand Canyon from Pennsylvania in 1901 and 1902, respectively. The pioneering brothers built their photography studio in 1904 and made their living photographing parties traveling the Bright Angel Trail. In 1911, after having boats custom-made for the expedition, they filmed their own trip down the Green and Colorado Rivers, and canyon

visitors flocked to their small auditorium to see the film, in which both brothers repeatedly tumble into the water. Emery continued to show the film to audiences twice daily until his death at 95 in 1976.

Today, their studio, perched on the edge of the canyon, holds a small but well-stocked bookstore and an art gallery with changing exhibits. You can still see clips of the original Kolb river film, though not projected on the big screen (nor introduced by the late Emery). Their home, built on two stories and beneath the bookstore, is maintained by the

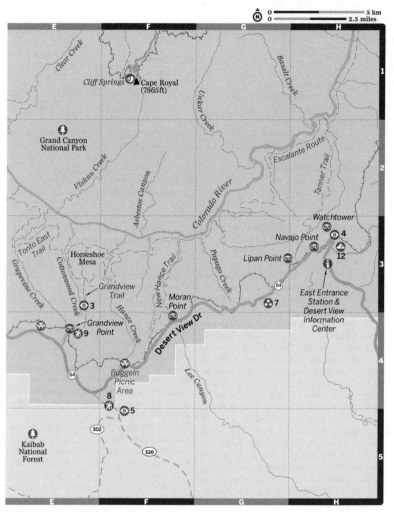

Grand Canyon Association and occasionally opened to the public for tours.

Yavapai Geology Museum & Observation Station
MUSEUM

(Map p60; ⊗8am-7pm) Panoramic views of the canyon unfold behind the plate-glass windows of this observation station on Yavapai Point, one of the South Rim's best viewpoints. Plaques beneath the large windows identify and explain the formation of the landmarks upon which you're gazing. With a topographic relief model of the canyon itself and a model illustrating and explaining the canyon's sedimentary layers, this is an excellent place to bone up on Grand Canyon geology before hiking down. If the exhibits here spark your curiosity, consider attending a ranger talk about canyon geology (check *The Guide* for locations and times).

Bright Angel Lodge
HISTORIC BUILDING

(Map p60) By the 1930s, tourism to the park had boomed, and English immigrant Fred Harvey decided to build a more affordable alternative to El Tovar. Designed by Mary Colter, the log-and-stone Bright Angel Lodge was completed in 1935. Just off the lobby is the **History Room**, a small museum devoted to Harvey, who, in conjunction with the Atchison, Topeka & Santa Fe Railway, transformed the Grand Canyon into a popular tourist destination. Don't miss the fireplace, built of Kaibab limestone and layered with stones that represent the canyon strata from river to rim.

On the lodge grounds is the **Buckey O'Neill Cabin**, now a guesthouse. Built in the 1890s by William Owen O'Neill, the cabin is the longest continually standing building on the rim. Nicknamed 'Buckey' because he 'bucked the odds' in a card game, O'Neill moved to Arizona in 1879 and worked as an author, journalist, miner, politician and judge. Drawn to a copper deposit near Anita, about 14 miles south of today's Grand Canyon Village, he lived in this cabin and worked on the side as a tour guide. As was the case with so many other prospectors, Buckey found mining to be an unprofitable venture, so he eventually sold his land to the railways and went on to become mayor of Prescott, Arizona. He was one of Teddy Roosevelt's Rough Riders in the Spanish American War and died the day before the assault on San Juan Hill. Today, the lucky few who make reservations well in advance can stay in his cabin.

The first stagecoach to the South Rim left Flagstaff on May 19, 1892. Eventually, stages made the 11-hour ride to the park thrice weekly, and three stations along the way allowed visitors to stretch their legs, dust off and prepare for the next leg of the journey. **Red Horse** (originally called Moqui Station) was built 16 miles south of the village in the 1890s; in 1902 Ralph Cameron,

who controlled Bright Angel Trail, moved the building to its present site on the Bright Angel Lodge grounds and converted it into the Cameron Hotel. It served as a post office from 1907 to 1935. When Mary Colter designed Bright Angel Lodge in the early '30s, she insisted the station be preserved and incorporated into the lodge.

Lookout Studio   HISTORIC BUILDING
(Map p60; ⊙8am-sunset) Like Mary Colter's other canyon buildings, Lookout Studio (c 1914) was modeled after stone dwellings of the Southwest Pueblo Indians. Made of rough-cut Kaibab limestone – the stone that comprises one of the layers of the upper canyon walls – with a roof that mirrors the lines of the rim, the studio blends into its natural surroundings. The interior features an arched stone fireplace, stone walls and a timber-framed ceiling. Inside, you'll find a small souvenir shop and a tiny back porch that offers spectacular canyon views. There's also a stone stairway snaking below Lookout Studio leading to another terrace, which may be closed in bad weather.

Grand Canyon Train Depot HISTORIC BUILDING
(Map p60) Designed by Francis Wilson for the Atchison, Topeka & Santa Fe Railway, this train depot was completed in 1909, eight years after the first train arrived in the village from Williams. It's one of three remaining log depots in the country and one of only 14 log depots ever constructed in the US. The logs are squared on three sides to create a flat-walled interior. The 1st floor was used for passenger services, and the 2nd floor was a two-bedroom apartment for the ticket agent. Today, a Grand Canyon Railway

train pulls into the station daily from Williams (see the boxed text p226).

Verkamp's Visitor Center   HISTORIC BUILDING
(Map p60; ☺8am-7pm) In 1898 John G Verkamp sold souvenirs from a tent outside Bright Angel Lodge to persevering travelers who arrived at the canyon after long, arduous stagecoach rides. He was a little before his time, however, as there weren't enough customers to make a living, and he closed down his operation after only a few weeks. The arrival of the railroad in 1901 opened up the canyon to more and more tourists, and in 1905 Verkamp returned to build the modified Mission-style Verkamp's Curios at its present location beside Hopi House. After running the shop for more than 100 years, Verkamp's ancestors closed down the business, and the NPS revamped the building as a visitor center in 2008.

Grand Canyon Cemetery   CEMETERY
(Map p60) More than 300 people are buried at Grand Canyon Cemetery; the lives of many of them are intricately woven into the history of the canyon. They include the Kolb brothers, John Verkamp, Ralph Cameron and John Hance, who ran a hotel a few miles from Grandview Point.

Desert View

Tusayan Ruins & Museum
(Map p56; admission free; ☺9am-5pm) The tiny Tusayan Ruins & Museum houses only a few displays of pottery and jewelry, but the 4000-year-old split-twig figures of animals (see p182) on exhibit are worth a stop at this beautiful little stone building. From here you can take a short self-guided walk through the remains of an **ancient Pueblo village** that was excavated in 1930. Tree-ring analyses date the structure to 1185, and archaeologists estimate that about 30 people lived here. Much of the village has been left only partially excavated in order to prevent excessive erosion damage to the unrestored room sections and kiva (ceremonial chamber). Look in *The Guide* for details on ranger-led tours. This is a shaded area with bathrooms, but there are no canyon views.

Watchtower
(Map p56) The top floor of the Watchtower, at 7522ft, edges out Navajo Point as the highest spot on the rim itself. Designed by Mary Colter and built in 1932, the 70ft circular

stone Watchtower was inspired by ancient Pueblo watchtowers. You'll enter through the gift shop, above which a small terrace offers beautiful views. Continue up a small flight of stairs to the **Hopi Room**, where you can rest on a bench and admire the wall murals that depict the snake legend and a Hopi wedding, among other scenes. Second- and 3rd-floor balconies also overlook this room. A final flight of steps leads to the 4th floor, where binoculars and big windows offer expansive views in every direction. From here you can see the canyon and the Colorado River, the San Francisco Peaks, the Navajo Reservation, Echo Cliffs and the Painted Desert.

OVERLOOKS

Even if your visit to the canyon is very short, try to carve out some time to quietly sit and contemplate this monumental work of nature.

The best times of day to watch the light and shadow bring out the canyon's sculpted features are at sunrise and sunset – of course, these are also prime times for busloads of like-minded visitors to pull up and pile out for photo ops at the most popular overlooks. But you'd be surprised how few of them actually roam beyond the parking lots. Hiking a few minutes along the rim from any overlook is usually all it takes to get you to a secluded spot all your own.

Overlooks are listed here west to east.

Hermits Rest (p63) Stone archway welcomes you to the end of the line.

Pima Point (p63) Good views of Hermit Camp on the Tonto Platform and Hermit

---

TOP FIVE OVERLOOKS

Mohave Point (p63) For a look at the river and three rapids.

Hopi Point (p63) Catch huge sunset views.

Lipan Point (p64) Creeks, palisades, rapids and sunrises.

Desert View (p64) Climb to the top of the Watchtower and wave down at the river.

Yaki Point (p64) A favorite point to watch the sunrise warm the canyon's features.

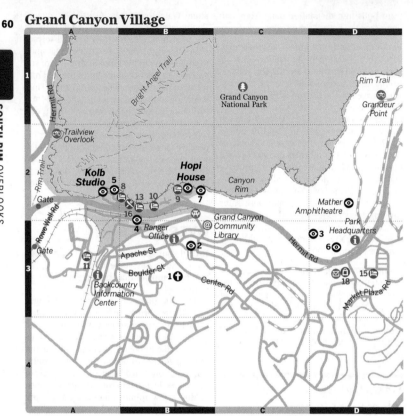

Rapids on the Colorado River as well as some sections of the Hermit Trail. A great spot to watch sunrise/sunset.

Abyss (p63) Good place to see very steep walls.

Mohave Point (p63) Great spot to watch sunrise/sunset.

Hopi Point (p63) Great views of various temples and buttes, and the river.

Powell Point (p62) Standing at this overlook and sharing its name is the Powell Memorial, a monument to the brave John Wesley Powell.

Maricopa Point (p62) Good views of Bright Angel Canyon.

Trailview Overlook (p62) Offers an excellent view of most of the Bright Angel Trail and is a very good spot from which to watch hikers and mule trains ascending and descending the trail.

Yavapai Point (p57) A westward alternative to Mather Point, Yavapai gives a good introduction to the lay of the canyon.

Mather Point (p64) With two outcrops, this overlook boasts a fantastic look into the canyon.

Pipe Creek Vista (p64) A quieter alternative to Mather Point on the same section of the South Rim.

Yaki Point (p64) A superb place to watch the sunrise, with knockout views of several formations.

Shoshone Point (p64) Accessible only by walking, Shoshone Point will reward you with a rocky promontory and some of the canyon's best views.

Grandview Point (p64) Take in expansive views of the canyon from the overlook, or hike down a short way for a bit more solitude.

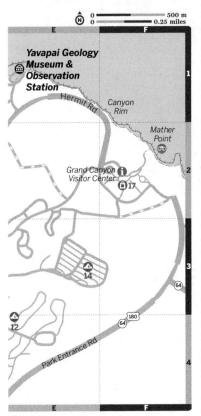

Moran Point (p64) Excellent view down both directions of the Colorado and of the colorful walls of Red Canyon.

Lipan Point (p64) Magnificent panoramic views taking in the curvy Colorado and the Palisades of the Desert.

Navajo Point (p64) This spot overlooks the river below and vast Navajo Reservation to the east.

Desert View (p64) The South Rim's highest overlook affords views in all directions from the top floor of the Watchtower, as well as from a lower terrace.

DRIVING

Two scenic drives follow the contour of the rim on either side of the village: Hermit Rd to the west and Desert View Dr to the east. The rim dips in and out of view as the road passes through the piñon-juniper and ponderosa stands of Kaibab National Forest. Pullouts along the way offer spectacular views and interpretive signs that explain the canyon's features and geology.

Millions of visitors drive up, jump out of their cars and snap a photo – but photos don't do justice to the enormity of this place.

Take a minute or 60 to walk out, find a quiet place to sit and absorb each view, unhurried. If you're short on time, select a few choice overlooks to enjoy at length. Breathe in the desert air, study the behavior of ravens and the swoop of turkey vultures, peer down at the river and wonder at the forces that carved this canyon.

Though you might expect bumper-to-bumper traffic, this is generally not the case. Yes, there's a constant stream of cars, but you'll rarely come to a standstill and can usually find plenty of parking at the viewpoints. The road to Yaki Point and the South Kaibab Trailhead is closed year-round to all traffic except bicycles and the green Kaibab Trail Route shuttle. From March 1 to November 30, Hermit Rd is closed to all traffic except bicycles and the red Hermits Rest Route shuttle. Both scenic drives may close due to snow or ice buildup from November through March; call ✆928-638-7888 for current road and weather conditions.

If you don't have a car or don't want to drive, bus tours (see p87) of both scenic drives leave several times daily year-round. Alternatively, you can hike the Rim Trail and hop on and off the free shuttle along the Hermit Rd route. Or rent a bike; shuttle racks can accommodate up to three bikes, and Bright Angel Bicycles (p86) even offers shuttle drop-offs and pickups.

Books & More Store (p84) sells an audio guide with more information on what you'll see along the rim. Some viewpoints offer good river views, while others are best for sunrises or sunsets.

🚗 Hermit Road Drive

Duration 2½ hours

Distance 8 miles

Start Grand Canyon Village

Finish Hermits Rest

Summary Hermit Rd heads out to the western reaches of the Rim Trail all the way to historic Hermits Rest, with exceptional views leading the way.

This popular road offers several exceptional views. It begins at the west end of Grand Canyon Village and ends at Mary Colter's distinctive Hermits Rest, built as a rest stop for early park tourists. Hermit Rd is closed to private vehicles from March through November, but the Hermits Rest shuttle route will take you to all the sites detailed here.

Although this drive also makes a great bike ride, the road is very narrow. Because shuttles are not allowed to pass bicycles along Hermit Rd, cyclists are required to pull off the road to allow vehicles to pass. However, starting from the Abyss, the Greenway Trail provides a multi-use path away from vehicle traffic all the way to Hermits Rest.

❶ **Trailview Overlook** offers a great view of Bright Angel Trail, the lush vegetation at Indian Garden and Grand Canyon Village on the rim to the east. If you arrive early in the morning, you may see the tiny specks of a faraway mule train descending into the canyon.

In 1890 prospector Daniel Lorain Hogan discovered what he believed to be copper 1100ft below ❷ **Maricopa Point**. He filed a mining claim for the area, including 4 acres on the rim, and set about making his fortune. After more than 40 years of minimal success, Hogan realized that the real money

at the canyon was in tourism, so in 1936 he built tourist cabins, a trading post and a saloon on the rim. In 1947 he sold the property to Madelaine Jacobs for $25,000.

Ironically, it was Jacobs who would make her fortune off mining interests here. Learning that the gray rock Hogan had ignored in his quest for copper was rich in uranium, she sold out to Western Gold & Uranium. From 1956 through 1969 the Orphan Mine just southwest of this point produced more than a half million tons of uranium ore. Tourists still visited the point during the mining, though the experience must have been somewhat marred by the noise and radioactive dust.

Today, in addition to the wide-angle views of the canyon from Maricopa Point, you can also see the metal remains of the tramway and elevator that moved the ore to the rim. Some areas above the rim are fenced off, in part due to a slight risk from radioactivity.

Perched at Powell Point, the ❸ **Powell Memorial** was erected in 1915 in honor of John Wesley Powell, the intrepid one-armed Civil War veteran, ethnologist and geologist who led the first white-water run through the canyon on the Colorado in 1869. It doesn't offer much of a river view, but it's a good spot to think about that first brave dive down the unexplored, wild Colorado.

The park was officially dedicated at this spot in 1920.

One of the park's best viewpoints, ④ **Hopi Point** juts out further than any other overlook along Hermit Rd and offers huge, spectacular views of plateau upon plateau and the Colorado River a mile below. Notable canyon features here include the Isis and Osiris Temples. Until completion of Hermit Rd in 1912, Hopi Point was the westernmost spot on guided tours. Nowadays, it's a popular place to watch the sunset and is often crowded on summer evenings. If you're here during shuttle season, walking the 0.3-mile segment of the Rim Trail between Powell Point and Hopi Point is a pleasant alternative to getting on the bus.

If you're doing the Grand Canyon speed-demon tour and only have time for a couple of stops, make them count at Mohave and Hopi Points. ⑤ **Mohave Point** serves up a delicious array of cliff views in all directions. It's also a particularly good place to see the Colorado, as three rapids – Salt Creek, Granite and Hermit – are visible below and downstream.

Aptly named, the ⑥ **Abyss** is a beautiful example of how steep some canyon drop-offs can be. If you're at all acrophobic, consider stopping at a different viewpoint – sheer cliffs drop 2600ft to the Redwall limestone below. If heights don't bother you, walk about a quarter mile westward along the Rim Trail and (carefully) check out the dizzying drop.

The overwhelming maw of the Grand Canyon can truly be appreciated from ⑦ **Pima Point**, where you can see for miles to the west, north and east. In 1912 the Atchison, Topeka & Santa Fe Railway completed Hermit Camp, a tourist hub with tent cabins, restrooms, showers and a blacksmith forge 3000ft below Pima Point, accessible from a trailhead at Hermits Rest. The camp was a popular mule-train destination, and a tramway was built in 1926 to transport supplies. By 1930, tourists favored Phantom Ranch, the stone lodge and cabins built along the river in 1922, and Hermit Camp was abandoned. In 1936 the railway intentionally torched the camp, the remains of which are still visible from the rim.

⑧ **Hermits Rest** (like Hermit Rd, and Hermit Rapid...) is one of the 13 canyon features named after one of the park's most famous residents, Louis Boucher (aka 'The Hermit'). Boucher was a Canadian immigrant who worked as a prospector and tourist guide and lived alone at Dripping Springs in Boucher Canyon, below Hermits Rest, from 1889 to 1912.

Hermit Road Driving Tour

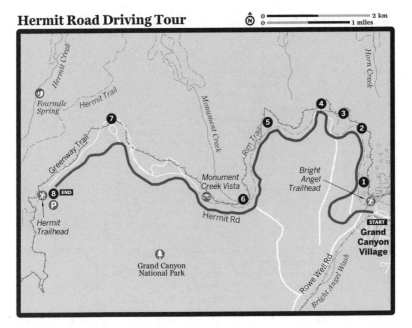

Back in the early 1900s, prospector Ralph Cameron held the rights to Bright Angel Trail, prompting the Atchison, Topeka & Santa Fe Railway to develop other trails and services for canyon tourists. In 1909 the railway began work on Hermit Rd. It commissioned none other than Mary Colter to design a resthouse at the end of the road, constructed an 8.5-mile trail from the rim into the canyon and built a camp at the end of the trail. Colter's Hermits Rest, a beautiful stone and wood shelter, offered tourists a place to freshen up before descending into the canyon or after the arduous journey back to the rim.

Today Hermits Rest features a small gift shop and snack bar. You can still take Hermit Trail into the canyon. If you just want to stretch your legs, hike down about 10 minutes and search the walls for exposed fossil beds.

 Desert View Drive

Duration 1-4 hours

Distance 25 miles

Start Grand Canyon Visitor Center

Finish East Entrance

Summary Desert View Dr is the red-carpet welcome to the Grand Canyon

(sans paparazzi and hype), starting at the East Entrance and including historic architecture, a Native American ruin and inspiring vistas.

Six well-marked viewpoints (plus several unmarked ones), an ancient Puebloan site with accompanying small museum and Mary Colter's Watchtower give you a dash of culture with your canyon views. A leisurely drive, with plenty of time for every stop, takes about four hours. Start early enough and you might be lucky enough to see a loping coyote or grazing mule deer near the road. Desert View Dr could also make an excellent one-way bike ride if you can be dropped off or picked up at one end, or if you don't mind the 50-mile round-trip.

As it sits beside the Grand Canyon Visitor Center parking lot (300 yards away), ❶ **Mather Point** can be the most crowded of all the viewpoints. However, its roomy overlooks extend to two promontories that jut out over the canyon, providing views of the Bright Angel and South Kaibab Trails ribboning down into the canyon. Or you can walk 1.3 miles east along the Rim Trail to ❷ **Pipe Creek Vista** to escape the crowds. Views from this overlook take in Brahma Temple and O'Neill Butte, as well as Pipe Creek, naturally, and it tends to be less of a

Desert View Driving Tour

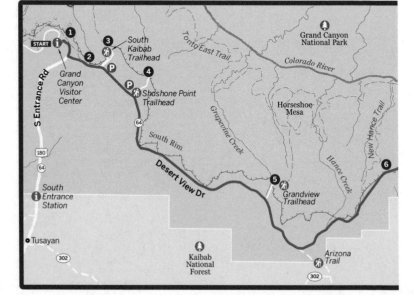

traffic circus than Mather Point. From Pipe Creek you can catch the Kaibab Trail Route shuttles back to the information plaza.

Closed year-round to private vehicles, ❸ **Yaki Point** lies just north of Desert View Dr and is accessed by the green Kaibab Trail Route shuttles. From Yaki Point in 1924 the NPS began the two-year process of blasting rock to create South Kaibab Trail, an effort to bypass Ralph Cameron's Bright Angel Trail. East of the trail, you'll get an excellent look at Zoroaster Temple and Wotan's Throne beyond.

If you don't see many cars as you drive by the unsignposted ❹ **Shoshone Point Trailhead** (p67), make time for the wonderful 1-mile walk to this peaceful picnic spot and viewpoint.

They didn't call the next overlook ❺ **Grandview Point** for nothing. Peter Berry (another prospector-turned-entrepreneur) and his partners built the Grandview Toll Trail in 1893 to access copper claims more than 2000ft below on Horseshoe Mesa. In 1897 he built the Grand View Hotel here on the rim, and when he wasn't hauling copper, he led tourists into the canyon on foot and by mule. When the railroad arrived 13 miles west of here in 1901, tourists naturally gravitated toward those facilities, forcing Berry to close up shop in 1908. Un-

fortunately, his mining venture petered out about the same time. Today thousands make a steep descent into the canyon via Berry's Grandview Trail, while others enjoy impressive canyon views from the spot where his hotel once thrived.

The oft-visited ❻ **Moran Point** is named after Thomas Moran, the landscape painter who spent just about every winter at the canyon from 1899 to 1920 and whose romantically dramatic work was instrumental in securing the canyon's national-park status. From here you can see down the river in both directions, and peer down onto the reddish-orange Hakatai shale of Red Canyon below. Particularly in the early morning or evening light, it's easy to see what drew Moran and hundreds of other artists to the canyon.

See p86 for details about the Tusayan Ruins and Museum.

One of the most spectacular viewpoints on the South Rim, ❼ **Lipan Point** gives a panoramic eyeful of the canyon and makes a magnificent spot to watch the sunset. From here, you'll get an unobstructed view of Unkar Rapid just to the west. You can also catch glimpses of both 75-Mile Creek and Unkar Creek, which feed into either side of the Colorado; on the north bank, look for the gentle slopes of Unkar Delta at the sinuous kink in the river. To the northeast, the sheer cliffs called the Palisades of the Desert define the southeastern wall of the Grand Canyon, beyond which the Echo and Vermilion Cliffs lie in the distance.

The Escalante and Cardenas Buttes are the immediate features you'll see from ❽ **Navajo Point** (7498ft), beyond which you'll get good views of several miles' worth of the Colorado River. You can also look to the east back at Desert View and the ❾ **Watchtower** (p59).

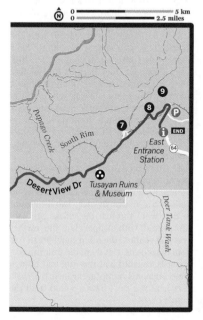

DAY HIKES

Hiking along the South Rim is among park visitors' favorite pastimes, with options for all levels and persuasions. The popular river-bound corridor trails (Bright Angel and South Kaibab) span the 7 to 10 miles to the canyon floor, following paths etched thousands of years ago by drainage routes. Several turnaround spots make these trails ideal for day hikes of varying lengths. Both can get packed during summer with foot and mule traffic. For more solitude, opt for a less trodden trail like Hermit or Grandview.

GETTING AWAY FROM IT ALL

It's easy to get away if you know where to find the 'emergency exits.'

» Arrive through the East Entrance (p53)

» Take the 1-mile trail to Shoshone Point (p67)

» Walk along the rim just east of Pima Point (p63) or east of Mather Point (p64)

» Avoid the Rim Trail through Grand Canyon Village between 9am and 5pm

» Hike into the canyon on the steep and narrow Hermit Trail to Santa Maria Spring (p71)

» Camp at Desert View Campground (p80) rather than Mather Campground

Most of the trails start with a super-steep series of switchbacks that descend quickly to the dramatic ledge of Coconino sandstone about 2 miles beneath the rim. Hike another 3 miles and you'll hit the sun-baked Tonto Platform, which after another couple of miles opens up to inner gorge vistas. From the platform it's a fast and furious pitch to the canyon floor and Colorado River. Most day hikers will want to stay above the Tonto Platform, particularly in summer.

Day hiking requires no permit, just preparation and safety. In the following descriptions, we specify whether the listed distances are one way or round-trip. (Hiking time depends largely on each hiker's ability.) Day hikes that can extend into overnight excursions are noted in the text.

The first two hikes listed here are excellent for families, as neither involve significant elevation change.

To help you decide which hikes to do, see the hiking chart on p30. Day hikes are listed here in ascending order of difficulty and duration.

🏃 Rim Trail

Duration Varies

Distance Varies (up to 12 miles one way)

Difficulty Easy-moderate

Start Hermits Rest

Finish Pipe Creek Vista

Transportation Shuttle

Summary The Rim Trail can be walked in its entirety in a day with stops at scenic viewpoints, or explored in short segments by hopping on and off the shuttles.

The Rim Trail makes a lovely stroll at sunrise, sunset or under a starry sky, times when the crowds really thin out. Runners also favor this trail before the heat hits. When you first arrive in the park, stretch your legs along the trail to take in the canyon air and get the lay of the land. The trail includes the Trail of Time exhibit (boxed text, p198), with examples of stone from geologic layers within the canyon, interpretive signs and viewing spots.

Stretching from Hermits Rest on the rim's western edge through Grand Canyon Village to Pipe Creek Vista and with an elevation change of a mere 200ft, the Rim Trail connects a series of scenic points and is hands down the easiest long walk in the park. By no means a nature trail, it's paved from Powell Point (2 miles west of Kolb Studio) to the South Kaibab Trailhead (4.6 miles east of Kolb Studio), which makes it accessible to wheelchairs and more easily navigable for those with mobility issues.

Still, flexibility is a big draw, with the shuttles making it simple to jump on for a segment and hike for as long as you like. Every viewpoint from Hermits Rest to Yaki Point is accessed by one of three shuttle routes, which means you can walk to a vista and shuttle back, or shuttle to a point, walk to the next and shuttle from there. A helpful map inside *The Guide* shows the shuttle stops and hiking distances along each segment of the trail.

The trail passes many of the park's historical sights, including **El Tovar**, **Hopi House**, **Kolb Studio**, **Lookout Studio** and **Verkamp's Visitor Center**. The 3 miles or so that wind through the village are usually packed with people, but the further west you venture, the more you'll break free from the crowds. Out there the trail runs between Hermit Rd and the rim, and though some segments bump up against the road, elsewhere you can't hear a sound from the shuttle buses.

One very pretty stretch is the mile east of **Pima Point**, where the trail is set far back from the road, offering stunning views and relative solitude. Winding through piñon-juniper woodlands, it passes several viewpoints; see the Hermit Rd drive (p61) for details. **Mohave** and **Hopi Points** offer great views of the Colorado River, with three visible rapids (Salt Creek, Granite and Hermit) below and downstream.

Shoshone Point

Duration 40 minutes round-trip

Distance 2 miles round-trip

Difficulty Easy

Start/Finish Shoshone Point Trailhead

Transportation Car

Summary With an elevation change of only 50ft and a sandy trail through ponderosa forest, Shoshone Point puts solitude within easy reach.

The gentle and cool amble out to Shoshone Point, accessible only by foot or bike, can be a welcome pocket of peace during the summer heat and crowds. This little-known hike is also ideal for children. Chances are you won't see another person, which means you can have the spectacular views all to yourself.

The trail starts from a dirt pullout along Desert View Dr, 1.2 miles east of Yaki Point or 6.3 miles west of Grandview Point. There's no official trailhead or signpost, so look for the dirt road barred by a closed and locked gate. The park service deliberately downplays this trail, which it makes available from May to October for weddings and other private events. If the parking lot is full of cars, refrain from hiking out, out of respect for any private events taking place. When it hasn't been reserved for a special gathering, and during winter months, hikers are welcome on the trail. Because the trail is sandy, it isn't wheelchair-friendly, and if you're cycling you'll have to saddle up a mountain bike to ride out here.

It's a fast and mostly flat out-and-back walk along the forested trail, which weaves through fragrant ponderosa pines before opening up in a clearing. This is a great spot for a family gathering, as you'll find picnic tables, BBQ grills and portable toilets. Nearby Shoshone Point juts out into the canyon, offering magnificent views of the North Rim's full sweep. Unlike the other scenic points, there are no safety railings here. You can walk to the tip of the slender plateau and its Easter Island *moai*-like formation, where it feels almost possible to reach out and touch **Zoroaster Temple**.

Bright Angel Trail – Short Day Hike

Duration Mile-and-a-Half Resthouse 2-3 hours round-trip; Three-Mile Resthouse 4-5 hours round-trip

Distance 3 miles round-trip; 6 miles round-trip

Difficulty Moderate-difficult

Start/Finish Bright Angel Trailhead

Transportation Shuttle

Summary Test out your canyon legs with a hike to either resthouse on the well-traveled Bright Angel Trail; bonuses on the Bright Angel are merciful shade and water.

The most popular of the corridor trails, the Bright Angel is wide, well graded and easy to follow. It's equally attractive to first-time canyon hikers and seasoned pros, as well as mule trains, making it a heavily trafficked route. But the din doesn't lessen the sheer beauty. The steep and scenic 7.8-mile descent to the Colorado is punctuated with four logical turnaround spots, including two well-appointed resthouses for opportunities to seek shade and hydration. Even if you're wary of crowds, you won't regret taking a jaunt of some length on the Bright Angel.

The trail follows a natural route along the Bright Angel Fault and was first used by the Havasupai to reach the glistening water source at Indian Garden and the inner-canyon recesses. In the late 19th century, miners improved the trail, enlisted the help of mules and began charging a toll for usage. While numerous individuals and groups, including the Atchison, Topeka & Santa Fe Railway, wrangled for control, the reins eventually went to the NPS in 1928.

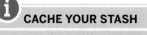

CACHE YOUR STASH

If you plan to do some hiking and don't want to leave laptops, passports or other valuables in the car, Bright Angel Lodge offers a storage service for a small fee. Keep in mind that the service is offered on a space-available basis.

Bright Angel Trail – Day Hikes

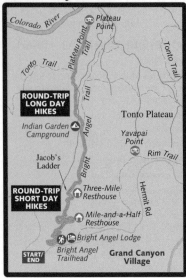

There is both shade and seasonal water on the Bright Angel (unlike the South Kaibab). Still, the summer heat can be crippling; day hikers should either turn around at one of the two resthouses (a 3- to 6-mile round-trip) or hit the trail at dawn to safely make the longer hikes to Indian Garden and Plateau Point (see p68). Hiking to the Colorado for the day is not an option during the summer.

The trailhead of the oft-crowded Bright Angel Trail is smack in Grand Canyon Village, just west of Kolb Studio and Bright Angel Lodge. There's ample nearby parking, or you can take the shuttle bus to the Hermits Rest transfer stop and walk from there. The piñon-fringed trail quickly drops into some serious switchbacks as it follows a natural break in the cliffs of Kaibab limestone, the Toroweap formation and Coconino sandstone. The trail soon passes through two tunnels – look for the Indian pictographs on the walls of the first. After passing through the second, **Mile-and-a-Half Resthouse**, 1131ft and nearly an hour's hike from the top, comes into view. It has restrooms, an emergency phone and drinking water from May to September. Turning around here makes for a 2½-hour round-trip.

Continuing downward through different-colored rock layers, more switchbacks finally deposit you 2112ft down at **Three-Mile Resthouse**, which has seasonal water and an emergency phone but no restrooms. Down below, you'll see the iridescent green tufts of Indian Garden tucked into a canyon fold, as well as the broad expanse of Tonto Platform, a nice visual reward before beginning the ascent back to the rim. First-time Grand Canyon hikers should strongly consider making this their turnaround point.

Bright Angel Trail – Long Day Hike

Duration Indian Garden 5-7 hours round-trip; Plateau Point 8-10 hours round-trip

Distance 9.2 miles round-trip; 12.2 miles round-trip

Difficulty Difficult

Start/Finish Bright Angel Trailhead

Transportation Shuttle

Summary Continuing down the Bright Angel brings you to the shady oasis of Indian Garden; for a more challenging and very exposed hike, cross Tonto Platform to reach Plateau Point for gorgeous views of the inner gorge. Distances and durations for these hikes reflect round-trips from trailhead to turnaround and back. Follow the Short Day Hike description and continue from Three-Mile Resthouse using the following hike description.

If you're continuing down from Three-Mile Resthouse, you'll soon hit a grueling set of switchbacks known as **Jacob's Ladder**, which twist through Redwall limestone cliffs. A bridge ferries you across the transcanyon water pipeline, and soon after you descend into the cool leafiness of **Indian Garden**, where Havasupai still farmed up until a century ago. These days, it's a popular campground, with a ranger station, toilets, year-round drinking water, shaded picnic tables and a mule corral. If this is your day-hike destination, linger in the soothing, albeit crowded, spot: eat lunch under a cottonwood, nap on the grass and splash your feet in the creek. With an elevation gain of 3060ft, it's a hard and hot 4.6-mile climb back up to the rim – particularly the thigh-burning Jacob's Ladder. The round-trip takes about seven hours with a rest here.

From the campground, if you turn left and head west across Garden Creek, you'll soon reach the **Plateau Point Trail** junction, a spur off the Tonto Trail. This ribbon of a trail unfurls north for just under a mile over the barren and yucca-studded **Tonto Plateau**, which is not as flat as it looks from above. The trail dead-ends at **Plateau Point** (3120ft below the rim) for a stunning view of the inner gorge. Though it's a popular year-round destination for strong day hikers, rangers nonetheless discourage anyone from making the round-trip trek in summer. The long, exposed stretch can be brutally hot, with the 12-mile round-trip taking up to 10 hours.

🚶 South Kaibab Trail

Duration Cedar Ridge 1-2 hours round-trip; Skeleton Point 3-5 hours round-trip

Distance 3 miles round-trip; 6 miles round-trip

Difficulty Moderate; moderate-difficult

Start/Finish South Kaibab Trailhead

Transportation Shuttle

Summary Day-hike destinations on the South Kaibab give hikers a steep, stark and rewarding challenge on this spectacular South Rim spine, but this party is BYO water, as the trail has no water sources.

One of the park's prettiest trails, the South Kaibab combines stunning scenery and adventurous hiking with every step. The only corridor trail to follow a ridgeline instead of a drainage route, the red-dirt path traverses the spine of a crest, allowing for unobstruct-

South Kaibab Trail

ℹ️ DO LOOK DOWN

When hiking out of the canyon, it helps to gauge your progress by stopping occasionally to look back at how far you've climbed – instead of only up toward the rim, which can feel daunting and overwhelming, especially when you're tired.

ed 360-degree views. Blasted out of the rock by rangers in the mid-1920s, the South Kaibab is steep, rough and wholly exposed. The dearth of shade and water, combined with the sheer grade, make ascending the South Kaibab particularly dangerous in summer, and rangers discourage all but the shortest of day hikes. The main passersby during summer are mule trains taking the shortest route to Phantom Ranch, backpackers planning to ascend Bright Angel and day hikers out for a quick peek. The trail sees a fair number of rescues, with up to a half-dozen on a hot June day. Even if you're just hiking a few miles, plan on bringing a gallon of water.

Summer day hikers should turn around at **Cedar Ridge**, perhaps the park's finest short day hike. Up to a two-hour round-trip with a 1140ft change in elevation, Cedar Ridge is a dazzling spot, particularly at sunrise, when the deep ruddy umbers and reds of each canyon fold seem to glow from within. This hike can also be done with a ranger; see p79. During the rest of the year, the continued trek to Skeleton Point, 1.5 miles beyond Cedar Ridge and 2040ft below the rim, makes for a fine day hike – though the climb back up is a beast in any season.

The trailhead is 4.5 miles east of Grand Canyon Village along Yaki Point Rd, just shy of the point itself. To keep crowds in check during the high season, you're only permitted to park at the trailhead between December and February; all other times require a ride aboard either the Kaibab Trail Route shuttle (p86) or the far more direct Hikers' Express shuttle (p87). Water and toilets are available at the trailhead.

From the mule corral the trail starts out deceptively gentle, with a long, well-graded switchback that leads to the end of a promontory about 20 minutes from the top. Here the cliff-hugging trail opens up to a shaggy promontory, which juts off the elbow of a switchback and offers a sweeping panorama of the purplish Tonto Platform far below. The ledge, unfortunately dubbed 'Ooh Aah Point,' is a nice spot for rest and refreshment. It's also a good juncture to gauge how you're feeling and consider turning back, ascending the 780ft to the top for a round-trip hike of a little over 1.5 miles.

Soon after, things turn serious, as the trail takes a sharp nosedive and begins to zigzag down a series of steep, tight switchbacks, making its way down the red sandstone. After about 30 minutes, the trail straightens out some when it hits the gorgeous **Cedar Mesa** and its namesake ridge, a striking red-tinged mesa. Stop long enough for a snack and perhaps a visit to the pit toilet. But what you'll linger for are the lovely vast views of Bright Angel Canyon, Devil's Corkscrew and the North Rim. This is considered the last 'safe' turnaround in summer, and the ascent from here takes one to two hours.

The trail then meanders off the mesa toward **O'Neill Butte**, wraps around to the east, then levels out onto another plateau known as **Skeleton Point**, where you can enjoy views of the Colorado River while you refuel with a snack.

🏃 Grandview Trail

Duration Coconino Saddle 1-2 hours round-trip; Horseshoe Mesa 4-6 hours round-trip

Distance 1.5 miles round-trip; 6 miles round-trip

Difficulty Moderate-difficult; difficult

Start/Finish Grandview Trailhead

Transportation Shuttle

Summary The Grandview is the bee's knees for stunning views and solitude – but it's also a knee-killer. In this case, the pain is your grand gain.

One of the steepest trails in the park – dropping 1200ft in the first three-quarters of a mile – Grandview is also one of the finest and most popular day hikes. The payoff following the stunning (and grueling) descent is an up-close look at one of the inner canyon's sagebrush-tufted mesas and a wonderful sense of solitude. The trail spirals down to a sprawling horseshoe-shaped mesa, where Hopi people once collected minerals.

In 1892 miner Pete Berry improved the former Native American route and constructed the current trail to access his Last Chance Mine at Horseshoe Mesa. For the next 15 years mules carted high-grade copper from there to the rim, even after Berry established his Grand View Hotel in 1897 and guided mule tours into the canyon.

The trailhead, right beside where the hotel once stood, is at Grandview Point, 12 miles east of the village on Desert View Dr, with year-round parking. While rangers don't recommend the trek to Horseshoe Mesa in summer (there's no water on the very exposed trail, and the climb out is a doozy), it's not overly long and certainly doable for strong hikers strapped with a hydration system and hiking early or late. For a shorter but still rewarding option, you can hike to Coconino Saddle and turn around there. Though it's only a 1.5-mile round-trip, it packs a quick and precipitous punch as you plunge 1600ft over less than a mile. With the exception of a few short level sections, the Grandview is a rugged, narrow and rocky trail and probably not the best choice for those skittish of heights or occasional loose footing. The steep drop-offs can be a bit scary, but although the trail is no longer maintained, Berry's metal-reinforced switchbacks have held up quite nicely.

Steep from the start, the trail first wends down the north end of **Grandview Point**, passing through Kaibab limestone along cobbled and cliff-edged rock stairs fringed with occasional flowers like fiery orange Indian paintbrush, straw-yellow arnica and blue delphinium. The views from the trailhead and just below are extraordinary, so even if you don't plan to hike, do walk down the trail a short way to take in the vistas. After about 30 or so minutes, you'll reach the **Coconino Saddle**, where the trail crosses the slender spur between Hance and Grapevine Canyons.

The saddle is a stunning overlook and a nice leafy spot for a snack and a rest in the shade. From here the trail is more exposed and eventually narrows to a ribbon as it traverses the ruddy Supai sandstone. A little over 2 miles past Coconino you'll hit a second saddle, connecting to **Horseshoe Mesa**, then a short dip later you reach pit toilets and remnants of old miners' cabins. There are traces of mining all over the mesa, from the speckled soil to old machinery and mine shafts. Although the many hollowed-out caves may look enticing, it's forbidden, not to mention very dangerous, to enter them.

For backpackers, three different trails descend 1000ft from Horseshoe Mesa to the Tonto Trail; the easiest to follow is the one that heads west near the pit toilets. Take it to hike a 7-mile loop around the foot of the mesa, following the Tonto and East Horseshoe Mesa Trails and rejoining Grandview a little ways up from the mesa, making for a 16.6-mile round-trip from the rim. Camping overnight on Horseshoe Mesa or the Tonto requires a backcountry permit. From the Tonto you can also hike 7 miles east to join the primitive New Hance Trail, or 20 miles west to the South Kaibab Trail.

🚶 Hermit Trail

Duration 2-4 hours round-trip

Distance 5 miles round-trip

Difficulty Moderate-difficult

Start/Finish Hermit Trailhead

Transportation Shuttle

Summary Unmaintained Hermit Trail winds down into the often-shady and usually unpopulated Hermit Canyon, connecting with several other trails to secluded canyon treks.

This wilderness trail descends into lovely Hermit Canyon by way of a cool spring. It's a rocky trip down, with some knee-wrenching switchbacks and long traverses that wend through the Supai cliffs. But if you set out early in the morning and take it slow, the Hermit offers a wonderfully serene day hike and glimpses into hidden corners. Offering several good turnaround spots and a clear shot to the Colorado River, the trail is equally appealing to both day hikers and backcountry adventurers.

In 1912 the Atchison, Topeka & Santa Fe Railway developed the trail (originally called El Tovar) for tourists to avoid tolls on the then privately controlled Bright Angel Trail. Mule trains ferried travelers to cushy Hermit Camp, which boasted a fancy stone cabin outfitted with a stove, glass windows, beds, and wood floors adorned with Navajo rugs. Supplies arrived via tram from Pima Point.

The trail was eventually renamed in honor of Louis 'The Hermit' Boucher (p63). When the NPS gained control of Bright Angel in 1928, luring away the mule tourism business, the Hermit was abandoned. Though officially untended since then, the trail is in remarkably good condition.

The best destination for day hikers is Santa Maria Spring. For a shorter but still worthwhile hike, turn around at the Waldron Trail junction in Waldron Basin, a round-trip of just under 3 miles with 1240ft of elevation change. The upper section of the Hermit is well shaded in the morning, making it a cool option in summer.

The **Hermit Trailhead** is at the end of its namesake road, 8 miles west of Grand Canyon Village and about 500ft from Hermits Rest. Although the road is only accessible via shuttle bus during the summer peak season, overnight backpackers are permitted to park at the lot near the trailhead throughout the year, and day hikers may do so in winter.

The rocky trail weaves down Hermit Basin toward Hermit Creek along a cobblestone route indented with steps and fraught with washouts. You'll reach the rarely used **Waldron Trail** (jutting off to the south) after about 1.5 miles and 1240ft of descent, followed some 30 minutes later by the spur trail headed for Dripping Springs. The trail then traces over some flat rocks (a perfect picnic spot) before descending steeply to **Santa Maria Spring**, a cool, shady haven, marked by a pretty stone shelter adorned with green foliage and a welcome wooden bench. The lush scene belies the spring, however, which is actually more of a trickle. You can drink the water provided you treat it.

🚶 Dripping Springs Trail

Duration 3-5 hours round-trip

Distance 7 miles round-trip

The three-day South Kaibab to North Kaibab trek is the classic Grand Canyon rim-to-rim hike and one of the finest trips in the canyon. You can start on either rim, but the climb up the South Kaibab is the hottest and most exposed in the park (thus, when hiking from north to south, it's best to ascend via the Bright Angel Trail instead). Most hikers begin on the South Kaibab and descend 6.4 miles to the Colorado River and Bright Angel Campground. From there it's 7 miles to Cottonwood Campground for the second night, and a final 6.8-mile climb up to the North Rim.

You'll need a backcountry permit (p34) to do the hike and get a lift home. Between mid-May and mid-October, the nifty **Trans-Canyon Shuttle** (see p223 for booking information). departs daily from Grand Canyon Lodge on the North Rim at 7am, arrives at Bright Angel Lodge on the South Rim around 11:30am, and then makes the return trip at 1:30pm, arriving back at the North Rim around 6pm. You must reserve a seat beforehand by sending in a deposit for half the fare. Cash, travelers checks and money orders are accepted; credit cards are not.

Remember that no facilities on the North Rim are open between mid-October and mid-May, and that the weather can be unpredictable – you could leave warm, sunny weather on the South Rim and walk into a snowstorm on the North Rim. There is a year-round ranger station that can provide shelter if you turn left at the North Kaibab trailhead and walk about a mile, but if you turn right at the trailhead, you will encounter a whole lotta nothing for 43 miles.

Difficulty Moderate-difficult

Start/Finish Hermit Trailhead

Transportation Shuttle

Summary An excellent day hike with an elevation change of 1440ft, Dripping Springs is a must-do for South Rim hikers curious to see why Louis Boucher made this secluded spot his home.

What better reason to tackle a hike than to answer the question: 'What would the Hermit do?' The trailhead at which you will address this inquiry is at Hermits Rest, and for the first 2 miles you will be on the Hermit Trail. At the junction with the Dripping Springs Trail, turn left and head west along the narrow path as it climbs and meanders along the slope's contours. In a mile you'll hit the junction with the Boucher Trail; turn left here to continue following the Dripping Springs Trail as it wends up toward the water source, which sprouts from an overhang not far beneath the rim. Droplets shower down from the sandstone ceiling, misting a myriad of maidenhair ferns, and here you will find your answers.

🏃 Tonto Trail (South Kaibab to Bright Angel)

Duration 7-9 hours one way

Distance 13.1 miles one way

Difficulty Very difficult

Start South Kaibab Trailhead

Finish Bright Angel Trailhead

Transportation Shuttle

Summary A stellar choice for strong hikers seeking solitude, this full-day excursion links two popular corridor trails along a peaceful, winding section of the Tonto Trail – but time it right to avoid charring your epidermis and brain. Distance and duration given for this hike are from start to finish; the hike description, however, details only the section linking the South Kaibab and Bright Angel trails. See Map p75 for this hike.

This is a long, difficult hike that's best suited for any season but summer. That said, it is doable in the hot months, provided you're on the trail by 5am and are a truly (be honest with yourself) experienced desert hiker. The Tonto is an unpatrolled wilderness trail with no facilities along its undulating, sun-baked desert terrain – under no circumstances is this route an option for moderate hikers during the summer.

The full Tonto is a 95-mile east–west passage along the entire length of the Tonto Platform, from Red Canyon to Garnet Canyon. Unlike the corridor trails, the Tonto does not extend to the rim, and nor does it involve significant elevation change, remaining around 4000ft. But it is by no means easy or level – this 4.1-mile section of the Tonto linking the South Kaibab and Bright Angel Trails jumps up and down as it follows the contours and drainage routes while paralleling the river and rim. Most hikers hop on the Tonto to connect to other trails. The segment described here – from the Tipoff on South Kaibab to Indian Garden on Bright Angel – is considered the central portion and is officially referred to as the Tonto Trail.

From the South Kaibab Trailhead it's a bone-jarring, hot 4.4-mile descent to the Tonto Trail junction, dropping 3260ft in elevation to the edge of the Tonto Platform. Just past the junction there's an emergency telephone and a toilet, a final reminder you're about to set foot on wilder, unpatrolled terrain.

Heading west on the Tonto, you'll hug the contours as the trail crosses the agave-dotted plateau and darts in and out of gulches. Deep in a canyon fold, the trail skirts through a canopy of cottonwoods near a drainage; just past here on the left is a terrific spot for camping. The trail remains in shade through midmorning. As the day progresses, however, the Tonto bakes and the surrounding landscape is completely parched – you don't want to be caught here midday in summer, so it's imperative you time your start accordingly. After about two hours you'll stumble into lush **Indian Garden**, the perfect shady oasis for cooling off before the haul up to the rim. From here it's a steep, hot and mule-churned 4.6 miles up the Bright Angel – but take heart, the first 1.5 miles are the toughest.

OVERNIGHT HIKES

Without venturing below the rim, it's impossible to truly appreciate the grandeur and depth – both literal and figurative – of the Grand Canyon, one of the world's deepest chasms. Hiking down through ancient layers of rock is a singularly surreal journey through geologic time, and the difference in ecology between rim and river is truly unique. Outdoor enthusiasts should plan to spend at least a night or two in the inner gorge to explore side canyons and tributaries of the rich wilderness along the Colorado.

Overnight hikes into the canyon require a backcountry permit, applications for which are taken up to four months in advance. If you didn't secure a backcountry permit be-

forehand, try your luck at the Backcountry Information Center, where walk-ins can fill vacancies or cancellations. Typically, you'll be wait-listed for several days before snagging one; see p34 for more detailed information.

🏃 Bright Angel Trail

Duration 3 days round-trip

Distance 18.6 miles round-trip

Difficulty Difficult

Start/Finish Bright Angel Trailhead

Transportation Shuttle

Summary The most popular path from the rim to the river, the Bright Angel is well maintained and easy to follow – fun for first-time canyon hikers and veterans alike.

The Bright Angel, a corridor trail that's wide and well-maintained, opens onto sweeping canyon views that take your mind off the knee-pounding 7.8-mile, 4380ft descent to the Colorado River. Because of its accessibility, it tends to be well traveled at all times of day, but its benefits include shady spots on the trail and seasonal water sources.

The path follows a natural break in the cliffs along Bright Angel Fault as it winds down to the productive freshwater spring at Indian Garden and on to the inner canyon. Native Americans were the first to use the route. Arriving in the late 19th century, prospectors improved the trail, introduced mules and began charging a toll. Tourism quickly outpaced mining, and by 1928 the NPS gained control.

Between mid-May and mid-September, extreme heat and sun mandate shorter hiking days; it's recommended that you stay off the trail between 10am and 4pm. Plan to start hiking at first light – 4:30am in summer and 6:30am in spring and fall. Take advantage of the trail's four day-use resthouses to get out of the sun and hydrate. These open-walled, roofed enclosures offer shade, picnic tables, nearby toilets and an emergency telephone. The two upper resthouses provide drinking water from May to September.

Mules have the right of way, so hikers must step aside to let mule trains pass by them. In winter and early spring the upper reaches can be icy, and you may want to wear crampons.

DAY 1: BRIGHT ANGEL TRAILHEAD TO INDIAN GARDEN CAMPGROUND
2-3 HOURS; 4.6 MILES

The Bright Angel Trailhead (6860ft) is both exhilarating and intimidating. The canyon unfolds before you in all its glory, hikers bustle around making last-minute adjustments to their backpacks, and wranglers acquaint first-time mule riders (is there any other kind?) with the curious beasts. You may even reread the interpretive sign at the trailhead to delay your first steps down a trail that looks like it drops off the edge of the planet.

Start slowly. If you suffer vertigo, look to the left for a while or just stop and close your eyes – the first five minutes are the hardest. Before you know it, you'll grow accustomed and the trail gets interesting.

Quickly pass through **First Tunnel**. Indian pictographs adorn the wall above the piñon- and juniper-lined trail. After passing through **Second Tunnel**, you'll reach **Mile-and-a-Half Resthouse** (5720ft), about 45 minutes from the trailhead. Anyone starting late or hiking for the first time should turn around here, allowing two to three hours round-trip.

About 200 yards before **Two-Mile Corner** look for more pictographs on a boulder. As you approach **Three-Mile Resthouse** (4920ft), about 90 minutes from the trailhead, your views expand over the Redwall limestone cliffs to Indian Garden and Tonto Platform below. Day hikers turning back here should allow four to five hours round-trip.

The switchbacks of **Jacob's Ladder** descend through sheer Redwall cliffs. Beyond, mesquite clumps grow from seasonal streambeds as you cross the transcanyon water pipeline and reach Indian Garden, 45 minutes from Three-Mile Resthouse. Havasupai Indians farmed here until the early 20th century.

Bright Angel Trail – Overnight Hikes

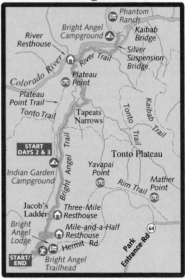

The year-round **Indian Garden Campground** (3800ft; 50-camper limit) is an inviting stop, with cottonwoods, a ranger station, a toilet and a resthouse with picnic tables. Year-round drinking water is available just before the Plateau Point Trail junction. Each of the campground's 15 sites offers a picnic table shaded by an open-walled, roofed enclosure. Indian Garden is a day-hike destination only for stronger hikers, who should allow five to seven hours round-trip.

DAY 2: DAY HIKE TO COLORADO RIVER
6-8 HOURS; 9.4 MILES

Passing the Tonto Trail junction after a half-mile, the Bright Angel Trail follows year-

HISTORY OF THE BRIGHT ANGEL

In one form or another, the Bright Angel Trail has been in continuous use for thousands of years. It was originally forged by the Havasupai Indians to access present-day Indian Garden, where they grew crops and farmed until the early 20th century. In the early 1890s prospectors Ralph Cameron and Pete Berry – who built the Grand View Hotel – improved the trail, eventually extending it to the river. Seeing a golden opportunity, in 1903 Cameron imposed a $1 toll on anyone using the trail, a widely criticized decision. In response, the Atchison, Topeka & Santa Fe Railway and others constructed toll-free alternative trails, such as the Hermit, to draw the burgeoning mule-tourism trade. In 1928 the park service took the reins of the Bright Angel and lifted the toll, thus ending mule traffic on the Hermit.

round Garden Creek as it cuts through the dramatic sandstone cliffs of **Tapeats Narrows**. Below, you'll cross the creek twice before arriving at a barren saddle.

In front of you is **Devils Corkscrew**, a massive set of switchbacks through the arid Vishnu schist (the oldest exposed rock of the canyon's layers) and the trail's last big descent. At the base of the switchbacks, the trail meets Pipe Creek, where the lush streamside habitat contrasts sharply with the desert. To the west, Garden Creek tumbles over a dramatic waterfall to join Pipe Creek. Ninety minutes from Indian Garden is the **River Resthouse**.

The welcome sight of the Colorado and Pipe Creek Beach below heralds the unsigned junction (2446ft) with the **River Trail**. Follow this undulating trail upstream for 30 minutes, enjoying views of Zoroaster Temple (7123ft), then cross the **Silver Suspension Bridge**. Linking the Bright Angel and South Kaibab Trails, the trail continues a short distance to the black Kaibab Suspension Bridge.

A ranger station, a toilet, drinking water and a telephone are just prior to the Bright Angel Creek footbridge. Cross the bridge, turn left at the junction and follow the creek upstream to Bright Angel Campground, 1.5 miles from the start of the River Trail. **Phantom Ranch** (2546ft) is 0.3 miles further. A right turn at the junction leads to the boat beach, **Anasazi ruins** and **Kaibab Suspension Bridge**. After a picnic, return to Indian Garden to camp. For different campgrounds, hike to Bright Angel Campground the first night, then Indian Garden Campground the second night, breaking the ascent into two days.

DAY 3: INDIAN GARDEN CAMPGROUND TO BRIGHT ANGEL TRAILHEAD
4-5 HOURS; 4.6 MILES

Retrace your steps up to the South Rim.

🚶 South Kaibab to Bright Angel

Duration 2 days one way

Distance 16.1 miles one way

Difficulty Difficult

Start South Kaibab Trailhead

Finish Bright Angel Trailhead

Transportation Shuttle

Summary This excellent South Rim hike takes you down the exposed spine of the South Kaibab and returns up the more forgiving Bright Angel; or make it a three-day rim-to-rim hike, trekking up the North Kaibab.

If you only have time to spend one night in the canyon, or you want to start and finish on the South Rim, this hike is a terrific choice.

This hike can also easily be adapted to do the classic rim-to-rim from the South Kaibab to the North Kaibab. For more details on this rim-to-rim hike, see the boxed text on p72.

DAY 1: SOUTH KAIBAB TRAILHEAD TO BRIGHT ANGEL CAMPGROUND
4-6 HOURS; 6.8 MILES

From the South Kaibab Trailhead (7260ft) the trail starts out at a gentle decline before spiraling steeply down to **Cedar Mesa** (6320ft), where you'll gain a slight reprieve. Past Skeleton Point the trail continues its precipitous drop over scree and through the Redwall cliffs, eventually opening up onto the **Tonto Platform**.

Traverse the agave-studded plateau past the Tonto Trail junction, then take a long pause and a deep breath at the **Tipoff** (3870ft), which provides an emergency phone and toilet and marks the beginning of the steep descent into the inner gorge.

South Kaibab to Bright Angel

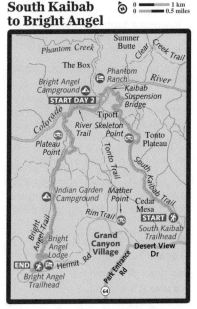

After hiking another challenging 1.5 miles and drinking in pretty views of Phantom Ranch, you'll reach the **River Trail**, which skirts the south side of the Colorado River and connects up with the Bright Angel Trail. Soon you'll cross the river via the skinny black **Kaibab Suspension Bridge**; turn left after crossing the bridge and you'll see an ancient Anasazi dwelling.

Just shy of a mile from here is the Bright Angel Campground.

As an alternative to camping at Bright Angel Campground, you may prefer spending the night at Phantom Ranch. This picturesque riverside ranch is the only accommodation within the canyon. Dating from 1922, the cluster of buildings – which includes a main lodge and cabins – is fringed with towering cottonwoods and fruit orchards planted more than a century ago.

Used predominantly by people who descend the corridor trails on mules, the ranch is very popular and often fully booked. Spots not taken by mule excursions go to hikers who don't feel like toting camping gear. Reservations must be made far in advance, and you must check in at the transportation desk at Bright Angel Lodge by 4pm on the day prior to your hike. You can also see if there are any same-day openings by calling ☎928-638-2631, as cancellations for dorm beds do occur and are doled out on a first-come, first-served basis each morning at Bright Angel Lodge.

Family-style breakfasts and dinners are served here, but they must be reserved at the same time as you book your lodgings.

DAY 2: BRIGHT ANGEL CAMPGROUND TO SOUTH RIM
6-9 HOURS; 9.3 MILES

To return to the South Rim, take the River Trail from the campground, pick up the Bright Angel and begin the 9.3-mile ascent, which takes between six and nine hours. Provided you have planned ahead, you could also spend a second night on the trail at Indian Garden Campground.

If you're hiking to the North Rim, head up the North Kaibab to Cottonwood Campground, where you can spend your second night.

🏃 Hermit Trail to Hermit Creek

Duration 2 days round-trip

Distance 15.6 miles round-trip

Difficulty Difficult

Start/Finish Hermits Rest Trailhead

Transportation Shuttle

Summary Tracing the path of the Hermit, this steep but rewarding out-and-back hike goes down to the river and Vishnu schist, the oldest exposed rock of the canyon's layers.

DAY 1: HERMITS REST TRAILHEAD TO HERMIT CREEK
4-6 HOURS; 7.8 MILES

From the Hermit Trailhead a steep, rocky path descends 2.5 miles to Santa Maria Spring (for a full description of the day hike, see p71). Backpackers continue past the spring as the trail levels for a mile or so before zigzagging over loose rocks.

Soon after descending the Redwall via a series of extremely steep, compressed switchbacks known as the **Cathedral Stairs**, the Hermit hits the Tonto (6.6 miles from the trailhead, at 3120ft). One mile west of the junction are stone remnants of the old **Hermit Camp** and near that the cliff-rimmed **Hermit Creek Campground** (3000ft), a glorious place to sleep.

From the campground it's another 1.5 miles to the Colorado, which you can reach by turning down Hermit Creek just before Hermit Camp or following the creek right from the campground. Down at the river, the canyon walls are exquisite black Vishnu schist shot through with veins of pink Zoroaster granite. **Hermit Rapids** mark the confluence of Hermit Creek and the Colorado.

DAY 2: HERMIT CREEK TO HERMITS REST TRAILHEAD
6-8 HOURS; 7.8 MILES

To return to Hermits Rest, retrace your steps for the arduous but gorgeous climb back to the trailhead. For a longer wilderness excursion, you can pick up the eastbound Tonto and intercept the Bright Angel, as detailed below.

🏃 Hermit Trail to Bright Angel

Duration 3-4 days one way

Distance 26.9 miles one way

Difficulty Difficult

Start Hermits Rest Trailhead

Finish Bright Angel Trailhead

Transportation Shuttle

Summary Not for first-time canyon hikers, this stunning trek may require some

Hermit Trail to Hermit Creek

Hermit Trail to Hermit Creek — map showing 0–1 km / 0–0.5 miles scale; Colorado River, Tonto Trail, Hermit Trail, Travertine Canyon, START DAY 2, Hermit Creek Campground, Cathedral Stairs, Eremita Mesa, Pima Point, Hermits Rest, Santa Maria Spring, Hermit Trailhead, START/END, Boucher Trail, Dripping Springs Trail, Waldron Trail

route finding – particularly along the undulating and unmaintained Tonto – but you'll find ample water sources and plenty of camping spots.

Following in the steps of the Hermit, this backcountry hike begins with solitude and wends its way along the curves of the Colorado and across the Tonto Platform to connect with the Bright Angel Trail at Indian Garden.

DAY 1: HERMITS REST TRAILHEAD TO MONUMENT CREEK
5-7 HOURS; 11.6 MILES

Descend 4 miles past Santa Maria Spring, then turn right at the Tonto Trail junction for the 14.5-mile eastbound passage to the Bright Angel Trail. From the junction it's 3.8 miles to **Monument Creek**, providing water and designated trailside campsites, after a descent of 3640ft this first day. Alternatively, you can spend the first night at Hermit Creek Campground, then backtrack a mile to embark on the Tonto your second morning.

For a quick side trip, head 2 miles down the drainage to **Granite Rapids**, one of the bigger rapids on the Colorado. If you're lucky, you might catch a raft or kayak running the rapid when you get down to the

river; look for the trail sign just south of the monument spire.

DAY 2: MONUMENT CREEK TO INDIAN GARDEN CAMPGROUND
4-6 HOURS; 10.7 MILES

The Tonto snakes along the contour with a mild elevation change of 600ft, reaching Cedar Spring after 1.3 miles and Salt Creek in another 30 minutes; there's seasonal water and camping, as well as a pit toilet just above the campsite at Salt Creek. From there it's just under 5 miles to Horn Creek – don't even think about drinking the water here, as it's been found to have a high radioactive level. In under an hour you'll be at verdant Indian Garden, with treated water available year-round.

DAY 3: INDIAN GARDEN CAMPGROUND TO BRIGHT ANGEL TRAILHEAD
3-5 HOURS; 4.6 MILES

Load up on water at the campground before beginning the hot grind back to the South Rim, the first 2 miles of which are the toughest. It's best to get a very early start so that you're still in the shade for the grueling Jacob's Ladder switchbacks. You'll stay cool and have a spectacular view as the sun inches its way down the red Supai sandstone.

OTHER ACTIVITIES

For information on rafting, see the Colorado River chapter and p37.

Cycling

Cyclists have limited options inside the park, as bicycles are only allowed on paved roads and the Greenway Trail. The multi-use Greenway Trail, open to cyclists as well as pedestrians and wheelchairs, stretches about 13 miles from Hermits Rest all the way to the South Kaibab Trailhead. Keep your ears open for news on paths possibly added since this book's publication. For more information about the Greenway Trail, see p178.

Hermit Rd offers a scenic ride west to Hermits Rest, about 16 miles round-trip from the village. Shuttles ply this road every 10 to 15 minutes between March and November (the rest of the year, traffic is minimal). They are not permitted to pass cyclists, so for the first 4 miles you'll have to pull over each time one drives by. However, starting from the Abyss, a completed section of the Greenway Trail diverges from the road and continues separately all the way to Hermits Rest.

Alternatively, you could ride out to the East Entrance along Desert View Dr (p64), a 50-mile round-trip from the village. The route is largely shuttle-free but sees a lot of car traffic in summer. Just off Desert View Dr, the 1-mile dirt road to Shoshone Point (p67) is an easy, nearly level ride that ends at this secluded panoramic vista, one of the few places to escape South Rim crowds.

See p86 for bike-rental details.

Mule Rides

Mosey into the canyon the way tourists traveled a century ago, on the back of a sure-footed mule. Half-day and overnight mule trips into the canyon depart every day of the year from the corral west of Bright Angel Lodge.

Due to erosion concerns, the NPS has limited inner-canyon mule rides to those traveling all the way to Phantom Ranch. Rather than going below the rim, three-hour day trips ($119) now take riders along the rim, through the ponderosa, piñon and juniper forest to the Abyss overlook. Riders dismount to enjoy the view and a snack before heading back to the village.

Overnight trips (one/two people $482/850) and two-night trips (one/two people $701/1170) still follow the Bright Angel Trail to the river, travel east on the River Trail and cross the river on the Kaibab Suspension Bridge. Riders spend the night at Phantom Ranch. It's a 5½-hour, 10-mile trip to Phantom Ranch, but the return trip up the 8-mile South Kaibab Trail is an hour shorter. Overnight trips include dorm accommodations and all meals at Phantom.

Don't plan a mule trip assuming it's the easiest way to travel below the rim. It's a bumpy ride on a hard saddle, and unless you're used to riding a horse regularly you will be saddle-sore afterwards. Riders must be at least 4ft 7in tall, speak fluent English and weigh no more than 200lb fully clothed. Personal backpacks, waist packs, purses or bags of any kind are not allowed on the mules. Anything that could possibly fall off and injure someone in the canyon below will be kept for you till your return. For complete regulations and more information, consult the Xanterra website. Keep in mind that these rules are in place for the safety of the riders, the mules and others on the trails.

Mule trips are popular and fill up quickly; to book a trip more than 24 hours and up to 13 months in advance, call **Xanterra** (☑888-297-2757, 303-297-2757; www.grandcanyonlodges.com/mule-rides-716.html). If you arrive at the park and want to join a mule trip the following day, ask about availability at the transportation desk at Bright Angel Lodge (your chances are much better during the off season). If the trips are booked, join a waiting list, cross your fingers and show up at the lodge at 6:15am on the day of the trip and hope there's been a cancellation. Or make tracks to the other side of the canyon: mule rides on the North Rim (p143) are usually available the day before the trip.

If you're not planning a mule trip, just watching the wranglers prepare the mules can be fun, particularly for young children. In summer stop by the mule corral at 8am; in winter they get going about an hour later.

Flyovers

At press time, over 300 flyovers of the Grand Canyon were still departing daily from Tusayan and Las Vegas. However, the NPS and the Federal Aviation Administration were also inviting public comments on a draft environmental impact report in June 2011, which may have implications for the number or existence of scenic flyovers at Grand

---

TOP POST-HIKE TREATS

Recharge and reward yourself with a tasty snack after a long, hot day on the trail:

» **Chocolate milkshake** (Bright Angel Fountain, p84) The best milkshake you will ever taste in your life will be waiting for you to savor on the circular stone bench outside Bright Angel Fountain.

» **Hiker's Caesar** (Bright Angel Restaurant, p84) Romaine lettuce, grilled chicken breast, tomatoes and crisp veggies dressed in Parmesan.

» **Prickly-pear margarita** (El Tovar, p83) Tequila, prickly-pear syrup and lime over ice; for complete electrolyte replenishment (ahem), be sure to order this pink drink with salt.

Canyon National Park. Flights have already been restricted in number, altitude and routes to reduce noise pollution affecting the experience of other visitors and wildlife. If a flyover isn't the way you want to travel, consider enjoying an aerial view from the comfort of the IMAX Theater (p90).

Standard routes include a 30-minute flight over the western canyon, a 40-minute eastern tour along the rim to the confluence of the Colorado and Little Colorado Rivers, and a 50-minute loop that bridges the two by crossing the North Rim forest. On most flights you'll see Coconino Plateau, Dragon Head (a dramatic ridge jutting from the North Rim) and the Painted Desert.

Contact the following companies for specific rates, as each offers several options, but note that their prices are fairly competitive. If you're concerned about flight noise, ask whether company uses quiet technology (QT) helicopters, which provide a quieter experience. Flights from Tusayan operate year-round, departing daily at regular intervals between 8am and 5pm.

Grand Canyon Airlines (☑866-235-9422, 928-638-2359; www.grandcanyonairlines.com)

Grand Canyon Helicopters (☑928-638-2764, 702-835-8477; www.grandcanyonhelicop tersaz.com)

Maverick Helicopters (☑888-261-4414; www.maverickhelicopter.com)

Papillon Grand Canyon Helicopters (☑888-635-7272, 702-736-7243; www.papillon. com)

Scenic Airlines (☑866-235-9422; www.scenic. com)

Ranger Programs

Free ranger programs are one of the park's greatest treasures. Lasting 30 minutes to four hours, the talks and walks cover subjects ranging from fossils to condors to Native American history. Programs are held throughout the park and often involve a short walk. *The Guide* provides a complete listing of current ranger programs, including a short description and the location, time and duration of each program. A kiosk at Grand Canyon Visitor Center also clearly explains current ranger programs.

The **Cedar Ridge Hike** is one regular offering. It involves a strenuous 3-mile hike (two to four hours round-trip) 1140ft below the rim on the South Kaibab Trail. While you can take this trail by yourself, the ranger will explain canyon geology and history as you hike. It departs from the South Kaibab Trailhead at 8am. Take the green Kaibab Trail Route shuttle from Grand Canyon Visitor Center to access the trailhead.

On the one-hour **Geology and Fossil Walks**, both offered daily, you can brush up on your knowledge of brachiopods and learn about the canyon's rich history. The Fossil Walk is an easy half-mile one-way walk to exposed fossil beds along the rim, a particularly nice activity if you plan on hiking into the canyon from Hermits Rest. If you attend the ranger talk, you'll be able to recognize fossils that lie about 10 minutes down the trail.

Each **evening program** at McKee Amphitheater examines a significant aspect of the canyon's natural or cultural history. Subjects change nightly; check the kiosk at the Grand Canyon Visitor Center.

Cross-country Skiing

From November through March, depending on snowfall, the surrounding national forest offers several trails for cross-country skiing and snowshoeing. Trails around Grandview Point may be groomed. Contact the **Tusayan Ranger Station** (☑928-638-2443) for current information. You can rent skis from several outdoor shops in Flagstaff, where you'll also find plenty of cross-country and downhill trails.

SLEEPING

At the South Rim, you can sleep under the stars in one of the park's three campgrounds or choose a cabin or comfortable lodge room. Mather and Trailer Village campgrounds take reservations and are open year-round, while Desert View is open May through September and does not accept reservations. There's a seven-day limit at all three campgrounds. If you don't find a spot in the park, you can always pitch your tent free of charge in the surrounding Kaibab National Forest (see p88).

Xanterra (☑888-297-2757; www.grand canyonlodges.com) operates all park lodges, as well as Trailer Village. You can make reservations up to 13 months in advance; visit the website for more information and photos. For same-day reservations or to reach any lodge, call the **South Rim switchboard** (☑928-638-2631).

In summer or during the holidays, you may find that there are no rooms left at the village inns; instead, consider a chain hotel or motel in Tusayan or a roadside joint in Valle. If you want more than just a place to lay your head, however, head to Flagstaff, Williams or Sedona. Several historic hotels and B&Bs in Flagstaff and Williams and gorgeous but expensive inns in Sedona offer far more character than you'll find at most lodgings in or near the park.

Camping

The **National Park Service** (☎877-444-6777; www.recreation.gov) operates Mather and Desert View Campgrounds. Reservations for Mather are accepted up to six months in advance until the day before your arrival. From mid-November through February, sites at Mather Campground are first-come, first-served.

Along the banks of the Colorado River on the canyon floor, Bright Angel Campground is one of three backcountry campgrounds, along with Indian Garden and Cottonwood, that lie along the main corridor trails between the North and South Rims. You must obtain a backcountry permit if you intend to stay anywhere below the rim overnight. If you're staying at the campground but don't want to pack down your own stove and food, you can reserve meals at nearby Phantom Ranch.

Desert View Campground CAMPGROUND $
(Map p56; campsites $12; ☺May–mid-Oct) Set back from the road in a quiet piñon-juniper forest near the East Entrance, this first-come, first-served campground is a peaceful alternative to the more crowded and busy Mather Campground. The lovely sites are spread out enough to ensure some privacy. You'll find toilets and drinking water but no showers or hookups. A small cafeteria/snack shop near the campground serves breakfast, lunch and dinner, and there's also a general store that offers basic camping supplies and staples like pasta, canned food, milk, beer and wine. The best time to secure a spot is midmorning, when people are breaking camp. Don't drive in after dark assuming you'll get a site, as it's at least 25 miles to another campground. Call the **Desert View Information Center** (☎928-638-7893; ☺9am-5pm) to confirm the campground's operating dates.

Mather Campground CAMPGROUND $
(Map p60; ☎928-638-7851; campsites/group sites $18/50; ☺year-round) Though Mather has over 300 campsites, it's actually a pleasant and relatively quiet place to camp. Piñon and juniper trees offer plenty of shade, sites are well dispersed and the flat ground offers a comfy platform for your tent. If you're longing for pristine wilderness, look elsewhere, but if you just want a guaranteed site with ample facilities, this is your best bet. You'll find pay showers, laundry facilities, drinking water, toilets and grills. There are no hook-

---

GETTING HITCHED AT THE GRAND CANYON

To be married in the park, you must first obtain a state marriage license from any Arizona courthouse. The nearest location is the **Clerk of the Superior Court** (☎928-679-7600; 200 N San Francisco St, Flagstaff, AZ 86001; ☺8am-5pm Mon-Fri) in Flagstaff.

If you want an outdoor wedding, you'll need to download, fill out and mail in a detailed special-use application to the **NPS** (www.nps.gov/grca/parkmgmt/sup.htm; Grand Canyon National Park, Attn: Special Use Permits, PO Box 129, Grand Canyon, AZ 86023). Special-use permits cost $175, to be mailed with the permit application. Find application instructions, approved locations, local justices of the peace and other information at the NPS website.

Indoor weddings can be held at Shrine of the Ages (the special-use permit here also costs $175). Indoor weddings and/or receptions held at park lodges should be arranged through **Xanterra** (☎928-638-2525; www.grandcanyonlodges.com).

Remember that summer showers are prevalent from late June to September; consider a morning wedding to minimize the possibility of rain.

It's also possible to get married on the North Rim, though logistics are more complicated, given its remote location. Between May 1 and October 15, contact the **North Rim District Ranger** (☎928-638-7749; Concessions Management Asst, Attn: Special Use Permits, Grand Canyon National Park, North Rim, AZ 86052) using the same form. During the rest of the year, contact the North Rim Program Assistant at the permit address listed for the South Rim.

ups, though there's a dump station, and the maximum length for trailers and RVs is 30ft. Next door a small general store stocks camping supplies, drinks and basic food items. It even has its own shuttle stop on the Village Route. Sites for disabled travelers are closer to the facilities and on more level ground. If you don't have a car or would just like some distance between you and your fellow campers, ask for a backpacker site. As crowds diminish in September, some loops are closed. By December only one loop remains open. Winter fees drop slightly.

Trailer Village   RV CAMPGROUND $
(Map p60; ☎888-297-2757, same-day reservations 928-638-2631; sites from $35; ⊘year-round) As the name implies, this is basically a trailer park, offering little in the way of natural surroundings. Expect RVs lined up tightly at paved pull-through sites with hookups amid a rather barren, dry patch of ground. Check for spots with trees on the far north side. You'll find picnic tables and BBQ grills, while a coin laundry and showers are a quarter-mile away at Mather Campground. A dump station operates in all but the winter months.

Lodging

TOP CHOICE El Tovar   LODGE $$$
(Map p60; d $178-273, ste $335-426; ❋☎) Its exposed beams, dark-wood interiors, bronzes and stately presence continue to define El Tovar as a quintessential 1905 national-park lodge. It appeals to those visitors seeking more than a roadside motel, and even day trippers are lured in by the wide, inviting porches that wreathe the rambling wood structure, offering pleasant spots for people-watching and canyon sunsets. The original guestrooms were remodeled to accommodate private baths, thus many of the standard double rooms are incredibly small, ask for the slightly more expensive deluxe room. You can put a cot or a crib in a deluxe double at no extra charge for children (extra charge for adults), but if your party is more than three people, consider getting a suite rather than multiple doubles. The capacity varies by suite: standard suites sleep three, four or seven, while porch suites sleep three, four or five. Those in a mood to splurge can stay in one of three rim-view suites, all with sitting rooms and private porches looking out onto full canyon views. These are the only rooms in the park with a full rim view,

and they're often booked more than a year in advance. Themed suites are the next best choice, but standard king rooms (renovated in 2005) also have some atmospheric appeal befitting this elegant institution.

Bright Angel Lodge   LODGE $$
(Map p60; d without/with private bath $81/92, cabin $113-178; ⊘year-round; ❋@☎) Built in 1935 (see p57), this log-and-stone lodge on the ledge offers travelers more historic charm and nicer rooms than you'll find at most other accommodations on the South Rim. You will find two restaurants, a snack bar and a small, nondescript bar with a TV. In 2001 all rooms at Bright Angel were refurbished in keeping with architect Mary Colter's original design. The least expensive rooms in the park are the doubles with shared (immaculate) bath, which offer a double bed, a desk and a sink. The bathroom is down the hall, there are no TVs and the pleasant rooms are nothing extraordinary, but this is a great price for a perch right on the rim (no views, however). Powell suites feature two bedrooms and a tub but no shower or TV; each holds up to seven people.

Cabins at Bright Angel, many decorated in rustic Western style, offer more character. There are several options, starting with standard cabin and ranging up to the excellent value of rim-view cabins, which are bright and airy, with a queen bed, a full bath, a refrigerator, a partial canyon view and doors that open right out onto the Rim Trail.

One of the more interesting places to stay on either rim, the Buckey O'Neill Cabin is a spacious, Western-style cabin with a king bed, separate sitting room, refrigerator, dry bar, two TVs, a full bath and front and back doors. Built in the 1890s, the cabin was home to prospector Buckey O'Neill (p57). Canyon breezes more than compensate for the lack of an air conditioner. The cabin is usually booked more than a year in advance through the Bright Angel Lodge.

Phantom Ranch   CABINS $
(Map p56; ☎888-297-2757; dm $43; ❋) At the bottom of the canyon floor, which means it can only be reached on foot, mule or floating river conveyance. Built along the north bank of the Colorado River, stone cottages offer cozy private cabins sleeping four to 10 on bunks, as well as dormitory-style bunks in single-sex cabins outfitted for 10 people. Bunk prices include bedding, soap, shampoo and towels; meals are extra. The ranch

SOUTH RIM CAMPGROUNDS

CAMPGROUND	LOCATION	DESCRIPTION	NO OF SITES	ELEVATION
Desert View Campground	Desert View	First-come, first-served campground with well-dispersed sites on the peaceful eastern side of the South Rim	50	7450ft
Grand Canyon Camper Village	Tusayan	Large campground with showers and playground but little shade; RV sites have full hookups	300	6612ft
Mather Campground	Grand Canyon	Park's biggest campground, with wooded, well-dispersed sites; no hookups; trailers & RVs limited to 30ft	317	7000ft
Ten-X Campground	2 miles south of Tusayan	Spacious campground with picnic tables and fire rings, no showers; pull-through sites have no hookups	70	6650ft
Trailer Village	Grand Canyon Village	Near Mather Campground dump station (closed in winter); hookups and pull-through sites for vehicles up to 50ft	84	7000ft

	Drinking Water		Flush Toilets		Ranger Station Nearby		Wheelchair Accessible		Great for Families

– a mule, rather – also provides a duffel delivery service for about $65 each way, but these must be soft-sided duffels weighing no more than 30lb apiece. Reservations for the family-style meals (breakfast/dinner from $21/27) must be made at the same time as room reservations. If you'd rather skip the expensive meals, you may bring your own food and stove. After dinner each night, the dining room converts into a canteen that serves beer, wine and hot drinks, a good venue to meet fellow riverside ramblers.

Maswik Lodge LODGE $$
(Map p60; d South/North $92/173, cabins $92; ❄@🗢) Located a quarter-mile from the rim near the Backcountry Information Center, the Maswik Lodge is named for the Hopi kachina who guards the canyon. The lodge comprises 16 two-story wood-and-stone buildings set in the woods. Rooms at Maswik North feature private patios, high ceilings and forest views, while rooms at the less expensive Maswik South are smaller and don't offer much of a view. Here you'll encounter much less foot traffic and general bustling about than at the rim, but the rooms are standard motel rooms. You'll find a cafeteria and a bar here with a pool table and big-screen TV. Small cabins are available in the summer only.

Kachina & Thunderbird Lodges LODGE $$
(Map p60; d streetside/rimside $173/184; ❄) Beside the Rim Trail between El Tovar and Bright Angel, these institutional-looking lodges offer standard motel-style rooms with two queen beds, full bath and TV. It's worth spending up a little for the rimside rooms, some with partial canyon views. Neither lodge has a lobby or front desk – guests at Kachina check in at El Tovar, while those at Thunderbird check in at Bright Angel, just to keep things interesting.

Yavapai Lodge LODGE $$
(Map p60; d West/East $114/163; ☺Apr-Oct; ❄🗢) Sure, it's your basic motel, but there are some hidden pluses to the Yavapai Lodge. It lies more than a mile from the traffic and chaos of the central village, is close to Grand Canyon Visitor Center and within walking distance of the grocery store, post office and bank in Market Plaza. The lodgings are stretched out amid a peaceful piñon and juniper forest, yet you can pull your car right up to your door. Rooms in Yavapai East are in six air-conditioned, two-story buildings, while rooms in Yavapai West are spread out in 10 single-story buildings without air-conditioning. These are basic, clean motel rooms with tubs, showers and TVs. Yavapai closes from January to March but opens up briefly for the Thanksgiving and Christmas holidays.

OPEN	RESERVATIONS	DAY FEE	FACILITIES	PAGE
May–mid-Oct	No	$12		p80
Mar-Oct	No	$35-50		p89
year-round	Yes, up to 6 months in advance	$18		p80
mid-Apr–Sep	No	$10		p88
year-round	Yes	$35		p81

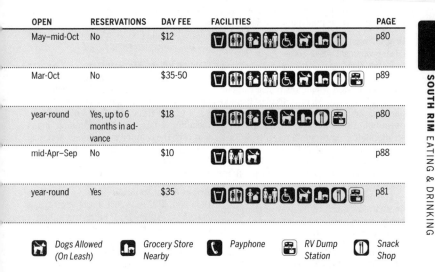

Legend: Dogs Allowed (On Leash) · Grocery Store Nearby · Payphone · RV Dump Station · Snack Shop

EATING & DRINKING

Grand Canyon Village has all the eating options you will need, whether it's picking up picnic parts at Canyon Village Marketplace, an après-hike ice-cream cone at Bright Angel Fountain or a sit-down celebratory dinner at El Tovar. Hours listed here are for the summer and may vary in slower seasons.

All South Rim bars close at 11pm, and drinks are prohibited along the rim itself.

TOP CHOICE El Tovar
Dining Room INTERNATIONAL $$$

(Map p60; 928-638-2631, ext 6432; El Tovar; mains $18-31; 6:30-11am, 11:30am-2pm & 5-10pm) If at all possible, treat yourself to at least one meal at historic El Tovar. The memorable surroundings feature dark wood, tables set with china and white linen, and huge picture windows with views of the rim and canyon beyond. The service is excellent, the menu creative, the portions big and the food very good – much better than you might expect at a place that knows it's the only gig in town. Breakfast options include fresh-squeezed orange juice, El Tovar's pancake trio (buttermilk, blue cornmeal and buckwheat pancakes with pine-nut butter and prickly-pear syrup) and cornmeal-encrusted trout with two eggs. Lunch and dinner menus are

equally creative. Though you're welcome to dress up to match the elegant setting, you'll be perfectly comfortable in jeans as well.

Though reservations are not taken for breakfast or lunch, they are required for dinner; call to make dinner reservations up to six months in advance. To avoid lunchtime crowds, eat before the Grand Canyon Railway train arrives at 12:15pm, as many passengers make lunch at El Tovar their first stop.

Inside the bar at El Tovar is a dark and cozy lounge, with big, cushioned chairs and stained glass. But if you prefer a sunnier outlook, the patio just outside the bar is a great spot to sit with a glass of sustainable sauvignon blanc and watch people strolling along the rim.

Arizona Room AMERICAN $$

(Map p60; Bright Angel Lodge; mains $8-28; 11:30am-3pm Mar-Oct & 4:30-10pm Mar-Dec) A wonderful balance between casual and up-scale, this busy restaurant is one of the best options for dinner on the South Rim. Antler chandeliers hang from the ceiling, and picture windows overlook a small lawn, the rim walk and the canyon beyond. Try to get on the wait-list when doors open at 4:30pm; because by 4:40 you may have an hour's wait – reservations are not accepted. Enjoy a drink while you wait in the tiny foyer or outside on the small deck, watching passersby on the Rim Trail. Mains include steak, chicken and fish dishes, while appetizers include such creative options as pulled-pork quesadillas.

Bright Angel Restaurant
AMERICAN $$

(Map p60; Bright Angel Lodge; mains $10-26; ⊗6:30am-10pm; 🔃) With exposed wood beams and an adobe-style interior, this busy family-style restaurant is not without its simple charm. Menu offerings include burgers, fajitas, salads, pasta and other down-home sorts of dishes. Families with small children gravitate here, so it can get loud, and the harried staff provide the most perfunctory service of the three waitstaffed restaurants on the South Rim. Reservations not accepted.

The dark, windowless bar off the hallway doesn't offer much in the way of character, but it's a cozy spot for a beer or espresso and the historic photos are interesting.

Phantom Ranch Canteen
AMERICAN $$$

(Map p56; mains $27-42; ⊗5am & 6:30am breakfast seatings, 5pm & 6:30pm dinner seatings) On the canyon floor, Phantom Ranch offers family-style meals on a set menu: hearty stew, steaks and vegetarian chili, as well as hearty breakfasts and sack lunches for the trail. Seating hours change seasonally. You must make meal reservations before your descent, ideally when you reserve your accommodations. The canteen is open to the public for cold lemonade and packaged snacks between 8am and 4pm, and for beer, wine and hot drinks from 8pm to 10pm.

Canyon View Deli
CAFETERIA $

(Map p60; ☑928-631-2262; Market Plaza; mains $4-7; ⊗7am-8pm) This counter in the village grocery store is the best place to find a fresh-made sandwich for a picnic, as well as pre-made salads and hot dishes like pizza and fried chicken. Morning offerings include breakfast burritos, doughnuts and coffee.

Maswik Cafeteria
CAFETERIA $

(Map p60; Maswik Lodge; mains $4-10; ⊗6am-10pm) The term 'cafeteria' should tip you off to the fare, setup and seating. Though fairly predictable, the food encompasses a nice variety and isn't too greasy. The various food stations serve burgers, sandwiches, fried chicken, Mexican food and even Vietnamese *pho*.

The adjoining Maswik Pizza Pub shows sporting events on TV and serves a decent selection of draft beer and wine.

Canyon Café
CAFETERIA $

(Map p60; Yavapai Lodge; mains $4-10; ⊗6am-10pm) At Yavapai Lodge, this cafe has the same sort of food and setup as at Maswik Cafeteria, and you can get boxed lunches to go. Hours vary seasonally.

Canyon Village Marketplace
MARKET $

(Map p60; ☑928-631-2262; Market Plaza; ⊗8am-8pm) The biggest source for supplies on either rim, this market offers everything you'd expect from your local grocery store, including a fair selection of organic items and over-the-counter medications. You may prefer to stock up on groceries in Williams, Flagstaff or Sedona, as prices and selection are better outside the park.

Bright Angel Fountain
FAST FOOD $

(Map p60; ☑928-638-2631; Bright Angel Lodge; mains $2-5; ⊗10am-8pm) On the rim at Bright Angel Lodge, this cafeteria-style fountain serves hot dogs, premade sandwiches, ice cream, fruit, juice and bottled water. The milkshakes are heavenly after a summer hike out of the canyon. Cash only.

Hermits Rest Snack Bar
FAST FOOD $

(Map p56; ☑928-638-2351; Hermits Rest; mains $2-5; ⊗9am-5pm) This walk-up window outside Hermits Rest is basically a human-powered vending machine, and is cash only.

Desert View Trading Post Snack Bar
FAST FOOD $

(Map p56; ☑928-638-2360; Desert View Trading Post; mains $2-5; ⊗9am-4pm) Small snack bar serving a limited menu, including burgers, corn dogs, premade sandwiches and soda, plus cold cereal, eggs and French toast in the morning.

SHOPPING

In Grand Canyon Village, **Market Plaza** (map p60) is the tiny but crucial commercial hub of the South Rim. Whether you need cash, crushed ice or crampons, this is where you'll find them.

Desert View Marketplace
MARKET

(Map p56; ☑928-638-2393; Desert View; ⊗9am-5pm) At the East Entrance, this general store sells simple groceries and souvenirs.

Books & More Store
BOOKSTORE

(Map p60; ⊗8am-8pm) The most extensive bookstore in the park is located at Grand Canyon Visitor Center. Here you will find a huge variety of books about the Grand Canyon and surrounding region, as well as DVDs, posters, postcards, prints, photographs and gifts. South Rim visitor centers and points of interest such as Hermits Rest, Kolb Studio and Tusayan Museum also carry a selection of books and gifts.

INFORMATION

Almost all services on the South Rim are in Grand Canyon Village, easily accessible via the blue Village Route shuttles. On the east side, **Market Plaza** (Map p60) includes the grocery/deli/outdoors shop **Canyon Village Marketplace** (☎928-631-2262; ☉8am-8pm), **Chase Bank** (☎928-638-2437; ☉9am-5pm Mon-Thu, 9am-6pm Fri) with a 24-hour ATM, and a **post office** (☎928-638-2512; ☉9am-4:30pm Mon-Fri, 11am-1pm Sat) where stamps are available via a vending machine from 5am to 10pm. The main visitor center is **Grand Canyon Visitor Center** (Map p60; ☎928-638-7644; ☉7:30am-6:30pm), just behind Mather Point.

Limited hours go into effect between October and March. If you have questions, NPS rangers and people who staff the hotels, restaurants and services are typically helpful and friendly.

Internet Access

Grand Canyon Community Library (Map p60; ☎928-638-2718; per 50min $3; ☉10:30am-5pm Mon-Fri) Just behind the garage, this little brown building houses the community library and several terminals providing internet access; hours vary seasonally, so call ahead.

Park Headquarters Library (Map p60; ☉8am-noon & 1-4:30pm Mon-Thu & alternate Fri) At the back of the courtyard at Park Headquarters, the small library offers free internet access when someone's staffing it.

Tourist Information

Backcountry Information Center (Map p60; ☎/fax 928-638-7875; ☉8am-noon & 1-5pm) Located near Maswik Lodge, this is the place to get wait-listed for a backcountry permit if you haven't reserved one ahead of time.

Grand Canyon Visitor Center (Map p60; ☎928-638-7644; ☉8am-5pm) Three hundred yards behind Mather Point, Grand Canyon Visitor Center encompasses this visitor center and the Books & More Store. Outside the visitor center, bulletin boards and kiosks display information on ranger programs, the weather, tours and hikes. The center's bright, spacious interior includes a ranger-staffed information desk and a lecture hall, where rangers offer daily talks on a variety of subjects.

TEN PRIME PICNIC PICKS

Terrific picnic spots abound in thousands of shady, secluded sites you can find simply by roaming along the rim, away from the shuttle-stop overlooks. Find your own favorite perch and look for circling condors or faraway mule trains, or take a hike to reach these prime picnic spots.

Cedar Ridge (p69) Lunch atop one of the outcrops to stake out photo ops before heading up the South Kaibab.

Indian Garden (p68) Heading up or down, this cool oasis on the Bright Angel makes a restful picnic stop.

Yavapai Point (p57) Poke around the Observation Station, then picnic at the point.

Santa Maria Spring (p71) Spirit yourself away with a sandwich to this secluded spring.

Widforss Point (p136) Pad across pine needles to take in peaceful views of five temples.

Uncle Jim Point (p140) No need to stray too far for the Uncle Jim Trail to reward you with views.

Shoshone Point (p67) Wander under the shade of ponderosa to this atypical South Rim picnic site.

Point Imperial (p135) Chow down as you get the lowdown on the layout from the highest point on the North Rim.

Hermits Rest (p63) BYO lunch or hit the snack bar before venturing down the trail a little way.

Cape Royal Wedding Site (p134) Best bench for a sunrise brunch.

Desert View Information Center (Map p56; ☎928-638-7893; ⊙9am-5pm) Housed in a small stone building near the East Entrance, this staffed information center also offers books and maps.

El Tovar (Map p60; ⊙8am-5pm) This hotel's helpful concierge can answer questions, arrange same- or next-day bus tours and sell stamps.

Transportation Desks (Map p60; ☎928-638-2631, ext 6015; ⊙8am-5pm) In the lobbies of Bright Angel, Yavapai and Maswik Lodges, these service desks can book bus tours and same- or next-day mule trips. They can also answer questions about horseback rides, scenic flights and smooth-water float trips. Bright Angel can arrange last-minute lodgings at Phantom Ranch, if available.

Tusayan Ruins & Museum (Map p56; ☎928-638-2305; ⊙9am-5pm) Three miles west of Desert View, this museum (p59) features exhibits on the park's indigenous people and has an information desk staffed by rangers.

Verkamp's Visitor Center (Map p60; ⊙8am-7pm) Next to Hopi House, also features a display about the building's history.

GETTING AROUND

Though the park can seem overwhelming when you first arrive, it's actually quite easy to navigate, especially when you leave it to shuttle drivers. *The Guide* contains a color-coded shuttle-route map in the centerfold.

Bicycle

See p77 for details about cycling around the South Rim.

Bright Angel Bicycles (☎928-814-8704; www.bikegrandcanyon.com; full-day adult/child $35/25; ⊙8am-6pm May-Sep, 10am-4:30pm Mar-Apr & Oct-Nov, weather permitting) rents 'comfort cruiser' bikes on the South Rim. The friendly folks here custom-fit each bike to the individual before sending cyclists on their way. Rates include helmet and bicycle-lock rental; child trailers also available. You can even arrange for private shuttle pickups and/or drop-offs.

Car

Once parked outside your hotel or in a public lot, your car can remain there as long as you're on the South Rim. All services and points of interest are accessible via the free shuttles, a hassle-free alternative to traffic and parking.

If you do drive, consult the Grand Canyon Village map (Map p60) or *The Guide* for parking-lot locations. You'll find four large parking lots at Grand Canyon Visitor Center, where you can catch shuttles eastbound and west.

Though Desert View is only 25 miles east of the village, allow at least 45 minutes by car, even if you plan to drive nonstop. While traffic usually moves rather smoothly, the speed limit is 45mph, and cars often turn unexpectedly into the many pullouts.

Note that from March through November, cars are not allowed on Hermit Rd, which heads west from the village to Hermits Rest.

See p226 for more information on gas stations and car repair.

Shuttle

Free shuttle buses ply three routes along the South Rim. In the pre-dawn hours, shuttles run every half-hour or so and typically begin running about an hour before sunrise; check *The Guide* for current sunrise and sunset information. From early morning until after sunset, buses run every 15 minutes. *The Guide* features exact seasonal operating hours relevant to your visit, along with a map of shuttle stops. Maps are also posted at all shuttle stops and inside the shuttles themselves.

Hermits Rest Route

The red Hermits Rest Route runs west along Hermit Rd from March through November, during which time the road is closed to private vehicles.

You can hop off at any of the viewpoints (it stops eight times from the village to Hermits Rest), enjoy the view and a hike, then catch another shuttle further west or back to the village. Alternatively, walk part of the way along the Rim Trail (p66) and catch the shuttle.

The shuttle stops only at Pima Point, Mohave Point and Powell Point on its return trip (eastbound) to the village.

Word to the wise: bring water with you on the shuttle – there's no water available until Hermits Rest.

Village Route

The blue Village Route provides year-round transportation between most village facilities, including Grand Canyon Visitor Center, Yavapai Point, Market Plaza, the Backcountry Information Center, hotels, restaurants, campgrounds and parking lots.

Kaibab Trail Route

The green Kaibab Trail Route provides service to and from the Yavapai Geology Museum, Mather Point, Grand Canyon Visitor Center, Pipe Creek Vista, South Kaibab Trailhead and Yaki Point.

South Kaibab Trailhead and Yaki Point are on a spur road off Desert View Dr that is closed to cars year-round.

Hikers' Express

The early-bird Hikers' Express shuttle leaves daily from Bright Angel Lodge, stopping at the Backcountry Information Center before heading to the South Kaibab Trailhead.

Hikers' Express departs at 4am, 5am and 6am from June to August; 5am, 6am and 7am in May and September; 6am, 7am and 8am in April and October; and 8am, 9am and 10am between November and March.

Tusayan Route

Running from mid-May to early September, the Tusayan shuttle loops between Tusayan and Grand Canyon Visitor Center. Visitors wishing to ride the shuttle must have a park pass, available for purchase at the National Geographic Visitor Center (p90).

Taxi

Grand Canyon South Rim Taxi Service (☑928-638-2822) offers taxi service to and from Tusayan and within the park. Service is available 24 hours, but there are only a couple of taxis, so you may have to wait for one.

Tours

Narrated bus tours depart daily from Maswik, Yavapai and Bright Angel Lodges. Tours offer a good introduction to the canyon, as drivers stop at the best viewpoints, point out the various buttes, mesas and plateaus, and offer historical anecdotes. Tour tickets are available at the lodge transportation desks or from the El Tovar concierge, or you can book by calling ☑928-638-2631. Children under 16 ride for free when accompanied by an adult, and wheelchair-accessible vehicles are available with a day's advance notice.

» Two-hour tours to **Hermits Rest** ($25) depart daily at 9am and 4pm. A 90-minute sunrise tour or two-hour sunset tour to Hermits Rest ($14.50) departs at various times throughout the year (the sunrise tour can leave as early as 4am in summer).

» Four-hour **Desert View Dr tours** ($44) include a stop at Lipan Point and an hour at the Watchtower. In summer a sunset tour of Desert View Dr departs at 4pm.

» Six-hour **combination tours** ($57) allow you to take in both western and eastern reaches of the South Rim, in one day or over multiple days.

BEYOND THE SOUTH RIM

Carved into the stunning landscape of the Southwest, the Grand Canyon has more than its own unique splendor to offer visitors. Stretching both north and south of the canyon is the Kaibab National Forest, the southern ecosystem of which is characterized by piñon and juniper. Grand Canyon National Park itself is bordered on the west by the Hualapai and Havasupai Reservations, where you can hike to turquoise waterfalls in the inner canyon, tiptoe on the glass-floored Skywalk on the West Rim, and raft along the Colorado for a day. Further west, where the Colorado River has been reined in by the massive engineering feat that is Hoover Dam, Lake Mead is a popular recreation area for desert dwellers thirsting for fishing, houseboating and water sports.

The gateway towns leading to the South Rim are destinations in their own right: Las Vegas for its slick excess and cardinal sins, Flagstaff for its cool, outdoorsy feel, Sedona for surreal natural beauty and metaphysical mystique, and Williams for its small-town, Route 66 atmosphere.

Kaibab National Forest (South Rim)

The park's South Rim is bordered by the piñon-juniper and ponderosa-pine woodland of **Kaibab National Forest** (☑928-635-8200; www.fs.fed.us/r3/kai/); its Tusayan Ranger Station sits just outside the park's South Entrance. Offering several great mountain-biking trails, unlimited camping, hiking and cross-country skiing, the forest extends outdoor-recreation options beyond the park. You won't find spectacular canyon views, but you won't find the crowds either. Bring plenty of water, as natural water sources are scarce in this arid region. You'll likely spot elk, mule deer, turkeys and coyotes, and on rare occasions you may encounter a mountain lion, black bear or bobcat.

The forest's Tusayan Ranger District (327,267 acres) borders Grand Canyon National Park to the north, the Navajo Reservation to the east, private and state-owned lands to the south and the Havasupai Reservation to the west. The main road through the forest is Hwy 64/180, which connects Williams and Flagstaff with the canyon. Hwy 64 accesses the district's northeast corner.

Sights & Activities

Grandview Lookout Tower   LOOKOUT
(Map p56) Built by the Civilian Conservation Corps in 1936 as a fire tower, the 80ft Grand-

view Lookout Tower offers great views of the region for those willing and able to climb all those stairs. From the park's Desert View Dr (p64), turn at the sign for 'Arizona Trail' between mileposts 252 and 253, about 2 miles east of Grandview Point. You can **hike** or **bike** 1.3 miles on a dirt road to the lookout. Alternatively, take unpaved Forest Rd 302, just past Grand Canyon National Park Airport, in Tusayan.

You can also ride or hike here via the **Tusayan Bike Trail**, a moderate bike trail on an old logging road. The trailhead is 0.3 miles north of Tusayan on the west side of Hwy 64/180. It's 16 miles from the trailhead to the lookout. If you don't want to ride all that way, three interconnected loops offer 3-, 8- and 9-mile round-trips.

From the lookout you can hike or ride part or all of the still-evolving **Arizona Trail** (boxed text, p34), a 24-mile one-way ride to the south boundary of the Tusayan Ranger District. This is an excellent and relatively easy ride. The northern segment of the trail unfolds beneath ponderosa pines and gambel oaks; further south, the trail passes piñon-juniper stands, sage and grasslands. Bring plenty of water, as there are no dependable sources along the trail. Ask at the ranger station about other hikes.

In the winter the United States Forest Service (USFS) maintains a groomed **cross-country skiing loop** 0.3 miles north of Grandview Lookout.

Apache Stables   HORSEBACK RIDING
(Map p56; ☑928-638-2891, 928-638-3105; www.apachestables.com; Moqui Dr/Forest Service Rd 328; 1/2hr rides $49/89, trail & wagon ride $59) Offers horseback rides through the forest. You can also take a one-hour evening trail ride to a campfire and return on a wagon. For riders of all ages, the outfitter offers a campfire wagon ride, in which trail riders rendezvous with the wagon for a cookout beneath the stars. For both campfire trips you must bring your own food (think hot dog and s'mores components), drinks and paper plates; if you bring a small cooler, the staff will put it on the wagon.

Sleeping

Free dispersed camping is allowed in the national forest as long as you refrain from camping in meadows, within a quarter-mile of the highway or any surface water, or within a half-mile of any developed campground. Dispersed camping is not allowed inside Grand Canyon National Park.

Tusayan
☑928 / POP 562 / ELEV 6612FT

The friendly little town of Tusayan, situated 1 mile south of the park's South Entrance along Hwy 64, is basically a half-mile strip of hotels and restaurants catering to Grand Canyon visitors. It makes a good base if accommodations inside the park are booked up, and it does offer conveniences like a general store, gas station, souvenir shop and espresso bar with internet access. The Tusayan Ranger Station sits just outside the park's South Entrance.

Sleeping

Some of these motels offer a touch more character than you'd find at most other American roadside motels, but don't expect anything particularly memorable.

Grand Hotel   HOTEL $$$
(☑928-638-3333, 888-634-7263; www.grandcanyongrandhotel.com; 149 Hwy 64; d $190-220; ❄︎⊛☎︎☒) The distinct Western motif in its open public spaces – including a big fireplace, high ceilings, woven rugs, stone floors and faux pine beams – gives this newish hotel an old look, and it works. And with appropriate Western hospitality, the friendly staff complete the theme. Relatively large, comfortable rooms are filled with pleasing Mission-style furniture, and the ones in back face the woods. You may catch Navajo dance performances in the evening (schedule varies), and nightly live country music draws locals and visitors from around 10:30pm. The hotel also features an indoor pool and a hot tub.

Ten-X Campground   CAMPGROUND $
(Map p56; ☑928-638-7851; sites per vehicle $10; ◯May-Sep) Woodsy and peaceful, this first-come, first-served USFS campground lies 2 miles south of Tusayan on Hwy 64. It has 70 sites and can fill up early in the summer. You'll find large sites, picnic tables, fire rings and BBQ grills (the campground host sells firewood), water and toilets, but no showers. There are pull-through sites for RVs but they don't have hookups. Pine needles make for soft sleeping grounds. An amphitheater sometimes hosts programs on everything from canyon geology to nature programs for children; check the bulletin board for times.

Seven Mile Lodge
MOTEL $

(928-638-2291; 208 Hwy 64; d $90; ❄️🌐) This simple, friendly motel doesn't take reservations, but you can show up as early as 9am to see if there are any vacancies; rooms are usually filled by early afternoon in the summer.

Grand Canyon Camper Village
CAMPGROUND $

(Map p56; 928-638-2887, 877-638-2887; www .grandcanyoncampervillage.com; 549 Camper Village Lane; tent sites $25, RV sites $35-50; 🌐📶) A mile south of the park on Hwy 64, this private campground has a ton of sites, a playground on the premises, and is convenient for walking into town for dinner. Sites are on dirt with no shade or natural surroundings, but there are toilets and pay showers. If you really need a place to camp, it's a safe and relatively quiet choice. Full hookups are available.

Best Western Grand Canyon Squire Inn
HOTEL $$$

(928-638-2681, 800-622-6966; www .grandcanyonsquire.com; 100 Hwy 64; d $260; ❄️@📶🌐📶) Rooms range from standard doubles in a two-story 1973 annex, sans elevator, to spacious interior rooms in the main hotel, with elevator. With plenty of stuff to keep kids and adults alike busy, this is the only resort-style accommodation in Tusayan. Amenities include a restaurant, popular sports bar, bowling alley, pool tables, fitness center, coin laundry and outdoor pool (open seasonally).

Canyon Plaza Resort
MOTEL $$

(928-638-2673, 800-995-2521; www.grand canyonplaza.com; 406 Canyon Plaza Lane; d/ ste $160/210; ❄️@🌐📶) Popular with tour groups, this huge motel is one of the bigger options in Tusayan, featuring spacious rooms and suites, a bright restaurant, an outdoor pool and hot tub and an 8ft indoor hot tub set in an atrium. All suites have two rooms, while suites with king beds include pullout couches in the sitting area.

Red Feather Lodge
MOTEL $$

(928-638-2414, 866-561-2425; www.redfeather lodge.com; 300 Hwy 64; d $140-170; ❄️@🌐📶) This motel offers well-kept rooms in two buildings, as well as a fitness center and an outdoor pool. Built in 1997, the three-story hotel features elevators and interior doors, while the older two-story motor lodge offers outside entrances and stairs.

Eating

Considering the number of tourists that pass through Tusayan annually, the village manages to retain a sort of old-fashioned, roadside-hub pace. There's an OK variety of eateries to choose from, but as yet no one has established a notable culinary presence.

Sophie's Mexican Kitchen
MEXICAN $$

(928-638-1105; 110 Hwy 64; mains $10-16; 🕙11am-9pm; 🍴) Festooned with colorful *papel picado* (cut-paper banners), this cheery restaurant in Tusayan's Grand Canyon Village Shops offers Mexican food like street-style tacos, fajitas and a few vegetarian options like chile rellenos. There's a selection of domestic and Mexican beers, as well as *horchata* (sweet Mexican rice drink), super-sweet desserts and a limited kids' menu.

RP's Stage Stop
CAFE $

(928-638-3115; 400 Hwy 64; mains $3-7; 🕙7am-8pm; 🌐) The only place in Tusayan to grab an espresso drink and pick up a sandwich for your picnic lunch; also a good spot to find wi-fi if you don't have access where you're staying.

We Cook Pizza & Pasta
PIZZERIA $$

(928-638-2278; 504 Hwy 64; mains $10-20; 🕙11am-10pm; 🍴) This cavernous, busy pizza joint is the kind of place where you order, take a number, and unceremoniously chow down at one of the big tables. The pizza isn't particularly compelling, but it's good and no-nonsense like its name, and whaddaya mean you want something fancier than broccoli and Asiago? It also has children's portions, a salad bar and pasta, of course.

Coronado Room
AMERICAN $$$

(928-638-2681; 100 Hwy 64; mains $13-30; 🕙5-10pm; 🍴) In a town where the pickings are very slim, the house restaurant at the Best Western Grand Canyon Squire Inn serves the classiest cuisine around. Wild game such as venison, elk and bison figure prominently, but tamer options like chicken and crab cakes are equally good. A surprisingly decent wine list complements the menu, which includes a children's menu.

Entertainment

Nightlife in Tusayan is mostly limited to the popular sports bar in the Best Western Grand Canyon Squire Inn, which also features live music nightly and Navajo dance performances on some weekend evenings.

National Geographic Visitor Center
THEATER

(Map p56; ☑928-638-2468; www.exploreth ecanyon.com; 450 Hwy 64; adult/child $13/10; ☺8:30am-8:30pm Mar-Oct, 10:30am-6:30pm Nov-Feb) Hourly, on the half-hour, the IMAX theater here screens a terrific 34-minute film called *Grand Canyon – The Hidden Secrets*. With exhilarating river-running scenes and virtual-reality drops off canyon rims, the film plunges you into the history and geology of the canyon through the eyes of ancient Native Americans, John Wesley Powell and a soaring eagle.

The IMAX experience affords you a safer, cheaper alternative to a canyon flyover, but if you do have your heart set on a helicopter ride, you'll also find **Grand Canyon National Park Airport** (Map p56) in Tusayan.

Information

Park passes are available at the **National Geographic Visitor Center** when a ranger is on duty.

Getting Around

You can walk to most places along the highway through Tusayan. From May to September, the free Tusayan Route (p87) shuttle stops at several spots in Tusayan before heading up to the South Rim. Stops include Grand Canyon Airport, Grand Canyon Squire Inn and the National Geographic Visitor Center. Shuttles run between 8am and 9:30pm.

Valle

About 25 miles south of the park, Valle marks the intersection of Hwy 64 to Williams and Hwy 180 to Flagstaff. There isn't much to it apart from a couple of curiosities, as well as a gas station, minimart and rooms at the **Grand Canyon Inn** (☑800-635-9203, 928-635-9203; www.grand-canyon-inn.com; cnr Hwys 180 & 64; d $120; ❄🛜🏊). This family-run motel offers standard motel rooms, a restaurant (open 7:30am to 2pm and 6pm to 9pm) and a heated outdoor pool.

Flintstones Bedrock City   AMUSEMENT PARK
(☑928-635-2600; tent sites $12, RV sites $16, admission $6; ☺7am-9pm Mar-Oct) It's a little worse for wear, but of course Bedrock City is old! You probably won't want to stay at the barren, windswept campground, but kids and lovers of camp (the kitsch kind) will love this slightly spooky roadside attraction. Built in 1972, it features a constant loop of Flintstones episodes in the tiny concrete movie theater, a Flintmobile that circles a volcano (complete with looming pterodactyl) and a clutch of Bedrock-style buildings to explore. The gift shop and basic diner are straight out of a David Lynch film. It's a must-stop for Flintstones fanatics and connoisseurs of kooky Americana.

Planes of Fame Air Museum   MUSEUM
(☑928-635-1000; www.planesoffame.org; cnr Hwys 64 & 180; adult/child/under 5yr $6.95/1.95/ free; ☺9am-5pm) Housed in a hangar at Valle Airport, this air museum has a collection of over 150 vintage airplanes on display, most of them fully functional and in immaculate condition. Aviation enthusiasts will find it fascinating.

Williams

☑928 / POP 2910 / ELEV 6780FT

A pretty slow spot by day, Williams comes to life in the evening when the Grand Canyon Railway train returns with passengers from the South Rim...and then closes down on the early side. Though this small town can't compete with Flagstaff's restaurants, historic downtown or myriad sights, it is a friendly town and caters to canyon tourists. Route 66 passes through the main historic district as a one-way street headed east; one-way Railroad Ave parallels the tracks and Route 66 and heads west.

Lining these two thoroughfares is downtown Williams.

Sights & Activities

There are plenty of opportunities for **hiking** and **biking** in nearby Kaibab, Coconino and Prescott National Forests. Ask at the visitor center or at the ranger station for maps and information.

Grand Canyon Railway   RAIL TOUR
(☑800-843-8724; www.thetrain.com) Following a 9:30am **Wild West show** by the tracks, the historic Grand Canyon Railway train (see boxed text p226) departs for its two-hour ride to the South Rim. If you're only visiting the rim for the day, this is a fun and hassle-free way to travel. You can leave the car behind and enjoy the park by foot, shuttle or tour bus.

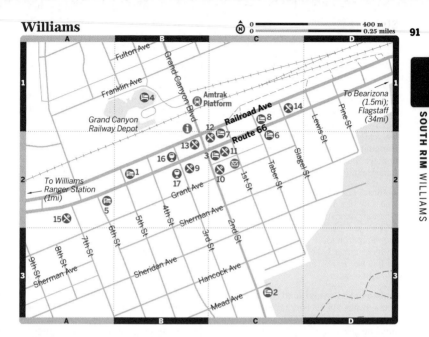

SOUTH RIM WILLIAMS

Williams

🛏 Sleeping

1 Canyon Country Inn	B2
2 FireLight B&B	C3
3 Grand Canyon Hotel	C2
4 Grand Canyon Railway Hotel	B1
5 Highlander Motel	A2
6 Lodge on Route 66	C2
7 Red Garter Bed & Bakery	C2
8 Rodeway Inn & Suites Downtowner Rte 66	C1

✗ Eating

9 Cruiser's Café 66	B2
10 Dara Thai Café	C2
11 Grand Canyon Coffee & Café	C2
12 Pancho McGillicuddy's Mexican Cantina	C2
13 Pine Country Restaurant	B2
Red Raven Restaurant	(see 11)
14 Rod's Steak House	C1
15 Safeway	A2

🍷 Drinking

16 American Flyer Coffee Company	B2
17 World Famous Sultana Bar	B2

Bearizona ZOO
(📞928-635-2289; www.bearizona.com; 1500 E Route 66; adult/child/under 4yr $16/8/free; ⏰8am-5pm Mar-Nov) Established in 2010, the awesomely named Bearizona is a drive-through 'wildlife park' inhabited by indigenous North American fauna. Visitors drive themselves along a road that winds through various fenced enclosures over 160 acres, where they can see roaming gray wolves, bison, bighorn sheep and black bears up close. There's also a walk-through section that features bobcats, javelinas, skunks and heart-meltingly adorable baby bears.

Grand Canyon Deer Farm PETTING ZOO
(📞928-635-4073, 800-926-3337; www.deerfarm .com; 6769 E Deerfarm Rd; adult/child/under 3yr $9.95/5.95/free; ⏰9am-6pm) Children love the deer farm. Blanketed in wood chips, a trail leads through an open area where the deer roam free. A smaller pen is home to goats (always eager to munch on food, shirts, strollers, whatever). Just $3 buys enough deer food to keep kids busy for a while. Among the more exotic animals in residence (that visitors are asked not to feed) are marmosets, wallabies, coatimundis, camels and 'mini-cattle.' It's 8 miles east of Williams, off I-40's exit 171.

Sleeping

Camping

Free dispersed camping is allowed in the national forest provided you refrain from camping in meadows, within a quarter-mile of the highway or any surface water, or within a half-mile of any developed campground.

The following three places are pleasant USFS campgrounds near Williams that offer year-round camping without hookups. Swimming is not allowed in any of the lakes. Contact the visitor center or the Williams Ranger Station for information.

Cataract Lake Campground CAMPGROUND $
(tent & RV sites $14; ⊙May-Sep) To get to this pleasant, woodsy campground, take exit 161 off I-40 and head north 2 miles. Note that the campground is not only right next to pretty Cataract Lake but also the BN-Santa Fe Railway tracks, and trains run regularly all night long.

Kaibab Lake Campground CAMPGROUND $
(tent & RV sites $18-35) Four miles northeast of town; take exit 165 off I-40 and go north 2 miles on Hwy 64.

**White Horse Lake
Campground** CAMPGROUND $
(tent & RV sites $18) Nineteen miles southeast of town, this campground offers a hiking trail and fishing; from town, drive 8 miles on 4th St and turn left on FR 110.

Railside RV Ranch RV CAMPGROUND $
(✆928-635-4077, 888-635-4077; www.railsidervranch.com; 877 Rodeo Rd; RV sites $36-38; 🐾♿) The closest campground to downtown Williams, with 96 RV hookups. There's no shade, but the campground has coin showers, a pet wash, free wi-fi and a playground. To get here, turn east from Grand Canyon Blvd onto Edison Ave (three blocks north of the tracks), then left on Airport Rd. After one block, turn right onto Rodeo Rd; the campground is on the left, just before the tracks.

Circle Pines KOA DEVELOPED CAMPGROUND $
(✆928-635-2626, 800-562-9379; www.circlepineskoa.com; 1000 Circle Pines Rd; tentsites $26, RV sites $45, cabins $52-228; 🐾♿♨) Amid 27 acres of ponderosa-pine forest a half-mile north of I-40 (take exit 167), Circle Pines is open year-round and offers plenty of activities for children and adults alike. Options include live music and hayrides on the weekends, miniature golf, an indoor pool, two hot tubs, bike rentals and horse stables. A cafe with outdoor seating serves breakfast and dinner during the high season.

Lodging

TOP CHOICE Red Garter Bed & Bakery B&B $$
(✆928-635-1484, 800-328-1484; www.redgarter.com; 137 W Railroad Ave; d $120-145; 🐾🐾) Up until the 1940s, gambling and girls were the draw at this 1897 bordello-turned-B&B across from the tracks. Nowadays, the place trades on its historic charm and reputation for hauntings. Of the four restored rooms, the suite was once reserved for the house's 'best gals,' who would lean out the window to flag down customers. Set back from the road, the other three rooms are smaller and quieter. All rates include a 'continental-plus' breakfast including freshly baked pastries. Sociable innkeeper John Holst knows the area well and is happy to get out a map, offer suggestions and relate the saucy history of the bordello and the town.

Grand Canyon Hotel BOUTIQUE HOTEL $
(✆928-635-1419; www.thegrandcanyonhotel.com; 145 W Route 66; dm $28, d with shared bath $60, d $70-125; 🐾@🐾) This charming spot is just what this town needed – a European-style hotel in a historic 1889 building right on Route 66. There's air-con in interior rooms, but in the exterior rooms you can get a good breeze going with the window open and the ceiling fan whirring. Private rooms are individually themed and decorated, some with clawfoot tubs or colorful Mexican textiles, and the place is run by friendly proprietors.

Lodge on Route 66 MOTEL $$
(✆928-635-4534, 877-563-4366; www.thelodgeonroute66.com; 200 E Route 66; r $85-100, ste $135-185; 🐾🐾) The Lodge is a beautifully designed blend of a Route 66 motel with low-key Southwestern style (ie no Kokopelli motif). Sturdy dark-wood furniture and wrought-iron accents give an elegant feel. Standard rooms are on the cramped side, with the big beds and little else taking up most of the available space, but roomier suites feature kitchenettes. Continental breakfast included.

Rodeway Inn & Suites Downtowner Rte 66 MOTEL $$
(✆928-635-4041; www.rodewayinn.com/hotel-williams-arizona-AZ302; 201 E Route 66; d $130, ste $150-160; 🐾🐾) Owned by the same friendly folks who run the Lodge across the highway,

the Downtowner has slightly larger rooms with a similar aesthetic and includes continental breakfast.

Canyon Motel & RV Park
MOTEL $

(928-635-9371, 800-482-3955; www.thecanyon motel.com; 1900 E Rodeo Rd; RV sites $35-38, cottages $74-78, train cars $78-160;) Stone cottages and rooms in two railroad cabooses and a former Grand Canyon Railway coach car offer a quirky alternative to a standard motel. Kids love the cozy train cars, which sport bunk beds and private decks. Cottages feature wood floors and kitchenettes. There's a heated indoor pool and a playground on the premises. To get here, turn east from Grand Canyon Blvd onto Edison Ave (three blocks north of the tracks), then left on Airport Rd. Drive one block, then turn right onto Rodeo Rd.

FireLight B&B
B&B $$

(928-635-0200, 888-838-8218; www.firelightbe dandbreakfast.com; 175 W Meade Ave; r $160-175, ste $250;) Four well-appointed and tastefully decorated rooms in this Tudor-style house all have their own fireplaces. Among the vintage amusements here are the 1940s jukebox and restored shuffleboard, while modern entertainment includes a Wii. A gourmet breakfast is served every morning by your hosts Debi (the interior designer) and Eric, and this romantic spot is adults only.

Grand Living Bed & Breakfast
B&B $$

(928-635-4171, 800-210-5908; www.grandliving bnb.com; 701 Quarter Horse Rd; r & ste $140-290;) Spacious rooms are named after flowers in this bigger B&B, grandly designed with antique oak and cherry furniture, king- or queen-sized beds, TVs and fireplaces. Gourmet breakfasts in the airy dining room are served by gracious hosts Gloria and Bill. To get here, turn east from Grand Canyon Blvd onto Edison Ave (three blocks north of the tracks), then left on Airport Rd. Drive one block, then turn right onto Rodeo Rd. Grand Living is just past the tracks, on the corner of Rodeo and Quarter Horse Rds.

Grand Canyon Railway Hotel
HOTEL $$

(928-635-4010, 800-843-8724; www.thetrain. com; 235 N Grand Canyon Blvd; d $190;) This sprawling hotel caters primarily to Grand Canyon Railway passengers (railway packages also available; see boxed text p226). While the spacious lobby – with a flagstone fireplace and gorgeous, large-scale canyon paintings by local Kenny McKenna – hints at elegance of days past, the Southwestern-style rooms are what you'd expect at any standard hotel. A restaurant, lounge and coffee house cover the dining and drinking bases. You'll also find a fitness room, heated indoor pool and hot tub.

Canyon Country Inn
MOTEL $

(928-635-2349, 877-405-3280; www.thecanyon countryinn.com; 422 W Route 66; r $66-98;) Rooms at this family-run inn are a step up from typical motel rooms and give you more of a B&B feel at a reasonable rate. Country-style decor includes frilly curtains, floral bedspreads and a teddy bear on the bed to make you feel at home. An 'extended' continental breakfast includes yogurt, fresh fruit, bagels and muffins.

Highlander Motel
MOTEL $

(928-635-2541, 877-635-2541; 533 W Route 66; d $49-59;) Good, clean budget choice with cutesy Old West decor, microwave, fridge, cable TV and spacious bathrooms.

Eating & Drinking

American Flyer Coffee Company
CAFE $

(928-635-0777; www.americanflyercoffeeco.com; 326 W Route 66; mains $2-6; 7am-2pm Sun-Thu, 7am-6pm Fri & Sat;) This extremely friendly cafe/bike-repair shop offers wi-fi access, freshly baked pastries and healthy items like salads and wraps along with its excellent house-roasted coffee. Board games, mellow music and cushy couches create a welcoming space.

Pancho McGillicuddy's Mexican Cantina
MEXICAN $$

(928-635-4150; www.vivapanchos.com; 141 W Railroad Ave; mains $11-15; 11am-10pm) Directly across from the train station, this bustling place serves up decent American-style Mexican food to hungry passengers. The restaurant is housed in an 1893 tavern and has a lively bar serving local microbrews on tap. Musicians perform on the outdoor patio on summer evenings.

Pine Country Restaurant
AMERICAN $$

(928-635-9718; www.pinecountryrestaurant. com; 107 N Grand Canyon Blvd; mains $9-22; 6am-9pm) This family restaurant offers reasonably priced American basics and gigantic pies. Though the menu offers few surprises, the price is right. Just across the street from the visitors center, it has wide windows and plenty of room to relax in a home-style setting.

Dara Thai Café   THAI $

(☎928-635-2201; 145 W Route 66, Suite C; mains $8-12; ☺11am-2pm & 5-9pm Mon-Sat) A breath of fresh lemongrass on the Williams culinary scene, Dara Thai offers a lighter alternative to meat-heavy menus elsewhere in town. Lots of choice for vegetarians, and all dishes are prepared to your specified spiciness. Despite its address, the front door is found along S 2nd St.

Red Raven Restaurant   AMERICAN $$

(☎928-635-4980; www.redravenrestaurant.com; 135 W Route 66; mains $10-22; ☺11am-2pm & 5-9pm Tue-Sun) White tablecloths and candlelight set the mood at the family-run Red Raven, delivering the most upscale dining experience you'll find in Williams. Simple but creative dishes (such as medallions of pork loin with pineapple and cranberry salsa) are complemented by a straightforward wine list.

Rod's Steak House   STEAKHOUSE $$

(☎928-635-2671; www.rods-steakhouse.com; 301 E Route 66; mains $13-26; ☺11am-9:30pm Mon-Sat) Locals say service here can be inconsistent. But the cow-shaped sign and menus spell things out – if you want steak and potatoes, this has been the place to come since 1946 (though there are a few non-cow items on the menu). Diners with limited mobility should note that restrooms are down a flight of stairs.

Cruisers Café 66   AMERICAN $$

(☎928-635-2445; www.cruisers66.com; 233 W Route 66; mains $10-20; ☺3-10pm) Housed in an old Route 66 gas station and decorated with vintage gas pumps and old-fashioned Coke ads, this cafe is a fun place for kids. Expect BBQ fare, such as burgers, spicy wings, pulled-pork sandwiches and mesquite-grilled ribs (cooked on the outdoor patio). In summer you can sit outside and enjoy live music.

Grand Canyon Coffee & Café   DINER $

(☎928-635-4907; www.grandcanyoncoffeeand cafe.com; 125 W Route 66; mains $6-8; ☺7am-3pm Sun-Thu, 7am-8pm Sat) Skip the coffee, but if you have a hankering for cheese enchiladas with your breakfast eggs, seat yourself at this local spot. Sandwiches, Americanized Asian dishes, diner stand-

bys and children's favorites round out the eclectic menu.

World Famous Sultana Bar   BAR $

(☎928-635-2021; 301 W Route 66; ☺10am-2am) Expect the once-over when you walk in, as this place seems to spook most tourists. But if you like the sort of bar that's kitted out with dusty taxidermied animals, crusty locals and a jukebox, stop by for a beer and a game of pool.

Safeway   SUPERMARKET $

(☎928-635-0500, pharmacy 928-635-5977; 637 W Route 66; ☺5am-10pm) Groceries and pharmacy.

Information

Library (☎928-635-2263; 113 S 1st St; ☺9am-5pm & 6-8pm Tue-Thu, 9am-5:30pm Fri, 9am-1pm Sat)

Police station (☎928-635-4461; 501 W Route 66; ☺9am-5pm Mon-Fri)

Post office (☎928-635-4572; 120 S 1st St; ☺9am-5pm Mon-Fri, to noon Sat)

Visitor center (☎928-635-4061, 800-863-0546; www.williamschamber.com; 200 W Railroad Ave; ☺8am-5pm) Inside the historic former train depot; offers a small bookstore with titles on the canyon, Kaibab National Forest and other areas of interest.

Williams Health Care Center (☎928-635-4441; 301 S 7th St; ☺8am-8pm)

Williams Ranger Station (☎928-635-5600; 742 S Clover Rd; ☺8am-4pm Mon-Fri) You'll find USFS rangers at both the visitor center and here.

Getting There & Around

Amtrak (☎800-872-7245; www.amtrak.com; 233 N Grand Canyon Blvd) Trains stop at Grand Canyon Railway Depot.

Arizona Shuttle (☎928-225-2290, 800-563-1980; www.arizonashuttle.com) Offers three shuttles a day to the canyon (per person $22) and to Flagstaff (per person $19).

Havasupai Reservation

One of the Grand Canyon's true treasures is Havasu Canyon, a hidden valley with four stunning, spring-fed waterfalls and inviting azure swimming holes in the heart of the 185,000-acre Havasupai Reservation. Parts of the canyon floor, as well as the rock underneath the waterfalls and pools, are made up of limestone deposited by flowing water.

These limestone deposits are known as travertine, and they give the famous blue-green water its otherworldly hue.

Because the falls lie 10 miles below the rim, most trips are combined with a stay at either Havasu Lodge in Supai or at the nearby campground. Supai is the only village within the Grand Canyon, situated 8 miles below the rim, and is the most remote village in the lower 48 states. For more on the Havasupai tribe, see p211.

The Havasupai Reservation lies south of the Colorado River and west of the South Rim. From Hualapai Hilltop, a three- to four-hour drive from the South Rim, a well-maintained trail leads to Supai, waterfalls and the Colorado River. For detailed information on traveling into Havasu Canyon, see www.havasupaitribe.com (note that the website is not officially affiliated with the tribe).

Before heading down to Supai, you *must* have reservations to camp or stay in the lodge. Do not try to hike down and back in one day – not only is it dangerous, but it doesn't allow you enough time to see the waterfalls.

Hiking

Two moderate to difficult trails are on the reservation, leading to waterfalls and a gorgeous swimming hole.

Hualapai Hilltop to Supai   HIKE

The initial hike to Havasu Canyon begins at the Hualapai Hilltop parking lot. The 8-mile hike to Supai village is not terribly strenuous, taking about three to five hours with a 2000ft elevation change.

The trail from Hualapai Hilltop descends steep switchbacks for 1.5 miles before leveling off in a dry creek bed. In this part of the canyon you'll see beautiful layers of the **Toroweap formation**, **Coconino sandstone**, **Hermit shale**, and **Esplanade sandstone**. The trail then winds through the canyon for the remaining 6.5 miles to Supai. About 1.5 miles before Supai, the trail meets Havasu Creek; follow this trail downstream to the village. Shade trees line the creek, and the sheer walls of the canyon rise dramatically on either side of the trail.

Havasu Canyon to Waterfalls   HIKE

The stunning waterfalls and travertine-bottomed pools of Havasu Canyon begin about a mile past Supai. The 6-mile round-trip hike to Beaver Falls makes for a good six-hour day with stops at the pools; be prepared for an extremely steep climb down to Mooney Falls.

About a mile beyond Supai are the newly formed (and as yet unofficially named) **New Navajo Falls** and **Rock Falls** and blue pools below. The new falls developed above the former Navajo Falls, which was completely destroyed in a major flash flood in 2008. After another mile, you will reach beautiful **Havasu Falls**. This waterfall drops 100ft into a sparkling blue pool surrounded by cottonwoods and is a popular swimming hole. Havasu Campground sits a quarter-mile beyond Havasu Falls. Just beyond the campground, the trail passes **Mooney Falls**, which tumbles 200ft down into another blue-green swimming hole. To get to the swimming hole, you must climb through two tunnels and descend a very steep trail – chains provide welcome handholds, but this trail is not for the faint of heart. Carefully pick your way down, keeping in mind that these falls were named for prospector DW James Mooney, who fell to his death here. After a picnic and a swim, continue about 2 miles to **Beaver Falls**. The Colorado River is 5 miles beyond.

The trail passes small pools and cascades and crosses the creek many times; use extra caution when the water is high. The Colorado lies 10.5 miles from Supai and 8 miles beyond the campground, and camping is prohibited beyond Mooney Falls. It's a strenuous hike to the river and back that may involve bushwhacking and route-finding. It's generally recommended that you don't attempt to hike to the river; in fact, the reservation actively discourages this.

Sleeping

It is essential that you make phone reservations in advance; if you hike in without a reservation, you will not be allowed to stay in Supai and will have to hike 8 miles back up to your car at Hualapai Hilltop.

Havasu Campground   CAMPGROUND $

(☏928-448-2121, 928-448-2141, 928-448-2180; per night per person $17) Two miles past Supai, the campground stretches three-quarters of a mile along the creek between Havasu and Mooney Falls. It's often packed in summer, so be sure to hike its length before choosing a site. Sites have picnic tables and the campground features several composting toilets, as well as drinking water at Fern Spring. Fires are not permitted but gas stoves are allowed.

Havasupai Lodge LODGE $$
(📞928-448-2111, 928-448-2101; r $145; ❄) The only lodging in Supai offers motel rooms, all with canyon views, two double beds, air-conditioning and private showers. There are no TVs or telephones. Reservations are essential; the lodge is often booked months in advance for the entire summer.

Eating

The **Sinyella Store** (⊘7am-7pm) is the first shop you'll see as you walk through the village. Take off your pack for a minute and lounge on the lawn with an ice-cream bar and the owner's friendly dogs and cats. In Supai, the **Havasupai Tribal Cafe** (📞928-448-2981; ⊘6am-6pm) serves breakfast, lunch and dinner daily, and the **Havasupai Trading Post** (📞928-448-2951; ⊘6am-6pm) sells basic but expensive groceries and snacks. Remember that all supplies are still carried down by mule, which affects the availability and variety of food in the canyon; if you can't survive without Nutella or fresh arugula, pack it down yourself.

Information

The local **post office** is the only one in the country still delivering its mail by mule, and mail sent from here bears a special postmark to prove it. There's also a small emergency **clinic** (📞928-448-2641) in Supai.

Liquor, recreational drugs, pets and nude swimming are not allowed, nor are trail bikes allowed below Hualapai Hilltop.

Havasupai Tourist Enterprise (📞928-448-2141, 928-448-2237; www.havasupai-nsn.gov; PO Box 160, Supai, AZ 86435; adult/under 13yr $35/free; ⊘5:30am-7pm) Visitors pay an entry fee and $5 environmental-care fee when they arrive in Supai.

Getting There & Around

Seven miles east of Peach Springs on historic Route 66, a signed turnoff leads to the 62-mile paved road ending at Hualapai Hilltop. Here you'll find the parking area, stables and the trailhead into the canyon, but no services.

To get to Supai, park at Hualapai Hilltop and then hike, ride or fly the 8 miles down to the village. If you plan on hiking or riding down, you should spend the night in Peach Springs (ideally), Grand Canyon Caverns or in one of the motels along Route 66. Motels in Seligman are about 90 miles from Hualapai Hilltop.

Be aware that Hualapai Hilltop is a good (ie not so good) three- to four-hour drive from the South Rim. Don't let place names confuse you:

Hualapai Hilltop is on the Havasupai Indian Reservation, not the Hualapai Reservation, as one might think.

Helicopter

On Sunday, Monday, Thursday and Friday from mid-March through mid-October, a helicopter ($85 one way) shuttles between Hualapai Hilltop and Supai from 10am to 1pm. Advance reservations are not accepted; you just show up at the parking lot and sign up; however, service is prioritized for tribal members and those offering services and deliveries to the reservation. Call Havasupai Tourist Enterprise before you arrive to be sure the helicopter is running. From mid-October to mid-March the helicopter operates on Sunday and Friday only.

Horse & Mule

If you don't want to hike to Supai, you can ride a **horse** (round-trip to lodge/campground $120/187). It's about half that price if you hike in and ride out, or vice versa. You can also arrange for a **pack horse or mule** (round-trip $85) to carry your pack into and out of the canyon.

Horses and pack mules depart Hualapai Hilltop at 10am year-round. Call the lodge or campground (wherever you'll be staying) in advance to arrange a ride.

Hualapai Reservation & Skywalk

Home to the much-hyped Skywalk, the Hualapai Reservation borders many miles of the Colorado River northeast of Kingman, covering the southwest rim of the canyon and bordering the Havasupai Reservation to the east and Lake Mead National Recreation Area to the west. The reservation includes the only road to the river within the Grand Canyon.

In 1988 the Hualapai Nation opened Grand Canyon West, a less chaotic alternative to the South Rim. Though the views here are lovely, they're not as sublime as those on the South Rim – but the unveiling of the glass bridge known as Grand Canyon Skywalk in 2007 added a completely novel way to view the canyon. Note that Grand Canyon West is a three- to four-hour drive from the South Rim.

Sights & Activities

Grand Canyon West GUIDED TOUR
(📞928-769-2636, 888-868-9378; www.grandcanyonwest.com; per person $43-87; ⊘7am-7pm Apr-Sep, 8am-5pm Oct-Mar) Nowadays, the only way to visit Grand Canyon West,

---

ⓘ PACKING A MULE

If hiring a pack mule to carry your backpack into Havasu Canyon, your best bet is to stuff your backpack into a duffel bag (preferred by mule wranglers). Later, when you pick up your bag at the lodge or campground, you can remove your pack from the duffel and hoist it normally, rather than schlepping an awkward, heavy duffel.

---

the section of the west rim overseen by the Hualapai Nation, is to purchase a package tour. A hop-on, hop-off shuttle travels the loop road to scenic points along the rim. Tours can include lunch, horse-drawn wagon rides from an ersatz Western town, and informal Native American performances. Tours depart several times a day from the Grand Canyon West visitor center. Allow at least a half-day to get there, have a look around, and drive back out. Day tours from Las Vegas (see p87), including a round-trip flight in either a helicopter or a small plane, can also be arranged.

Grand Canyon Skywalk　　　　BRIDGE
All but the cheapest packages to Grand Canyon West include admission to the Grand Canyon Skywalk, the horseshoe-shaped glass bridge cantilevered 4000ft above the canyon floor. Jutting out almost 70ft over the canyon, the Skywalk allows visitors to see the canyon through the glass walkway. The only way to visit the Skywalk is on a package tour, which makes the experience of peering past your feet into the gorge below quite a pricey prospect. Note that no cameras, cell phones or other personal belongings are allowed on the Skywalk. Free lockers are provided, and photographers are on hand to take your picture for an additional fee.

Diamond Creek Road　　　　DRIVING TOUR
(entry permit per person $16 plus tax) This 22-mile unpaved scenic road heads north from Peach Springs to the Colorado River. At road's end you'll find picnic tables and a camping area. Don't forget to purchase an entrance permit from the Hualapai Lodge front desk before driving down the road.

Hualapai River Runners　　　　RAFTING
(www.grandcanyonwest.com/rafting.php) Offers one-day rafting on the Colorado from Diamond Creek to Pierce Ferry Landing. Its motorized rafts hold up to 10 people. This is your only opportunity for a one-day white-water rafting trip in the Grand Canyon. The Hualapai Lodge can arrange packages that include accommodations with the river trip.

Sleeping & Eating

Thirty-five miles east of Peach Springs, along the Route 66 strip in Seligman, you'll find several inexpensive, simple motels.

Hualapai Lodge　　　　MOTEL **$$**
(☎928-769-2230; 900 Route 66, Peach Springs; d $110; ❀🛜❄) The only place to stay in Peach Springs is this modern lodge, which has a saltwater swimming pool and occasional Native American performances in the lobby. Connected to the hotel is Diamond Creek Restaurant (mains $7 to $13; open breakfast, lunch and dinner), serving standard American fare.

Diamond Creek Campground　　CAMPGROUND **$**
(sites incl entrance fee $25) At the end of Diamond Creek Rd is this small, basic beach campground along the Colorado River. The elevation here is 1900ft, so the campground is extremely hot in summer. You'll find toilets and picnic tables but no drinking water. The campground holds about 10 people and is first-come, first-served; contact the **Hualapai Office of Tourism** (☎928-769-2230) for availability.

Information

Hualapai Office of Tourism (☎928-769-2219, 888-255-9550) staffs a desk at Hualapai Lodge in the microscopic town of Peach Springs.

Getting There & Around

There are no regular shuttles or buses to Peach Springs or the Hualapai Reservation. At the time of research, 12 of the 21 miles of Diamond Bar Rd to Grand Canyon West were paved, and the middle 9 miles were being graded regularly. Call the Hualapai Lodge to check road conditions before heading out, especially if it's been raining, as the road may be impassable. If you don't feel up to driving, take advantage of the **park-and-ride service** (☎702-260-6506; per person round-trip $15) that departs from Meadview, Arizona; advance reservations required.

To get to Grand Canyon West from Kingman, fill up your gas tank and drive north on Hwy 93 for approximately 26 miles. Then head northeast along the paved Pierce Ferry Rd for about another 30 miles, before turning onto Diamond Bar Rd for the final 21-mile stretch. Directions from other towns are detailed on the **Grand Canyon West website** (www.grandcanyonwest.com).

Bypass the driving completely by booking a Grand Canyon West tour with a round-trip flight from Las Vegas (see p87).

Flagstaff

📞 928 / POP 65,870 / ELEV 6910FT

Flagstaff's laid-back charms are myriad, from its pedestrian-friendly historic downtown crammed with eclectic vernacular architecture and vintage neon to its high-altitude pursuits like skiing and hiking. Buskers play bluegrass on street corners while bike culture flourishes like a regional religion. Locals are generally a happy, athletic bunch, skewing more toward granola than gunslinger. Northern Arizona University (NAU) gives Flag its college-town flavor, while its railroad history still figures firmly in the town's identity. Throw in a healthy appreciation for craft beer, freshly roasted coffee beans and an all-around good time and you have the makings of a town you want to slow down and savor.

From downtown, I-17 heads south toward Phoenix, splitting off at Hwy Alt 89 (also known as 89A), a spectacularly scenic winding road through Oak Creek Canyon to Sedona. While Hwy 180 is the most direct route to the South Rim, Hwy 89 beelines north to Cameron to meet Hwy 64, leading westward to the East Entrance. Those headed to the North Rim (193 miles) stay on Hwy 89 past Cameron, link up with Alt 89 to Jacob Lake, then take Hwy 67 to the rim.

Sights

Flagstaff's laid-back appeal is hard to pin down – it could be the wonderful mix of cultural sites, its historic downtown, the access to outdoorsy pursuits – better you should investigate yourself.

Museum of Northern Arizona MUSEUM
(Off map p100; 📞928-774-5213; www.musnaz.org; 3101 N Fort Valley Rd; adult/child $7/4; ⏲9am-5pm) If you have time for only one sight in Flagstaff, this is it. In an attractive Craftsman-style stone building amid a pine grove, this small but excellent museum features exhibits on local Native American archeology, history and culture, as well as geology, biology and the arts. Don't miss the extensive collection of Hopi katsina (the correct Hopi pronunciation for 'kachina') dolls and a wonderful variety of Native American bas-

ketry and ceramics. The bookstore specializes in regional subjects. Check the website for information on changing exhibits, weekend craft demonstrations and one- to three-day workshops for children and adults. The museum also offers customized trips to the Grand Canyon (see p216).

Riordan Mansion State Historic Park HISTORIC SITE
(Map p100; 📞928-779-4395; www.azstateparks. com/Parks/RIMA; 409 W Riordan Rd; adult/child $7/3; ⏲9:30am-5pm May-Oct, 10:30am-5pm Nov-Apr) Centered on a beautiful 13,000-sq-ft mansion, this park is a must for anyone interested in the Arts and Crafts movement. Having made a fortune from their Arizona Lumber Company, brothers Michael and Timothy Riordan had the house built in 1904. The Craftsman-style design was the brainchild of Atchison, Topeka & Santa Fe Railway architect Charles Whittlesey, who also designed El Tovar, on the South Rim. The exterior features hand-split wooden shingles, log-slab siding and rustic stone. Filled with Edison, Stickley, Tiffany and Steinway furniture, the interior is a shrine to Arts and Crafts and looks much as it did when the Riordans lived here. Visitors are welcome to walk the grounds and picnic, but entrance to the house is by guided tour only. Tours leave daily and on the hour; advance reservations are accepted. The site's visitor center has a good selection of books on the Arts and Crafts movement, and exhibits on Flagstaff's history and architecture.

Lowell Observatory OBSERVATORY
(Map p100; 📞928-774-3358; www.lowell.edu; 1400 W Mars Hill Rd; adult/child $6/3; ⏲9am-5pm Mar-Oct, noon-5pm Nov-Feb, call for evening hours) On top of the very aptly named Mars Hill, about a mile west of downtown, this national historic landmark was built in 1894 by Percival Lowell. In 1896 Lowell bought a 24in Clark refractor telescope for $20,000 (around $6 million in today's dollars) and spent the next 20 years looking for life on Mars. Though he never did spot a Martian, the observatory has witnessed many important discoveries, the most famous of which was the first sighting of Pluto, in 1930.

In the '60s NASA used the Clark telescope to map the moon. Weather permitting, visitors can stargaze through the telescope; check the website for the evening schedule. The short, paved Pluto Walk climbs through

Arizona claims bragging rights for having the longest continuous stretch of Route 66, running east to west from Seligman to Topock. Getting off I-40 for part of a long road trip can be a beautiful alternative to simply blowing through this part of the country, especially on this section of the Mother Road. Driving some parts of this byway can be equal parts eerie, nostalgic and melancholy, while other parts are strongly redolent of scrub and dust, and still others are delightfully thriving.

Nineteen miles west of Williams, Ash Fork is an oft passed-over town left in the dust of first the railroad and then the interstate. Founded in 1882 when the Atlantic and Pacific Railroad established a stop here, Ash Fork became home to the Escalante Harvey House several years later, making it a destination for locals and tourists. These days its claim to fame is as the 'Flagstone Capital of the World,' as smooth vermilion slabs of Coconino sandstone are quarried in the area. You can stay for the night at **Ash Fork Inn** (928-637-2514; 859 W Route 66), try the green chili at **Ranch House Cafe** (928-637-2710; 111 W Park Ave) and poke around the free **Ash Fork Historical Museum** (928-637-0204; www.ashforkrt66museum.com; 901 W Route 66).

Several miles west of Ash Fork, if you take exit 139 and follow Crookton Rd for a few miles, you'll come upon the Partridge Creek Bridge, out of which a cottonwood tree grows. The area is slated for development, but with any luck both bridge and tree will remain unmolested.

A worthy stop west of Williams is Seligman, where Juan Delgadillo once reigned prankishly supreme at his famous **Delgadillo's Sno Cap Drive-In** (928-422-3291; 22235 E Route 66; mains $2-6). We won't ruin the fun for you, but his son and family carry on the merry traditions as they serve you frosty (or are they incredibly warm?) shakes and cheeseburgers with cheese. Along both sides of Seligman's stretch of Route 66 are the historic buildings that have survived over the years, as well as cafes, restaurants (Road Kill Café, anyone?) and souvenir shops where they lay the kitsch on thick. One of Seligman's handful of clean, basic budget hotels is the **Historic Route 66 Motel** (928-422-3204; 500 W Route 66; r $47-57;).

Getting back on the westward highway reveals miles upon miles of rolling hills and canyon country, punctuated by the Route 66 attraction of **Grand Canyon Caverns & Inn** (928-422-3223; www.grandcanyoncaverns.com; milepost 115, Route 66; adult/child $15/10; 8am-6pm May-Sep, call for off-season hours). You'll be greeted by a huge plaster dinosaur and can escape the desert heat in the cool subterranean caverns here, 21 stories below ground via elevator. You'll encounter a model of the gigantic Harlan's ground sloth (*Glossotherium harlani*) whose well-preserved skeleton was found inside the cave with a broken hip. The cavern **restaurant** (7am-7pm), about a mile off the highway, is a great little roadside resting spot with a small playground, and you can even stay the night at the **inn** (d $77-86;) or the very quiet, underground suite ($700) within the caverns.

Next stop west is Peach Springs, the biggest town on the Hualapai Reservation, with a motel where you can arrange one-day rafting trips on the Colorado. Moving westward, you'll pass tiny towns like Truxton and Valentine, and teeny Hackberry, whose Old Route 66 Visitor Center lures passersby with its eccentrically decorated gas station. Vintage cars in faded disrepair, old toilet seats and rusted-out ironwork adorn the 1934 general store and dusty parking lot. It's run by a Route 66 memorialist and makes a lovely spot to stop for a cold drink and souvenirs.

For more information on the history of this old highway, check out the **Historic Route 66 Association of Arizona** (928-753-5001; www.azrt66.com).

a scale model of our solar system, providing descriptions of each planet. You can stroll the grounds and museum on your own, but the only way to see the telescopes and lovely observatories is on a tour (on the hour from 10am to 4pm in summer; on the hour from 1pm to 4pm in winter). Even those with a passing interest in astronomy will enjoy the tours, as guides do a great job of explaining things in everyday terms.

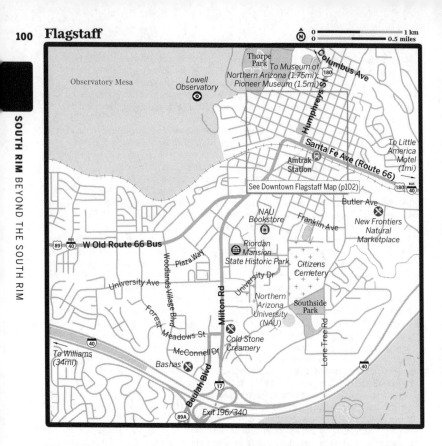

The Arboretum
PARK

(☎928-774-1442; www.thearb.org; 4001 S Woody Mountain Rd; adult/child $7/3; ⊗9am-5pm Apr-Oct; 🖫) More than just an attraction for gardeners and plant lovers, this 200-acre arboretum is a lovely spot to take a break and rejuvenate your spirit. Two short wood-chip trails hug a meadow and wind beneath ponderosa pines, passing an herb garden, native plants, vegetables and wildflowers, among other growing things. Plan a picnic at one of the tables scattered throughout the gardens. The arboretum offers tours (11am, 1pm and 3pm), as well as a summer adventure program for children aged four to 12.

Pioneer Museum
MUSEUM

(Map p100; ☎928-774-6272; www.arizona historicalsociety.org/museums/flagstaff.asp; 2340 N Fort Valley Rd; adult/child $5/free; ⊗9am-5pm Mon-Sat) Housed in the old 1908 county hospital, the Pioneer Museum preserves Flagstaff's early history in photographs and an eclectic mix of memorabilia – for example, a 1920s-era permanent-wave machine (for curling hair) that looks more like a science-fiction torture device.

Coconino Center for the Arts

(Map p100; ☎928-779-2300; www.culturalpart ners.org; 2300 N Fort Valley Rd; ⊗vary) Behind the Pioneer Museum, the Coconino Center for the Arts exhibits work by local artists and hosts various performances and programs. Check its website for current exhibitions and events. The adjacent **Art Barn** (☎928-774-0822; 2320 N Fort Valley Rd; ⊗vary) has been displaying and selling local artisans' work for three decades. Here you'll find a good selection of jewelry, photography, painting, pottery and kachina dolls, among other objects.

Activities

Hiking & Biking

Ask at the USFS ranger stations for maps and information about the scores of hiking and mountain-biking trails in and around Flagstaff. Another useful resource is *Flagstaff Hikes: 97 Day Hikes Around Flagstaff*, by Richard and Sherry Mangum (Hexagon Press, 2007), available at the visitor center and Babbitt's Backcountry Outfitter, among other places.

Consider tackling the steep, 3-mile one-way hike up 9299ft **Mt Elden** to the ranger station at the top of the peak's tower, which has stairs you can climb to the ranger's lookout. Arizona Snowbowl (p102) offers several trails, including the strenuous 4.5-mile one-way hike up 12,633ft **Humphreys Peak**, the highest point in Arizona; wear decent boots, as sections of the trail cross crumbly volcanic rock. In summer, ride the scenic **chairlift** (adult/child $12/8; ☺10am-4pm Fri-Sun & Mon hols Memorial Day-Labor Day) at Arizona Snowbowl to 11,500ft, where you can hike, hear ranger talks and take in the desert and mountain views. Children under eight ride for free.

There's also a beautiful stretch of the Arizona Trail (boxed text, p34) running through the area. If you head toward Walnut Canyon (p109), you'll see a turnoff on the right, leading to the **Walnut Canyon Trailhead.** Drive 1.7 miles down the graded dirt road and you'll come to the trailhead. There are no restrooms, no water, no nothin' – come prepared with a map and supplies if you want to do the Fisher Point Trail (6.7 miles one way) or hike up to Marshall Lake (13.4 miles one way).

An original, fabulous series of local mountain-biking and hiking guides is penned by local character Cosmic Ray. Pick up a copy of *Fat Tire Tales and Trails* (Cosmic Ray, 2010), with hand-drawn, to-scale maps and colorful, entertaining summaries of each trail – 'epic-didlyicious!' – accompanied with elevation gain, distance, difficulty level and detailed route descriptions. Cosmic Ray also self-publishes the guide *50 Favorite Hikes: Flagstaff and Sedona* (2007), as well as laminated, shove-in-your-pocket trail maps for both Flagstaff and Sedona. Look for his books and maps at Macy's, Absolute Bikes and regional branches of REI (Recreational Equipment, Inc) – and then hit the trail.

Absolute Bikes   BIKE RENTAL
(Map p102; ☑928-779-5969; www.absolutebikes. net; 202 E Route 66; bike rentals per day from $40; ☺9am-7pm Mon-Fri, 10am-6pm Sat, 10am-4pm Sun) For an inside track on the local mountain-biking scene, check out the super-friendly gearheads at Absolute Bikes. Though Flagstaff is blessed with several excellent bike shops, this is the only one that offers rentals.

Other Activities

If you can't guess by glancing around at the physically fit townsfolk, Flagstaff is full of active citizens. So there's no shortage of outdoors stores and places to buy or rent camping, cycling and skiing equipment. For ski rentals, swing by Peace Surplus.

Thorpe Park (Map p100; 191 N Thorpe Rd) has a great playground for letting the little ones run loose, and a dog park.

FLAGSTAFF FUN STUFF FOR KIDS

» Call on Cold Stone Creamery (p106) for a creative cone

» Feed the fawns at Grand Canyon Deer Farm (p91)

» Picnic and play at Thorpe Park playground (p101)

» Browse books in the children's section of the library (p108)

» Ride the scenic chairlift at Arizona Snowbowl (p102)

» Hike through lava flows at Sunset Crater Volcano National Monument (p109)

» Board the Grand Canyon Railway (boxed text p226) to the South Rim

» Learn about native flora in the Arboretum (p100) summer adventure program

» Groove to the tunes of the Summer Concert Series at the Arboretum (p100) on the first Saturdays of June, July and August

» Pull up a chair in Heritage Sq (p107) and catch a family-friendly flick on a warm summer weekend

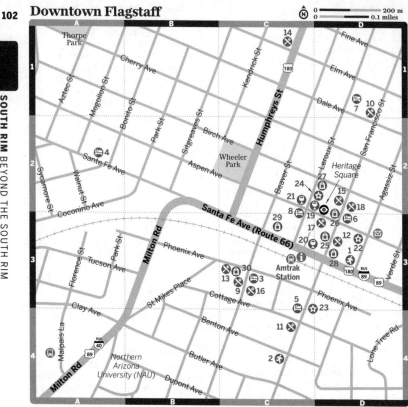

Arizona Snowbowl
SKIING

(928-779-1951; www.arizonasnowbowl.com; Hwy 180 & Snowbowl Rd; lift ticket adult/child $49/26; 9am-4pm) Seven miles north of downtown, AZ Snowbowl is small but lofty, with four lifts and 30 ski runs between 9200ft and 11,500ft.

Flagstaff
Nordic Center
CROSS-COUNTRY SKIING

(928-220-0550; www.flagstaffnordiccenter.com; milepost 232, Hwy 180; from $16 Sat & Sun, from $10 Mon-Fri; 9am-4pm weather permitting) Fifteen miles north of Flagstaff, the Nordic Center offers 30 groomed trails for cross-country skiing, as well as lessons, rentals and food. Past the Nordic Center off Hwy 180, you'll find plenty of USFS cross-country skiing pullouts, where you can park and ski for free.

Vertical Relief Rock Climbing
ROCK CLIMBING

(Map p102; 928-556-9909; www.verticalrelief. com; 205 S San Francisco St; rock gym day pass $16; 10am-11pm Mon-Fri, noon-8pm Sat & Sun) Provides 6500 sq ft of artificial indoor climbing walls. Routes range from beginner to the most difficult grades. The center also offers indoor and outdoor classes as well as information on local climbing routes.

Northern Arizona
Trail Rides
HORSEBACK RIDING

(928-225-1538; www.northernarizonatrailrides. com; 3090 S Old Munds Hwy) Offers trail rides, including breakfast and happy-hour rides. Call ahead for reservations. To get to the stables, take Hwy Alt 89 south of town for about a mile before turning onto S Old Munds Hwy.

Sleeping

Dozens of nondescript, independent motels, with rates ranging from $30 to $50, line Old Route 66 and the railroad tracks east of downtown (exit 198 off I-40). Check the room before you pay – some are much worse than others. For the money, you're far better off at one of the hostels or historic hotels downtown.

Chain motels and hotels line Milton Rd, Beulah Blvd and Forest Meadows St, clustering around exit 198 off I-40.

Flagstaff has too many wonderful B&Bs to list here, most of which are detailed at www.flagstaff-bed-breakfast.com.

TOP CHOICE **Inn at 410**   B&B $$
(Map p102; ☑928-774-0088, 800-774-2008; www.inn410.com; 410 N Leroux St; r $125-200; ❄@) This elegant and fully renovated 1894 house offers nine spacious, beautifully decorated and themed bedrooms, each with a refrigerator and private bathroom. Most rooms also have a fireplace or whirlpool bath and many have four-poster beds and views of the garden or the San Francisco Peaks. A short stroll from downtown, the inn has a shady garden with fruit trees and a cozy dining room, where the full gourmet breakfast and afternoon snacks

are served and where you can mix yourself a cocktail on a lazy afternoon.

England House   B&B $$
(Map p102; ☑928-214-7350, 877-214-7350; www.englandhousebandb.com; 614 W Santa Fe Ave; r $129-199; ❄@) Exquisitely restored and decorated by owners Richard and Laurel, this Flagstaff B&B has a distinctive stone exterior made of local Moenkopi and Coconino sandstones. Even more elegant is the meticulously designed interior, from the original stamped-tin ceilings to the carefully curated antique French furniture. Gourmet meals are as healthy as they are delicious, and guests are encouraged to raid the refrigerator for treats like bottled beers and ice-cream bars.

Starlight Pines   B&B $$
(☑928-527-1912, 800-752-1912; www.starlight-pinesbb.com; 3380 E Lockett Rd; r $135-189; ❄@) On the east side of town, Starlight Pines has four spacious rooms in a Victorian-style house, each decorated with Tiffany-style lamps, antique clawfoot tubs, Stickley chairs and other lovely touches. Each room has individual extras like a private balcony overlooking Mt Elden or a fireplace. Your hosts, Michael and Richard, are as

welcoming and warm as the house itself and are happy to give travel advice on the canyon and local attractions.

Comfi Cottages
BUNGALOW $$$

(☎928-774-0731, 888-774-0731; www.comfi cottages.com; cottages $140-285; 🖥🛇🐾) If you're tired of hotels and motels, consider these bungalows, which are spread out in residential areas around town and all less than a mile from the historic district. Most were built in the 1920s and '30s and have a homey old feel to them, with wood floors, Craftsman-style kitchens and little lawns. Cabinets are filled with breakfast foods, and each cottage includes a TV, VCR, telephone, bicycles, tennis rackets, a BBQ grill, a picnic table and picnic baskets.

Arizona Mountain Inn
CABINS $$

(☎928-774-8959, 800-239-5236; www.arizona mountaininn.com; 4200 Lake Mary Rd; cabins $130-230; 🛇🐾) A-frame and wood cabins outfitted with kitchenettes, some with mountain views and lofts, are scattered around this ponderosa-forested property about 10 minutes' drive south of downtown. This is a great getaway for those craving quiet, and kids will love the playground, complete with play cabin. Dogs are allowed in most cabins for an extra fee.

Grand Canyon
International Hostel
HOSTEL $

(Map p102; ☎928-779-9421, 888-442-2696; www .grandcanyonhostel.com; 19½ S San Francisco St; dm $18-20, r with shared bath incl breakfast $36-43; 🖥@🛇) Housed in a historic building with hardwood floors and Southwestern decor, this bright, homey hostel offers private rooms or dorms with a four-person maximum. It has a slightly more mellow feel than the DuBeau, which is owned by the same proprietors. The kitchens are spotless, and there's a TV room with a video library.

DuBeau International Hostel
HOSTEL $

(Map p102; ☎928-774-6731, 800-398-7112; www .grandcanyonhostel.com; 19 W Phoenix Ave; incl breakfast dm $21-24, r $46-66; 🖥@🛇🐾) This independent hostel offers the same friendly service and clean, well-run accommodations as the Grand Canyon International Hostel. There are also laundry facilities and bright kitchens. Convivial common areas include a nonsmoking lounge with a fireplace, as well as a jukebox, foosball and a pool table – it's a bit livelier over here.

Weatherford Hotel
HOTEL $

(Map p102; ☎928-779-1919; www.weatherford hotel.com; 23 N Leroux St; r with shared bath $49-79, r $89-139; 🛇🛇) Standing on the corner of Aspen and Leroux, this historic three-story brick hotel offers 11 charmingly decorated rooms with turn-of-the-20th-century feel. Three newly renovated rooms also incorporate modern amenities such as TVs, phones and air-conditioning. Since the Weatherford's three bars often feature live music, it can get noisy here – if you need silence for sleeping, consider staying elsewhere. If you do stay, note that there's a 2am curfew.

Hotel Monte Vista
HOTEL $$

(Map p102; ☎928-779-6971, 800-545-3068; www .hotelmontevista.com; 100 N San Francisco St; d $65-130, ste $120-175; 🛇) A huge, old-fashioned neon sign towers over this allegedly haunted 1926 hotel, hinting at what's inside: feather lampshades, vintage furniture, bold colors (just try to find a plain white wall) and eclectic decor. Rooms named for movie stars who slept in them include the Humphrey Bogart room, with dramatic black walls, yellow ceiling and gold-satin bedding. Even more intriguing are the several resident ghosts who supposedly make regular appearances. Though lacking in high-end amenities, the Monte Vista's appeal comes from all of its glorious funkiness.

Little America Motel
MOTEL $$

(Off map p100 ☎928-779-7900, 800-352-4386; www.flagstaff.littleamerica.com; 2515 E Butler Ave; d & ste $149-179; 🖥🛇🛇🐾) When you reach the Sinclair truck stop, don't drive away thinking you have the wrong place. A little further down the side driveway is a sprawling boutique-style motel with spacious rooms, which are immaculately decorated in French Provincial style and furnished with goosedown bedding, refrigerators and large bathrooms. Small patios in each room open on 500 acres of grass and woods, through which a flat 2-mile trail winds. You'll also find a playground, fitness center, restaurant and heated outdoor pool at this oasis in the most unexpected of places.

Camping

Free dispersed camping is permitted in the national forest surrounding Flagstaff. Also check out p112 for information about USFS campgrounds in Oak Creek Canyon, 15 to 30 miles south of town.

Woody Mountain Campground

CAMPGROUND $

([928-774-7727, 800-732-7986; www.woody mountaincampground.com; 2727 W Route 66; tent sites $20, RV sites $30; ☺Mar-Oct; @🔊🏊]) Has 146 sites, playground and coin laundry; off I-40 at exit 191.

Fort Tuthill County Park

CAMPGROUND $

([928-679-8000; tent & RV sites $16; ☺May-Sep) Fort Tuthill sits 5 miles south of downtown at exit 337 off I-17; has 100 family sites with water and sewer only, and 150 group sites without utilities.

Flagstaff KOA

CAMPGROUND $

([928-526-9926, 800-562-3524; www .flagstaffkoa.com; 5803 N Hwy 89; tent & RV sites $26-44; 🔊) One of the biggest campgrounds lies a mile north of I-40 off exit 201, 5 miles northeast of downtown.

Eating

TOP CHOICE Criollo Latin Kitchen

FUSION $$

(Map p102; [928-774-0541; www.criollolatinkitch en.com; 16 N San Francisco St; mains $13-30; ☺11am-10pm Mon-Thu, 11am-11pm Fri, 9am-11pm Sat, 9am-2pm & 4-10pm Sun) Weekend brunch may not sound like the time to come to Criollo, since this Latin fusion spot has such a romantic, industrial setting for cozy cocktail dates and delectable late-night small plates, but the blue-corn blueberry pancakes make a strong argument for showing up in the light of day. Whatever time you choose to dine, the food is sourced locally and sustainably whenever possible, and the wine list is divine.

Josephine's

AMERICAN $$$

(Map p102; [928-779-3400; www.josephinesres taurant.com; 503 N Humphreys St; mains $18-30; ☺11am-2:30pm & 5-9pm Mon-Fri, 8am-2pm & 5-9pm Sat & Sun) Josephine's feels more like someone's home than a restaurant, occupying a 1911 Craftsman bungalow. There's pleasant patio dining, although Humphreys St is a bit loud; inside, you'll encounter a great old stone bar, a fireplace, Craftsman light fixtures and dining tables in each room. Dinner features such creative dishes as carnitas with a muscat reduction and Manchego potato cakes or wok-charred salmon with cranberry citrus sauce. Though a bit pricey, it's a reliable option for an upscale meal. Consider stopping for lunch – pecan-encrusted fish tacos or a fried green tomato and turkey sandwich are welcome changes

from typical lunch fare. Josephine's also has an extensive wine list.

Beaver Street Brewery

BREWPUB $$

(Map p102; [928-779-0079; www.beaverstreet brewery.com; 11 S Beaver St; mains $10-16; ☺11am-11pm Sun-Thu, 11am-midnight Fri & Sat) Beaver Street Brewery, located on the block south of the tracks that's also home to popular Flagstaff haunts like Macy's and La Bellavia, is a bustling place to go for a bite to eat with a pint of local microbrew. It usually has five handmade beers on tap, like its Railhead Red Ale or R&R Oatmeal Stout, and some seasonal brews. The menu is typical brewpub fare, with delicious pizzas, burgers and salads. This place packs them all in – families, river guides, ski bums and businesspeople.

Macy's

CAFE $

(Map p102; [928-774-2243; www.macyscoffee. net; 14 S Beaver St; mains $3-7; ☺6am-8pm Mon-Wed, to 10pm Thu-Sun; 🔊) This crowded coffeehouse is a Flagstaff institution, where students rub shoulders with superior court judges. The delicious house-roasted coffee has kept Flagstaff buzzing for over 30 years now. The vegetarian menu includes many vegan choices, with traditional cafe grub like pastries, steamed eggs, bagels, yogurt and granola. A coin laundry is sandwiched between here and La Bellavia, so you can pop in a load and relax with your latte and book. Macy's is cash only.

Pato Thai Cuisine

THAI $$

(Map p102; [928-213-1825; www.patothai.com; 104 N San Francisco St; mains $7-14; ☺11am-9:30pm Mon-Sat, noon-8:30pm Sun) Pato Thai welcomes guests into a warmly hued dining room redolent with galangal, Thai basil and lemongrass. The attractive environs are matched by well-executed, authentic Thai cuisine with a few Chinese dishes thrown in for good measure. Spiciness level is adjusted to your taste (err on the mild side).

Fratelli Pizza

PIZZERIA $$

(Map p102; [928-774-9200; www.fratellipizza.net; 119 W Phoenix; mains $10-20; ☺10:30am-9pm Sun-Thu, to midnight Fri & Sat) Consistently voted Flagstaff's best pizza joint, Fratelli still pulls them in with its handmade, stone oven–baked pizza. Sauce choices include red, BBQ, pesto and white (olive oil with garlic, basil and oregano), and toppings range from standard pepperoni to grilled chicken, walnuts, artichoke hearts and cucumber. It's located just south of the Amtrak station, and offers free parking. But if you'd rather just pop in and out, it also does simple slices for about $2.50.

MartAnne's Burrito Palace
MEXICAN $

(Map p102; ☎928-773-4701; 10 N San Francisco St; mains $7-10; ⊗7:30am-2pm Mon-Fri, 8:30am-1pm Sun) This local-favorite hole-in-the-wall specializes in chilaquiles (scrambled eggs, red enchilada sauce, cheese and onions on a tortilla). Just about everyone in town recommends it for quick, tasty, low-key Mexican. Finish an entire breakfast here and you probably won't need to eat for the rest of the day. Cash only.

La Bellavia
BREAKFAST $

(Map p102; ☎928-774-8301; 18 S Beaver St; mains $4-9; ⊗6:30am-2pm) Be prepared to wait in line at this popular, cash-only breakfast spot. The seven-grain French toast with bananas, apples or blueberries is excellent, or try one of its egg dishes like Eggs Sardo – with sautéed spinach and artichoke hearts. Swedish pancakes and French toast with strawberry butter are *substantial*. Lunch includes a grilled portobello-mushroom sandwich and a grilled salmon salad, as well as standard options like grilled cheese, burgers and a tuna melt. If you're lucky, one of the few tables outside will be free.

Brix
AMERICAN $$$

(Map p102; ☎928-213-1021; www.brixflagstaff .com; 413 N San Francisco St; mains $23-34; ⊗11am-2pm & 5-9pm Mon-Fri, 5-9pm Sat) Situated in a renovated brick carriage house, Brix brings a breath of fresh, unpretentious sophistication to Flagstaff's dining scene. The menu varies seasonally, using to delicious advantage what is fresh and ripe, sometimes organic, for classics like salade Niçoise and roasted rack of lamb. Artisanal cheeses and the well- balanced wine list feature selections whose provenance is as near as Chino Valley, Arizona and as far as South Australia. Though the dining room feels a bit too cramped, it does speak of this restaurant's popularity, and there's also a leafy patio out back if weather permits alfresco dining. Reservations are highly recommended.

Café Olé
MEXICAN $

(Map p102; ☎928-774-8272; 119 S San Francisco St; mains $6-12; ⊗11am-3pm & 5-8pm Tue-Sat; 🕿) For some of the best Mexican food in the region, stop by this brightly colored joint (complete with chili-pepper strings and interior murals). It's a friendly, family-run place – the Aguinaga family has been perfecting its recipes for more than a decade. The food veers towards New Mexican–style, featuring green and red chili sauce, and everything is fresh and healthy (there's no lard in the beans, and they keep frying to a minimum).

Mountain Oasis
INTERNATIONAL $$

(Map p102; ☎928-214-9270; 11 E Aspen; mains $9-19; ⊗11am-9pm; 🍴) Vegetarians and vegans will find a bunch of options on this internationally spiced menu. Tasty specialties include the TBLT (tempeh bacon, lettuce and tomato), Thai veggies and tofu with peanut sauce and brown rice, and stuffed grape leaves. Steak and chicken are also featured on the menu, so meat eaters need not shy away from this relaxed, plant-filled oasis. The fresh-fruit lemonades are just the thing to revive your spirit on a hot afternoon.

Late for the Train
CAFE $

(Map p102; ☎928-773-0100; www.lateforthetrain .com; 107 N San Francisco St; mains $2-6; ⊗6am-6pm Sun-Thu, 6am-9pm Fri & Sat; 🕿) High-ceilinged and full of light, the downtown shop is spare on decor but manages a warm atmosphere. Beans are roasted in-house, so the coffee and espresso drinks are some of the best in town; but on those really frigid winter days, try the habanero hot cocoa. Late for the Train has a larger location in a converted gas station along Hwy 180.

New Frontiers
Natural Marketplace
GROCERY $

(☎928-774-5747; 320 S Cambridge Lane; mains $4-10; ⊗8am-9pm Mon-Sat, 8am-8pm Sun; 🍴) Cobble together healthy picnics and stock up on groceries at our favorite area health-food market. Some of the organic produce is grown on its own farm in California; it's on offer alongside an extensive array of natural and organic foods. Plus, there's a bakery, soup and salad bar, deli and premade items.

Cold Stone Creamery
ICE CREAM $

(Map p100; ☎928-779-2856; 2080 S Milton Rd; ice cream $4-15; ⊗11am-10pm Sun-Thu, 11am-11pm Fri & Sat; 🖐) If you're not familiar with Cold Stone, this ice-cream shop offers all kinds of treats, from gummy bears and brownies to fruit, which are folded into your ice cream on a chilled granite countertop. Don't be surprised if the staff burst into song.

Bashas' SUPERMARKET $

(Map p100; ☎928-774-3882; www.bashas.com; 2700 S Woodlands Village Blvd; ☺5am-11pm) For groceries, Bashas' is a good local chain supermarket that carries a respectable selection of organic foods.

Drinking

Flagstaff Brewing Company BREWPUB

(Map p102; ☎928-773-1442; www.flagbrew.com; 16 E Route 66; ☺11am-midnight) Flag Brew serves up its own handcrafted beer ('beer like your mom used to make') as well as guest brews, hearty pub food and a variety of live music. Popular with students and outdoors types, it also features a convivial patio, a ping-pong table and a totally unpretentious vibe.

Pay 'n' Take BAR

(Map p102; ☎928-226-8595; www.payntake.com; 12 W Aspen Ave; ☺7am-10pm Mon-Wed, 7am-1am Thu-Sat, 9am-10pm Sun; 🛜) The name is self-explanatory, but it's more like stay 'n' hang. This kick-back spot has a great bar where you can enjoy a beer or a coffee. Help yourself to whatever you'd like from the wall refrigerators, and take it to one of the small tables inside or out on the back patio. You can even have pizza delivered or bring your own takeout if you like. Folks here are always happy to shoot the breeze, *and* there's free wi-fi.

Cuvee 928 WINE BAR

(Map p102; ☎928-214-9463; www.cuvee928 winebar.com; 6 W Aspen Ave, Suite 110; ☺11:30am-9pm Mon & Tue, to 10pm Wed-Sat) With a central location on Heritage Sq and patio seating, this wine bar makes a pleasant venue for people-watching as well as wine tasting. It has a relaxed but upscale ambience, well-rounded menu and full bar if brewpubs aren't your cup of tea.

Entertainment

Flagstaff hosts all sorts of festivals and music programs; call the visitor center or log on to its website for details. On summer weekends, people gather on blankets for fun evenings at **Heritage Sq**. Live music (folk, Celtic, children's etc) starts at 6:30pm, followed at 9pm by a kid-friendly movie projected on an adjacent building. Various activities keep (sometimes PJ-clad) kids entertained until the film starts.

Pick up a free copy of local rag *Flagstaff Live!* or check out www.flaglive.com for current shows and happenings around town.

If you're just after a game of pool and a beer, head to the smoke-free **Uptown Billiards** (Map p102; ☎928-773-0551; www.uptown-billiards.net; 114 N Leroux St; ☺1pm-1am Mon-Sat, 3-11pm Sun). Or catch live music and mingle on the patio with a fun mix of locals at **Mia's Lounge** (Map p102; ☎928-774-3315; 26 S San Francisco St; ☺noon-2am Mon-Sat, 2pm-2am Sun).

Flagstaff Symphony Orchestra CLASSICAL MUSIC

(Map p102; ☎928-774-5107; www.flagstaff symphony.org; 113 E Aspen Ave, Suite A; ☺10am-3pm) Holds eight annual performances in the Ardrey Memorial Auditorium, on the NAU campus.

Charly's Pub & Grill LIVE MUSIC

(Map p102; ☎928-779-1919; www.weatherford hotel.com; 23 N Leroux St; ☺8am-10pm) This restaurant at the Weatherford Hotel has regular live music. Its fireplace and brick walls provide a cozy setting for the blues, jazz and folk played here. Head upstairs to stroll the wraparound verandah outside the popular 3rd-floor Zane Grey Ballroom, which overlooks the historic district. Inside, check out the 1882 bar, a fireplace and an original Thomas Moran painting.

Monte Vista Cocktail Lounge MUSIC

(Map p102; ☎928-779-6971; www.hotelmontevista .com; Hotel Monte Vista, 100 N San Francisco St; ☺from 4pm) In the Hotel Monte Vista, this hopping lounge hosts DJs most nights, and on weekends welcomes diverse bands, from country to hip-hop to rock.

Museum Club BAR

(☎928-526-9434; www.themuseumclub.com; 3404 E Route 66; ☺11am-2am Mon-Sat, to 9pm Sun) Housed in a 1931 taxidermy museum (hence its nickname, 'The Zoo'), this log cabin–style club has been a roadhouse since 1936. Today, its Route 66 vibe, country music and spacious wooden dance floor attract a lively crowd.

Shopping

The Artists' Gallery ARTS & CRAFTS

(Map p102; ☎928-773-0958; www.flagstaffartists gallery.com; 17 N San Francisco St; ☺9:30am-7:30pm Mon-Sat, 9:30am-5:30pm Sun) This art co-op, locally owned and operated since 1992, carries the work of over 40 northern Arizona artists, including two-dimensional art, jewelry, ceramics and glasswork.

SOUTH RIM FLAGSTAFF

Old Town Shops
MALL

(Map p102; ☑928-774-3100; www.oldtownshops.net; 120 N Leroux St) A cluster of several independent stores, including a hip novelty shop, a wine merchant and a few stylish indie boutiques, occupies this two-floor space. Local musicians often liven up the open hall space.

Painted Desert Trading Co
HANDICRAFTS

(Map p102; ☑928-226-8313; www.painteddeserttrading.com; 2 N San Francisco St; ☺10am-6pm Mon-Sat, noon-5pm Sun) Carries quality Native American crafts and an excellent selection of books on regional topics.

Zani
GIFTS

(Map p102; ☑928-774-9409, 800-294-9409; www.zanicardsandgifts.com; 107 W Phoenix Ave; ☺10:30am-6pm Mon-Sat) Zani carries beautiful handmade paper, locally made jewelry of silver or fused glass, stamped leather goods and Asian-inspired gifts and homewares.

NAU Bookstore
BOOKS

(Map p100; ☑800-426-7674; www.bookstore@nau.edu; cnr S San Francisco St & Mountain View Dr; ☺8am-5pm Mon-Fri) The university bookstore offers one of the best selections of books about Native Americans and the region, as well as field guides and children's books. From downtown Flagstaff, take San Francisco St south past Butler Ave onto the NAU campus. Park in one of the lots at the intersection of S San Francisco and Mountain View and follow the signs to the bookstore.

Outdoor Equipment

Since it's probably the biggest, baddest metropolis you hit before your Grand Canyon backpacking adventure, Flagstaff is a good place to get last-minute advice and gear up with the best deals on outdoor equipment. You'll find these locally owned shops downtown.

Babbitt's Backcountry Outfitter

(Map p102; ☑928-774-4775; www.babbittsbackcountry.com; 12 E Aspen Ave; ☺9am-8pm Mon-Sat, 10am-6pm Sun) Rents only backpacks and tents, but sells quality outdoor gear, books and USGS maps.

Peace Surplus

(Map p102; ☑928-779-4521; www.peacesurplus.com; 14 W Route 66; ☺8am-9pm Mon-Fri, to 8pm Sat, to 6pm Sun) Sells and rents a huge array of outdoor clothing and equipment, including snowboards and downhill and cross-country skis.

Aspen Sports

(Map p102; ☑928-779-1935; www.flagstaffsportinggoods.com; 15 N San Francisco St; ☺8am-7pm Mon-Sat, 9am-5pm Sun) For gear that's more climbing- and backpacking-oriented; no rentals.

Information

Coconino National Forest Supervisor's Office (☑928-527-3600; www.fs.fed.us/r3/coconino; 1824 S Thompson St; ☺8am-4:30pm Mon-Fri) For information on hiking, biking and camping in the surrounding national forest.

Flagstaff Medical Center (☑928-779-3366; www.flagstaffmedicalcenter.com; 1200 N Beaver St; ☺emergency 24hr)

Flagstaff Public Library (☑928-774-7670; www.flagstaffpubliclibrary.org; 300 W Aspen Ave; ☺10am-9pm Mon-Thu, to 7pm Fri, to 6pm Sat; @☎) Library internet access and wi-fi available.

Police station (☑928-779-3646; 911 E Sawmill Rd; ☺emergency 24hr)

Post office (Map p102; ☑928-714-9302; 104 N Agassiz St; ☺9am-5pm Mon-Fri, to 1pm Sat)

USFS Flagstaff Ranger Station (☑928-526-0866; 5075 N Hwy 89; ☺8am-4:30pm Mon-Fri) Provides information on the Mt Elden, Humphreys Peak and O'Leary Peak areas north of Flagstaff.

Visitor center (Map p102; ☑928-774-9541, 800-379-0065; www.flagstaffarizona.org; 1 E Route 66; ☺8am-5pm Mon-Sat, 9am-4pm Sun) Inside the Amtrak station, the visitor center has a great Flagstaff Discovery map and tons of information on things to do.

Getting There & Away

Flagstaff Pulliam Airport is 4 miles south of town off I-17. **US Airways** (☑800-428-4322; www.usairways.com) offers several daily flights from Phoenix Sky Harbor International Airport. **Greyhound** (☑928-774-4573, 800-231-2222; www.greyhound.com; 399 S Malpais Lane) stops in Flagstaff en route to/from Albuquerque, Las Vegas, Los Angeles and Phoenix. **Arizona Shuttle** (☑928-226-8060, 877-226-8060; www.arizonashuttle.com) has shuttles that run to the Grand Canyon National Park, Williams and Phoenix Sky Harbor Airport.

Operated by **Amtrak** (☑928-774-8679, 800-872-7245; www.amtrak.com; 1 E Route 66; ☺3am-10:45pm), the *Southwest Chief* stops at Flagstaff on its daily run between Chicago and LA.

Getting Around

Mountain Line Transit (☑928-779-6624; www.mountainline.az.gov; adult/child $1.25/0.60) services six fixed bus routes daily; pick up a user-friendly map at the visitor center. Those with disabilities can use the company's on-call VanGo service.

If you need a taxi, call **A Friendly Cab** (☎928-774-4444) or **Sun Taxi** (☎928-779-1111). Several major car-rental agencies operate from the airport and downtown; see p226.

Around Flagstaff

Covered by a single $5 entrance fee (valid for seven days), both Sunset Crater Volcano and Wupatki National Monuments lie along Park Loop Rd 545, a well-marked 36-mile loop that heads east off Hwy 89 about 12 miles north of Flagstaff then rejoins the highway 26 miles north of Flagstaff. Visitors can choose from among several picnic grounds. Rangers offer interpretive programs in summer.

SUNSET CRATER VOLCANO NATIONAL MONUMENT

In AD 1064 a volcano erupted on this spot, spewing ash across 800 sq miles, spawning the Kana-A lava flow and leaving behind 8029ft **Sunset Crater**. The eruption forced farmers to vacate lands they had cultivated for 400 years. Subsequent eruptions continued for more than 200 years. The **visitor center** (☎928-526-0502; www.nps.gov/sucr; admission $5; ☉visitor center 8am-5pm May-Oct, 9am-5pm Nov-Apr, monument sunrise-sunset) houses a seismograph and other exhibits pertaining to volcanology, while viewpoints and a 1-mile interpretive trail through the **Bonito lava flow** (formed c 1180) grant visitors a firsthand look at volcanic features; a shorter 0.3-mile loop is wheelchair accessible. You can also climb **Lenox Crater** (7024ft), a 1-mile round-trip that climbs 300ft. More ambitious hikers and mountain bikers can ascend **O'Leary Peak** (8965ft; 8 miles round-trip), the only way to peer down into Sunset Crater (aside from scenic flights).

Across from the visitor center, the USFS-run **Bonito Campground** (☎928-526-0866; tent & RV sites $18; ☉May–mid-Oct) provides running water and restrooms but no showers or hookups.

WUPATKI NATIONAL MONUMENT

The first eruptions here enriched the surrounding soil, and ancestors of today's Hopi, Zuni and Navajo people returned to farm the land in the early 1100s. By 1180 thousands were living here in advanced multistory buildings, but by 1250 their pueblos stood abandoned. About 2700 of these structures lie within **Wupatki National Monument** (☎928-679-2365; www.nps.gov/wupa; admission $5; ☉9am-5pm), though only a few are open to the public. A short self-guided tour of the largest dwelling, **Wupatki Pueblo**, begins behind the visitor center. **Lamaki**, **Citadel** and **Nalakihu Pueblos** sit within a half-mile of the loop road just north of the visitor center, and a 2.5-mile road veers west from the center to **Wukoki Pueblo**, the best preserved of the buildings. In April and October rangers lead visitors on a 16-mile round-trip weekend backpacking tour ($50; supply your own food and gear) of **Crack-in-Rock Pueblo** and nearby petroglyphs. Chosen by lottery, only 13 people may join each tour; apply two months in advance via the website or in writing.

WALNUT CANYON NATIONAL MONUMENT

The Sinagua cliff dwellings at **Walnut Canyon** (☎928-526-3367; www.nps.gov/waca; admission $5, valid for 7 days; ☉8am-5pm May-Oct, 9am-5pm Nov-Apr) are set in the nearly vertical walls of a small limestone butte amid this forested canyon. The mile-long **Island Trail** steeply descends 185ft (more than 200 stairs), passing 25 rooms built under the natural overhangs of the curvaceous butte. A shorter, wheelchair-accessible **Rim Trail** affords several views of the cliff dwelling from across the canyon. Even if you're not all that interested in the mysterious Sinagua people, whose origins are unknown and whose site abandonment are still not understood today, Walnut Canyon itself is a beautiful place to visit, only about 11 miles from Flagstaff.

METEOR CRATER

A huge meteor crashed into our planet almost 50,000 years ago and produced this **crater** (☎928-289-5898, 800-289-5898; www.meteorcrater.com; adult/child $15/8; ☉7am-7pm Jun–mid-Sep, 8am-5pm mid-Sep–May) about 43 miles east of Flagstaff. It is 570ft deep and almost a mile across. It was used as a training ground for some of the *Apollo* astronauts; the on-site museum has exhibits about meteors and space missions. Descending into the crater is not allowed, but you can walk the 3.5-mile Rim Trail. However, apart from a big hole in the ground, there's not much to see, and some readers suggest it's an overpriced attraction. The crater is privately owned and operated, and national-park passes are not accepted.

Meteor Crater RV Park (☏928-289-4002, 800-478-4002; RV sites $32) has 71 RV sites with hookups. There are showers, a coin laundry, a playground, a small grocery store and a Subway sandwich shop.

Sedona

☏928 / POP 10,031 / ELEV 4500FT

Sedona's a stunner, but it's intensely spiritual as well – and some say sacred. If you're driving to or from Flagstaff, it's a challenge to keep your eyes on the road. Winding your way through the ponderosas that give way to oaks growing in the riparian lushness of Oak Creek Canyon, you'll dip through shady curves in the canyon and rise alongside beautiful red-rock walls. The closer you get to Sedona, the more magical the landscape becomes.

Nestled amid alien-looking red sandstone formations at the south end of the 16-mile gorge that is Oak Creek Canyon, Sedona attracts spiritual seekers, artists and healers, and day trippers from Phoenix trying to escape the oppressive heat. Many New Age types believe that this area is the center of vortexes (not 'vortices' in Sedona) that radiate the Earth's power, and Sedona's combination of scenic beauty and mysticism draws throngs of tourists year-round. You'll find all sorts of alternative medicines and practices, from psychic channeling, past-life regression, crystal healing, shamanism and drumming workshops to more traditional massages, yoga, tai chi and acupressure. The surrounding canyons offer excellent hiking and mountain biking, and the town itself bustles with art galleries and expensive gourmet restaurants. Unlike nearby Flagstaff, Sedona's economy is almost entirely driven by tourism, and in summer the traffic and the crowds in town and on the trails can make you feel the antithesis of peace. Remember to breathe, channel those good vibrations and see if you can't feel some of Sedona's essential magic.

Sedona's navigational center is the roundabout at the intersection of Hwys Alt 89 and 179, known as the 'Y.' Northeast of the Y is Uptown Sedona, the pedestrian center where you'll find most of Sedona's hotels, boutiques and restaurants. Turning south at the Y will take you to Tlaquepaque Village. West of the Y is West Sedona, where strip malls line the highway and eventually lead to Red Rock State Park.

A **Red Rock Pass** (per day/week/year $5/15/20) is required to park anywhere in the surrounding national forest and several cultural sites. You can buy one at the visitor centers, various local businesses and hotels and at some trailheads.

Sights

Chapel of the Holy Cross   CHURCH
(☏928-282-4069; www.chapeloftheholycross.com; 780 Chapel Rd; ⊙9am-5pm Mon-Sat, 10am-5pm Sun) Situated between spectacular, statuesque red-rock columns 3 miles south of town, this modern, nondenominational chapel was built in 1956 by Marguerite Brunwig Staude in the tradition of Frank Lloyd Wright. There are no services, but even if you're not affiliated with any religion, the soaring chapel and the perch it occupies may move you as it did its architect. There are no restrooms on the site.

Slide Rock State Park   PARK
(☏928-282-3034; www.azstateparks.com/Parks/SLRO; 6871 N Hwy Alt 89; per car Memorial Day-Labor Day $20, Sep-May $10; ⊙8am-7pm Memorial Day-Labor Day, 8am-5pm Sep-May) Popular for picnicking and swimming, this state park features a natural rock chute that whisks swimmers through Oak Creek. Bring a blanket and a cooler, or buy drinks and snacks at the small park store. To avoid the long lines and entrance fee, you can park your car on the shoulder just north of the entrance and hike down to the rock slide – just follow the crowds. Drive carefully, as lots of pedestrians will be picking their way along and across the highway, about 7 miles north of town.

Red Rock State Park   PARK
(☏928-282-6907; www.azstateparks.com/Parks/RERO; 4050 Red Rock Loop Rd; per car/bicycle or pedestrian $10/3; ⊙8am-5pm) This park includes an environmental education center, a visitor center (open 9am to 5pm), picnic areas and 5 miles of well-marked trails in a riparian habitat amid gorgeous scenery. Ranger-led activities include nature walks, bird walks and full-moon hikes during the warmer months. While popular, it doesn't pack quite as exciting a punch as Slide Rock, meaning it's not so packed, and pleasant because of it.

Sedona Arts Center   ARTS CENTER
(☏928-282-3809, 888-954-4442; www.sedonaartscenter.com; 15 Art Barn Rd; ⊙10am-5pm)

At the time of research, controversy had been brewing among Sedona locals regarding Red Rock Pass fees, and whether it was fair to impose such fees on residents. In response, the USFS held several public meetings to solicit public comment on how they might change or better implement the Red Rock Pass system. Because Red Rock Country is federal land, the government cannot waive the fee for some people (locals, for example) and not others (visitors to the area). And since the area receives about the same number of visitors as does Grand Canyon National Park – that is, over 4 million annually – fees are crucial for maintaining and preserving the 500,000 acres of heavily used land, trails, visitor centers and facilities.

Pending any decisions, Red Rock Passes (per day/week/year $5/15/20) are still required when visiting national forest land in Red Rock Country. Note that if you have a valid Federal Interagency Annual Pass (if you purchased an annual National Parks pass at the Grand Canyon, that's the one), you need not purchase a Red Rock Pass and should display your pass in your windshield when parking in national-forest lands.

The arts center features changing exhibits of local and regional artists, a gift shop, classes in performing and visual arts, and a variety of cultural events like the Sedona Plein Air Festival (p24).

Sedona Heritage Museum   MUSEUM
(📞928-282-7038; www.sedonamuseum.org; 735 N Jordan Rd; adult/child $5/free; ⏰11am-3pm) At this small heritage museum you'll find out who the founding families of Sedona were, and get to know them through quotidian artifacts. Set on the historic farmstead of the Jordan family, the museum displays photos, domestic tools and historical information inside the main house. Outside, the property is home to native flora. Be sure to poke around in the tractor shed out back, where the vintage fire engine and apple-sorting machine reside.

Activities

Hiking and **mountain-biking** trails crisscross the surrounding red-rock country and the woods and meadows of green Oak Creek Canyon. Available at the visitors centers and ranger stations, the free *Red Rock Country* recreation guide describes hiking and biking trails for all skill levels and includes a map of scenic drives. One popular hiking trail in Oak Creek Canyon is the **West Fork Trail**, which follows the creek for 7 miles – the canyon walls rise more than 200ft in places. Wander up as far as you want, splash around and turn back when you've had enough. The trailhead lies about 3 miles north of Slide Rock, in Call of the Canyon Recreation Area.

Oak Creek holds several good **swimming** holes. If Slide Rock is too crowded, check out **Grasshopper Point** ($8 per car), a few miles south. Southwest of town you can splash around and enjoy splendid views of Cathedral Rock at **Red Rock Crossing**, a USFS picnic area along a pretty stretch of Oak Creek; look for the turnoff about 2 miles west of the hospital on Hwy Alt 89.

Another stunningly beautiful place to hike is through the red rock of **Boynton Canyon**, an area that exudes spiritual energy and where some have reported experiencing the antics of energetic spirits. Look for the rock formation known as **Kachina Woman** and try not to be moved. Boynton Canyon is about 5 miles north of Hwy Alt 89 up Dry Creek Rd; get an early start to avoid crowds.

Hike House   HIKING GOODS
(📞928-282-5820; www.thehikehouse.com; 431 Hwy 179, Suite B-1; ⏰9am-6pm) For more itinerary ideas, stop by the Hike House, an innovative concept shop integrating its proprietary, interactive hike-finding system with a high-end hiking shop and snack bar. If you're experienced enough to skip its free guided introductory hike, and don't need new boots or cool hiking equipment, the front patio is still a great place to put up your feet and sip a smoothie after a long hike.

Fat Tire Bike Shop   BIKE RENTAL
(📞928-852-0014; www.thefattire.com; 325 Jordan Rd; per day $75; ⏰9am-5pm Mon-Sat) Rent bikes at the Fat Tire Bike Shop. It also does group rides several days a week; call the shop for more info.

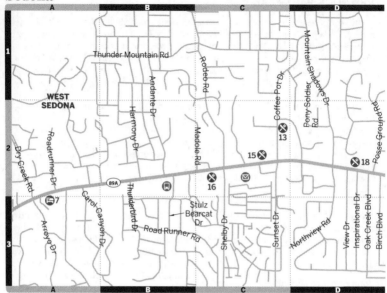

Sleeping

As you might expect from such a scenic town, Sedona is rich with beautiful B&Bs, creekside cabins and full-service resorts, for which you should also expect to pay accordingly. Rates at chain motels range from $75 to $130, reasonable by Sedona standards. Contact the **Sedona Bed & Breakfast Guild** (www.bbsedona.net) for lodging information and suggestions.

Apart from camping, Sedona doesn't have many options for the budget traveler.

Lodging

TOP CHOICE **Briar Patch Inn**   CABINS $$$
(☑928-282-2342, 888-809-3030; www.briar patchinn.com; 3190 N Hwy Alt 89; cottages $219-395; 🛜🐾) Nestled in nine wooded acres along Oak Creek, this lovely inn offers 19 log cottages with Southwestern decor and Native American art. All cottages include patios, many have fireplaces, and several lie beside the burbling creek. In summer, a hearty buffet breakfast – including homemade granola, fresh fruit, home-baked breads and pastries, and a quiche of the day – is served on a stone patio that overlooks the creek and is accompanied by live chamber music (Wednesday to Sunday). There's a two-night minimum on weekends and it's best to book at least a few months ahead.

El Portal   B&B $$$
(☑928-203-9405, 800-313-0017; www.elportal sedona.com; 95 Portal Lane; r $259-459; @🛜🐾) This discreet little inn is a beautiful blend of Southwestern and Craftsman style, a pocket of relaxed luxury tucked away in a corner near Tlaquepaque. The look is rustic but sophisticated, incorporating reclaimed wood, river rock and thick adobe walls. Each room is meticulously designed and decorated with authentic Stickley and Wright furnishings, exposed beams and antique doorknobs and fixtures. Rooms at the back have incredible red-rock views, and the inn surrounds a peaceful courtyard perfect for sipping a glass of wine. It's one of the few Sedona inns that welcomes dogs, and guests have free pool and spa privileges at the large Los Abrigados resort next door.

Garland's Oak Creek Lodge   LODGE $$$
(☑928-282-3343; www.garlandslodge.com; Hwy Alt 89; cabins $180-295; ☉closed Sun & mid-Nov – Apr 1; 🛜) Set back from Oak Creek on eight secluded acres with broad lawns, an apple orchard and woods, this lodge offers nicely appointed Western log cabins, many with

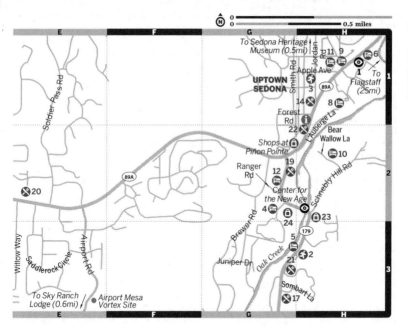

Sedona

fireplaces. Rates include a full hot breakfast, 4pm tea and a superb gourmet dinner. There's a yoga gazebo overlooking the creek, and you can arrange for massages or spa treatments in its tiny spa cabin, or just enjoy

cocktails at 6pm and the absence of ringing phones or TVs. Catering to guests who crave peace and quiet amid verdant surroundings, Garland's is 8 miles north of Sedona and is often booked up a year in advance. If you can't stay overnight, booking dinner is a delicious alternative; a few spots are sometimes available for nonguests.

L'Auberge de Sedona
RESORT $$$

(☎928-282-1661, 800-905-5745; www.lauberge.com; 301 L'Auberge Lane; r $205-295, ste $410-560, cottages $290-620; ✲🕿🐾) If you're lucky enough to wake at L'Auberge, you'd never know it was in the center of uptown Sedona. It's situated creekside, with well-appointed cabins amid green lawns, and the red-rock backdrop looms within reaching distance. Luxuries include whirlpool baths, wine and cheese every evening, free yoga classes and a gift bag for your dog, who is welcome here ($35 to $50 fee applies). Pool and spa are being constructed at the time of research. Service is impeccable, the setting elegant.

Lantern Light Inn
B&B $$

(☎928-282-3419, 877-275-4973; www.lanternlightinn.com; 3085 W Hwy Alt 89; r $139-195, ste $195-309; @🕿) The lovely couple running this small inn in West Sedona put you right at ease in their comfortable antique-filled rooms. Rooms range from small and cozy, overlooking the back deck and garden, to the huge guesthouse in back (breakfast not included), but all feel comfortably overstuffed. There's a common room, more of a family library with musical instruments, that can be used for meetings. Credit cards not accepted.

Junipine Resort
LODGE $$$

(☎928-282-3375, 800-742-7463; www.junipine.com; 8351 N Hwy Alt 89; creekhouses $135-400; @🕿🛗) In the Oak Creek Canyon woodland, 8 miles north of Sedona, this resort offers spacious, lovely one- and two-bedroom 'creekhouses,' all with kitchens, living/dining rooms, wood-burning stoves and decks – and some with lofts. Some units have creekside views, others have hot tubs, and a few offer both. Two-bedroom units sleep up to four, a great option for families ($25 for each additional person, children under 12 free). The on-site restaurant serves great food as well as microbrews and wine, so you needn't trek all the way into town if you're too relaxed to leave.

Inn on Oak Creek
B&B $$$

(☎928-282-7896, 800-499-7896; www.innonoakcreek.com; 556 Hwy 179; r $200-295; ✲@🕿) Just around the corner from Tlaquepaque, this bright and welcoming country-style B&B boasts an enviable location directly above Oak Creek. Each immaculate, eminently cozy room is decorated according to some individual theme, ranging from old Hollywood to roosters, and all have whirlpool baths and gas fireplaces. Breakfast is a decadent treat here, consisting of several courses that feature freshly squeezed juices, house-baked breads and gourmet mains, served in the sunny dining room or on the deck above the creek.

Rose Tree Inn
MOTEL $$

(☎928-282-2065, 888-282-2065; www.rosetreeinn.com; 376 Cedar St; r $95-145; ✲@🕿) The five homey rooms nestled around this inn's peaceful courtyard garden immediately make you feel as though you're settling in at a friend's place. Some rooms have fireplaces, and all have kitchenettes. It's much cozier and more personable than a hotel and feels a world away from busy Hwy Alt 89 just a block south.

Sky Ranch Lodge
MOTEL $$

(☎928-282-6400, 888-708-6400; www.skyranchlodge.com; Airport Rd; r $80-164, cottages $194; ✲🕿🛗🐾) At the top of Airport Rd, with spectacular views of the town and surrounding country, this lodge offers spacious motel rooms, six landscaped acres, and a pool and hot tub. Rates vary according to type of bed and your view. Some include balconies, fireplaces, kitchenettes and/or refrigerators; also available are cottages with vaulted ceilings, exposed beams, kitchenettes and private decks. Away from the main drag and its tourist hordes, this family-run lodge is an excellent deal.

La Vista Motel
MOTEL $

(☎928-282-7301; www.lavistamotel.com; 500 N Hwy Alt 89; r $66-90, ste $90-100; ✲🕿) Right on the side of the highway leading into Oak Creek Canyon, this friendly family-run motel has clean rooms and suites. Some suites are decked out with full kitchens, porches, tile floors, sofas, refrigerators and bathtubs. Rooms on the lower level, off the highway, tend to be quieter but more expensive.

Sedona Motel
MOTEL $

(☎928-282-7187, 877-828-7187; www.thesedonamotel.com; 218 Hwy 179; r $79-89; ✲) Directly south of the Y, this friendly little motel offers big value within walking distance of Tlaquepaque and Uptown Sedona. Rooms are basic but clean, but the fantastic red-rock views may be all the luxury you need.

Matterhorn Inn MOTEL $$
(928-282-7176, 800-372-8207; www.matter
horninn.com; 230 Apple Ave; r $150;) All
rooms at this friendly, central motel in-
clude refrigerators and have balconies or
patios overlooking Uptown Sedona and Oak
Creek. Its terraced location is right in the
middle of town, above the highway, and is
within walking distance of the shops and
restaurants.

Slide Rock Lodge MOTEL $$
(928-282-3531; www.sliderocklodge.com; 6401 N
Hwy Alt 89; r $99-149, ste $179;) If you want to
stay in Oak Creek Canyon, this is an affordable way to do it. This log-cabin longhouse
has rooms along the canyon wall that tend
toward the simple and rustic. Some rooms
have fireplaces, all are clean and there's a
large grassy area outside to relax and grill.
The atmosphere is friendly, quiet and con-
ducive to a laid-back stay.

Camping
Rancho Sedona RV Park (928-282-7255,
888-641-4261; www.ranchosedona.com; 135 Bear
Wallow Lane; RV sites $31-63) includes a laun-
dry, showers and 30 RV sites, most with full
hookups.

Dispersed camping is not permitted in
Red Rock Canyon. The **USFS** (928-282-
4119, 877-444-6777; www.recreation.gov) runs the
following campgrounds along Hwy Alt 89 in
Oak Creek Canyon (none with hookups). All
are nestled in the woods just off the road. It
costs $20 to camp, but you don't need a Red
Rock Pass. Reservations are accepted for all
campgrounds but Pine Flat East.

Manzanita 18 sites; open year-round; 6
miles north of town.

Cave Springs 82 sites; showers; 11.5 miles
north.

Pine Flat East and Pine Flat West 57
sites; 12.5 miles north.

Eating

Pick up groceries and healthy picnic components at **New Frontiers Natural Marketplace** (928-282-6311; 1420 W Hwy Alt 89; mains
$4-10; 8am-9pm Mon-Sat, to 8pm Sun;) or
stop by for smoothies, vegetarian salads or
panini from the deli. Another good Arizona
grocery chain is **Bashas'** (928-282-5351; 160
Coffee Pot Dr; 6am-11pm).

TOP CHOICE **Elote Café** MEXICAN $$
(928-203-0105; www.elotecafe.com; King's Ran-
som Hotel, 771 Hwy 179; mains $17-22; 5pm-late,
Tue-Sat) Some of the best, most authentic
Mexican food you'll find in the region, with
unusual traditional dishes you won't find
elsewhere, like the fire-roasted corn with
lime and cotija cheese, or tender, smoky
pork cheeks. Reservations are not accepted,
so if you want to eat at a reasonable hour,
line up by 4:30pm or resign yourself to wait-
ing with a white sangria.

**L'Auberge Restaurant on
Oak Creek** AMERICAN $$$
(928-282-1661; www.lauberge.com; 301 L'Auberge
Lane; mains $34-52; 7am-9pm Mon-Sat, 9am-
2pm & 5:30-9pm Sun) Featuring refined American cuisine with a French accent, the menu
at L'Auberge changes seasonally (you might
find ramps and morels in the spring, and
roast duck and beets in the fall). This creekside spot is a local favorite for celebrating
special occasions in elegant environs, with
a select wine list to complement your meal.

Dahl & DiLuca Ristorante ITALIAN $$$
(928-282-5219; www.dahlanddiluca.com; 2321
Hwy Alt 89; mains $13-33; 5-10pm) Though
this lovely Italian place fits perfectly into

VORTEXES 101

While Sedona's surreal beauty makes itself plain to see, its more subtle attraction won't
be obvious to the naked eye...apart from the many ads for vortex tours. Several vortexes
(swirling energy centers where the Earth's power is said to be strongly felt) are located
around Sedona, which is one of the reasons it has become a mecca for spiritual seekers
and New-Age types.

The four best-known vortexes are in Sedona's Red Rock Mountains. These include
Bell Rock, near the village of Oak Creek, **Cathedral Rock**, near Red Rock Crossing,
Airport Mesa, along Airport Rd, and **Boynton Canyon**. Local maps show these four
main sites, although some individuals claim that others exist. Stop by the Sedona Cham-
ber of Commerce Visitor Center to find out about the myriad of local vortex tours – in-
volving everything from chakra cleansings to yoga to meditation.

the groove and color scheme of Sedona, at the same time it feels like the kind of place you'd find in a small Italian seaside town. It's a bustling, welcoming spot serving excellent, authentic Italian food.

Heartline Café   AMERICAN $$$

(☎928-282-0785; www.heartlinecafe.com; 1600-1610 W Hwy Alt 89; mains $18-28; ⊗8am-4pm & 5-9:30pm) This restaurant's name refers to a Zuni Indian symbol for good health and long life, and indeed the imaginative menu offers fresh and clean gourmet victuals. A cozy ambience and creative, seasonal menu make it a long-running favorite. Nowadays, the Heartline Gourmet Express next door serves breakfast and lunch; both venues have pleasant garden patios for dining alfresco.

Wildflower Bread Company   DELI $

(☎928-204-2223; www.wildflowerbread.com; 101 N Hwy Alt 89; ⊗6am-9pm Mon-Fri, 7am-9pm Sat, 7am-8pm Sun; 🛜🍴) In the same complex as the visitor center, Wildflower is a great place to recharge with a fresh sandwich (or salad, soup, frittata...) in the cool, spacious dining room or on either of the shaded patios. There's free wi-fi, a kids' menu and plenty of delicious house-baked breads, bagels, pastries and cakes to take with you.

The Hideaway   ITALIAN $

(☎928-282-4204; 251 Hwy 179; mains $7-15; ⊗11am-9pm) The best reason for coming to the Hideaway is to dine on the deck at sunset, when gorgeous red-rock views serve as the appetizer. As the name suggests, this hidden-away, casual spot is easy to get to and equally easy to miss. Retreat from Uptown madness and enjoy a glass of wine with down-home, American-style Italian food, while drinking in the spectacular colors of Sedona's fading daylight.

Shugrue's Hillside Grill   AMERICAN $$$

(☎928-282-5300; www.jamrestaurants.com; Hillside Plaza, 671 Hwy 179; mains $15-38; ⊗11:30am-3pm & 5-9pm, plus brunch 8am-3pm Sat & Sun) Promising panoramic views, an outdoor deck from which to enjoy them and consistently excellent food, this restaurant is a great choice for an upscale meal. If it's too chilly to sit outside, don't fret – the walls are mostly glass, so you can still enjoy the scenery. The menu offers everything from steak to ravioli, but it is best known for its wide variety of well-prepared seafood. A jazz ensemble plays on the weekends.

Coffee Pot Restaurant   BREAKFAST $

(☎928-282-6626; www.coffeepotsedona.com; 2050 W Hwy Alt 89; mains $4-11; ⊗6am-2pm; 🍴) This has been the go-to breakfast and lunch joint for decades. It's always busy, and service can be slow, but it's friendly, the meals are reasonably priced and the selection is huge – 101 types of omelets, for a start (jelly, peanut butter and banana omelet, anyone?).

Sedona Memories   DELI $

(☎928-282-0032; 321 Jordan Rd; mains $7; ⊗10am-2pm Mon-Fri) This tiny local spot assembles gigantic sandwiches on slabs of homemade bread (which it doesn't sell, so don't bother asking). There are several vegetarian options, and you can nosh on the quiet porch. Cash only.

Black Cow Café   ICE CREAM $

(☎928-203-9868; 229 N Hwy Alt 89; ice creams $4-5; ⊗10:30am-9pm) Many claim the Black Cow has the best ice cream in town, and it certainly hits the spot on a hot, dusty day. If you don't want dessert, it also does sandwiches and soup.

Drinking & Entertainment

Check the listings at *Sedona Red Rock News* (www.redrocknews.com) for current local entertainment. The **Sedona Performers Guild** (☎928-282-0549; www.sedonaperformer sguild.org, www.studiolivesedona.com) has information on local performers, and upcoming live shows appearing in town.

The **Sedona International Film Festival** (☎928-282-1177; www.sedonafilmfestival. com) usually takes place during the month of February, but screenings and events occur throughout the year.

Heart of Sedona   CAFE

(☎928-282-5777; 1370 W Hwy Alt 89; coffee $2-5; ⊗6am-11pm; 🛜) Offering a pleasant outdoor patio with good views, this coffee shop is the best spot for a jolt of caffeine and a pastry while you check your email on its free wi-fi network. Despite being on the main drag of West Sedona, it's an oasis of tranquility.

Oak Creek Brewery & Grill   BREWERY

(☎928-282-3300; www.oakcreekpub.com; 336 Hwy 179; beers $5.75; ⊗11:30am-9pm) At Tlaquepaque Village, this spacious brewery serves a full menu that includes upmarket pub-style dishes like crab cakes and 'fire-kissed pizzas.' All of the menu offerings are best washed down with a house brew, of course – we're partial to the Oak Creek Am-

In this town, you can't really go wrong at sundown if you have its red rocks in sight. But for a more sublime Sedona sunset, many suggest seeing it from the **airport** (with about 600 other people). If you seek solitude, hike up to **Eagle's Nest** at the top of the Eagle's Nest Loop in Red Rock State Park and you may have the 360-degree view all to yourself. If you've procured a Red Rock Pass, drive up **Dry Creek Road** or **Schnebly Hill Road**, find a deserted trailhead, and mosey off into the sunset.

ber. While several flagship brews are always on tap, seasonal specialties vary.

Shopping

Shopping is a big draw in Sedona, and visitors will find everything from expensive boutiques to T-shirt shops. Uptown along Hwy Alt 89 is the place to go souvenir hunting.

Tlaquepaque Village   MALL
(928-282-4838; www.tlaq.com; 10am-5pm shops) Just south of Alt 89 on Hwy 179, this is a series of Mexican-style interconnected plazas that is home to dozens of high-end art galleries, shops and restaurants. It's easy to lose a couple of hours meandering the lovely maze here.

Garland's Navajo Rugs   HANDICRAFTS
(928-282-4070; www.garlandsrugs.com; 411 Hwy 179; 10am-5pm) If you miss the entrance to Tlaquepaque (which is easy enough to do), you'll quickly come upon this place on the other side of the roundabout. It offers the area's best selection of rugs and also sells other Native American crafts. It's an interesting shop to visit even if you don't plan on buying anything – it displays naturally dyed yarns with their botanical sources of color, as well as bios of the weavers and descriptions of how many hours it takes to create a handwoven rug.

ℹ Information

Police station (928-282-3100; www.sedonaaz.gov; 100 Roadrunner Dr; emergency 24hr)

Post office (928-282-3511; 190 W Hwy Alt 89; 8:45am-5pm Mon-Fri, 9am-1pm Sat)

Sedona Chamber of Commerce Visitor Center (928-282-7722, 800-288-7336; www.visitsedona.com; 331 Forest Rd; 8:30am-5pm Mon-Sat, 9am-3pm Sun) Located in Uptown Sedona; pick up free maps and brochures, and get last-minute hotel bookings.

Sedona Public Library (928-282-7714; www.sedonalibrary.org; 3250 White Bear Rd;

10am-6pm Mon, Tue & Thu, to 8pm Wed, to 5pm Fri & Sat; @) A statue of the town's namesake (Sedona Arabelle Miller Schnebly, that is) greets visitors at the entrance.

USFS South Gateway Visitor Center (928-203-7500; www.redrockcountry.org; 8379 Hwy 179; 8am-5pm) Get a Red Rock Pass here, as well as hiking guides, maps and local national-forest information. It's just south of the Village at Oak Creek.

Verde Valley Medical Center (928-204-3000; www.verdevalleymedicalcenter.com; 3700 W Hwy Alt 89; 24hr)

ℹ Getting There & Away

While scenic flights depart from Sedona, the closest commercial airport is Phoenix (two hours) or Flagstaff (30 minutes).

Ace Express (928-649-2720, 800-336-2239; www.acexshuttle.com; one way/round-trip $60/99) Door-to-door shuttle service running between Sedona and Phoenix Sky Harbor.

Amtrak (800-872-7245; www.amtrak.com) Stops in Flagstaff, about 25 miles north of Sedona.

Greyhound (800-231-2222; www.greyhound.com) Stops in Flagstaff.

Sedona-Phoenix Shuttle (928-282-2066, 800-448-7988; www.sedona-phoenix-shuttle.com; one way/round-trip $50/90) Runs between Phoenix Sky Harbor and Sedona eight times daily; call to make reservations.

ℹ Getting Around

Barlow Jeep Rentals (928-282-8700, 800-928-5337; www.barlowjeeprentals.com; 3009 W Hwy Alt 89; 9am-6pm)

Bob's Taxi (928-282-1234) Local cab service.

Enterprise (928-282-2052; www.enterprise.com; 2090 W Hwy Alt 89; 8am-6pm Mon-Fri, 9am-noon Sat) Rental cars available here.

Cameron

A tiny, windswept community 32 miles east of the park's East Entrance and 54 miles north of Flagstaff, Cameron sits on the western edge of the Navajo Indian Reservation. There's not much to it; in fact, the town basically comprises just the **Cameron Trading Post & Motel** (☑928-679-2231, 800-338-7385; www.camerontradingpost.com; RV sites $15, r $99-109, ste $149-179; ☻❀☎). In the early 1900s Hopis and Navajos came to the trading post to barter wool, blankets and livestock for flour, sugar and other goods. Today visitors can browse a large selection of quality Native American crafts, including Navajo rugs, basketry, jewelry and pottery. Of course, you'll also find the ubiquitous T-shirts, roadrunner knickknacks and other canyon kitsch.

The spacious rooms, many with balconies, feature hand-carved furniture and a Southwestern motif. They are spread out in three two-story adobe-style buildings: the Navajo (doubles with two double beds), the Hopi (two-room suites and doubles with one or two queen beds) and the Apache (doubles with two queen beds). The nicest is the Hopi, set around a lovely, lush garden with fountains and benches – a peaceful spot to sit and relax. Ask for a room with a garden view or a view of the Little Colorado River Gorge, which winds around the back of the hotel. RV sites offer hookups, and you can take your meals at **Cameron Trading Post Dining Room** (☑928-679-2231, 800-338-7385; mains $9-23; ☻6am-10pm), a good place to try the Navajo taco (fried dough with whole beans, ground beef, chili and cheese). If you're driving to the North Rim and need a place to stay en route, or if rooms in the park are booked, this is a great option.

Cameron is also a good spot to break up a long drive: relax at the restaurant for lunch, poke around the **art gallery** (☻9am-5pm), and sip a cold drink in the shade of the garden before getting back into the car. Even if the gallery itself is closed, look for the dinosaur footprints left in the flagstone of the gallery's entrance.

Lake Mead & Hoover Dam

Lake Mead and Hoover Dam are the most-visited sites within the **Lake Mead National Recreation Area** (www.nps.gov/lame), which encompasses 110-mile-long Lake Mead, 67-mile-long Lake Mohave and many miles of desert around the lakes. The excellent **Alan Bible Visitors Center** (☑702-293-8990; ☻8:30am-4:30pm), on Hwy 93 halfway between Boulder City and Hoover Dam, has information on recreation and desert life. From there, North Shore Rd winds around the lake and makes a great scenic drive.

Straddling the Arizona-Nevada border, the graceful curve and art-deco style of the 726ft **Hoover Dam** (www.usbr.gov/lc/hoover dam) contrasts superbly with the stark landscape. Visitors can either take the 30-minute **power plant tour** (adult/child $11/6; ☻9:15am-5:15pm, to 4:15pm winter) or the more in-depth, one-hour **Hoover Dam tour** (no children under 8; tour $30).

Tickets for both tours are sold at the **visitor center** (exhibits adult/child $8/free; ☻9am-6pm). Tickets for the power plant tour only can be purchased online.

Would-be river rats should check out **Desert Adventures** (☑702-293-5026; www .kayaklasvegas.com; 1647 Nevada Hwy, Suite A, Boulder City; trips from $149) for lots of half-day, full-day and multiday kayaking adventures, and hiking and horseback trips.

For a relaxing lunch or dinner break, head to nearby downtown Boulder City, where **Milo's** (538 Nevada Way; dishes $4-18; ☻11am-10pm Sun-Thu, to midnight Fri & Sat) serves fresh sandwiches, salads and gourmet cheese plates at sidewalk tables outside the wine bar.

Las Vegas

☑702 / POP 583,756 / ELEV 2001FT

It's three in the morning in a smoky casino when you spot an Elvis lookalike sauntering by arm in arm with a glittering showgirl just as a bride in a long white dress shrieks 'Blackjack!'

Vegas is Hollywood for the everyman, where you play the role instead of watching it. It's the only place in the world you can see ancient hieroglyphics, the Eiffel Tower, the Brooklyn Bridge and the canals of Venice in a few short hours. Sure, they're all reproductions, but in a slice of desert that's transformed itself into one of the most lavish places on earth, nothing is halfway – even the illusions.

Las Vegas is the ultimate escape. Time is irrelevant here. There are no clocks, just never-ending buffets and ever-flowing drinks. This is a city of multiple personalities, constantly reinventing herself since the days of the Rat Pack. Sin City aims to infatuate, and its reaches are all-inclusive. Hollywood bigwigs gyrate at A-list ultralounges, while college kids seek cheap debauchery and grandparents whoop it up at the penny slots. You can sip designer martinis as you sample the apex of world-class cuisine or wander the casino floor with a 3ft-high cocktail tied around your neck.

If you can dream up the kind of vacation you want, it's already a reality here. Welcome to the dream factory.

History

Contrary to Hollywood legend, there was much more at the dusty crossroads than a gambling parlor and some tumbleweeds the day mobster Ben 'Bugsy' Siegel rolled in and erected a glamorous tropical-themed casino, the Flamingo, under the searing sun.

Las Vegas boomed in the 1920s. The legalization of gambling in 1931 then carried Vegas through the Great Depression. WWII brought a huge air-force base and big aerospace bucks, plus a paved highway to Los Angeles. Soon after, the Cold War justified the Nevada Test Site. Monthly aboveground atomic blasts shattered casino windows downtown yet attracted curious visitors.

A building spree sparked by the Flamingo in 1946 led to mob-backed tycoons upping the glitz ante at every turn. Big-name entertainers, like Frank Sinatra, Liberace and Sammy Davis Jr, arrived on stage at the same time as topless French showgirls.

Since then, Sin City continues to exist chiefly to satisfy the desires of visitors. Once it was North America's fastest-growing metropolitan area, but the recent housing crisis hit residents here especially hard. Now among the glittering lights of the Strip, you'll spot unlit, vacant condominium towers that speak to a need for economic revival. Yet Vegas has always been a boom-or-bust kind of place, and if history is any judge, the city will double down and resume its winning streak in no time.

Sights

The Strip, aka Las Vegas Blvd, is the center of gravity in Sin City. Roughly 4 miles long, Circus Circus Las Vegas caps the north end of the Strip and Mandalay Bay is on the south end near the airport. Whether walking or driving, distances on the Strip are deceiving. A walk to what looks like a nearby casino usually takes longer than expected.

Downtown Las Vegas is the original town center and home to the city's oldest hotels and casinos: expect a retro feel. Its main drag is fun-loving Fremont St, four blocks of which are a covered pedestrian mall that runs a groovy light show every night.

Major tourist areas are safe. However, Las Vegas Blvd between downtown and the Strip gets shabby, and Fremont St east of downtown is rather unsavory.

Casinos

TOP CHOICE **Cosmopolitan** CASINO
(www.cosmopolitanlasvegas.com; 3708 Las Vegas Blvd S) Hipsters who have long thought they were too cool for Vegas finally have a place to go where they don't need irony to endure – much less enjoy – the aesthetics. Like a new Hollywood 'it' girl, the Cosmo looks good at all times of the day or night, full of ingenues and entourages, plus regular folks who enjoy contemporary design. With a focus on pure fun, it avoids utter pretension, despite the constant wink-wink, retro moments: the Art-o-Matics (vintage cigarette machines hawking local art rather than nicotine), and possibly the best buffet in town, **The Wicked Spoon.**

TOP CHOICE **Encore** CASINO
(www.encorelasvegas.com; 3121 Las Vegas Blvd S) With this slice of the French Riviera in Las Vegas – and it's classy enough to entice any of the Riviera's regulars – Steve Wynn has upped the wow factor, and the skyline, yet again. Filled with indoor flower gardens, a butterfly motif and a dramatically luxe casino, it's an oasis of bright beauty. **Botero**, the restaurant headed by Mark LoRusso, is centered on a large sculpture by Fernando Botero himself. Encore is attached to its sister property, the $2.7-billion **Wynn Las Vegas** (☎702-770-7100; www.wynnlasvegas. com; 3131 Las Vegas Blvd S). The entrance is obscured from the Strip by a $130-million artificial mountain, which rises seven stories tall in some places. Inside, the Wynn resembles a natural paradise – with mountain views, tumbling waterfalls, fountains and other special effects.

Hard Rock CASINO
(www.hardrockhotel.com; 4455 Paradise Rd) Beloved by SoCal visitors, this trés-hip casino hotel is home to one of the world's most impressive collections of rock 'n' roll memorabilia, including Jim Morrison's handwritten lyrics to one of the Door's greatest hits and leather jackets from a who's who of famous rock stars. **The Joint** concert hall, **Vanity Nightclub** and Rehab summer pool parties

attract a pimped-out, sex-charged crowd flush with celebrities.

Bellagio
CASINO

(www.bellagio.com; 3600 Las Vegas Blvd S) The Bellagio dazzles with Tuscan architecture and an 8-acre artificial lake, complete with don't-miss choreographed dancing fountains. Look up as you enter the lobby: the stunning ceiling is adorned with a backlit glass sculpture composed of 2000 hand-blown flowers by world-renowned artist Dale Chihuly. The **Bellagio Gallery of Fine Art** (☎702-693-7871; admission $15; ◷10am-6pm Sun-Thu, 10am-7pm Fri & Sat) showcases temporary exhibits by top-notch artists. The free **Bellagio Conservatory & Botanical Gardens** features changing exhibits throughout the year.

Venetian
CASINO

(www.venetian.com; 3355 Las Vegas Blvd S) Hand-painted ceiling frescoes, roaming mimes, gondola rides and full-scale reproductions of famous Venice landmarks are found at the romantic Venetian. Next door, the **Palazzo** (☎702-414-1000; www.venetian.com; 3355 Las Vegas Blvd S) exploits a variation on the Italian theme to a less interesting effect: despite the caliber of the **Shops at Palazzo** and the star-studded dining – including exhilarating ventures by culinary heavyweights Charlie Trotter, Emeril Legasse and Wolfgang Puck – the luxurious casino floor and common areas somehow exude a lackluster brand of excitement.

Caesars Palace
CASINO

(www.caesarspalace.com; 3570 Las Vegas Blvd S) Quintessentially Las Vegas, Caesars Palace is a Greco-Roman fantasyland featuring marble reproductions of classical statuary, including a not-to-be-missed 4-ton Brahma shrine near the front entrance. Towering fountains, goddess-costumed cocktail waitresses and the swanky haute-couture **Forum Shops** all turn up the glitz.

Paris-Las Vegas
CASINO

(www.parislasvegas.com; 3730 Las Vegas Blvd S) Evoking the gaiety of the City of Light, Paris-Las Vegas strives to capture the essence of the grande dame by recreating her landmarks. Fine likenesses of the Opéra, the Arc de Triomphe, the Champs-Élysées, the soaring Eiffel Tower and even the Seine frame the property.

Mirage
CASINO

(www.mirage.com; 3400 Las Vegas Blvd S) With a tropical setting replete with a huge atrium filled with jungle foliage and soothing cascades, the Mirage captures the imagination. Circling the atrium is a vast Polynesian-themed casino, which places gaming areas (including a popular high-limit poker room) under separate roofs to evoke intimacy. Don't miss the 20,000-gallon saltwater aquarium, with 60 species of critters hailing from Fiji to the Red Sea. Out front in the lagoon, a fiery faux volcano erupts hourly after dark until midnight.

Flamingo
CASINO

(www.flamingolasvegas.com; 3555 Las Vegas Blvd S) Another quintessentially Vegas hotel is the Flamingo. Weave through the slot machines to the free **Wildlife Habitat** to see the flock of Chilean flamingos that call these 15 tropical acres home.

New York-New York
CASINO

(www.nynyhotelcasino.com; 3790 Las Vegas Blvd S) A mini metropolis featuring scaled-down replicas of the Empire State Building, the Statue of Liberty, ringed by a September 11 memorial, and the Brooklyn Bridge.

Aria
CASINO

(www.arialasvegas.com; 3730 Las Vegas Blvd S) The flagship hotel of the CityCenter complex is its only gaming property. The contemporary, sleek design and the sophisticated casino provide a stylish backdrop to the real star of the show – which is the drop-dead gorgeous restaurants, guaranteed to sate the most hard-to-wow foodie.

Mandalay Bay
CASINO

(M-Bay; www.mandalaybay.com; 3950 Las Vegas Blvd S) Not trying to be any one fantasy, the tropically themed Mandalay Bay is worth a walk-through. Standout attractions include the multilevel **Shark Reef** (www.sharkreef.com; adult/child $17/11; ◷10am-11pm; 🚻), an aquarium home to thousands of submarine beasties with a shallow pool where you can pet pint-sized sharks.

Palms
CASINO

(www.palms.com; 4321 W Flamingo Rd) Equal parts sexy and downright sleazy, the Palms attracts loads of notorious celebrities (think Paris Hilton and Britney Spears) as well as a younger, mostly local crowd. Its restaurants and nightclubs are some of the hottest in town, and the buzzing casino holds its own.

Other highlights include a 14-screen cinema with IMAX capabilities and a live music club, **The Pearl**. Just don't take the elevator to the **Playboy Club** expecting debauchery à la Hef's mansion: while a few bunny-eared, surgically enhanced ladies deal blackjack in a stylishly appointed lounge full of mostly men, the sexiest thing about it is the stunning skyline view.

Golden Nugget
CASINO

(www.goldennugget.com; 129 E Fremont St) Looking like a million bucks, this casino hotel has set the downtown benchmark for extravagance since opening in 1946. No brass or cut glass was spared inside the swanky casino, known for its nonsmoking poker room; the **Rush Lounge**, where live local bands play; the utterly lively casino and some of downtowns' best restaurants. Don't miss the gigantic 61lb Hand of Faith, the world's largest gold nugget, around the corner from the hotel lobby.

Wynn Las Vegas
CASINO

(www.wynnlasvegas.com; 3131 Las Vegas Blvd S) Steve Wynn's signature casino hotel stands on the site of the imploded 1950s-era Desert Inn. The curvaceous, copper-toned 50-story tower exudes secrecy – the entrance is obscured from the Strip by an artificial mountain of greenery. Inside, the resort comes alive with vibrant colors, inlaid flower mosaics, natural-light windows, lush foliage and waterfalls. The sprawling casino – especially the poker room – sees plenty of action.

Other Attractions

TOP CHOICE **Atomic Testing Museum** MUSEUM
(www.atomictestingmuseum.org; 755 E Flamingo Rd; adult/child $12/9; ⊘9am-5pm Mon-Sat, 1-5pm Sun) Recalling an era when the word 'atomic' conjured up modernity and mystery, the Smithsonian-run Atomic Testing Museum remains an intriguing testament to the period when the fantastical – and destructive – power of nuclear energy was tested just outside of Las Vegas. Don't skip the deafening Ground Zero Theater, which mimics a concrete test bunker.

TOP CHOICE **Neon Museum** MUSEUM
(☑702-387-6366; www.neonmuseum.org; cnr Fremont & 4th Sts; displays free, guided tours $15; ⊘displays 24hr, guided tours noon & 2pm Tue-Sat) It isn't really a museum at all, but a fascinating walking tour of the 'neon boneyard,' where irreplaceable vintage neon signs – the

original art form of Las Vegas – spend their retirement.

Fremont Street Experience
STREET

(www.vegasexperience.com; Fremont St; ⊘hourly 7pm-midnight) A four-block pedestrian mall topped by an arched steel canopy and filled with computer-controlled lights, the Fremont Street Experience, between Main St and Las Vegas Blvd, has brought life back to downtown. Every evening, the canopy is transformed into a six-minute light-and-sound show enhanced by 550,000 watts of wraparound sound. It doesn't hurt that the table limits are lower in this part of town and the free drinks seem to appear a little faster.

Downtown Arts District
ARTS CENTER & FESTIVAL

On the **First Friday** (www.firstfriday-lasvegas .org) of each month, a carnival of 10,000 art lovers, hipsters, indie musicians and hangers-on descend on Las Vegas' downtown arts district. These giant monthly block parties feature gallery openings, performance art, live bands and tattoo artists. The action revolves around the **Arts Factory** (101-109 E Charleston Blvd), **Commerce Street Studios** (1551 S Commerce St) and the **Funk House** (1228 S Casino Center Blvd).

Citycenter
SHOPPING CENTER

(www.citycenter.com; 3780 Las Vegas Blvd S) Just when you thought you'd seen it all on the Strip – where themed hotels compete to outdo each other with over-the-top special effects – comes the CityCenter, which beats the competition by not competing at all. Yes, we've seen this symbiotic relationship before (think giant hotel anchored by a mall 'concept') but this super-modern (nearly futuristic) complex places a small galaxy of hypermodern, chi-chi hotels in orbit around the glitzy **Crystals** (www.crystalslasvegas.com; 3750 Las Vegas Blvd S) shopping center. The uber-upscale spread includes the subdued, stylish **Vdara**, the hush-hush opulent **Mandarin Oriental** and the dramatic architectural showpiece **Aria**.

Activities

TOP CHOICE **Qua Baths & Spa** SPA
(☑702-731-7776; www.harrahs.com/qua; Caesars Palace, 3570 Las Vegas Blvd S; ⊘6am-8pm) Social spa-going is encouraged in the tea lounge, herbal steam room and arctic ice room, where dry-ice snowflakes fall.

Papillon Helicopter Tours   HELICOPTER TOUR
(☏702-736-7243; www.papillon.com; 275 E Tropicana Ave; tours from $245) To view Las Vegas and nearby natural wonders at high altitude, float over to Papillon Helicopter Tours. Helicopter trips to the Grand Canyon range from flyovers to a champagne toast at the bottom of the canyon.

Escape Adventures   MOUNTAIN BIKING
(☏800-596-2953; www.escapeadventures.com; 8221 W Charleston Blvd; trips incl bike from $120) The source for guided mountain-bike tours of Red Rock Canyon State Park.

Las Vegas for Children

Few places in Vegas bill themselves as family-friendly. State law prohibits people under 21 from loitering in gaming areas.

Circus Circus   CASINO HOTEL & AMUSEMENT PARK
(www.circuscircus.com; 2880 Las Vegas Blvd S; 🖲) This hotel complex is all about the kids, and its **Adventuredome** (adult/child $25/15; ⊙10am-7pm Sun-Thu, 10am-midnight Fri & Sat; 🖲) is a 5-acre indoor theme park with fun ranging from laser tag to bumper cars and a roller coaster. The **Midway** (admission free; ⊙11am-midnight; 🖲) features animals, acrobats and magicians performing on center stage.

Pinball Hall of Fame   MUSEUM
(www.pinballmuseum.org; 3330 E Tropicana Ave at S Pecos Rd; admission free, games $0.25-0.50; ⊙11am-11pm Sun-Thu, to midnight Fri & Sat;🖲) This interactive museum is more fun than any slot machines.

Excalibur   CASINO HOTEL
(www.excalibur.com; 3050 Las Vegas Blvd S; 🖲) A video arcade and shopping at themed stores like Dragon's Lair, for all your dragon and wizard sculpture needs.

Sleeping

Rates rise and fall dramatically depending on demand. Most hotel websites feature calendars with day-by-day room rates listed.

THE STRIP

Cosmopolitan   CASINO HOTEL $$$
(☏702-698-7000; www.cosmopolitanlasvegas.com; 3708 Las Vegas Blvd S; r $200-400; ✳@🛜🏊) Are the too-cool-for-school, hip rooms worth the price tag? The indie set seems to think so. The rooms are impressive exercises in mod design, but the real delight of staying here is stumbling out of your room at 1am to play some pool in the upper lobbies before going on a mission to find the 'secret' pizza joint.

Encore   CASINO HOTEL $$$
(☏702-770-8000; www.encorelasvegas.com; 3121 Las Vegas Blvd S; r $250-850; ✳@🛜🏊) Classy and playful more than overblown and opulent – even people cheering at the roulette table clap with a little more elegance. There's a definite French Riviera colorful theme in the public spaces, but the rooms themselves are studies in subdued luxury.

Mandalay Bay   CASINO HOTEL $$$
(☏702-632-7777, 877-632-7800; www.mandalaybay.com; 3950 Las Vegas Blvd S; r $100-380; ✳@🛜🏊) The ornately appointed rooms have a South Seas theme, and amenities include floor-to-ceiling windows and luxuri-

---

DON'T MISS

COOL POOLS

» **Hard Rock** Seasonal swim-up blackjack and killer 'Rehab' pool parties at the beautifully landscaped and uber-hip Beach Club.

» **Mirage** Lush tropical pool is a sight to behold, with waterfalls tumbling off cliffs, deep grottos and palm-studded islands for sunbathing.

» **Mandalay Bay** Splash around an artificial sand-and-surf beach built from imported California sand and boasting a wave pool, lazy-river ride, casino and DJ-driven topless Moorea Beach Club.

» **Caesars Palace** Corinthian columns, overflowing fountains, magnificent palms and marble-inlaid pools make the Garden of the Gods Oasis divine. Goddesses proffer frozen grapes in summer, including at the topless Venus pool lounge.

» **Golden Nugget** Downtown's best pool offers lots of fun and zero attitude. Play poolside blackjack, or sip on a daiquiri in the Jacuzzi and watch the sharks frolic nearby.

ous bathrooms. Swimmers will swoon over the sprawling pool complex, with a sand-and-surf beach.

Tropicana
CASINO HOTEL $

(702-739-2222; www.troplv.com; 3801 Las Vegas Blvd S; r from $40, ste from $140; ❄@🅰🛜🏊) As once-celebrated retro properties go under, the Tropicana – keeping the Strip tropical vibe going since 1953 – just got (surprise!) cool again. The multimillion-dollar renovation shows, from the airy casino to the lush, relaxing gardens with their newly unveiled pool and beach club. The earth-toned, breezy rooms and bi-level suites are bargains.

Caesars Palace
CASINO HOTEL $$

(866-227-5938; www.caesarspalace.com; 3570 Las Vegas Blvd S; r from $90; ❄@🏊) Send away the centurions and decamp in style – Caesars' standard rooms are some of the most luxurious you will find in town.

Bill's Gamblin' Hall & Saloon
CASINO HOTEL $$

(702-737-2100, 866-245-5745; www.billslasvegas.com; 3595 Las Vegas Blvd S; r $65-150; ❄@🛜) Set smack bang mid-Strip with affordable rooms nice enough to sport plasma TVs, Bill's is great value, so book far ahead. Rooms feature Victorian-themed decor, and guests can use the pool next door at the Flamingo without charge.

Paris-Las Vegas
CASINO HOTEL $$

(702-946-7000, 877-603-4386; www.parislasvegas.com; 3655 Las Vegas Blvd S; r from $100; ❄@🛜🏊) Nice rooms with a nod to classic French design; the newer Red Rooms are a study in sumptuous class.

DOWNTOWN & OFF STRIP

Downtown hotels are generally less expensive than those on the Strip.

TOP CHOICE Hard Rock
CASINO HOTEL $$$

(702-693-5544, 800-473-7625; www.hardrockhotel.com; 4455 Paradise Rd; r $109-450; @🛜🏊) Everything about this boutique hotel spells stardom. French doors reveal skyline and palm-tree views, and brightly colored Euro-minimalist rooms feature souped-up stereos and plasma-screen TVs. While we dig the jukeboxes in the HRH All-Suite Tower, the standard rooms are nearly as cool. The hottest action revolves around the lush Beach Club.

TOP CHOICE Artisan Hotel
BOUTIQUE HOTEL $

(800-554-4092; www.artisanhotel.com; 1501 W Sahara Ave; r from $40; ❄@🛜🏊) A Gothic baroque fantasy with a decadent dash of rock 'n' roll, this boutique hotel is veritably covered in art. At the visually intoxicating Artisan, each suite is themed around the work of a different artist, although with one of Vegas' best after-parties raging on weekend nights downstairs (a fave with the local alternative set), you may not spend much time in your room. The libidinous, mysterious vibe here isn't for everyone, but if you like it, you'll love it. Artisan's sister hotel, **Rumor** (877-997-8667; www.rumorvegas.com; 455 E Harmon Ave; ste from $69; ❄@🛜🏊), is across from the Hard Rock and features a carefree, Miami-cool atmosphere; its airy suites overlook a palm-shaded courtyard dotted with daybeds and hammocks perfect for lounging around the pool.

El Cortez Cabana Suites
BOUTIQUE HOTEL $

(800-634-6703; www.eccabana.com; 651 E Ogden Ave; ste $45-150; ❄@🛜) You probably won't recognize this sparkling little boutique hotel for its brief movie cameo in Scorcese's *Casino* (hint: Sharon Stone was murdered here) and that's a good thing, because a massive makeover has transformed it into a vintage oasis downtown. Mod suites decked out in mint green include iPod docking stations and retro tiled bathrooms. Plus the coolest vintage casino in town – El Cortez – is right across the street.

Platinum Hotel
BOUTIQUE HOTEL $$

(702-365-5000, 877-211-9211; www.theplatinumhotel.com; 211 E Flamingo Rd; r from $120; ❄@🛜🏊) Just off the Strip, the coolly modern rooms at this spiffy, non-gaming property are comfortable and full of nice touches – many have fireplaces and they all have kitchens and Jacuzzi tubs.

Red Rock Resort
RESORT $$$

(702-797-7878; www.redrocklasvegas.com; 11011 W Charleston Blvd; r $200-625; ❄@🛜🏊) Red Rock touts itself as the first off-Strip billion-dollar gaming resort, and most people who stay here eschew the Strip forever more. There's free transportation between the Strip, and outings to the nearby Red Rocks State Park and beyond. Rooms are well appointed and comfy.

Eating

Sin City is an unmatched eating adventure. Since Wolfgang Puck brought Spago to Caesars in 1992, celebrity chefs have taken up residence in nearly every megaresort. Reservations are a must for fancier restaurants; book in advance.

THE STRIP

On the Strip itself, cheap eats beyond fast-food joints are hard to find.

TOP CHOICE Sage   AMERICAN $$$

(☑877-230-2742; www.arialasvegas.com; Aria 3730 Las Vegas Blvd S; mains $25-42; ◎5-11pm Mon-Sat) Acclaimed chef Shawn McClain meditates on the seasonally sublime with global inspiration and artisanal, farm-to-table ingredients in one of Vegas' most drop-dead gorgeous dining rooms. Don't miss the seasonal cocktails doctored with housemade liqueurs, French absinthe and fruit purees.

TOP CHOICE Joël Robuchon   FRENCH $$$

(☑702-891-7925; MGM Grand, 3799 Las Vegas Blvd S; menu per person $260-420; ◎5:30-10pm Sun-Thu, to 10:30pm Fri & Sat) A once-in-a-lifetime culinary experience; block off a solid three hours and get ready to eat your way through the multicourse seasonal menu of traditional French fare. This intimate little restaurant has garnered a veritable constellation of stars from foodie organizations, and many a celeb has called this red-and-gold palace of opulence home for an evening. **L'Atelier de Joël Robuchon**, next door, is where you can belly up to the counter for a slightly more economical but still delicious meal.

DOCG Enoteca   ITALIAN $$

(☑702-891-3199; Cosmopolitan, 3799 Las Vegas Blvd S; mains $13-28; ◎10am-5pm) Among the Cosmopolitan's alluring dining options, this is one of the least glitzy – but most authentic – options. That's not to say it isn't loads of fun. Order up to-die-for fresh pasta or a wood-fired pizza in the stylish *enoteca*-inspired room that feels like you've joined a festive dinner party. Or head next door to sexy **Scarpetta**, which offers a more intimate, upscale experience by the same fantastic chef, Scott Conant.

Social House   JAPANESE $$$

(☑702-736-1122; www.socialhouselv.com; Crystals Mall, CityCenter, 3720 Las Vegas Blvd S; mains $24-44; ◎5-10pm Mon-Thu, noon-11pm Fri & Sat, noon-10pm Sun) Nibble on creative dishes inspired by Japanese street food in one of the Strip's most serene yet sexy dining rooms. Water-marked scrolls, wooden screens and loads of dramatic red and black conjure visions of Imperial Japan, while the sushi and steaks are totally contemporary.

RM Seafood   SEAFOOD $$$

(☑702-632-9300; www.rmseafood.com; Mandalay Place, 3930 Las Vegas Blvd S; mains $27-62; ◎cafe 11am-10pm, restaurant 5-11pm) From ecoconscious chef Rick Moonen, modern American seafood dishes, such as Cajun popcorn and Maine lobster, come with comfort-food sides (like gourmet mac 'n' cheese), a raw shellfish and sushi bar, and a 'biscuit bar' serving savory salads.

Fiamma   ITALIAN $$$

(☑702-891-7600; www.mgmgrand.com; MGM Grand, 3799 Las Vegas Blvd S; meals $50-60; ◎5-11pm) Fiamma is set in a row of outstanding restaurants at MGM Grand, but what sets it apart is that it's a top-tier dining experience you won't be paying off for the next decade. You haven't had spaghetti until you've had Fiamma's take on it, made with Kobe-beef meatballs.

Victorian Room   STEAKHOUSE $$

(www.billslasvegas.com; Bill's Gamblin' Hall & Saloon, 3595 Las Vegas Blvd S; mains $8-20; ◎24hr) A hokey old-fashioned San Francisco theme belies one of the best deals in sit-down restaurants in Las Vegas. The prime rib or New York steak specials ($14.95) are delicious around the clock.

Society Café   CAFE $$

(www.wynnlasvegas.com; Encore, 3121 Las Vegas Blvd S; mains $14-30; ◎7am-midnight Sun-Thu, 7am-3am Fri & Sat) A slice of reasonably priced culinary heaven in the midst of Encore's loveliness. The basic cafe here is equal to fine dining at other joints. The sliders are a good appetizer or light meal, and the lobster-roll club sandwich makes eating with your hands classy again.

'wichcraft   SANDWICH SHOP $

(www.mgmgrand.com; MGM Grand, 3799 Las Vegas Blvd S; sandwiches $7-10; ◎10am-5pm) This designy little sandwich shop, the brainchild of celebrity chef Tom Colicchio, is one of the best places to taste gourmet on a budget.

Olives
MEDITERRANEAN **$$$**

(☎702-693-8181; www.bellagio.com; Bellagio, 3600 Las Vegas Blvd S; mains $16-52; ☺lunch & dinner) Bostonian chef Todd English dishes up homage to the life-giving fruit. Flatbread pizzas, house-made pastas and flame-licked meats get top billing, and patio tables overlook Lake Como. Try his new comfort-food and sports-bar venture, **Todd English PUB**, in the CityCenter complex.

DOWNTOWN & OFF THE STRIP
Traditionally off the culinary radar, Downtown's restaurants offers better value than the Strip, whether you're at a casino buffet or a retro steakhouse.

Just west of the Strip, the Asian restaurants on Spring Mountain Rd in Chinatown are also good budget options, with lots of vegetarian choices.

TOP CHOICE **Rosemary's**
INTERNATIONAL **$$$**

(☎702-869-2251; 8125 W Sahara Ave; dinner mains $30-42, 3-course prix-fixe menu $55; ☺lunch Fri, dinner daily) Words fail to describe the epicurean ecstasy you'll encounter here. Yes, it's a very long drive from the Strip. But once you bite into heavenly offerings like Texas BBQ shrimp with Maytag blue cheese 'slaw, you'll forget about everything else.

TOP CHOICE **Firefly**
TAPAS **$$**

(3900 Paradise Rd; small dishes $4-10, large dishes $11-20; ☺11:30am-2am Sun-Thu, to 3am Fri & Sat) Locals seem to agree on one thing about the Vegas food scene: a meal at Firefly can be twice as fun as an overdone Strip restaurant, and half the price. Is that why it's always hopping? Nosh on traditional Spanish tapas, while the bartender pours sangria and flavor-infused mojitos.

Lotus of Siam
THAI **$$**

(www.saipinchutima.com; 953 E Sahara Ave; mains $9-29; ☺11:30am-2pm Mon-Fri, 5:30-9:30pm Mon-Thu, 5:30-10pm Fri & Sat) The top Thai restaurant in the US? According to *Gourmet Magazine*, this is it. One bite of simple pad Thai – or any of the exotic northern Thai dishes – nearly proves it.

Pink Taco
MEXICAN **$$**

(www.hardrockhotel.com; Hard Rock, 3900 Paradise Rd; mains $8-15; ☺7am-11pm Mon-Thu, to 3am Fri & Sat) Whether it's the 99-cent taco and margarita happy hour, the leafy poolside patio or the friendly rock 'n' roll clientele, Pink Taco always feels like a worthwhile party.

WORTHY INDULGENCES: BEST BUFFETS

Wicked Spoon Buffet (www.cosmopolitanlasvegas.com; The Cosmopolitan, 3655 Las Vegas Blvd S)

Le Village Buffet (www.parislv.com; Paris-Las Vegas, 3655 Las Vegas Blvd S)

Spice Market Buffet (Planet Hollywood, 3667 Las Vegas Blvd S)

Sterling Brunch at Bally's (☎702-967-7999; Bally's, 3645 Las Vegas Blvd S; ☺Sun)

The Buffet (☎702-693-7111; www.bellagio.com; Bellagio, 3600 Las Vegas Blvd S)

Sunday Gospel Brunch (☎702-632-7600; www.hob.com; House of Blues, Mandalay Bay, 3950 Las Vegas Blvd S; ☺seatings 10am & 1pm Sun)

N9NE
STEAKHOUSE **$$$**

(☎702-933-9900; www.palms.com; Palms, 4321 W Flamingo Rd; mains $26-43; ☺dinner) At this hip steakhouse heavy with celebs, a dramatic dining room centers on a champagne and caviar bar. Chicago-style aged steaks and chops keep coming, along with everything from oysters Rockefeller to Pacific sashimi.

Golden Gate
SEAFOOD **$**

(www.goldengatecasino.com; 1 E Fremont St; ☺11am-3am) Famous $1.99 shrimp cocktails (super-size 'em for $3.99).

Drinking
For those who want to mingle with the locals and drink for free, check out **SpyOnVegas** (www.spyonvegas.com). It arranges an open bar at a different venue every weeknight.

THE STRIP
TOP CHOICE **Mix**
LOUNGE

(www.mandalaybay.com; 64th fl, Mandalay Bay, 3950 Las Vegas Blvd S; cover after 10pm $20-25) THE place to grab sunset cocktails. The glassed-in elevator has amazing views, and that's before you even glimpse the mod interior design and soaring balcony.

EMERGENCY ARTS

A coffee shop, an art gallery, studios and a de facto community center of sorts, all under one roof and right smack downtown? While the most prized art in Las Vegas may hang in the Bellagio's gallery, some of the most interesting art being *made* in Las Vegas happens right here at the **Emergency Arts** (Hard Rock, 3900 Paradise Rd) building, also home to **The Beat Coffeehouse** (www.thebeatlasvegas.com; sandwiches $6-7; ⊙7am-midnight Mon-Fri, 9am-midnight Sat, 9am-3pm Sun), a friendly bastion of laid-back cool and strong coffee where vintage vinyl spins on old turntables. If you're aching to meet some savvy locals who know their way around town, this is your hang-out spot.

TOP CHOICE Gold Lounge LOUNGE & NIGHTCLUB
(www.arialasvegas.com; Aria, 3930 Las Vegas Blvd S; cover after 10pm $20-25) A fitting homage to Elvis; you won't find watered-down Top 40 at this luxe ultralounge, but you will find gold, gold and more gold. Make a toast in front of the giant portrait of the King himself, and try not to pass out in the toilets.

Parasol Up – Parasol Down BAR & CAFE
(www.wynnlasvegas.com; Wynn, 3131 Las Vegas Blvd S; ⊙5pm-2am) Unwind with a fresh fruit mojito by the soothing waterfall at the Wynn to experience one of Vegas' most successful versions of paradise.

Red Square BAR
(www.mandalaybay.com; Mandalay Bay, 3950 Las Vegas Blvd S; ⊙5pm-2am) Heaps of Russian caviar, a solid ice bar and over 200 frozen vodkas, infusions and cocktails. Don a Russian army coat to sip vodka in the subzero vault.

Chandelier Bar BAR
(www.cosmopolitanlasvegas.com; Palazzo, 3950 Las Vegas Blvd S; ⊙5pm-2am) In a city full of lavish hotel lobby bars, this one pulls out the stops. Kick back with the Cosmopolitan hipsters and enjoy the curiously thrilling feeling that you're tipsy inside a giant crystal chandelier.

LAVO LOUNGE & NIGHTCLUB
(www.palazzo.com; Palazzo, 3325 Las Vegas Blvd S) One of the sexiest new Italian restaurant-lounge-nightclub combos for the see-and-be-seen set, Lavo's terrace is the place to be at happy hour. Sip a cocktail in the dramatically lit bar or stay to dance among reclining Renaissance nudes in the club upstairs.

DOWNTOWN & OFF THE STRIP
Want to chill out with the locals? Head to one of their go-to favorites.

TOP CHOICE Fireside Lounge COCKTAIL BAR
(www.peppermilllasvegas.com; Peppermill, 2985 Las Vegas Blvd S; ⊙24hr) The Strip's most unlikely romantic hideaway is inside a retro coffee shop. Courting couples flock here for the low lighting, sunken fire pit and cozy nooks built for supping on multistrawed tiki drinks and for acting out your most inadvisable 'what happens in Vegas, stays in Vegas' moments.

Double Down Saloon BAR
(www.doubledownsaloon.com; 4640 Paradise Rd; ⊙24hr) You just can't get more punk rock than a dive where the tangy, blood-red house drink is named Ass Juice. The jukebox vibrates with New Orleans jazz, British punk, Chicago blues and surf-guitar king Dick Dale.

Beauty Bar COCKTAIL BAR
(www.thebeautybar.com; 517 E Fremont St; cover $5-10) At the salvaged innards of a 1950s New Jersey beauty salon, swill a cocktail while you get a makeover demo or chill out with the hip DJs and live local bands. Then walk around the corner to the **Downtown Cocktail Room**, a speakeasy.

Frankie's Tiki Room THEME BAR
(www.frankiestikiroom.com; 1712 W Charleston Blvd; all drinks $8; ⊙24hr) At the only round-the-clock tiki bar in the US, the drinks are rated in strength by skulls and the top tiki sculptors and painters in the world have their work on display.

Entertainment

Las Vegas has no shortage of entertainment on any given night, and **Ticketmaster** (☎702-474-4000; www.ticketmaster.com) sells tickets for pretty much everything.

Tix 4 Tonight (☎877-849-4868; www.tix4tonight.com; Bill's Gamblin' Hall & Saloon, 3595 Las Vegas Blvd S; ⊙10am-8pm) offers half-price tix for a limited lineup of same-day shows and small discounts on 'always sold-out' shows.

Nightclubs & Live Music

Admission prices to nightclubs vary wildly based on the mood of door staff, male-to-female ratio, and how crowded the club is that night.

Marquee
CLUB
(www.cosmopolitanlasvegas.com; Cosmopolitan, 3708 Las Vegas Blvd) When someone asks what's the coolest club in Vegas, Marquee is the undisputed answer. Celebrities (we spotted Macy Gray as we danced through the crowd), an outdoor beach club, hot DJs, and that certain *je ne sais quoi* that makes a club worth waiting in line for.

Tryst
CLUB
(www.trystlasvegas.com; Wynn, 3131 Las Vegas Blvd S) All gimmicks aside, the flowing waterfall makes this place ridiculously (and literally) cool. Blood-red booths and plenty of space to dance ensure that you can have a killer time even without splurging for bottle service.

Drai's
CLUB
(Bill's Gamblin' Hall & Saloon, 3595 Las Vegas Blvd S; ⊙midnight-8am Wed-Sun) Feel ready for an after-hours scene straight outta Hollywood? Things don't really get going until 4am, when DJs spinning progressive discs keep the cool kids content. Dress to kill.

Stoney's Rockin' Country
LIVE MUSIC
(www.stoneysrockincountry.com; 9151 Las Vegas Blvd S; cover $5-10; ⊙7pm-late Thu-Sun) An off-Strip place worth the trip. Friday and Saturday has $20 all-you-can-drink draft beer and free line-dancing lessons from 7:30pm to 8:30pm. The mechanical bull is a blast.

Bank
CLUB
(Bellagio, 3600 Las Vegas Blvd S; cover men from $30, women free-$30; ⊙10:30pm-4:30am) Service and an upscale vibe are what sets this place apart. Spring for VIP treatment (starting at $475) and you will be treated like a celebrity.

Moon
CLUB
(www.n9negroup.com; Palms Casino Resort, 4321 W Flamingo Rd; cover Mon-Fri $20, Sat & Sun $40; ⊙10:30pm-4am Tue & Thu-Sun) Stylishly outfitted like a nightclub in outer space; the retractable roof opens for dancing to pulsating beats under the stars. Admission includes entry to the only Playboy Club in the world.

Production Shows

There are hundreds of shows to choose from in Vegas. Any Cirque du Soleil show tends to be an unforgettable experience.

TOP CHOICE LOVE
PERFORMING ARTS
(☏702-792-7777; www.cirquedusoleil.com; tickets $99-150) At the Mirage, this is a popular addition to the Cirque du Soleil lineup and locals who have seen many a Cirque production come and go say it's the best one yet.

TOP CHOICE Steel Panther
LIVE MUSIC
(☏702-617-7777; www.greenvalleyranchresort.com; Green Valley Resort, 2300 Paseo Verde Pkwy, Henderson; admission free; ⊙11pm-late Fri) A hair-metal tribute band makes fun of the audience, themselves and the 1980s with sight gags, one-liners and many a drug and sex reference.

O
PERFORMING ARTS
(☏702-796-9999; www.cirquedusoleil.com; tickets $99-150) Still a favorite is Cirque du Soleil's aquatic show, O, performed at the Bellagio.

Zumanity
PERFORMING ARTS
(☏702-740-6815; www.cirquedusoleil.com; tickets $69-129) Sensual and sexy adult-only show at New York-New York.

Shopping

Bonanza Gifts
GIFTS
(☏702-385-7359; 2440 Las Vegas Blvd S) The best place for only-in-Vegas kitsch souvenirs.

The Attic
VINTAGE
(1018 S Main St; ⊙10am-5pm Mon-Thu, to 6pm Fri, 11am-6pm Sat) Be mesmerized by fabulous hats and wigs, hippie-chic clubwear and lounge-lizard furnishings.

Fashion Show Mall
MALL
(3200 Las Vegas Blvd S) Nevada's biggest and flashiest mall. There's a branch of **Borders Express** (www.borders.com) here.

Forum Shops
MALL
(Caesars Palace, 3500 Las Vegas Blvd S) Upscale stores in an air-conditioned version of Ancient Rome.

Grand Canal Shoppes
MALL
(Venetian, 3355 Las Vegas Blvd S) Italianate indoor luxury mall with gondolas.

The Shoppes at the Palazzo
MALL
(Palazzo, 3327 Las Vegas Blvd S) International designers flaunt their goodies.

Mandalay Place MALL
(3930 Las Vegas Blvd S) On the sky bridge between the Mandalay Bay and the Luxor. An airy promenade with unique, fashion-forward boutiques.

Miracle Mile Shops MALL
(Planet Hollywood, 3663 Las Vegas Blvd S) A staggering 1.5 miles long; get a tattoo, drink and duds.

Information

Emergency & Medical Services

Gamblers Anonymous (☎702-385-7732) Assistance with gambling concerns.

Police (☎702-828-3111)

Sunrise Hospital & Medical Center (☎702-731-8000; 3186 S Maryland Pkwy)

University Medical Center (☎702-383-2000; 1800 W Charleston Blvd)

Internet Access

Wi-fi is available in most hotel rooms (about $10 to $24 per day, sometimes included in the 'resort fee') and there are internet kiosks with attached printers in most hotel lobbies ($5 per five minutes).

Internet Resources & Media

Las Vegas Review-Journal (www.lvrj.com) Daily paper with a weekend guide, *Neon,* on Friday.

Las Vegas Tourism (www.onlyinvegas.com) Official tourism website.

Las Vegas Weekly (www.lasvegasweekly. com) Free weekly with good entertainment and restaurant listings.

Las Vegas.com (www.lasvegas.com) Travel services.

Lasvegaskids.net (www.lasvegaskids.net) The lowdown on what's up for the wee ones.

Vegas.com (www.vegas.com) Travel information with booking service.

Money

Every hotel-casino and bank and most convenience stores have an ATM. The ATM fee at most casinos is around $5. Best to stop at off-Strip banks if possible.

American Express (☎702-739-8474; Fashion Show Mall, 3200 Las Vegas Blvd S; ☉10am-9pm Mon-Fri, 10am-8pm Sat, noon-6pm Sun) Changes currencies at competitive rates.

Post

Post office (☎702-382-5779; 201 Las Vegas Blvd S) Downtown.

Tourist Information

Las Vegas Visitor Information Center (☎702-892-7575; www.visitlasvegas.com; 3150 Paradise Rd; ☉8am-5pm) Free local calls, internet access and maps galore.

Getting There & Around

Just south of the major Strip casinos and easily accessible from I-15, **McCarran International Airport** (LAS; ☎702-261-4636; www.mccarran. com) has direct flights from most US cities, and some from Canada and Europe. **Bell Trans** (☎702-739-7990; www.bell-trans.com) offers a shuttle service ($6.50) between the airport and the Strip. Fares to downtown destinations are slightly higher. At the airport, exit door 9 near baggage claim to find the Bell Trans booth.

All of the attractions in Vegas have free self-parking and valet parking available (tip $2). Fast, fun and fully wheelchair accessible, the **monorail** (☎702-699-8299; www.lvmonorail. com) connects the Sahara to the MGM Grand, stopping at major Strip megaresorts along the way, and operating from 7am to 2am Monday to Thursday and until 3am Friday through Sunday. A single ride is $5, a 24-hour pass is $12, and a three-day pass is $28. The **Deuce** (☎702-228-7433; www.rtcsouthernnevada.com), a local double-decker bus, runs frequently 24 hours daily between the Strip and downtown (one ride/24-hour pass is $3/7).

North Rim

Best Hikes

» Bright Angel Point (p136)
» North Kaibab (p141)
» Widforss Trail (p136)
» Cape Final (p137)
» Cliff Springs (p136)

Best Places to Stay

» Grand Canyon Lodge (p144)
» Best Friends Animal Sanctuary (p155)
» Parry Lodge (p155)
» Purple Sage Inn (p155)
» Kaibab Lodge (p150)

Why Go?

A single stone-and-timber lodge with floor-to-ceiling windows is perched directly on the canyon rim, and miles of trails wind through meadows thick with wildflowers, willowy aspen and towering ponderosa pines. At the end of every day the lodge's small rimside sun porch fills with dusty, weary hikers, doffing baseball caps, Camelbaks and backpacks. They grab a beer from the saloon and mingle on the porch, settling into the Adirondack chairs, comparing notes and sharing experiences. After the sun sets, when most of the children have gone to sleep and darkness has subdued the canyon's ferocity, folks bundle in their fleeces and sit quietly, studying the stars, breathing in the canyon's emptiness, listening to the silence. This is the kinder, gentler Grand Canyon, and once you've been here you'll never want to see the canyon from anywhere else.

When to Go
North Rim

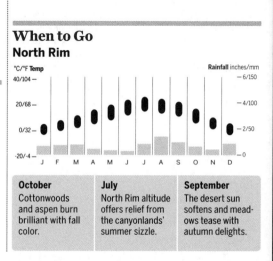

October	July	September
Cottonwoods and aspen burn brilliant with fall color.	North Rim altitude offers relief from the canyonlands' summer sizzle.	The desert sun softens and meadows tease with autumn delights.

PLANNING TIPS

Park accommodation is limited to Grand Canyon Lodge and the campground. All facilities at the Grand Canyon North Rim are closed mid-October through mid-May.

Fast Facts

» Miles of rim trails: 25

» Highest elevation: 8803ft

» Elevation change from rim to Colorado River: 5850ft

Reservations

Grand Canyon Lodge (☎877-386-4383; www .foreverlodging.com) takes reservations up to a year months in advance; no penalty for cancellations made before 72-hours. Call ☎928-638-2611 for same-day room reservations.

North Rim Campground (☎877-444-6777, 928-638-7814; www.recreation .gov) takes reservations up to six months in advance; hiker/cyclist sites are usually available without reservation.

Resources

» www.nps.gov/grca/

» www.foreverlodging.com

» www.kaneutah.com

Entrances

The North Rim Entrance sits 30 miles south of Jacob Lake on Hwy 67. A park pass of $25 per car, good for seven days on both rims, can be purchased at the gate. Those entering on foot, by bicycle or by motorcycle pay $12 per person. If you arrive after-hours, a posted note will direct you – remember to pay the fee when you depart. From here, it is 14 miles to Grand Canyon Lodge.

DON'T MISS

Just coming to the North Rim is getting away from it all, but once you're here there are a few easily accessible hideaways. **Uncle Jim's Cave**, once used as a ranger residence, lies in the rocks on the far side of **Harvey Meadow** on the way to the Widforss Trailhead – easy to get to and free of crowds, the meadow and cave make a great spot to hang out, particularly for children. The stone **Moon Room** below the sun porch of Grand Canyon Lodge offers a cool and quiet rimside refuge. Look for small, unmarked stairs along the trail that runs between the lodge and the canyon. On the road to Cape Royal, few folks bother stopping at **Greenland Lake**, and it's a peaceful place for a picnic. Unmaintained forest roads off Cape Royal Rd and the road to Point Sublime lead miles through the woods and meadows to **backcountry overlooks**. Ask at the visitor center for details, and secure a backcountry permit if you plan on primitive camping.

When You Arrive

» Upon entry, you'll receive a map and a copy of *The Guide*, a National Park Service (NPS) newspaper with information on ranger programs, hikes and park services.

» Do not lose your entrance receipt, as you'll need it if you intend on leaving and re-entering the park.

» The road dead-ends at Grand Canyon Lodge. At the lodge entrance you'll find the **North Rim Visitor Center** (☎928-638-7864; ⊙9am-6pm, closed mid-Oct–mid-May) as well as a cafeteria, a saloon and a cafe and other amenities.

Orientation

On a horseshoe-shaped boardwalk at the Grand Canyon Lodge entrance, you'll find a small cafeteria, a Western saloon that also serves coffee and pastries, a **postal window** (⊙8am-5pm Mon-Fri, closed mid-Oct–mid-May) and the North Rim Visitor Center. Note there is a bathroom and icemaker behind the center, and wheelchairs are available for loan. Just over a mile up the road, next to the campground, there are laundry facilities, a general store, fee showers, a gas station and the **North Rim Backcounry Office** (☑928-638-7875; ⊙8am-noon & 1-5pm, closed mid-Oct–mid-May). Both the 1.2-mile Transept Trail and a 1-mile leg of the Bridle Trail link the lodge and campground.

Park Policies & Regulations

See p19 for general information on park policies and regulations on both rims.

OVERLOOKS

Every drive and hike on the North Rim includes a canyon overlook, and one of the best is from the sun porch of Grand Canyon Lodge. From here, steps lead to two rocky overlooks (they don't have a name, but you can't miss them), and Bright Angel Point is an easy amble along a precipitous rocky outcrop. You can drive paved roads to Point Imperial and Cape Royal, or a dirt road to Point Sublime. Widforss Point, Cape Final and the North Kaibab down to Coconino Overlook make excellent day-hike destinations, and just outside the park boundary the Kaibab National Forest offers trails and dirt roads through aspen and meadows to remote overlooks.

DRIVING

Driving on the North Rim involves miles of slow roads through dense stands of evergreens and aspen to the region's most spectacular overlooks. To reach Cape Royal and Point Imperial Rds, head 3 miles north from Grand Canyon Lodge to the signed right turn. From here, it is 5 miles to the Y-turn for Point Imperial and Cape Royal Rds. The road to Point Sublime offers amazing views, but requires at least four hours round-trip navigating a treacherous dirt road. You can hike to Point Imperial but no trails connect the viewpoints.

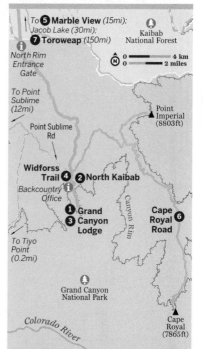

North Rim Highlights

❶ Sit in an Adirondack chair on the sun porch of **Grand Canyon Lodge** (p144), sip a North Rim Sunset and watch the canyon transform with every shifting nuance of light

❷ Listen to the silence of the sunrise from the Coconino Overlook on the **North Kaibab** (p141)

❸ Stargaze at a **ranger talk** (p144) on the sun porch of Grand Canyon Lodge

❹ Hike through aspen, ponderosa and meadows along **Widforss Trail** (p136) to Widforss Point

❺ Picnic and throw the frisbee among Indian paintbrush at **Marble View** (p147)

❻ Leisurely explore short hikes and sights along the **Cape Royal Rd** (p134) and take in the view from **Cape Royal Point**

❼ Belly-crawl to the sheer-drop view at **Toroweap** (boxed text p138)

North Rim

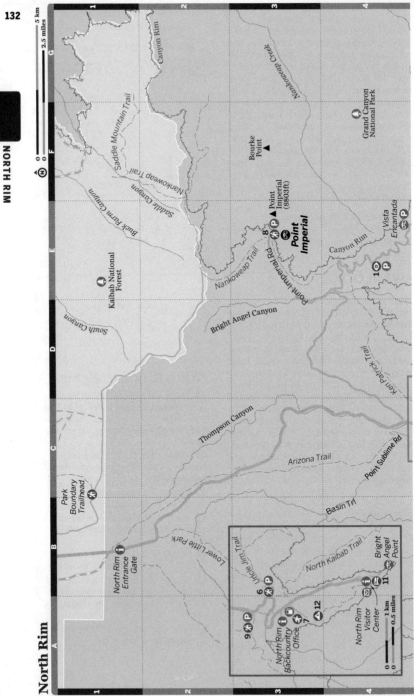

0 5 km
0 2.5 miles

Canyon Rim

Saddle Mountain Trail

Nankoweap Creek

Bourke Point

Grand Canyon National Park

Nankoweap Trail

Point Imperial (8803ft)

Point Imperial

8

Buck Farm Canyon

Saddle Canyon

Kaibab National Forest

Nankoweap Trail

Point Imperial Rd

Vista Encantada

Canyon Rim

1

South Canyon

Bright Angel Canyon

Kanabownits Trail

Thompson Canyon

Park Boundary Trailhead

Arizona Trail

Point Sublime Rd

North Rim Entrance Gate

Basin Trl

Lower Little Park

Uncle Jim Trail

North Kaibab Trail

Bright Angel Point

6

9

North Rim Backcountry Office

7

12

11

North Rim Visitor Center

0 1 km
0 0.5 miles

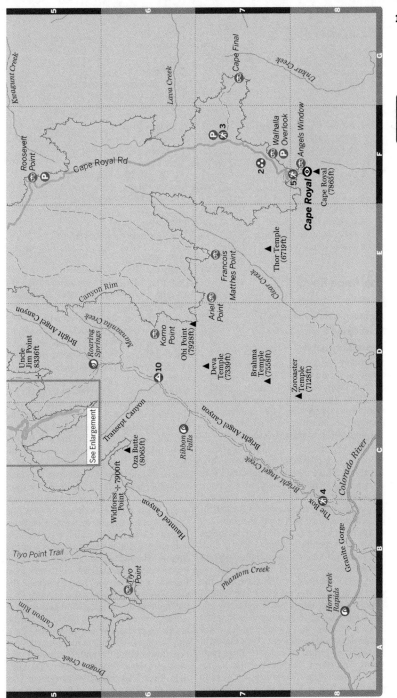

North Rim

🚗 Cape Royal

Duration 45 minutes one-way

Distance 23 miles one-way

Start Grand Canyon Lodge

Finish Cape Royal

Summary Descending gradually from 8200ft at Grand Canyon Lodge to 7685ft at Cape Royal, this paved road is a must and is the only spot on the North Rim where you can see the Colorado River; once at Cape Royal parking lot, it's an easy 15-minute walk to the overlook.

From the Y-turn for Point Imperial and Cape Royal Rds, it's 2.5 miles to **Greenland Lake**. Look for the small parking lot on the right. A two-minute walk leads to a meadow and alpine pond and, a few minutes further, an old, empty salt cabin. This is the only stop on the drive without rim views, and it makes an excellent spot for a picnic.

Cape Royal Rd continues 2 miles to **Vista Encantada**. Views from this overlook extend from Nankoweap Creek within the canyon to the Vermilion Cliffs and Painted Desert in the distance. You'll find a few picnic tables, but because the tables are right next to the road and parking lot it's not a particularly nice spot to eat. After taking in the view, continue 1.6 miles to **Roosevelt Point**. From here, you can see the confluence of the Little Colorado and Colorado Rivers, the Navajo Reservation, the Painted

Desert and the Hopi Reservation. The easy 0.2-mile round-trip rimside **Roosevelt Point Trail** loops through burnt-out forest to a small bench at the canyon edge.

The next stop is **Walhalla Overlook**, 6.5 miles past Roosevelt Point. Just below the rim lies Unkar Delta, a plateau composed of sand and rocks deposited by Unkar Creek. This was the winter home of ancestral Puebloans from AD 850 to 1200. On the north side of the parking lot, a path crosses the street and leads to **Walhalla Glades**, the ancient Puebloans' summer home. Because this area sits below most of the North Rim, snow here melted earlier and enabled villagers to grow beans, corn and squash. A short self-guided walk leads past six small ruins; pick up a walking-tour brochure from a small box at the trailhead just off the road.

The road ends 1.5 miles past Walhalla Overlook at the Cape Royal parking lot. From here, a 0.3-mile paved path, lined with piñon, cliffrose and interpretive signs, leads to **Angels Window**, a natural arch, and **Cape Royal Point**, arguably the best view from this side of the canyon. The path splits at the view of Angels Window, a few minutes from the trailhead. To the left, a short path leads to a precipice overlook that juts into the canyon and drops dramatically on three sides – here, you are literally standing atop Angels Window. To the right, the path continues to the rocky outcrop of Cape Royal Point. The Colorado River – 70 miles downstream of Lees Ferry, 18 miles upstream of Phantom Ranch and 207 miles upstream of Lake Mead – can be seen directly below the point.

While the path is plenty wide enough for strollers and wheelchairs, they can't access Angels Window and the point itself is rocky. Several pleasantly shaded picnic tables sit at the far end of the parking lot. The **Wedding Site** features great canyon views – an ideal spot for a sunrise picnic.

This road may be closed in the late fall and early spring, and during heavy wind. The only bathrooms are at the Cape Royal parking lot.

🚗 Point Imperial

Duration 20 minutes one-way

Distance 11 miles one-way

Start Grand Canyon Lodge

Finish Point Imperial

Summary At 8803ft, Point Imperial is an easy drive and the highest overlook on either of the rims.

Expansive views of the canyon's eastern half and the desert beyond include Nankoweap Creek, the Vermilion Cliffs, the Painted Desert and the Little Colorado River. An interpretive sign identifies the sights and geologic formations. The drive to Point Imperial passes the North Kaibab trailhead and the turn for the Widforss trailhead before cutting east. Though the road winds pleasantly through the ponderosa and aspen

---

TOP FIVE OVERLOOKS

Every drive and hike on the North Rim includes a canyon overlook, but unlike the South Rim there is no extended stretch of trail with panoramic canyon views.

» **Grand Canyon Lodge** Steps lead from the lodge's sun porch to two rocky overlooks.

» **Bright Angel Point** An easy amble along a precipitous rocky outcrop.

» **Cape Royal** Primarily paved trail leads from the parking lot to one of the park's best overlooks.

» **Point Imperial** Highest overlook on either rim.

» **Cape Final** Quiet, uncrowded and spectacular, well worth the wooded 2-mile hike.

---

dotted with mountain meadows, there are no overlooks or stops along the way.

🚗 Point Sublime

Duration 2 hours one-way

Distance 18 miles one-way

Start Widforss Trailhead

Finish Point Sublime

Summary Touted as one of the more spectacular and remote viewpoints within the park, Point Sublime lives up to its reputation for those with the time and inclination to tackle the forested drive along a road that is, in places, almost impassable.

From the Y intersection just past the Widforss Trailhead parking area, a dirt road veers left towards **Point Sublime**. About 4 miles west of Hwy 67, an old fire-access road heads south for about 7 miles to **Tiyo Point**, a quiet overlook and a beautiful backcountry campsite (no facilities). You can't drive, but it's a moderate hike through forests and meadows, and you'll more than likely have the canyon overlook to yourself. Just park on the side of the road to hike in, and be sure to get a permit if you're going to camp. Further down the road, about 70 minutes from Hwy 67, a lovely backcountry campsite nestled in a clearing among the trees offers side-canyon views. The road bumps and winds and bumps some more through ponderosa and aspen, and past several lovely side-canyon views before reaching the piñon and desert shrubs of Point Sublime, with some picnic tables and backcountry campsites.

Check road conditions before taking off, and absolutely do not attempt this drive in a 2WD. If you're looking for absolute solitude, you may be disappointed. It's amazing how many folks make their way out here.

DAY HIKES

Do not underestimate the effect of altitude. If you can, spend a few days acclimatizing with scenic drives, short walks and lazy days before conquering longer trails. The only maintained rim-to-river trail from the North Rim is the North Kaibab, a steep and difficult 14-mile haul to the river; day hikers will find multiple turnaround spots. Under no circumstances should anyone attempt to hike to the Colorado River and back in one day – as a ranger told us, the Grand Canyon wants to kill you.

In addition to the following official trails, a number of old unmarked and unmaintained fire roads off Cape Royal Rd lead several miles to rarely visited **Komo**, **Ariel** and **Francois Matthes Points**. They don't have the sweeping views of the North Rim's standard overlooks, but they promise solitude.

Ask at the visitor center for current conditions and details, and see the hiking charts in the Activities chapter (p29). The following hikes are listed in order from the most to the least recommended.

🚶 Bright Angel Point

Duration 30 minutes round-trip

Distance 0.5 miles round-trip

Difficulty Easy

Start/Finish Grand Canyon Lodge

Transportation Car

Summary More a walk than a hike, this paved trail wraps up, down and out along a narrow finger of an overlook that dangles between Transept Canyon and Roaring Springs Canyon.

This is one of the few trails on the North Rim where you feel like you're walking along a precipice, with the canyon dropping off from either side of the trail. Anyone with a fear of heights should think twice before strapping on their walking shoes. There are few guardrails, and the edges are crumbling rock and sand – hold onto your children's hands and do not veer from the established trail. While it is officially paved and easy, the few steep inclines, rocky spots and narrow path make this dangerous for strollers and prohibitive to wheelchairs. A few benches and boulders offer pleasant spots to rest along the way.

The overlook gives unfettered views of the mesas, buttes, spires and temples of Bright Angel Canyon, as well as a straight shot of the South Rim, 10 miles across the canyon as the crow flies, and the distant San Francisco Peaks towering over Flagstaff. Listen carefully and you can hear Roaring Springs below. The trail begins on the left side of the sun porch, or you can start at a second trailhead in the log shelter in the parking area by the visitor center.

🚶 Widforss Trail

Duration 6 hours round-trip

Distance 10 miles round-trip

Difficulty Moderate

Start/Finish Widforss Trailhead

Transportation Car

Summary A moderate hike through woods and meadows with peeping canyon views leads to a spectacular canyon overlook.

Named after Gunnar Widforss, an early-20th-century artist who lived, worked, died and was buried at the Grand Canyon, the Widforss Trail meanders through stands of spruce, white fir, ponderosa pine and aspen to **Widforss Point**. Tall trees offer shade, fallen limbs provide pleasant spots to relax, and you likely won't see more than a few people along the trail.

After a 15-minute climb, the canyon comes into view. For the next 2 miles, the trail offers wide views of the canyon to one side and meadows and woods to the other. Halfway into the hike, the trail jags away from the rim and dips into gullies of lupines and ferns; the canyon doesn't come into view again until the end. From Widforss Point (elevation 7900ft), take the small path to the left of the picnic table to a flat rock, where you can enjoy a sandwich, the classic view and the silence. Though the total elevation change is only 440ft, rolling terrain makes the first few miles a moderate challenge. The park service offers a self-guided trail brochure, available at the trailhead and the visitor center, for the first half of this hike. Follow the trail to the end of the guide and then turn around, and, though you'll miss the overlook at the point, you'll have hiked the best part of the trail. This is a really pretty hike in late September or early October when the leaves are golden, and the point makes an excellent backcountry campsite.

🚶 Cliff Springs

Duration 1 hour round-trip

Distance 1 mile round-trip

Difficulty Easy-moderate

Start/Finish Cliff Springs Trailhead, Cape Royal Rd

Transportation Car

Summary While this sweet little trail leads to a lovely hidden dell, stretches can be tricky to negotiate and it's not a particularly pleasant hike. Fortunately, it's short.

Look for the trailhead directly across the road from a small pullout on a curve 0.3

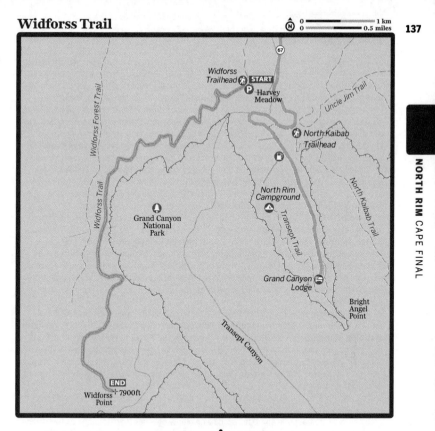

miles from Cape Royal. The trail immediately heads sharply downhill, over loose rock and through the woods. In about five minutes, you'll come to a stone **ancestral Puebloan granary**, used by the ancestral Puebloans to store corn, beans and squash. The path then makes its way through dry, barren pines and along a short, rocky descent into a ravine. It hugs the wall of a narrow side canyon, passing under the shade of a boulder overhang, for about 10 minutes to its end.

At **Cliff Springs**, a tiny trickle emerges from the ground, forming a large puddle fringed with ferns and verdant thistle, and a huge, flat rock, cooled by steady breezes, offers a shaded spot to sit. The view here is strikingly different from other North Rim trails. You are actually hidden in the canyon, as opposed to sitting on the canyon's edge, and you don't get a sense of the massive vista that so many overlooks boast.

Cape Final

Duration 2 hours round-trip

Distance 4 miles round-trip

Difficulty Easy

Start/Finish Cape Final Trail Trailhead, Cape Royal Rd

Transportation Car

Summary Forested walk to jutting rock over the canyon, with spectacular views.

Hike this trail for the destination, not the hike. It's so dry, with nothing but brown ponderosa and brittle needles for most of the hike, that it feels like you're walking through a box of kindling, and what you see at the trailhead is what you'll see for just about the entire hike. But it's almost completely flat, quite easy, and you're rewarded with an amazing canyon overlook.

TOROWEAP

One of the park's most impressive overlooks, Toroweap (also known as Tuweep) offers a landscape and views unlike anywhere else on the North Rim. Its 4552ft elevation, lower than either rim, supports piñon, junipers, cacti and small flowering desert plants, and sheer cliffs drop directly into the canyon and the Colorado River below. But Toroweap is not for everyone. It sits 150 miles from the North Rim Entrance Gate, requires at least two hours on a rough desert dirt road, there are no facilities and it's almost unbearably hot and dry during the summer. (*Toroweap* is, in fact, a Paiute term meaning 'dry or barren valley.') For those who venture out here, however, Toroweap promises a Grand Canyon experience like nothing else. You literally have to crawl on your belly to see the river below, and there are no guardrails. Lava Falls, perhaps the roughest water in the canyon, is visible 1.5 miles downstream, and Vulcans Throne, basalt remnants of a cinder cone eruption 74,000 years ago, rises from the Esplanade Platform. Across the canyon is the Hualapai Reservation and 25 miles east sits the mouth of Havasu Canyon, home to the Havasupai.

The most reliable way to get here is to drive 7 miles west of Fredonia on Hwy 389 and look for a dirt road and the sign 'Toroweap.' Take this road 55 miles south to the **Tuweep Ranger Station**, which is staffed year-round. **Tuweep Campground**, a free, first-come first-served primitive campground offering nine sites, lies 5.4 miles beyond the ranger station and a mile before the rim. Call up to four months in advance to reserve the group site that sleeps between seven and eleven people. A backcountry permit is required for camping beyond the designated camping area, but Toroweap does not require a park entrance fee.

About 46 miles after the turn onto BLM 109 from Hwy 389, turn west onto Mt Trumbull Rd and head 3 miles to **Nampaweap Petroglyphs**, inside **Grand Canyon-Parashant National Monument**. A small parking lot marks the short walk to the petroglyphs. Once at Toroweap, a few moderate and sparsely marked hikes offer chances to stretch your legs. The 2.9-mile **Esplanade Loop Trail** begins at the campground. For a shorter hike, try the easy **Saddle Horse Canyon Trail**, a 1.6-mile round-trip to the canyon rim. The easy-to-miss trailhead is 0.3 miles south of the Tuweep Campground.

The road to Toroweap, notorious for flattening tires, keeps garages in Kanab in business, and a tow can cost upwards from $1000! Drive under 25mph to minimize your chances, have at least one spare tire, and bring plenty of water (there is none at Toroweap, and shade is scarce). The ranger is not always available, and cell service is spotty at best.

After the initial, moderate 10-minute incline, the trail levels off. In about a half hour, a short side trail veers left to a beautiful view – take a few minutes to rehydrate, and return to the main trail. There is one more view before the trail narrows, turns rocky and heads a couple of minutes downhill. The ponderosa give way to piñon, sagebrush and cliffrose, and a flat, rocky triangle roughly 25ft by 25ft extends into the canyon with incredible views. Hike five more minutes through cactus and scramble up some boulders to **Cape Final**. Here, a small, rocky overlook sits at the edge of the canyon, offering a 270-degree view of lower Marble Canyon, Eastern Grand Canyon and one of the canyon's most famous formations, Vishnu Temple. The ease of this hike makes it great for children, but it's a frighteningly dangerous overlook and there are no guardrails.

🏃 Transept Trail

Duration 45 minutes one way

Distance 1.5 miles one way

Difficulty Easy

Start Grand Canyon Lodge

Finish North Rim Campground

Transportation Car

Summary Conveniently connecting Grand Canyon Lodge to the campground, this rocky dirt path with moderate inclines follows the rim and meanders through the aspen and ponderosa pine.

From the bottom of the steps off the Grand Canyon Lodge sun porch, follow the trail along the rim to the right. This is particularly nice in the evening, as you can relax in the woods and watch the sun set across a side canyon. In about 15 minutes, you'll come to a log bench with a quiet, lovely view of the canyon. With plenty of room to run, this is a nice spot for a picnic with children. From here, the trail veers from the edge and the path becomes relatively level, more a walk through the woods than a hike. The trail passes a small **ancient Puebloan site** and several viewpoints before reaching the rim-view tent sites of the campground, and the general store beyond. If hiking the trail from the campground to the lodge, look for the trailhead behind the general store.

🏃 Point Imperial

Duration 2 hours round-trip

Distance 4 miles round-trip

Difficulty Easy

Start/Finish Point Imperial Trailhead

Transportation Car

Summary Forested walk to jutting rock over the canyon with spectacular views.

From the Point Imperial parking lot this trail heads northeast along the rim, veers through areas burned by the 2000 fire and ends at the park's northern border, where it connects with the backcountry Nankoweap Trail and US Forest Service (USFS) roads. Expect to see a haunting landscape of blackened remains of burned forest mixed with tender regrowth and emerging meadows, and keep an eye out for the white-tailed Kaibab squirrel and mule-deer. Though this quiet trail rolls gently along the rim and through the woods, the high elevation (8800ft) can make it seem more difficult. Unlike other trails on the North Rim, it doesn't lead to a spectacular overlook and doesn't form a loop. You'll need to retrace your steps to return to the Point Imperial parking lot.

🏃 Clear Creek Trail

Duration 5 hours one way

Distance 8.4 miles one way

Difficulty Moderate-difficult

Start North Kaibab Trail, 0.3 miles north of Phantom Ranch

Finish Clear Creek

Transportation Foot

Summary Side hike off the North Kaibab (p141) offers spectacular views and backcountry camping.

In excellent condition and easy to follow, the enjoyable Clear Creek Trail is one of few inner-canyon trails on the north side of the Colorado and easily the most popular inner-canyon hike. Built in 1935, it was originally created as a mule trail so visitors to Phantom Ranch could access a side canyon and do some trout fishing in the stocked creek. The views into the gorge and across the canyon are magnificent. Even the first few miles provide gorgeous views, so hiking a couple of miles and turning around it makes a lovely day hike from Phantom Ranch or Bright Angel Campground. Be warned, however, that because it lies on the south-facing slope the entire trail bears the brunt of the sun from sunrise to sunset. It is unspeakably hot during the summer, and there's no shade or water anywhere. Bring plenty of water and get an early start.

Pick up the trail 0.3 mile north of Phantom Ranch. Heading east off the North Kaibab, the trail switchbacks up to the base of Sumner Butte, and in just under one mile stone benches at **Phantom Overlook** offer a pleasant rest and view of Phantom Ranch. The trail levels for a bit, offers spectacular views of the river, then ascends to the Tonto Platform, climbing just over 1000ft over the first 1.7 miles. It then meanders along the contours and canyon folds, passing beneath

---

TASTE OF THE CANYON INTERIOR

Except for the handful of hard-core wilderness trails into the canyon, the only option for hiking the canyon interior on the North Rim is the overnight North Kaibab Trail (p141). For a day hike you can stop at various points and turn around. Even a short jaunt gives a feel for the distinct world below the rim.

Coconino Overlook (1.4 miles, 1 hour round-trip) Flat Coconino Sandstone on the canyon edge.

Supai Tunnel (4 miles, 3 hours round-trip) Red-rock tunnel with seasonal water.

Redwall Bridge (5.2 miles, 4 hours round-trip) Wooden bridge crosses Roaring Springs Canyon.

Roaring Springs (9.4 miles, 8-9 hours round-trip) Primary source of water for both rims.

Zoroaster and Brahma Temples on the left, before dropping to the streambed and ending at a dry tributary creek. You need to hike the drainage about 100ft down to the lovely little cottonwood-fringed **backcountry campground** alongside tiny Clear Creek. You can spend the night with a backcountry permit, or retrace your steps to Phantom Ranch.

Several rough trails follow the creek's tributaries from the campground, and there's a 6-mile scramble along the creek to the Colorado River. The northeast fork of Clear Creek leads up to **Cheyava Falls**, but it only flows in the spring after heavy snowfall and it's 10 miles round-trip from Clear Creek. Do not attempt any side-hikes without a map, and always check conditions with rangers before setting out.

🚶 Ken Patrick Trail

Duration 6 hours one way

Distance 10 miles one way

Difficulty Moderate-difficult

Start North Kaibab Trail parking area

Finish Point Imperial

Transportation Car

Summary Offering rim and forest views, this challenging trail ascends and descends numerous ravines as it winds through an old, deep forest, crosses Cape Royal Rd after 7 miles and continues for another 3 miles to Point Imperial.

The trail starts with a gentle climb into the woods and winds through gambel oak, ponderosa pine, white fir and aspen woodland. Views are intermittent, offering quick glimpses of Roaring Springs Canyon. The trail sees a lot of mule traffic, and it shows – particularly on the first mile, where the soft dirt path, worn into sandy grooves by hooves and softened by mule urine, can be smelly and hard on the feet. After a mile the mules head off on the Uncle Jim Trail, while the Ken Patrick veers to the left. Beyond this junction the trail grows increasingly serene, at times faint but still discernible, and involves several difficult uphill stretches.

For excellent views and a shorter, easier, mule-free walk, start at Point Imperial and hike 3 miles to Cape Royal Rd, and turn around. This stretch is the steepest but also the prettiest and the quietest. The trail alternates between shady conifer forests and panoramic views of Nankoweap Canyon, the

Ken Patrick & Uncle Jim Trails

Little Colorado River gorge, Marble Platform and the Painted Desert, and the San Francisco Peaks far to the south. Allow four hours for this round-trip journey.

🚶 Uncle Jim Trail

Duration 3 hours round-trip

Distance 5 miles round-trip

Difficulty Easy-moderate

Start/Finish North Kaibab Trail parking area

Transportation Car

Summary Wooded loop to a canyon overlook.

This spur trail – named for a hunting advocate and forest-service warden who shot hundreds of mountain lions on the North Rim to protect resident deer – shares the Ken Patrick Trailhead. The two trails are the same for the first mile, then Uncle Jim heads right. After a bit of down and up, the trail soon reaches the 2-mile loop out to the point – it makes little difference if you go left or right. Near the tie-up area for mules at **Uncle Jim Point**, you'll have a terrific view of the North Kaibab switchbacks, Roaring Springs, the Walhalla Plateau and the South Rim. Tree trunks carved into chairs and stools offer a perfect resting spot before your return. Note that this trail is also used by mules.

🚶 Bridle Trail

Duration 40 minutes one-way

Distance 1.2 miles one-way

Difficulty Easy

Start Grand Canyon Lodge

Finish North Kaibab Trailhead

Transportation Car

Summary Hard-packed utilitarian trail and the only one in the park that allows dogs and bicycles.

This uninspiring trail offers visitors a means of walking from the lodge to the campground, and on to the North Kaibab Trailhead. It hugs the road for 1 mile to the campground before climbing a bit up through the woods to the North Kaibab parking area.

OVERNIGHT HIKES

Even the most able-bodied hikers emerge from the pines after a day hike on the North Kaibab and collapse, exhausted and hot, on the stone wall by the trailhead. The 3 miles just below the rim are steep switchback after steep switchback of grinding haul, with no shade and no relief from the heat, made all the more draining by the pools of mule urine blocking the trail. It's not so bad going down, but coming back up is tough – time your hike so you're not tackling this section during the heat of the day. The following description includes an overnight about halfway down the trail. With a dawn departure, you could hike down to the river in one day. Note that the trail drops 4170ft over 7.4 miles from the rim to Cottonwood Campground, but from Cottonwood it levels off to a pleasant 1680ft decline over 7.4 miles.

The clearly marked trailhead lies about 2 miles north of Grand Canyon Lodge. The modest parking lot often fills soon after dawn; you can also walk from the lodge or campground on the Bridle Trail or reserve a spot on the hikers' shuttle. Potable water is available mid-May through mid-October at Supai Tunnel, Roaring Springs and Cottonwood Campground (6.8 miles from the rim), and year-round at Phantom Ranch (at the canyon bottom). Rangers staff Phantom Ranch year-round, and Cottonwood Campground from mid-May through mid-October. The trail remains open year-round, even though the North Rim closes. Snowshoes may be necessary for the upper elevations, and the trail can be dangerous due to ice and snow. If you emerge from the canyon when the North Rim is closed, turn left out of the parking lot towards seasonal rangers – otherwise it's more than 40 miles to civilization. See the boxed text on p145 for information on the rigorous unmaintained trails into the canyon.

Backcountry permits ($10 per permit, plus $5 per camper below the rim and $5 per group above the rim) are required for overnight hiking, overnight camping at rim sites beyond North Rim Campground, and camping below the rim. Passes are available on the first of the month, four months prior to the proposed start month. The North Rim Backcountry Office reserves a limited number of last-minute walk-up permits for Cottonwood Campground, and maintains a waiting list for other sites, available in person only. Go to www.nps.gov/grca/planyour visit/backcountry-permit.htm for the rather complicated details on securing passes and the various regulations.

🏃 North Kaibab Trail

Duration 9 hours down, 12 hours up

Distance 14.2 miles one way

Difficulty Difficult

Start North Kaibab Trailhead

Finish Colorado River

Transportation Car or hikers' shuttle

Summary Spectacular two-day inner-canyon trek includes creekside stretches, strenuous switchbacks and a cottonwood-fringed campground.

DAY 1: NORTH KAIBAB TRAILHEAD TO COTTONWOOD CAMPGROUND
4½ HOURS; 6.8 MILES

The sandy trail begins at 8250ft, under the shade of aspens and pines. Within 10 minutes, the trail emerges from the trees and opens up to canyon views. At **Coconino Overlook** (7450ft), about 25 minutes from the trailhead, a flat ledge offers clear views of Roaring Springs and Bright Angel Canyon.

Forty minutes or so later, the trail comes to a tree-shaded glen with a seasonal water tap and pit toilets, the turn-around for half-day mule trips. Just around a bend is **Supai Tunnel** (6800ft), a short red corridor blasted through the rock when the trail was built in the 1930s. On the other side of the tunnel, views open to an intimidating set of switchbacks beside a knuckle-biting drop-off. It's a tough descent along the switchbacks to **Redwall Bridge** (6100ft). The bridge, built in 1966 when more than 14in of rain fell over

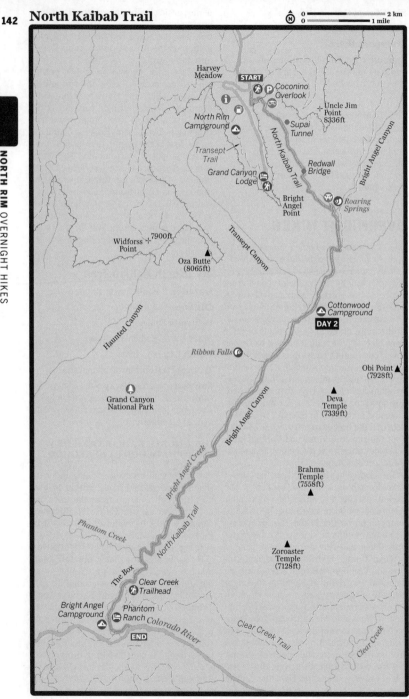

36 hours and washed away huge sections of the North Kaibab Trail, crosses Roaring Springs Canyon. Once you cross the bridge, the trail thins. It hugs the canyon wall to the right and hovers above dramatic sheer drops to the left.

A little over a mile after the bridge, you'll reach the cascading waterfall of **Roaring Springs** (5200ft) itself; take the short detour to the left, where you'll find picnic tables and a pool to cool your feet. Seasonal water is available at the restrooms or 10 minutes down the trail at the **Pumphouse Residence**. New York City–born Grand Canyon artist Bruce Aiken (www.bruce aiken.com) lived and worked here as the pump operator from 1973 until his retirement in 2006. Park rangers now live here during the summer only.

From Roaring Springs, the trail follows the small and inviting **Bright Angel Creek** 2.1 miles to **Cottonwood Campground** (4080ft). Here, tall cottonwoods offer a shaded spot to relax along the creek. It's a beautiful spot and a welcome oasis after the scorching canyon descent, but the campsites themselves are not shaded. The campground provides drinking water (May 15 to October 15), pit toilets, a phone, a ranger station and an emergency medical facility.

DAY 2: COTTONWOOD CAMPGROUND TO COLORADO RIVER
4 HOURS; 7.3 MILES

From the campground, the trail levels off considerably. The steepest grind is over, and it's a gentle downhill walk along Bright Angel Creek to the Colorado River.

After about 30 minutes, you'll see a turnoff on the right for **Ribbon Falls** (3720ft; 8.3 miles one way from rim). Take this 0.3-mile spur across the bridge and up to the falls. Here, water mists 100ft over moss-covered stone to a small pool surrounded by fern, columbine, and monkey flower, creating a hidden fairyland. Standing underneath feels like a cold shower, and it's an ideal spot to rest. Retrace your steps to the main trail, and continue to **The Box**, a narrow passage between 2000ft walls that tower over the trail. For about 4 miles, the trail, shaded by canyon walls but with no breeze, follows the stream along almost flat ground. It passes over several bridges before opening up about 20 minutes before **Phantom Ranch** (2546ft), **Bright Angel Campground** and, a few minutes later, the **Colorado River** (2400ft).

OTHER ACTIVITIES

Like everything on the North Rim, activities here are friendly, low-key affairs. If you're here for a few days, park rangers will know you by name.

⚙️ Cycling

Because bikes are allowed on blacktop roads only, options for biking on the North Rim are limited to Hwy 67 into the park, Point Imperial Rd, and Cape Royal Rd. The two exceptions are the 17-mile dirt road to Point Sublime and the utilitarian Bridle Trail that follows the highway from the lodge to the North Kaibab Trailhead. **North Rim Outfitter Station** (⏱7am-7pm, closed mid-Oct–mid-May), in the gas station next to the campground, rents surrey, mountain and tandem bikes as well as jogging strollers. Prices vary.

In the surrounding Kaibab National Forest just outside the park entrance, bikes are allowed on a seemingly endless network of forest roads and all trails, including the spectacular 18-mile **Rainbow Rim Trail** connecting five remote overlooks.

Mule Rides

Family-run **Canyon Trail Rides** (☏435-679-8665; www.canyonrides.com; ⏱mid-May–mid-Oct) take reservations anytime for the upcoming year. Unlike mule trips on the South Rim, however, you can usually book a trip upon your arrival at the park. Just duck inside the Grand Canyon Lodge to the **Mule Desk** (☏928-638-9875; ⏱7am-5pm). Mule rides from the North Rim don't go into the canyon as far as the Colorado River, but the half-day trip gives a taste of life below the rim, doesn't follow precipitous canyon ledges, and is suitable even for folks a bit shy around horses and scared of heights.

One Hour Rim of the Grand Canyon (7yr age limit, 220lb weight limit; $40) Wooded ride to an overlook. Several departures daily.

Half-Day Trip to Uncle Jim's Point (10yr age limit, 220lb weight limit; $75; ⏱7:30am & 12:30pm) Follow the Ken Patrick Trail through the woods.

Half-Day Canyon Mule Trip to Supai Tunnel (10yr age limit, 200lb weight limit; $75; ⏱7:30am & 12:30pm) Descend 1450ft into the canyon along the North Kaibab Trail.

Ranger Programs

Ranger programs are small, informal gatherings that reflect the summer-camp mood of the North Rim. Several afternoon and evening talks are held around the fireplace on the sun porch of Grand Canyon Lodge – a highlight of any visit. When skies are clear, guests gather to gaze through telescopes while a ranger describes the night sky. Other programs are conducted at the campground amphitheater, inside Grand Canyon Lodge, or at the Walhalla Overlook parking lot. *The Guide* publishes a seasonal schedule, and daily events are posted at the visitor center and at the campground.

Cross-Country Skiing

Once the first heavy snowfall closes Hwy 67 into the park (as early as late October or as late as January), you can cross-country ski the 44 miles to the rim and camp at the campground (no water, pit toilets). Camping is permitted elsewhere with a backcountry permit, available from rangers year-round. You can ski any of the rim trails, though none are groomed. The closest ski rental is in Flagstaff.

SLEEPING

The closest lodging outside the park is Kaibab Lodge, 18 miles from the rim, or Jacob Lake Inn, 44 miles from the rim. Beyond that, you'll have to drive 78 miles north to Kanab, Utah, 85 miles northeast to Marble Canyon or 125 miles northeast to Page, Arizona. Contact the backcountry office or Pipe Spring National Monument for permits to camp at remote North Rim overlooks or at backcountry sites below the rim; you can camp for free without a permit anywhere in the bucolic North Kaibab National Forest, just outside the park gate.

Grand Canyon Lodge   HISTORIC HOTEL **$$**
(☑928-638-2611 same-day reservation, 877-386-4383 reservations up to 12 months in advance, 480-337-1320 reservations from outside the USA; www.foreverlodging.com; r for 2 $116, cabin for 2 $121-187, $10 for each additional guest over 15yr; ☺mid-May–mid-Oct; 🐾🖶) Made of wood, Kaibab limestone and glass, with a 50ft-high sunroom, a spacious rimside dining room and panoramic canyon views, this is the canyon as it was meant to be. The original lodge, designed by Gilbert Stanley Underwood and built in 1928 by the Union Pacific Railroad in anticipation of a direct train link to the North Rim, burned down in 1932. It was rebuilt in 1937, but the train and masses of tourists never did come. The lodge, listed on the *National Register of Historic Places*, remains today much as it was then. Two small stone sun porches, each with Adirondack chairs and one with a massive fireplace, sit directly on the canyon edge. It just doesn't get any better than sitting here with a cold beer after a long, dusty hike, watching the sun set over the canyon. There are no rooms in the lodge itself.

Rustic Frontier cabins and Pioneer cabins cluster together, separated by patches of dirt and dirt paths, on the west side of the road just before the lodge. Frontier cabins, which actually occupy half a cabin, sleep three and include a double and a twin bed and a tiny bathroom (shower only). Pioneer cabins, renovated in 2009, offer two small rooms sleeping up to six (one with a queen bed, the other with a bunk-bed and a pull-out sleeper futon) connected by a bathroom (shower only). On the other side of the road, the bright, spacious and recommended Western cabins, made of logs and buffered by trees and grass, provide two queen beds, full bathrooms, gas fireplaces, refrigerators and porches with wicker rocking chairs. The best are numbers 304, 307, 308, 310, 320 and 318, and the worst (next to the visitor center) are numbers 356, 352 and 348. Four incredible rim-view Western cabins boast spectacular views of the Grand Canyon. They cost only $10 more than a standard Western cabin, but you'll need to call the last week of May the year *before* you want to go if you want one – they book as soon as the park starts accepting reservations for the next season. About 0.5 miles up the road are 40 simple motel rooms, each with a queen bed. No rooms or cabins have air-conditioning.

North Rim Campground   CAMPGROUND **$**
(☑877-444-6777, 928-638-7814; www.recreation.gov; sites $18-25; 🐾) Set back from the road beneath ponderosa, 1.5 miles north of Grand Canyon Lodge, North Rim Campground offers pleasant sites on level ground blanketed in pine needles. Sites 11, 14, 15, 16, 18 and 19 overlook the Transept (a side canyon) and cost a little more. Their proximity to the edge makes these sites unsuitable for children, and while they are beautiful they are

Experienced hikers with extensive wilderness experience and GPS navigational systems will find several unmaintained and roughly marked North Rim trails to tackle. These are intense, interior-canyon death traps that should not be attempted by the average canyon visitor.

The **Nankoweap Trail** descends from Marble Canyon 5240ft to the Colorado River. Considered by many to be the toughest hike in the canyon, the grueling 14-mile trail can be tricky to follow and requires a fair amount of maneuvering along steep ledges. Nankoweap Creek, 10.6 miles below the rim, provides a resplendent green oasis for back-country camping.

From Toroweap, the **Lava Falls Route** plummets 2540ft over a distance of 1.5 miles to the Colorado River. Do not try this treacherous, shadeless hike, described by the park service as 'one of the hottest, steepest, loosest, scariest chutes in the canyon' in the summer, when temperatures can reach upwards of 115°F.

Other trails include the **Tuckup Trail**, **Bill Hall Trail**, **Thunder River Trail** and **North Bass Trail**. Good day-hike options include Bill Hall 1 mile down to Muav Cabin, or North Bass 1.3 miles to Monument Point. Contact the backcountry office for maps, guides and current conditions.

---

particularly windy. Site 10, backed by woods, and site eight, nestled in a little aspen grove, are the nicest of the standard sites. The least desirable, with views of the bathrooms, are sites 20, 22, 50 and 51. Reservations are accepted up to six months in advance; hiker/cyclist sites are usually available without reservation. There are no hookups, and stays are limited to seven days per season. The campground remains open once snow closes the road from Jacob Lake, but there are no services (pit toilets only), no water and you must have a backcountry permit (available from on-site rangers after the backcountry office closes).

EATING & DRINKING

Part of the North Rim's charm lies in the striking contrast between the intimacy of its facilities and the wildness of the canyon. With only one restaurant, one cafeteria and one saloon, you'll find yourself bumping into the same folks, sharing stories over a glass of wine. Visitors can contact the following establishments through the **North Rim Switchboard** (☎928-638-2612, ☎928-638-2611).

TOP CHOICE **Grand Canyon Lodge**
Dining Room AMERICAN $$
(mains $12-24; ☺6:30-10am, 11:30am-2:30pm, 4:45-9:45pm, closed mid-Oct–mid-May) Some people get downright belligerent if they can't get a window seat, but the canyon-view win-

dows are so huge, it really doesn't matter where you sit. While the solid menu includes buffalo steak and several vegetarian options, don't expect culinary memories. Make reservations in advance of your arrival to guarantee a spot for dinner (reservations are not accepted for breakfast or lunch). With a day's notice, a boxed lunch can be ready for pick up at 6:30am. If you're calling between January 1 and April 15 to make reservations for the upcoming season, call ☎928-645-6865.

Grand Canyon Cookout
Experience AMERICAN $$
(adult $30-35, 6-15yr $12-22, under 6yr free; ☺6-7:45pm Jun-Sep) Chow down on BBQ, skillet cornbread and southwestern baked beans, served buffet style, while husband and wife Woodie and Cleda Jane entertain with Western songs and cheesy jokes. It sounds corny, but it's a lot of fun, very old-school national park and great for kids. A little train is supposed to shuttle folks from the lodge to the chuck wagon tent next to the campground, but most of the time it doesn't work so they have to use a van, or you can just walk the mile up the Bridle Trail. Buy tickets in advance, usually available same-day.

Roughrider Saloon & Coffee Shop BAR $
(snacks $2-5; ☺5:30-10:30am & 11:30am-11pm, closed mid-Oct–mid-May) If you're up to catch the sunrise or enjoy an early-morning hike, stop at this small saloon on the boardwalk beside the lodge for an espresso, a fresh-made cinnamon roll and a banana. Starting at 11:30am the saloon serves beer, wine and

ℹ️ TACKLING THE ELEVATION

Hikes and overlooks on the North Rim range from 8000ft to almost 9000ft in elevation, and it can take a couple days to acclimate. Simply drinking lots of water can often prevent headaches, nausea, shortness of breath and exhaustion, all symptoms of elevation sickness. There is an ice-maker (free) and a cold-water faucet for drinking water behind the visitors center. If you need ice to fill your cooler, the North Rim General Store sells bagged ice.

mixed drinks, as well as hot dogs and Anasazi chili. Teddy Roosevelt memorabilia lines the walls, honoring his role in the history of the park. This is the only bar in the lodge, so if you want to enjoy a cocktail on the sun porch or in your room, pick it up here.

Deli in the Pines   CAFETERIA $
(mains $4-8; ⊙7am-9pm, closed mid-Oct–mid-May) This small cafeteria beside the lodge serves surprisingly good food. The limited menu includes sandwiches, pizza and chili. There are a few indoor tables, but you're better off taking your plate outside to enjoy the high mountain air.

North Rim General Store   MARKET $
(⊙7am-8pm, closed mid-Oct–mid-May; 📶) Adjacent to the campground and just over a mile from the lodge, the general store primarily services the needs of campers. You'll find canned soup, instant oatmeal, pasta, beer, wine and frozen hamburgers and steak, as well as picnic supplies like bread, cheese, peanut butter and, if you're lucky, a few fresh fruits and vegetables. There's also camping gear, including tents and first-aid basics, and it's the only place to find children's Tylenol.

INFORMATION

All services on the North Rim are closed from mid-October through mid-May, but rangers are always on hand. Day-trippers are welcome year-round (no charge). You can stay at the campground (with water and a bathroom but no services) until the first heavy snowfall closes the road from Jacob Lake; after that you'll need a backcountry permit (available directly from winter rangers after the backcountry office closes).

Public showers and laundry facilities are next to the campground.

ATMs The only ATMs are at the Rough Rider Saloon and the North Rim General Store.

Emergency (📞911 or 9-911; ⊙24hr) EMT-certified rangers respond; dial from your cabin.

Kane County Hospital (📞435-644-5811; 355 N Main St, Kanab; ⊙emergency room 24hr) The closest medical facility, 78 miles away in Kanab, Utah.

North Rim Backcountry Office (📞928-638-7875; ⊙8am-noon & 1-5pm, closed mid-Oct–mid-May) Backcountry permits on and below the rim.

North Rim Grand Canyon Guide Pick up this publication when you arrive at the gate or in the visitor center.

North Rim Switchboard (📞928-638-2612) Call to reach all facilities on the North Rim, including the Grand Canyon Lodge front desk and restaurant, the saloon, gift shop, gas station, cafeteria and general store. Cell service is shaky at best; Verizon provides the best coverage.

North Rim Visitor Center (📞928-638-7864; ⊙8am-6pm, closed mid-Oct–mid-May) Maps, books, trail guides and current conditions.

Postal Window (⊙8am-5pm Mon-Fri, closed mid-Oct–mid-May) Sits next to the Rough Rider Saloon.

Wi-fi (Grand Canyon Lodge, North Rim General Store) The most dependable connections are from the store.

GETTING THERE & AROUND

There is no public transportation to the North Rim, and once there the only way to get around is by car, bicycle, motorcycle or foot. Both the 1.2-mile Transept Trail and a 1-mile leg of the Bridle Trail link the lodge and campground, and the Bridle Trail continues a mile or so to the North Kaibab Trailhead.

Car & Motorcycle

Chevron Service Station (⊙8am-5pm, 24hr pay at the pump, closed mid-Oct–mid-May) Next to the campground, has gas and sells oil, but does not have a garage or towing services. The closest full-service garage and 24-hour towing is located in Kanab, 78 miles north of Grand Canyon Lodge.

Shuttles

Hikers' Shuttle (⊙5:45am & 7:10am, seasonal variations) Complimentary shuttle takes folk from the Grand Canyon Lodge 2 miles to the North Kaibab Trailhead twice daily. You must sign up for it at the front desk; if no one signs up the night before, it will not run. Note that there is no service from North Kaibab Trailhead back to the lodge.

Trans-Canyon Shuttle (☏928-638-2820; one way/round-trip $80/150) Departs from the Grand Canyon Lodge at 7am daily to arrive at the South Rim at 11:30am. Cash only. Reserve at least two weeks in advance.

BEYOND THE NORTH RIM

The North Rim sits on the southern edge of the spectacular 1010-sq-mile North Kaibab Plateau, refreshingly cool and green at 8000ft and surrounded below by red-rock scenery, miles of trails and vast expanses of desert wilderness. You can easily spend a week exploring the dramatic diversity of the region, boating on Lake Powell one day, hiking a slot canyon the next and biking through the aspen and meadows of the Kaibab another. Combine a visit to the North Rim with Zion and Bryce National Parks (see Lonely Planet's *Zion & Bryce Canyon National Parks*), both within a few hours north of the park.

Kaibab National Forest (North Rim)

☏928 / ELEV 7900FT-9000FT

Hwy Alt 89 (also known as 89A) winds 5000ft up from the burning canyons of the Paria Canyon-Vermilion Cliffs Wilderness, past the Kaibab National Forest boundary and through the eerie black-timbered remains of a 2001 forest fire, to the outpost of **Jacob Lake**. Nearly everyone heading up to the canyon stops here, piling out of dusty vehicles to breathe in the mountain air, shop for canyon souvenirs and grab a cookie or ice cream before continuing south on Hwy 67 through the meadows, rolling hills, aspen and ponderosa pine of the Kaibab National Forest on their way to the North Rim. On the 30 miles between Jacob Lake and the park entrance, dirt forest-service roads on either side lure curious travelers, offering yellow canopies in the fall, wildflowers in the summer and miles of opportunities for hiking, biking, snowmobiling and cross-country skiing. While most folk simply pass through on their way to the rim, the Kaibab is an idyllic setting in its own right and well worth a couple days to enjoy.

Sights & Activities

The 68,340-acre **Kanab Creek Wilderness**, comprised of classic canyonland formations cut by Kanab Creek, lies in the southwestern corner of the Kaibab and abuts the western edge of the Kaibab Plateau. Here you'll find many desert trails for experienced hikers; the 21.5-mile **Snake Gulch** rewards hikers with loads of incredible petroglyphs. On the southeast corner, abutting the eastern edge of the Kaibab Plateau, is the **Saddle Mountain Wilderness**. Stop by the Kaibab Plateau Visitor Center in Jacob Lake for maps and information on the network of **hiking trails** throughout the region. In the winter, you can **cross-country ski** or **snowmobile** throughout the Kaibab. The Jacob Lake Inn is open year-round, but the 44-mile road from Jacob Lake to the North Rim Lodge (which is closed from mid-October through mid-May) is not plowed and there are no services north of Jacob Lake.

TOP CHOICE **Marble View**   LOOKOUT

A favorite of the many Kaibab Forest overlooks, this viewpoint makes a spectacular picnic or camping spot. From the 1-acre meadow, covered with Indian paintbrush and hiding Coconino sandstone fossils, views extend over the eastern edge of the canyon to the paper-flat expanse beyond. This is not a quintessential Grand Canyon overlook that you see in postcards and Grand Canyon books. Instead, you're looking down where the Colorado first cuts into the rocks from Lees Ferry, at the point where it only hints at the rapids and canyon beyond. The road seems to end at an overlook; be sure to take the narrow road through the woods to the right about 0.25 miles to Marble View.

East Rim View   HIKE

With views east into the Saddle Mountain Wilderness, Marble Canyon and the Vermilion Cliffs, this easily accessible overlook (elevation 8810ft) is suitable for strollers and wheelchairs. In fact, it's so easy to reach, it's amazing there aren't more people out here. East Rim doesn't offer the inviting picnic and camping opportunities of Marble View, and the views don't inspire comparable awe, but it's a beautiful spot. From the overlook you can hike the **East Rim Trail** 1.5 miles down into the Saddle Mountain Wilderness, and from there connect to longer hikes. The **Arizona Trail** runs past the overlook; turn right to take this trail about 6.5 miles to the

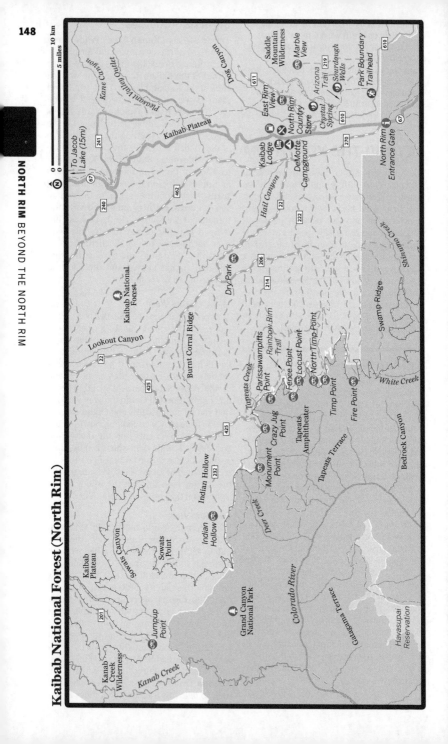

Kaibab National Forest (North Rim)

Park Boundary Trailhead. Look for the signed turn-off just on Hwy 67 just south of Kaibab Lodge; a parking lot with a bathroom is about 3 miles up a gravel road off the highway.

Arizona Trail: Park Boundary Trailhead to Crystal Spring HIKE

This narrow meander through wide meadows bordered by aspen and ponderosa is a hidden gem of the North Kaibab. There are no big views or cliffs, but plenty of room to run and scramble. Keep your eye out for fossils in the rocks along the trail. Perfect for families, this hike can be shortened considerably by hiking 2.3 miles to **Sourdough Wells** and turning around, or lengthen it by hiking an added 1.5 miles to **East Rim View**. With no grand vista awaiting you at the end, and no one section of the trail more lovely than another, this is the perfect path for strolling as far as you'd like, and then simply turning around. It also makes a great bike ride.

To get to the trailhead, turn east off Hwy 67 onto the well-marked sign for FR 611 toward East Rim View just south of Kaibab Lodge. Drive 1.2 miles to FR610. Turn right and go 4.6 miles to the Park Boundary Trailhead, a small, unmarked pullout on the right. There is a restroom but no water. From here, you can either head 0.2 miles east down the road and catch the trail on the left, after it crosses FR611, or you can head a couple of minutes down the path from the bathroom to a big meadow. The trail heads left toward Sourdough Wells and Crystal Spring, or right about 0.25 miles to the national park border.

Historic Fire Lookouts LOOKOUTS

Three steel towers, all on the National Register of Historic Places, are still used as fire lookouts: built in 1934, **Big Springs** and **Jacob Lake** stand 100ft tall, while **Dry Park** built in 1944, is 120ft tall. You can drive out to any of them and climb up and up and up for great views of the national forest and the Arizona Strip beyond, but be warned that they sway in any kind of wind – not for the faint of heart! Though the lookout rooms at the top are locked, someone staffs them May through October and they'll usually let you in. The easiest to reach is Jacob Lake, as it's on Hwy 67 about one mile south of Jacob Lake Inn.

Rainbow Rim Trail MOUNTAIN BIKING

The Rainbow Rim Trail connects **Parissawampitts, Fence, Locust, North Timp** and **Timp Points**, each a finger of the Kaibab Plateau that sticks out over the Grand Canyon. While the ride is beautiful, meandering through meadows, winding up and down with an elevation change of no more than 250ft and following the canyon edge for stretches at each overlook, none of the viewpoints stand out from one another and each point-to-point stretch drops into a steep side canyon with a bumpy downhill and a bumpy uphill. Less experienced bikers will find themselves walking their bikes for long stretches.

Shorten the ride by biking between any of the five overlooks, each accessed by a forest service road, and then retracing your steps or arranging for a shuttle to return you to your car. This is also an excellent hiking trail.

To get to Timp Point, turn right onto FR 22 0.7 miles south of Kaibab Lodge. Drive 2 miles to FR 270, turn left, and drive 1 mile to FR 222. Turn right and drive 5 miles to FR 206; turn right and go less than 0.25 miles to FR 271. Follow FR 271 for about 8 miles to the end of the road at Timp Point. Forest-service roads to each of the four other overlooks veer off FR 206. To drive to each view you must backtrack 45 minutes to FR 206, drive up or down a few miles to a different forest road, and then drive about 45 minutes back out to the rim. The rough FR 250 connects the overlooks, but it is only for high-clearance vehicles.

Distances from point to point:
» Timp Point to North Timp – 3 miles
» North Timp to Locust – 6.5 miles
» Locust to Fence – 3 miles
» Fence to Parissawampitts – 5.5 miles

Canyon Overlooks LOOKOUTS

Dirt roads veer off Hwy 67 in both directions to overlooks on the edge of the plateau. The drives are lovely, particularly in the fall when the aspen turn or in late summer when wildflowers and tall grass burst out of the meadows, but they are long and bumpy. Even in a 4WD, be prepared to drive at a snail's pace in some spots. Consider tackling the roads to **Fire Point, Crazy Jug, Indian Hollow** and the recommended **Jumpup** overlooks, all of which make nice backcountry camping sites. The five overlooks connected by **Rainbow Rim Trail** may see a few more people, but they have the advantage of excellent hiking and mountain biking from each point.

While they're certainly beautiful, don't expect classic canyon vistas at any of the Kaibab's overlooks; for that, head to the park itself. If you don't have a 4WD or don't fancy tackling the labyrinth of forest-service roads on your own, ask at the Kaibab Lodge about ATV tours to canyon overlooks.

Allen's Trail Rides   HORSEBACK RIDING
(☑435-644-8150) Offers one-hour, two-hour, half-day, full-day and custom-designed overnight or multiday horseback rides through the woods and to overlooks. Children must be at least five years old. Reservations are not required for short rides – just stop by the corrals just south of Jacob Lake Lodge. Prices carry.

Sleeping & Eating

You can camp for free anywhere in the national forest, including canyon overlooks.

Kaibab Lodge   LODGE $$
(☑928-638-2389; www.kaibablodge.com; Hwy 67; r $140-150, cabins $85-180; ☺closed mid-Oct–mid-May; ☎☀) There's something comforting about this lodge, 18 miles from the North Rim, hugged on two sides by a lovely meadow and on a third by ponderosa and aspen forest. It's a simple, quiet, low-key place, where the biggest excitement comes from counting deer that wander from the woods to graze. The accommodation options vary considerably – don't expect down comforters, feather pillows and luxurious bath supplies. The oldest, cabins one to six, offer simple, worn-out decor with wood floors and walls, plain beds and a porch overlooking the meadow. Newer cabins resemble one-room RVs more than cabins, are quite tiny and do not have porches with meadow views. Despite the feeling that you're staying in a room c 1952, or perhaps because of it, the older cabins are a better choice. The recommended and modern Eastview units, bright earthy orange rooms painted with petroglyphs and furnished with rough-hewn wood beds and nightstands, sit in two two-story log buildings. Each unit has a small porch overlooking the woods and field. Most cabins sleep up to four; Sam's Cabin has four beds and sleeps up to six.

A casual restaurant flanked by windows serves basic, tasty fish, burgers and pasta and offers a full bar. Breakfast features whole-wheat pancakes and yogurt with granola,

and it'll prepare a picnic lunch with one night's notice. Ask about ATV tours to canyon overlooks in the Kaibab National Forest.

DeMotte Campground   CAMPGROUND $
(Hwy 67; $17/8 1st/2nd vehicle, per site; ☺closed mid-Oct–mid-May; ☀) This quiet campground nestled in the forest 18 miles north of the North Rim sits on a slight hill with views of the adjacent meadow. Across the street is a small general store with basic supplies, and the restaurant and bar at Kaibab Lodge are within walking distance. The campground is first come, first served – choose a site before heading for the canyon. None of the 38 sites have hookups, and the best sites, on the eastern side of the first loop, sit under aspen and overlook the meadow. The weather dictates when the campground opens and closes for the year; call the Kaibab Plateau Visitor Center (☑928-638-2389).

Jacob Lake Inn   CABINS $$
(☑928-643-7232; www.jacoblake.com; Alt 89 & Hwy 67; r/cabins $119-138/89-103; ☺6:30am-9pm mid-May–mid-Oct, 8am-8pm mid Oct–mid-May; ☎) Accommodations here consist of basic cabins with tiny bathrooms (no bathtubs, TVs or phone) tightly packed amid the ponderosa forest, run-down motel rooms, or spacious doubles in the modern hotel-style building. Some cabins overlook the forest, a two-room family cabin costs $137, and there's a small, bedraggled playground. The busy, almost festive cafe is filled with visitors who are either coming from or heading to the North Rim, 44 miles south. An adjacent ice-cream counter offers diner fare, and the deli makes sandwiches and delicious cookies. Try the Cookie in a Cloud, a cakey cookie topped with marshmallow and chocolate, or the Six Grain, with sunflower seeds and oats.

North Rim Country Store   MARKET $
(☑928-638-2383; Hwy 67; ☺7am-7pm, closed mid-Oct–mid-May) Across Hwy 67 from Kaibab Lodge and DeMotte Campground, 18 miles north of North Rim, this small store and gas station sells a limited selection of groceries, including canned goods, cereal, cheese, wine and beer. In July and August, it may stay open until 8pm or 9pm.

Jacob Lake Campground   CAMPGROUND $
(☑877-444-6777; Alt 89 & Hwy 67; $17 per night; ☺closed Nov 1–mid-May; ☀) Nothing special sights scattered in the Ponderosa pine across from Jacob Lake Inn, 44 miles north of the North Rim.

Kaibab Camper Village CAMPGROUND $
(☑928-643-7804; www.kaibabcampervillage.com; RV sites/tentsites $35/17; ☺closed mid-Oct–mid-May) Set back a half-mile from Hwy 67 on a forest-service road just south of Jacob Lake Inn, this privately run campground offers the only RV hookups on the North Kaibab Plateau. It's friendly and fine if you need a hookup, but with so many idyllic spots in the surrounding national forest where you can pitch a tent for free, there's no reason to camp here except the shower and laundry facilities. The tentsites are crowded and next to an ugly aluminum-sided barn and bathroom.

Information

The Kaibab Lodge, North Rim Country Store and DeMotte campground, the only facilities between Jacob Lake and Grand Canyon Lodge, cluster together 18 miles north of the North Rim and 26 miles south of Jacob Lake. Jacob Lake itself is nothing more than a lodge and restaurant, visitor center, campground and gas station.

Kaibab Plateau Visitor Center (☑928-643-7298; Alt 89 & Hwy 67, Jacob Lake; ☺8am-5pm, closed mid-Oct–mid-May) The USFS visitor center features a small museum and bookstore and has maps on the region's many trails and forest roads.

Getting There & Around

There is no public transportation or shuttle service to or around Jacob Lake and the Kaibab National Forest.

Jacob Lake Inn Chevron (☑928-643-7232; ☺7:30am-8pm, credit-card sales 24hr) Services flat tires and can do basic mechanical work, but the closest towing services are in Fredonia and Kanab.

North Rim Country Store (☺7am-7pm, closed mid-Oct–mid-May) A gas station 26 miles south of Jacob Lake and 18 miles north of Grand Canyon Lodge.

Fredonia

☑435 / POP 1145 / ELEV 4672
Tiny blink-and-you-miss-it Fredonia lies along Alt 89, 72 miles northwest of the rim. There's nothing here for the traveler except the tiny **Grand Canyon Motel** (☑928-643-7646; 175 S Main; r $45; ☜). The welcoming grassy and shaded courtyard at holds a BBQ grill and a few picnic tables, but the interiors of the cute stone cabins that surround it are old and drab. Rooms are kept open for forest service personnel, so they only accept same-day reservations and they can

only be reached after 4pm. If you're looking for a last-minute, cheap place to stay, it's an option, but otherwise head to Kanab. If you need it, **Judd Auto Service** (☑928-643-7726, 623 S Main St) does towing, tire repair and simple mechanical work

Information

Kaibab National Forest District Headquarters (☑928-643-7395; 430 S Main; ☺8am-5pm Mon-Fri) On the main drag as you head to Kanab; from October to May, this is the best source for maps and information on the Kaibab National Forest.

Kanab

☑435 / POP 3804 / ELEV 4925FT
In 1874 Mormons settled remote Kanab, Utah. Hollywood, drawn by the desert backdrop and stunning red-rock formations, descended on the town in the 1920s. It has since served as a location for hundreds of movies and TV shows, including numerous Westerns and episodes of *The Lone Ranger* and *Gunsmoke*. Though the filmmaking craze here faded, the town still flaunts its silver-screen past. Small-town Kanab offers a tidy, pedestrian-friendly downtown, peaceful surroundings and some great food. This is a quiet, sleepy place that closes up early. While not a destination in itself, it offers a quirky taste of the American West and makes a good base for exploring the area.

Sights & Activities

Nestled under the brilliant red rocks on the far side of town and boasting modern facilities, this small city park is one of the most lovely in the Grand Canyon region. There's a playground, tennis courts, and a splash fountain perfect for children (turn the water on by pressing the small button on the shed by the fountain). Next door, the excellent **Kanab City Pool** (☑435-644-8952; $5, under 3yr free, $30 for 10 visits; ☺Mon-Sat seasonally), with a slide and a lap pool, is usually opened for general swimming from noon to 5pm. Mornings are reserved for lessons and lap swimming.

TOP CHOICE **Best Friends Animal Sanctuary** ANIMAL SANCTUARY
(☑435-644-2001; www.bestfriends.org; Angel Canyon, Hwy 89; admission free; ☺visitor center 9:30am-5:30pm, tours 4 times daily; ☜)

Surrounded by more than 33,000 acres of spectacular red-rock desert 5 miles north of Kanab, beautiful Angel Canyon is home to the largest no-kill animal rescue center in the country, housing up to 1700 sick, abused, abandoned and homeless animals from all over the country and the world. All of them, including critters at **Piggy Paradise** and **Horse Haven**, are up for adoption. Minivan tours of the sanctuary stop at **Dogtown**, made famous by the National Geographic show of the same name and home to Michael Vick's pitbulls, **Cat World**, and the strikingly moving hillside pet cemetery dotted with

Kanab

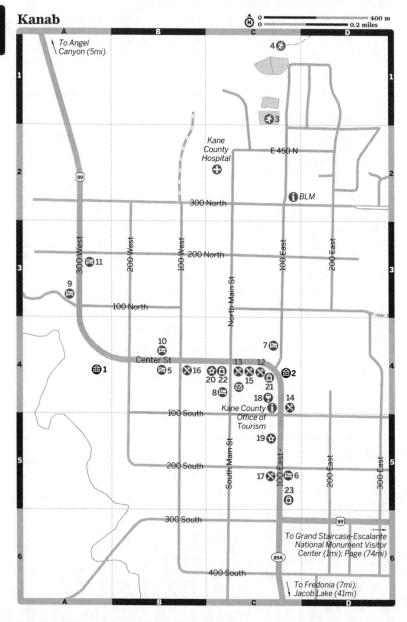

To Angel Canyon (5mi)

Kane County Hospital

E 450 N

BLM

300 North

200 North

100 North

Kane County Office of Tourism

100 South

200 South

300 South

400 South

To Grand Staircase-Escalante National Monument Visitor Center (1mi); Page (74mi)

To Fredonia (7mi); Jacob Lake (41mi)

wind chimes. Though you should call in advance to reserve a spot, walk-ins can usually be accommodated. Head directly to **Bunny House**, **Wild Friends** and **Parrot Garden** for scheduled daily tours of those habitats, and arrange in advance to volunteer for an afternoon, a week or longer; if you're staying at a cabin or cottage on-site and volunteer for at least a half-day, you can borrow a dog, cat or potbelly pig for the night!

Pipe Springs National Monument
HISTORIC SITE

(www.nps.gov/pisp; Hwy 389; admission $5, under 16yr free; ◉7am-5pm Jun-Aug, 8am-5pm Sep-May) Used by pioneers as a resting spot and cattle ranch, this small and quiet oasis in the desert 20 miles southwest of Kanab is both lovely and interesting. Visitors can experience the Old West amid cabins and corrals, an orchard, a pond and a garden. Built by Mormons in 1869 for church tithing and refuge from Indians, the stone **Winsor Castle** has tours every half-hour, and a small **museum** examines the history of Kaibab Paiutes and Mormon settlement. Follow the half-mile **Ridge Trail** for excellent views of the Arizona Strip, Kanab Canyon and the Kaibab Plateau. The visitors center provides backcountry permits camping in Grand Canyon National Park. Head south from Kanab on Hwy 89 to Fredonia, and west on Hwy 389.

Angel Canyon
DRIVING TOUR

During Kanab's Hollywood heyday Angel Canyon became the site of scores of movies and TV shows, including *The Lone Ranger*, Disney's *Apple Dumpling Gang* and *The Outlaw Josey Wales*. A dirt and gravel road winds up and down through Best Friends Animal Sanctuary, offering quintessential red-rock scenery and desert views. Just across from the Best Friends Animal Sanctuary Welcome Center, a dirt path veers east about 0.5 miles down to the **Kanab Creek**, a shallow, clear creek that's excellent for dogs and kids. A mile further, just beyond the horse corral on the left, is **Angel's Landing**. This small natural amphitheater borders a grassy field and makes a perfect picnic spot. To get to Angel Canyon, look for the signs for Best Friends Animal Sanctuary, 5 miles northwest of Kanab on Hwy 89; the road loops 5 miles and reconnects with Hwy 89.

FREE Frontier Movie Town
MUSEUM

(297 W Center St; ◉7:30am-11pm) This tiny, low-key, nonprofit roadside attraction is classic Americana tourism at its best. You have to walk through the gift shop to get to the **Little Hollywood Movie Museum**. Wander through the bunkhouse, saloon and other buildings used in Western movie sets and brush up on such tricks of the trade as short doorways (to make movie stars seem taller). You can a picnic and kick back in the tiny

grassy area while the kids act out movies. In the summer, tourists from around the world don feather boas, buckskin hats (aka coyote costume), Indian headbands and other Western attire and partake in a short Western spoof called *How The West Was Lost*. While this is generally only for tour groups, it's a hoot to watch. Call ahead for times. Winter hours, like so much in Kanab, are determined by mood and demand.

Squaw Trail   HIKING

Accessed just north of Jacob Hamblin Park at the end of 100 East, this short but steep 800ft scramble leads to spectacular views of Kanab and the surrounding desert wilderness. It's about a mile to the city overview; you can continue another 0.5 miles to the top, with 360-degree views, or retrace your steps. This hike is best in spring or fall, when the summer heat has faded and the cottonwoods turn brilliant yellow. Park next to the baseball fields and look for signs. An information kiosk at the trailhead gives directions for linking to trails to the east and west to create a series of loops for up to 6 miles.

Kanab Heritage Museum   MUSEUM

(13 S 100 East; admission by donation; ☺9am-5pm Mon-Fri Memorial Day-Labor Day) For a glimpse into the region's popular history, this small museum is worth a stop. While the few pieces of historical memorabilia aren't particularly riveting, it's fun to browse the 30-plus spiral-bound notebooks filled with movie newspapers, magazine articles, written histories and photographs.

Coral Pink Sand Dunes State Park   PARK

(www.stateparks.utah.gov; admission $6; ☺dawn-dusk; ⊕) Kids and adults alike can climb, slide and roll through coral-colored sand dunes dotted with junipers and piñon pines at this 3700-acre park. Bring spare clothes, as the dusty sand clings to everything, and don't come during the heat of a summer day unless you're wearing socks and shoes: the sand burns feet. The park's 1200-acre off-highway vehicle area is popular with locals. The park is located 20 miles northwestwest of Kanab; drive north on Hwy 89 about 10 miles and look for the sign.

Tours

Paria Outpost   GUIDED TOUR

(☏928-691-1047; www.paria.com) Susan and Steve Dodson specialize in customized 4WD tours and guided hikes through the rocks and sand of the Grand Staircase-Escalante National Monument and the Paria Canyon-Vermilion Cliffs Wilderness. They're friendly, flexible and knowledgeable, and can take you to desert secrets you'd have a hard time finding on your own.

Hummer Tours   GUIDED TOUR

(☏888-687-3006; www.wowhummertours.com) Ken, whose parents were the first to offer mule rides on the North Rim back in the 1950s, offers personalized backcountry excursions to slot canyons, petroglyphs and spectacular red-rock country. Tours range from two hours to all day, and can be customized to fit your personal interests.

Terry's Camera   PHOTO TOUR

(☏435-644-5981; 19 W Center St; ☺8am-6pm Mon-Sat) Terry has spent years roaming the back roads of the Southwest, photographing landscapes, wildlife, petroglyphs and whatever else he finds, and offers customized photo tours of the region.

Festivals & Events

Held in late August, the annual **Western Legends Roundup** (www.westernlegends roundup.com) honors Kanab's pioneer and Hollywood past, kicking off with a wagon train, followed by a film festival, a fiddle competition, cowboy poetry, Indian dances and wagon rides. At the **Kaibab Paiute Tribal Heritage Days** (☏928-643-7245), held the third weekend in August down the road from Pipe Springs National Monument, tribes of Southern Paiute celebrate with dancing, songs, competition, Native food and crafts and children's activities. All events are open to the public.

Sleeping

Tiny Kanab serves as overflow accommodation not only for the North Rim but for Zion and Bryce National Parks to the north as well, and during the high season of summer it can be surprisingly difficult to find a room. In addition to the following, try the recommended **Holiday Inn Express** (☏435-644-3100; www.hiexpress/kanabut.com; 217 S 100 East; r/ste $129/149; ✲❀@☞✲✲) or the clean and friendly independent motels **Treasure Trail Motel** (☏435-644-2687; www.treasuretrail kanab.com; 150 W Center St; r $66-88, ste $78-85; ✲❀✲✲) and **Aikens Lodge** (☏435-644-2625; www.aikenslodge.com; 79 W Center St; s/d $58/69. Ste $89-101; ✲✲@☞⊕).

Best Friends Animal Sanctuary CABIN $$
(☑435-644-2001, ext 4826; www.bestfriends
.org; Hwy 89; cabin $92-$140 for 2, $10 for each
additional person, under 16yr free; ✱♨🐾❄) With
peaceful surrounds and the spectacular
red-rock country of Angel Canyon out your
door, these bright, modern one-bedroom
cottages and two studio cabins overlook the
horse pasture at the animal sanctuary. And
best of all, if you volunteer for a few hours
at Best Friends, you can borrow a dog, cat
or potbelly pig for a sleepover! Two RV sites
($45 per night, closed November to March)
offer the perfect solution for those who want
the conveniences of a hookup without the
crowds of an RV park, but no tent camping
is allowed. The only way to reserve a cottage
is to leave a message at the phone contact
and they'll call you back, or email cottages@
bestfriends.org. Note that these popular cot-
tages book up months in advance.

Parry Lodge MOTEL $
(☑435-644-2601, 888-289-1722; www.parrylodge.
com; 89 E Center St; r $70-105; ✱🛜🐾❄🐕)
Rooms at this one-story 1929 motel are
set back from the road amid a large, tree-
covered parking lot. Some bear the names of
movie stars who stayed here while filming in
southern Utah, and while it's hard to believe
they were ever elegant enough for Gregory
Peck or Lana Turner, it's fun to imagine how
it must have once been. With a rough-at-the-
edges charm, this motel is like walking into
the tattered ghost of a more glamorous era.
The small, deep pool is a favorite, but avoid
the buffet breakfast and rooms in the newer,
two-story annex. In the summer, it shows
free Western movies in a barn in the parking
lot. One apartment, with a full kitchen and
two bedrooms, costs $120 and remodeled
rooms 'in the L' are the nicest.

Purple Sage Inn B&B $$
(☑435-644-5377; www.purplesageinn.com; r $120-
150; ✱🛜) Built in 1884 for Mormon pioneer
William Johnson Jr and his four wives, this
beautifully refurnished home with a lovely
grassy yard, garden terrace and red-rock
views is the only recommended bed and
breakfast in the region. It feels more like an
old home than an inn, and the full breakfast
is a low-key family-style affair. Some rooms
are quite small, but several on the second
floor boast a small balcony, perfect for
morning coffee or a glass of wine, and they
all are beautifully furnished with antiques,
quilts and period fixtures. The master bed-

room suite, with a massive brass bed and 6ft
vintage bathtub, is the nicest.

Quail Park Lodge MOTEL $$
(☑435-215-1447; www.quailparklodge.com; 125 N
300 West; r $100-130; ✱@🛜❄🐕) Though it
doesn't look like much from the outside, this
tiny roadside motel is several steps up from
the usual independent strip options. The
front desk is decidedly modern, the rooms
are spiffy, with contemporary design, bath-
robes and upscale bedding, and hosts are
friendly and helpful. The pool is hardly big-
ger than a postage stamp, but it's enough to
cool you off after a dusty day in the desert.

Victoria Inn HOTEL $$
(☑435-644-8660, 800-738-9643; www.kanab
victoriainn.com; 190 N 300 West; r incl hot breakfast
$119-130; ✱🛜🐕) Hardwood floors, a grand
staircase, quilts and four-poster beds lend
this handsome little hotel an old-time feel,
but the building is modern and the antiques
are new. There's no pool, but guests have access to the indoor pool at the Holiday Inn
Express, about a mile down the road.

Kanab Garden Cottages BUNGALOW $$
(☑435-644-2020, ext 102; www.kanabcottages
.com) Beautifully appointed, with homey fur-
niture and hardwood floors, Kanab Garden
rents three cottages, with varying prices,
spread throughout residential Kanab.

Eating & Drinking

Mormon-influenced Utah laws complicate
drinking options. The only place in town
where you can enjoy a drink without hav-
ing to order a meal is at Calvin T's Smoking
Gun. During the winter, most restaurants
reduce their hours according to need, mood
and available help. As the Rocking V puts
it, after Halloween they 'hold a summit to
determine the schedule through New Year's.'

TOP
CHOICE **Rocking V Café** AMERICAN $$
(☑435-644-8001; 97 W Center St; mains $12-25;
🕙5-10pm; 🍴) Housed in an 1892 storefront
and owned by Dallas transplants, this
brightly painted cafe offers a nice welcome
change from your standard basic and unin-
spired roadside fare. The food is fresh and
delicious, and the eclectic menu includes
buffalo steak, deep-dish vegetarian enchi-
ladas and risotto. There are a few sidewalk
tables, and local art is for sale at the gallery
upstairs.

Rewind Diner
AMERICAN $$

(18 E Center St; mains $8-15; ⊙11am-8:30 Tue-Thu, to 9pm Fri & Sat; 🖉) Betty Boop, draped in a red boa, holds the menu outside this retro diner. You can sit at the black-and-white-tiled soda fountain (try the excellent malt) or settle into a red vinyl booth. Vintage movie posters, a Coke-in-the-bottle vending machine and a chrome rotary public phone complete the 1940s ambiance. The menu extends beyond the classic hamburger and sandwich options to include falafel sandwiches, wild-mushroom pasta and salmon salad, as well as a complete vegetarian menu, beer and wine.

Houston's Trails End Restaurant
AMERICAN $$

(132 E Center St; mains $7-21; ⊙7am-10pm) Playing on the city's Western heritage, servers at this dependable family-style restaurant dress in cowboy/cowgirl regalia (complete with a gun in the holster), and the radio plays country music. Expect diner breakfast fare and carnivore classics like chicken-fried steak, burgers and ribs, but they don't serve alcohol.

Calvin T's Smoking Gun
BBQ $$

(78 E Center St; mains $12-24; ⊙11:30am-10pm; 🍴) Excellent BBQ, including pulled pork and slabs of ribs, served cafeteria style, but skip the watery and tasteless corn and uninspired baked beans. In the back courtyard, there's a replica of an Old West movie backdrop, with a pioneer wagon, a saloon, a jail and so on. Kids can act out their own movie while the parents relax over a cold beer or margarita, soaking in the cool desert night air. Like so much in Kanab, this is kitschy Western fun, complete with a giant wigwam chair, cowboy hats on the wall and deer-antler chandeliers.

Laid Back Larry's
HEALTH FOOD $

(98 S 100 East; ⊙varies) This tiny spot on Hwy 89 offers egg and cheese sandwiches on spelt English muffins for breakfast, one or two lunch options, and smoothies. In the back you'll find a limited but good selection of vegetarian and health-food groceries.

Jakey Leighs
SANDWICHES $

(4 E Center St; sandwiches $4-8; ⊙7am-10pm Tue-Sat, to 3pm Sun & Mon; 🍴) Come here for tasty quiche and a mediocre coffee on the pleasant patio, or grab a sandwich for the road.

Three Bears Creamery
ICE CREAM $

(210 S 100 East; ice cream $2-8; ⊙11am-9pm Mon-Fri, to 8pm Sat, closed Jan) Serving up fairytale themed sundaes like the Goldilocks (caramel sauce over vanilla ice cream – get it?) and the Big Bad Wolf (six scoops with four toppings), Three Bears is the best place for ice cream. It also serves sandwiches and soup. Cash only.

Entertainment

FREE Old Barn Playhouse
THEATER

During the summer, the Parry Lodge shows free classic Western films every night at 8pm in the Old Barn Playhouse behind the lodge. Seating ranges from overstuffed to folding wood, and the popcorn and ice cream are cheap. Movies open with two short films about the Western film industry and Kanab history, so come at about 8:30pm if you just want to catch the feature.

Crescent Moon Theater
PERFORMING ARTS

(📞435-644-2350; 150 S 100 East; adult/child $13/6.50; ⊙varies) Features cowboy music, comedy shows and Western poetry slams; cash only. Monday night is $2 Western Movie Night.

Kanab Theater
THEATER

(📞435-644-2334; 29 W Center St; adult/child $5/4; ⊙Wed-Sat) Tiny theater screening first-run movies.

Shopping

Willow Canyon Outdoor Co
OUTDOOR EQUIPMENT

(263 S 100 East; ⊙7:30am-8pm) This tiny place offers an excellent selection of hiking and field guides, camping gear, United States Geological Survey (USGS) maps, and clothes, as well as an eclectic mix of books, CDs and children's books. It's easy to spend hours just relaxing with a coffee and perusing the books at this markedly urban enclave.

Denny's Wigwam
GIFTS

(78 E Center St; ⊙8:30am-9:30pm Mon-Sat, 9am-9:30pm Sun) For all kinds of cowboy gear, as well as Native American pottery, jewelry and rugs. Dress up in old-fashioned duds and get your photo taken, or pick up anything from a John Wayne mug and toilet paper to rhinestone flip-flops – this is the place for touristy shopping.

Terry's Camera Trading Co   CAMERA GEAR
(☑435-644-5981; 19 W Center St) Terry specializes in camera gear and repair. Call for current hours.

Information

Good website include **www.visit kanab.info** and **www.kaneutah.com**.

Bureau of Land Management (☑435-644-4600; 318 N 100 East; ⊘7:45am-4pm Mon-Fri)

Grand Staircase-Escalante National Monument Visitor Center (☑435-644-4680; 745 E Hwy 89; ⊘8:30am-4:30pm) For information specific to the national monument.

Kane County Hospital (☑435-644-5811; 355 N Main St; ⊘emergency room 24hr) Best option for medical services close to the North Rim.

Kane County Office of Tourism (☑435-644-5033, 800-733-5263; www.kaneutah.com; 78 S 100 East; ⊘9am-7pm Mon-Fri, to 5pm Sat)

Police station (☑435-644-5854; 140 E South)

Post office (39 S Main St; ⊘9am-4pm Mon-Fri, to 2pm Sat)

Zion Pharmacy (☑435-644-2693; 14 E Center St; ⊘9am-6pm Mon-Fri, to noon Sat)

Getting There & Around

There is no bus, train or shuttle service to Kanab.

AIR The closest airline hubs are Las Vegas (four hours southwest) and Salt Lake City (five hours north). Flagstaff, 200 miles and almost four hours south, offers limited airline service.

CAR Kanab is about a 2½-hour drive northwest of the North Rim. The only car rental town is **Xpress Rent-a-Car** (☑435-644-3408; www .xpressrentalcarofkanab.com; 1530 S Alt 89). **Ramsey Towing and Service Garage** (☑435-644-2468; 115 S 100 East) offers a full-service garage with 24-hour towing service.

Along Highway 89 From Kanab to Page

☑435 / ELEV 3100FT TO 6500FT

The interior of the oval formed by Hwy 89 and Alt 89, and the surrounding area, is comprised of the Paria Canyon-Vermilion Cliffs Wilderness (including Vermilion Cliffs National Monument), the southern section of the 1.9-million-acre Grand Staircase-Escalante National Monument, the southeast corner of Glen Canyon National Recreation Area, the Navajo Indian Reservation and the northern tip of the Kaibab National Forest.

For the traveler, however, these are arbitrary distinctions. Whenever you peer out your car window, it's all simply desert. Dry, windy, seemingly endless desert. This is a lonely, desperate kind of wilderness that lures photographers and hikers with its brilliant red and chalky-white buttes, slot canyons and multihued rock formations. While dirt roads may tempt drivers into exploring, the roads are sandy and unpredictable; with a little bit of rain, they can become impassable within minutes and slot canyons can fill with torrents of water that wash away or kill anything or anyone in their path. Do not depend on GPS navigation beyond Hwy 89 and Alt 89, as it tracks roads that are, at best, rough 4WD trails and tragically miscalculates driving times.

Between the tourist hubs of Kanab and Page, there's mile after mile after mile of emptiness. Alt 89, the southern stretch of the oval, winds up from Lees Ferry and Marble Canyon several thousand feet and about 45 miles to Hwy 67 at Jacob Lake, 44 miles north of the North Rim, and then loops back down and north to Kanab; from Kanab, Hwy 89 passes several scenic drives, hiking trails, and two visitor centers on the 74-mile stretch to Page.

Sights & Activities

Paria Outpost offers **guided horseback rides** in Grand Staircase-Escalante Monument.

Johnson Canyon   DRIVING TOUR
This beautiful road escapes the grueling extremes of the desert, passing irrigated fields, cottonwood trees and working ranches. About 5 miles north of Hwy 89 look for remains of the *Gunsmoke* movie site on the right, where more than 20 episodes of the popular TV series were filmed. After 16 miles the road turns to dirt – turn around and return to Hwy 89, or continue through **Grand Staircase-Escalante National Monument** to Cannonville. This makes a lovely bike ride as well, particularly on a summer evening or fall afternoon.

Paria Townsite   FILM LOCATION
The town of Pahreah (rhymes with Maria) was originally settled in 1865, but Indian raids forced it to move upstream in 1870, and by 1910 floods forced settlers to leave the area altogether. In 1963 Hollywood chose the site to build a Western movie set, and it was used for films and TV shows until 1991.

Flooding in 2003 forced local volunteers and the Bureau of Land Management (BLM) to dismantle and move the set to drier ground, only to see it set alight by vandals a couple of years later. A small plaque and fence posts remain, and it is a lovely, quiet spot to poke around. From the picnic area, it is about 1.5 miles to the original site of the town of Pahreah, Pahreah Cemetery and the Paria River, where you can splash about in the muddy water. To get here, head 35 miles east of Kanab on Hwy 89 to the signed 5-mile dirt road (passable with a 2WD when dry).

Houserock Road DRIVING TOUR

While there isn't much in particular to see along the way, this beautiful drive passes through piñon and juniper, hugs the brilliant red sandstone cliffs of the Vermilion Cliffs National Monument and offers an excellent opportunity to get off the main drag. Ten miles south of Hwy 89, at the Utah-Arizona state line, the road changes from Utah County Rd 700 to BLM Rd 1065. Here you will find State Line Campground and a bathroom. The road passes a condor release site 2.9 miles before connecting with Alt 89. Look for Houserock Rd about 40 miles east of Kanab.

Wire Pass to Buckskin Gulch Trail HIKE

A perfect jaunt for anyone looking to experience Utah's slot canyons without a tour or a commitment to a wilderness expedition, this easily accessible hike requires a bit of scrambling and includes several stretches where the slot canyon is only about 30ft wide and walls tower more than 50ft high. After 1.7 miles the trail reaches **Buckskin Gulch**. You can make this a longer hike by turning right and exploring Buckskin Gulch a bit before retracing your steps, or the 12 miles to Paria Canyon. The trailhead sits on Houserock Rd, 8 miles south of Hwy 89 and 40 miles east of the Kanab. A day pass costs $6; free for children under 12.

Cottonwood Road DRIVING TOUR

This washboard dirt road heads through the magnificent rocky desert landscape of **Grand Staircase Escalante National Monument** and **Kodachrome Basin State Park**. The entrance, 3 miles west of the Paria Contact Station, heads north 49 miles to Cannonville, just outside **Bryce Canyon National Park**, and beyond. About 3.5 miles north of Hwy 89, the low cliffs of Dakota sandstone contain 95-million-year-old oysters clustered in the **Oyster Bed**, and Gros-

venor Arch, a 152ft-high double arch 28.9 miles north of Hwy 89, has a restroom and picnic tables. In dry conditions, the road can be driven by 2WD, but it's not recommended. Stop by the Paria Contact Station for a detailed overview of sights and hiking trails along Cottonwood Rd.

Toad Stools HIKE

This wander gives passersby a taste of the harsh Utah desert and cool rocks. The thin sand trail meanders through the scrubbrush, desert boulders and hoodoos about 1 mile to the first toadstool, a sandstone rock in the form of, you guessed it, a toadstool. The unmarked trailhead sits at a small parking area 1.4 miles east of the Paria Contact Station.

Big Water Visitors Center MUSEUM

(Hwy 89, Big Water, UT, Hwy 89; ☉9am-5:30pm Apr-Oct, 8am-4:30 Nov-Mar) A small dinosaur museum 16 miles northwest of Page, with displays on the extensive paleontology research in the area. Check out the tray of what looks like black stones – they're 200-million-year-old sharks' teeth, all found in the area.

Paria Outpost GUIDED TOUR

(☑928-691-1047; www.paria.com; Hwy 89) Steve and Susan Dodson, owners of the friendly and low-key outpost 30 miles east of Kanab, will arrange customized hiking and cycling itineraries, scenic tours and shuttle services for Grand Staircase Escalante National Monument, Buckskin Gulch, Coyote Buttes and other natural and Native American sights. Ask about catered two-day photography workshops.

Sleeping & Eating

White House Campground BASIC CAMPING $

(Hwy 89; primitive sites $6; ☀) Beautiful and quiet, White House offers five sheltered sites, set well apart from one another, each under the shade of a piñon. There are bathrooms, and water is available 3 miles up the dirt road at the Paria Contact Station. White House is 44 miles east of Kanab.

State Line Campground BASIC CAMPING $

(House Rock Rd; primitive sites free; ☀) There are bathrooms, but no water at this lovely desert spot. It's 40 miles east of Kanab and 10 miles south of Hwy 89.

Paria Outpost B&B $

(☑928-691-1047; www.paria.com; Hwy 89; r $65-95; ❀❀) Thirty miles west of Page and next

Three classic canyon hikes attract photographers and outdoor enthusiasts from around the world. Serious canyoneers can tackle the five-day trek along unforgettable 38-mile **Paria Canyon** from White House Campground to Lees Ferry. With numerous stretches of knee-deep muddy water, this hike winds in and out of a slot canyon, past sandstone cliffs, petroglyphs and a handful of campsites. The world-famous 20.3-mile **Buckskin Gulch** (best accessed from Wire Pass to Buckskin Gulch trailhead and White House Campground, both off Hwy 89 between Kanab and Page) is the longest and deepest slot canyon in the United States. Be prepared to wade, possibly swim, through sections and to squeeze through 15 miles of canyon with nothing more than glimpses of the sky above. Sandstone walls soar upwards of 200ft, and there are long stretches not much wider than your shoulders. Finally, only 20 people per day are allowed to hike 3.5 miles to **North Coyote Butte (the Wave)** a trail-free expanse of slickrock that ends at a smooth, orange-and-white striped rock, shaped into a perfect wave and big enough to climb over. To hike the Wave, reserve online up to seven months ahead; 10 walk-in next-day permits are given out by lottery at the Paria Contact Station on Hwy 89, 44 miles east of Kanab. Overnight permits are required for Paria Canyon and Buckskin Gulch. Absolutely do not attempt any of these hikes without checking trail conditions and the weather forecast at the Paria Contact Station. Call 435-688-3246 for details and access www.blm.gov/az for permits.

door to the Paria River Adventure Ranch, the Paria Outpost has one B&B room and a tipi, and they rent tents and sleeping bags. You're welcome to park your RV on site as well, but there are no hookups. On summer weekends from 5pm to 9pm it serves a tasty BBQ dinner buffet with open-mic Fridays. Throughout the year the outpost hosts Paria River Natural History Association lectures on local geology, paleontology and natural history.

Paria Canyon Guest Ranch CABINS $
(928-660-2674; www.pariacampground.com; Hwy 89; camping/dm $10/20, full hook-ups $35, cabin $50;) Offering horseback rides ($30 per hour) along the Paria River, and a game house with a pool table and a stereo system with an iPod hookup, this friendly, low-key ranch caters to folks looking for some action with their desert silence. It has one cabin (with a double and trundle bed) and a bunkhouse hostel that sleeps 14, and you can pitch your tent anywhere on its 30 acres. Cowboy steak dinners are available with advance notice. The ranch regularly hosts large groups but can be eerily quiet otherwise. The hostel is often booked with groups, so don't count on availability.

Information

Big Water Visitor Center (435-675-3200; Hwy 89, Big Water, UT; 9am-5:30pm Apr-Oct, 8am-4:3- Nov-Mar) Small museum and information on Grand Staircase-Escalante National Monument and the extensive paleontology research in the area.

Paria Contact Station (Hwy 89; 8:30am-4:15pm, closed mid-Nov–mid-Mar) Permits, maps and daily road and trail information for the Paria Canyon-Vermilion Cliffs Wilderness.

Getting There & Around

The only way to get to and around the region is by car, and you'll need a 4WD for most roads beyond the highway. **Paria Outpost** (928-691-1047; www.paria.com) offers a hikers' shuttle service for the area.

Page & Glen Canyon National Recreation Area

In 1972 Glen Canyon Dam, Lake Powell, Lees Ferry and more than a million acres of surrounding desert were established as Glen Canyon National Recreation Area (GCNRA). The main attraction here is the 186-mile-long Lake Powell, with 1960 miles of empty shoreline set amid striking red-rock formations, sharply cut canyons and dramatic desert scenery. The windy outpost of Lees Ferry (p165), best known as the jumping-off point for Grand Canyon raft trips, lies 15 miles below the dam but is an hour's drive from Page. Page, a small town that services Lake Powell and the Colorado River, sits 142 miles north of Flagstaff and 124 miles northeast of the North Rim. The N Lake Powell Blvd loops off Hwy 89 and forms Page's main strip.

Sights

The best view of the Colorado River snaking its way through the canyon to Glen Canyon Dam is from an overview just behind the Dennys in Page. A 940ft round-trip walk down stairs and over sandstone leads to a sheltered overlook.

Glen Canyon Dam   DAM

At 710ft tall, Glen Canyon Dam is the nation's second-highest concrete arch dam – Hoover Dam is 16ft taller. Construction lasted from 1956 through 1964. From April through October, free 45-minute guided tours depart from the **Carl Hayden Visitor Center** (☑928-608-6404; ☺8am-7pm Memorial Day-Labor Day, to 4pm Sep-May) and descend deep inside the dam in elevators. A display in the visitor center and three videos tells the story of the dam's construction, complete with all kinds of astounding technical facts.

John Wesley Powell Museum   MUSEUM

(www.powellmuseum.org; 64 N Lake Powell Blvd, Page; admission $6; ☺9am-5pm Mon-Sat, closed mid-Dec–mid-Feb) Back in 1869 the one-armed paddling pioneer John Wesley Powell led the very first expedition through the Grand Canyon on the Colorado River (see p187). This recommended spot displays memorabilia of those early river runners, including a model of Powell's boat, and photos and illustrations of Powell and his adventurous excursions.

Antelope Canyon   SLOT CANYON

Everywhere you look in Page, there seems to be another photo of Antelope Canyon, a scenic slot canyon on the Navajo Indian Reservation, a few miles east of Page and open to tourists by tour only. Year-round, but particularly in the summer, crowds of people pile into shuttles and schlep their tripods and cameras into the narrow canyon. Several tour companies offer trips into upper Antelope Canyon. For other slot canyons in the area, (see p159), the Wire Pass to Buckskin Gulch hike (p158) and guided 4WD trips from Kanab (p154).

Rainbow Bridge National
Monument   NATURAL BRIDGE

On the south shore of Lake Powell, Rainbow Bridge (50 miles by water from Wah-

weap Marina) is the largest natural bridge in the world, measuring 290ft high by 275ft wide. Most visitors arrive by boat and then hike a short trail, but serious backpackers can drive along dirt roads to access two unmaintained trails to the monument (each 28 miles round-trip). Both trailheads lie on the Navajo Indian Reservation; obtain a tribal permit from the **Navajo Parks & Recreation Department** (☑928-871-6647; PO Box 90000, Window Rock, AZ 86515).

Activities

Boating & Cruises

Most marinas rent kayaks, 18ft runabouts and 14ft fishing boats, as well as water skis and other 'toys.' Distances on Lake Powell are long. To take a powerboat from Page to Rainbow Bridge takes about three hours and at least 10 gallons of gas – that's upwards of $200 for fuel alone – and it's about five hours from the lake's northern to southern tips. Houseboating is hugely popular and, with its many coves and beaches to explore, Lake Powell is perfect for kayaking. Expect wind in the spring and monsoon rains in late July and August. See p161 for boat tours.

Fishing

The calm waters of the Colorado River, deep in a canyon between the dam and Lees Ferry, offer excellent and world-renowned nymph fly-fishing. Call **Lees Ferry Anglers** (☑928-355-2228; www.leesferry.com) for current conditions and to arrange a guided trip. To fish the Arizona portion of Lake Powell and the Colorado River, you must have an Arizona fishing license. Fishing the Utah portion of the lake requires a Utah fishing license. Children under 14 years old do not need a license. All marinas sell licenses, and several offer boat rental.

Hiking
Horseshoe Bend   HIKE

This popular 1.5-mile round-trip hike is short, but the soft sand, shadeless trail and moderate incline makes it a bit trying. Below the overlook, the river bends around a dramatic stone outcrop to form a perfect horseshoe, a view made famous in ubiquitous photos of the overlook. Toddlers should be secured safely in a backpack, as there are no guardrails at the viewpoint. Look for the parking area 5 miles south of the Carl Hayden Visitor Center on Hwy 89, just south of milepost 545.

Lake Powell is famous for its houseboating, and it's a huge attraction for families and college students alike. Though the lake hosts hundreds of houseboats daily, you can explore Lake Powell's secluded inlets, bays, coves and beaches for several days without seeing many folk at all. Contact the recommended **Antelope Point Marina** (☑800-255-5561; www.antelopepointlakepowell.com), which generally has more elegant boats and more personalized service, or **Aramark** (☑800-528-6154; www.lakepowell.com) for details and reservations.

Hanging Garden   HIKE

A 1-mile round-trip scramble across red rock leads to an oasis above the Colorado River and Lake Powell. Spot the trailhead sign on Hwy 89 just past the dam on the way into Page.

Swimming

The best place to enjoy Lake Powell's cold, clear water (short of jumping off your boat) is at the **Chains**. Look for the tiny hiking trail sign just east of the dam and turn left; from the parking lot, a short walk leads to flat, smooth sandstone that juts directly into the water. It's not exactly a trail, so just follow your nose to the water.

Nine miles northwest of Page, **Lone Rock** is basically a huge parking lot of sand and gravel set on a thin, mucky finger of Lake Powell. Tents and campers line the shore, there's no shade, and it can get crazy with partygoers during the weekend. A more peaceful option, particularly good for kids, is the boat launch at **Antelope Point Marina**, about 8 miles east of town on Hwy 89, where you can wade into the water from the small, rocky areas.

Tours

Colorado River Discovery   BOAT TOUR

(☑888-522-6644; www.raftthecanyon.com; 130 6th Ave, Page; adult/4-11yr $85/75; ☉Mar-Nov) Colorado River Discovery offers four-hour smooth water float trips down the Colorado from Glen Canyon Dam to Lees Ferry. Boats stop at petroglyphs, where you can also splash and cool off in the frigid water, and guides explain the natural and human history along the way. Despite the fact that several boats, each holding about 20 people, depart at the same time, the ride is peaceful, bucolic and a lot of fun. Don't be turned off by mayhem and busloads of people departing from headquarters in Page – once on the river, you barely see another boat, and it's a beautiful trip through the deep, sheer redrock sides of Glen Canyon. Trips depart once or twice a day, depending on the month, and it's a one-hour bus trip from the trip's end back to Page. Call ☑928-645-9175 one day in advance to reserve a Bistro Bag Lunch for the trip; complimentary water and lemonade provided. If you canoe or kayak the 15.2 miles from the dam to Lees Ferry, they'll meet you at Lees Ferry at the end of their raft trips and backhaul you ($23 per person, $23 per boat) upriver to an island just below the dam. You can camp at any of the six free, primitive campsites along the river (no permit required), or make it a day trip – it's about a six-hour float from the dam to Lees Ferry.

Hidden Canyon   BOAT TOUR

(☑888-522-6644; www.hiddencanyonkayak.com) This kayak touring company specializes in intimate kayak tours to Lake Powell's hidden canyons, quiet coves and iconic natural landmarks. Trips range from half-day jaunts to multiday backcountry camping expeditions, and guides boast years of experience both in and around Lake Powell and on the Colorado through the Grand Canyon. Meals are provided, and you're welcome to bring your own alcohol. If you'd rather explore on your own, Hidden Canyon rents kayaks ($40 per day) and camping gear, including tents, sleeping bags, folding chairs and camping stoves.

Lake Powell Resorts & Marinas   BOAT TOUR

(☑800-528-6154; www.lakepowell.com) Full-day boat tours to Rainbow Bridge (adult/child $113/84), half-day trips to Navajo Tapestry ($63/39) and 1½-hour rides to Antelope Canyon ($40/26), as well as summer dinner cruises to the dam ($73/34) from Wahweap Marina. Most boats seat up to 65 people, so don't expect an intimate ride.

Slot Canyon Hummer
Adventures   DRIVING TOUR

(☑928-645-2266; www.hummeradventures.net; 2/4hr tours per person $99/159; 12 N Lake Powell

Blvd, Page) Runs 4WD tours to several slot canyons on Navajo land. With only six people to a car, and no crowds vying for the perfect angle to shoot a photo, this is an excellent alternative to Antelope Canyon's mayhem. Ask about off-road buggy adventure trips.

Westwind Aviation SCENIC FLIGHTS
(☑800-245-8668; www.westwindaviation.com) Aerial tours of Grand Canyon and the area from Page Municipal Airport.

Roger Ekis's Antelope Canyon Tours CANYON TOUR
(☑928-645-9102; www.antelopecanyon.com; adult/5-12yr $32/20; 22 S Lake Powell Blvd, Page). Offers trips into Antelope Canyon (p160).

Sleeping

You can camp anywhere along the Lake Powell shoreline for free as long as you have a portable toilet or toilet facilities on your boat. Six designated primitive campsites, accessible by boat only, sit on the Colorado River between the dam and Lees Ferry. Bullfrog and Hite marinas offer primitive camping, and there are developed campgrounds at Wahweap (where you can also use the resort's two pools), Bullfrog and Halls Crossing marinas (call ☑800-528-6154 for reservations). In addition to the following, you'll find standard chain motels along Lake Powell Blvd in Page.

Courtyard by Marriott HOTEL $$
(☑928-645-5000, 800-321-2211; 600 Clubhouse Dr; r $150-160, no extra cost under 18yr; ❋◉🛜🏊) Surrounded by a golf course away from the strip's noise and traffic, with attractive, spacious rooms and a quiet garden courtyard with a large pool, this hotel is a peaceful alternative to other chain hotels. It has a bar and a restaurant, but you'd be better off going elsewhere for a meal.

Lake Powell Resort RESORT $$
(☑928-645-2433, 800-528-6154; www.lakepowell.com; 100 Lake Shore Dr; r $170-190, ste $250-280, no extra charge for children under 18; ❋🛜🏊🍽) This bustling resort on the shores of Lake Powell offers beautiful views and a lovely little pool perched on the rocks above the lake, but it is impersonal and frenetic. Several buildings spread out around the parking lot house basic hotel rooms; rates for lakeview rooms with tiny patios are well worth the extra money. In the lobby you can book boat tours and arrange boat rental. Prices are a bit lower weekdays, and the wi-fi is available in the lobby only.

Lu Lu's Sleep Ezze Motel MOTEL $
(☑928-608-0273, 800-553-6211; www.lulussleepezzemotel.com; cnr 8th Ave & Elm St; r $85-108; ❋◉🛜) Eight bright and tidy rooms share a small patio with two large tables, rattan umbrellas, two BBQs, and pebble landscaping. Elm St heads northeast off Lake Powell Blvd in the center of town, and 8th Ave cuts east off Lake Powell Blvd.

Debbie's Hide A Way MOTEL $$
(☑928-645-1224; www.debbieshideaway.com; 117 8th Ave; ste $129-199; ❋◉🛜) The owners encourage you to feel right at home – throw a steak on the grill, leaf through one of several hundred books that line the bookshelves, or just hang out with other guests among the rose and fruit trees. All accommodation is in basic suites, rates include up to seven people, and there are free laundry facilities. Head northeast off Lake Powell Blvd on Elm St and turn right on 8th Ave.

Lone Rock Beach BASIC CAMPING $
(camping $18; 🏊) Everyone here just pulls up next to the water and sets up house. It's a popular spot with college revelers, and can be busy and loud late into the night during the weekends. Escape to the dunes or the far edges of the lot if you're looking for quiet. There are bathrooms and outdoor cold showers.

Eating & Drinking

Unless otherwise noted, the following restaurants stretch along Dam Plaza, a back-to-back strip mall in the Safeway parking lot at the corner of Lake Powell Blvd and Navajo Dr. The best for big-city java with a punch is the Starbucks inside the Safeway.

Bean's Coffee CAFE $
(644F N Navajo Dr; mains $5-11; ⊙6:30am-6pm Mon-Fri, 7am-6pm Sat, 8am-2pm Sun; ◉🛜) While the coffee runs weak, this tiny cafe serves good breakfast burritos and sandwiches – try the tasty cashew chicken as a picnic lunch to go.

Slackers BURGERS $
(810 N Navajo Dr; mains $6-12; ⊙11am-9pm Mon-Fri) A chalkboard menu includes excellent burgers (though there's no kick to the green chili) and hot or cold sub sandwiches. Count on long lunch lines, or call and order in advance. Picnic tables offer shaded outdoor

strip-mall seating. Connects to **Big Dipper Ice-Cream and Yogurt** where, strangely, there's a DVD player with a selection of movies to pop in at your pleasure.

Blue Buddha Sushi Lounge SUSHI **$$**
(810 N Navajo; mains $14-26; ⏱5-10pm Mon-Sat, to 9pm Sun, closed Mon & Sun Oct-May) With cold sake and a relaxing blue-hued modern décor, this ultracool hideaway hits the spot after a hot and dusty day in the Arizona desert. Beyond sushi, there's a limited menu including teriyaki chicken and blackened tuna.

Bonkers AMERICAN **$$**
(660 Elm St; mains $8-16; ⏱11am-10pm) It doesn't look like much from the outside and the patio doesn't offer any kind of vista, but the service is excellent and food surprisingly tasty.

Dam Bar & Grille AMERICAN **$$**
(644 N Navajo Dr; mains $8-18; ⏱11am-10pm) Raft guides recommend the dependable pub

fare, including steak, pasta and ribs. There's a microbrewery feel here, and the patio is pleasant on summer evenings, despite the strip-mall view.

Ranch House Grille DINER **$**
(819 N Navajo Dr; mains $6-13; ⏱6am-3pm) The big, white room offers little in terms of ambiance, but the food is good, the portions huge and the service fast. This is your best bet for breakfast. To get here from the dam, turn left off of N Lake Powell Blvd onto N Navajo Dr.

Gunsmoke Saloon BBQ **$$**
(644 N Navajo Dr; mains $8-21; ⏱7pm-2am Tue-Sat) This cavernous spot next to the Dam Bar serves BBQ dinners, from sandwiches to racks of ribs with all the fixin's, but the main draw is the popular bar featuring alternative rock and plenty of drunken revelers. There are a couple of pool tables and a dance floor.

WORTH A TRIP

HOPI & NAVAJO RESERVATIONS

Many folk zoom past the Hopi and Navajo Reservations, registering them as nothing more than vast desert expanses and a few lonely souvenir huts standing windblown along the road between the North and South Rims. But for those with the time and a willingness to explore the unpolished reality of the American West, a side tour to this desolate area east of the Grand Canyon can be a highlight.

The surreal red-rock formations of **Monument Valley**, featured in hundreds of movies, advertisements, calendars and magazines, emerge magically from the flat and drab landscape 154 miles from Desert View and 246 miles from the North Rim.

Lying 208 miles east of Desert View on the New Mexico border, **Canyon de Chelly**, a many-figured canyon dotted with ancestral Puebloan ruins and etched with pictographs, strikes even the most jaded traveler as hauntingly memorable. Navajo families winter on the rims and move to traditional hogans (one-room structures traditionally built of earth, logs, stone and other materials, with the entrance facing east) on farms on the canyon floor in spring and summer.

Scenic rim drives offer breathtaking beauty, and you can explore the interior on guided hikes or horseback rides.

The private and isolated Hopi communities of **First**, **Second** and **Third Mesas**, about two hours from Grand Canyon's Desert View, consist of 12 traditional villages perched atop 7200ft mesas. At the end of First Mesa is the tiny village of **Walpi**, the most dramatic of the Hopi enclaves; Hopi guides offer 45-minute walking tours. The **Hopi Cultural Center**, on Second Mesa, has a small museum, and artisans sell woven baskets, kachina dolls and other crafts from roadside booths. On Third Mesa, **Old Oraibi** rivals Taos, New Mexico, and Acoma, New Mexico, as the oldest continuously inhabited village on the continent. Kachina dances are often open to the public, and tribe members sometimes personally invite visitors to other ceremonies. An invitation is an honor; be sure to respect local customs.

The Hopi strictly prohibit alcohol, as well as any form of recording, including sketching. Each of these spots has one or two motels, and there are a handful of chain motels in Kayenta, 24 miles south of Monument Valley.

Jadi Tooh
AMERICAN $$

(Antelope Point Marina; mains $12-23; ☉11am-10pm) A 'floating restaurant' with solid food at the Navajo-owned marina provides a peaceful respite from the bustling strip of Page, which is 8 miles southwest. Come for the relative quiet and the view.

Rainbow Room
AMERICAN $$$

(☎928-645-2433; Lake Powell Resort, 100 Lake Shore Dr; mains $16-25; ☉6-10am, 11am-2pm & 4-11pm) Though the food ranges from nothing special to downright bad, there's something to be said for a meal with a view. Perched above Lake Powell, picture windows frame dramatic red-rock formations against blue water. Your best bet is to eat elsewhere and come to the bar here for a beautiful sunset drink. Head west on Hwy 89 towards Kanab and follow signs to Wahweap Marina.

Entertainment

From May through August, movies are screened at Memorial Park, but the schedule varies from year to year.

Navajo Village Heritage Center
PERFORMING ARTS

(☎928-660-0304; www.navajo-village.com; adult/11-17yr/under 10yr $30/20/5; ☉6-8:30pm Jun-Aug, 5-7:30pm Apr, May, Sep & Oct) A rather touristy presentation of traditional Navajo storytelling, dancing and song. If the minimum of 10 guests are not booked, tours may be canceled. Located on the corner of Hwy 89 and Coppermine Rd, in the southeast part of Page.

Mesa Theater
THEATER

(☎928-645-9565; 42 S Lake Powell Blvd) A tiny theater screening first-run movies.

Information

The Glen Canyon National Recreation Area entrance fee, valid for seven days, is $15 per vehicle or $7 per individual entering on foot or bike.

Emergency

National Park Service 24-hour Dispatch Center (☎928-608-6300)

Police station (☎928-645-2463; 808 Coppermine Rd, Page)

Internet Access

Digital Lands (☎928-645-2241; 40 S Lake Powell Blvd; per hr $6; ☉10am-10pm) Next to movie theater

Bean's Coffee (☎928-645-6858; 644F N Navajo Dr; per 15min $3; ☉6:30am-6pm Mon-Fri, 7am-6pm Sat, 8am-2pm Sun)

Marinas

Marinas (except for Dangling Rope and Hite) rent boats, host rangers and small supply stores, and sell fuel. **Aramark** (☎800-528-6154; www.lakepowell.com) runs all the marinas except for Antelope Point, which is on Navajo Land.

Antelope Point (☎928-645-5900) Peaceful Navajo-owned marina 8 miles northeast of Page.

Bullfrog (☎435-684-3000) Connects to Halls Crossing marina by 30-minute ferry. On Lake Powell's west shore, 290 miles from Page.

Dangling Rope Smallest marina, accessible only by boat. Forty lake-miles from Page.

Halls Crossing (☎435-684-7000) Connects to Bullfrog marina by 30-minute ferry. On Lake Powell's east shore, 238 miles from Page.

Hite May be closed due to low water levels. At Lake Powell's north end, 148 lake-miles from Page.

Wahweap (☎928-645-2433) Frenetic place popular with tour buses. Six miles northwest of Page.

Medical services

Page Hospital (☎928-645-2424; cnr Vista Ave & N Navajo Dr)

Pharmacy (☎928-645-8155; 650 Elm St; 9am-8pm Mon-Fri, ☉9am-6pm Sat, 10am-4pm Sun) Inside the Safeway Food & Drug.

Post

Post office (☎928-645-2571; 44 6th Ave, Page; ☉8:30am-5pm Mon-Fri)

Ranger Stations

The following GCNRA ranger stations keep irregular hours.

Bullfrog Ranger Station (☎435-684-7400)

Escalante Ranger Station (☎435-826-5651)

Halls Crossing Ranger Station (☎435-684-7460)

Hite Ranger Station (☎435-684-2457)

Lees Ferry Ranger Station (☎928-355-2234)

Wahweap Ranger Station (☎928-608-6531)

Tourist information

Bullfrog Visitor Center (☎435-684-7423; ☉9am-5pm Wed-Sun, closed Apr-Oct) On the lake's north shore, this is a drive of more than 200 miles from Page.

Carl Hayden Visitor Center (☎928-608-6404; www.nps.gov/glca; ☉8am-7pm Memorial Day-Labor Day, to 4pm Sep-May) A well-stocked bookstore and the best source of regional information in Page. It's located at Glen Canyon Dam on Hwy 89, 2 miles north of Page.

Glen Canyon Natural History Association
(📞928-608-6072; www.glencanyonnha.com; ⊘8am-6pm) Excellent resource for entire region, with maps and guides to Glen Canyon Dam, Grand Staircase-Escalante National Monument, Lake Powell and Vermilion Cliffs National Monument.

Websites

Glen Canyon National Recreation Area (www.nps.gov/glca) Official website.

Lake Powell Resorts & Marinas (www.lakepowell.com) Marina lodging, boat rentals and boat tours for GCNRA.

Page/Lake Powell Tourism Bureau (www.pagelakepowelltourism.com)

Wayne's Words (www.wayneswords.com) Information on fishing in Lake Powell.

Getting There & Away

AIR Flights between Page Municipal Airport and Phoenix are offered by **Great Lakes Airline** (📞928-645-1355, 800-554-5111; www.flygreatlakes.com) and **Scenic Airlines** (📞800-634-6801).

CAR Page sits 125 northwest of the North Rim. Car rental is available through **Avis** (📞928-645-9347, 800-331-1212).

Lees Ferry & Marble Canyon

The town of Lees Ferry was named after polygamist John D Lee, who started the Lonely Dell Ranch and a primitive ferry service here in 1873. In 1877, Lee was executed for his role in the Mountains Meadow Massacre. Warren Marshall Johnson and his family ran the ferry ran until 1929, when the Navajo Bridge opened to a crowd of 5000 people. Today, Lees Ferry is best known as the jumping-off point for rafting trips, and it isn't much more than a boat launch, a couple of hiking trails, a campground and some historic buildings. The Colorado River cuts through red-rock Glen Canyon from the dam about 16 miles away, and the spectacular Vermilion Cliffs tower over what's referred to locally as Marble Canyon and House Rock Valley. A beautiful drive snakes 85 miles from here to the North Rim. Stop for an early dinner at Lees Ferry Lodge and head up to the canyon in the evening, when twilight settles over striking rock formations and the cool desert evening stretches across the flat expanse. Open the windows, listen to the silence and wind your way up to the high meadows of the Kaibab Plateau, past Jacob Lake, to the Grand Canyon Lodge, perched magnificently on the canyon edge.

Sights

Navajo Bridge   LANDMARK
Pedestrians are free to walk across the Colorado on the original 834ft-wide, 467ft-high Navajo Bridge, which offers great views south down Marble Canyon to the northeast lip of the Grand Canyon. Pop into the **Navajo Bridge Interpretive Center** (⊘9am-5pm, closed Nov-Apr) to see the small historical exhibit on the region and for maps, tourist information and books.

Historic Lees Ferry &
Lonely Dell Ranch   HISTORIC SITE
Walking-tour guides, one of Lees Ferry (along the river beyond the boat launch) and one of Lonely Dell Ranch (about a mile from the river) are available for purchase at the Rainbow Bridge Interpretive Center or the Carl Hayden Visitor Center in Page. Lees Ferry, the site of the original ferry crossing and of Charles Spencer's 1910 effort to extract gold from the surrounding hills, includes a couple of stone buildings and a sunken paddlewheel steamboat. Lonely Dell Ranch provided for families who worked at the crossing in the 1880s and 1890s. The log cabins, a stone ranch house and a pioneer cemetery remain. Look for the shared grave of the Johnson boys. As the story goes, a passing family didn't have money to pay for the ferry, and so Johnson granted them passage in exchange for the clothes of the travelers' dead child. Within weeks, the five Johnson boys were dead, infected with fever from the clothes.

Though the main ranch buildings lie only about 700ft up a dirt road from the parking area, a walking tour of the entire ranch is a 1-mile round-trip. You'll find picnic tables and an idyllic apricot orchard – a sheltered oasis that makes a wonderful picnic spot. From Alt 89 take the paved road north toward Lees Ferry for 5.1 miles, then turn left and drive 0.2 miles to signed Lonely Dell Ranch; for Lees Ferry, continue 0.7 miles beyond the turn for Lonely Dell Ranch.

Gravel Bar   SCENIC SPOT
Here, soft, white sand lines the Colorado River for several hundred feet and the water is calm and shallow halfway across. It makes an excellent, if windy, spot for a splash. Stick to wading in the shallows, far from the ripples

on the far side of the river – the deep water of the Colorado is dangerous for swimming.

Activities

The calm waters of the Colorado between the dam and Lees Ferry draw fly-fishers from around the world. It's primarily a nymphing river, with opportunities for dry **fly-fishing** at certain times. Strenuous scrambles into the canyon aside, the only access is by boat. **Lees Ferry Anglers** (🖉928-355-2261; www .leesferry.com; Cliff Dwellers Lodge, Alt 89, Marble Canyon) and **Marble Canyon Outfitters** (🖉928-645-2781; www.leesferryflyfishing.com; Marble Canyon Lodge, Alt 89, Marble Canyon), both in motels along Alt 89, offer guide services, including wade guiding.

Condor Release Site BIRDWATCHING

Your best shot at catching a glimpse of these massive birds in and around the North Rim, and well worth a detour. Look for the signed turn-off on Alt 89 about 20 miles west of Navajo Bridge and keep your eyes on the sky.

Sleeping & Eating

In the winter, things around here are pretty quiet. Restaurants may or may not be open. Three simple windswept motels dot Alt 89 in the shadow of the Vermilion Cliffs just west of Navajo Bridge, offering spectacular surrounds with panoramic views of the desert flatness to the south and rustic quiet.

Lees Ferry Lodge/Vermilion Cliffs Bar & Grill MOTEL $

(🖉928-355-2231; www.vermilioncliffs.com; Alt 89, Marble Canyon; s/d $64/74; ⊙6:30am-9pm; 🐾) This handsome stone building is perfect if you want something beyond a roadside motel. The 10 cozy rooms are decorated thematically. The cowboy room, for example, has animal skins and horseshoes on the wall, horse-print bed covers and a wood-burning stove, and there's a pleasant roadside courtyard with spectacular views. In the back they offer three trailers with basic accommodation for up to six ($85 to $130). Some of the rooms are showing their age. In a long room with a rough-hewn beamed ceiling and a pool table, the restaurant-bar serves hearty food and has an extensive beer selection.

Cliff Dwellers Lodge & Restaurant MOTEL $

(🖉928-355-2261, 800-962-9755; www.cliffdwellers lodge.com; Alt 89, Marble Canyon; r $80-90; ⊙6am-9pm; 🐾) Basic, but clean and friendly. Ask for a room in the newer section. The restaurant serves burgers (including vegetarian), steaks, fajitas and falafals. Owners, Terry and Wendy Gunn, run Lees Ferry Anglers (see below). It's 9.8 miles west of Navajo Bridge.

Marble Canyon Lodge MOTEL $

(🖉928-355-2225; www.marblecanyoncompany .com; Alt 89, Marble Canyon; s/d/apt $70/80/140; 🐾) Four miles west of Navajo bridge, simple rooms and deli sandwiches to go; the restaurant is open 6am to 10pm.

Lees Ferry Campground CAMPGROUND $

(camping $12) This GCNRA campground is a lovely, quiet spot, set up on a small hill with a few shade trees and views of the river, but it's windy, dry and barren. There are toilets and potable water, but no hookups or facilities.

Shopping

Lees Ferry Anglers OUTDOOR EQUIPMENT

(🖉928-355-2261; www.leesferry.com; Cliff Dwellers Lodge, Alt 89, Marble Canyon) A shop selling rods, reels, lines, flies and equipment for fly-fishing in the area and beyond, and giving anglers the lowdown on what's biting where.

Information

A post office, laundromat and pay showers are next to the gas station just west of Navajo Bridge. There's a wi-fi hotspot by Marble Canyon Lodge.
Lees Ferry Ranger Station (🖉928-355-2234) A ranger sometimes staffs this station, but don't count on it.
Navajo Bridge Interpretive Center (Alt 89, 39 miles southwest of Page; ⊙9am-5pm, closed Nov-Apr) Glen Canyon National Recreation Area Visitors Center offers historic exhibits in a beautiful stone building next to Navajo Bridge.

Getting There & Around

Marble Canyon and Lees Ferry are a 1½-hour drive northeast from the North Rim and an hour's drive southwest of Page. There is no public transportation to either.

Colorado River

Best Hikes

» Tapeats Creek to Thunder Spring (p174)

» Deer Creek (p175)

» Matkatamiba (p175)

» Nankoweap to Granaries (p174)

» Beaver Falls (p176)

Best Rapids

» Hance (p173)

» Horn Creek (p174)

» Hermit (p174)

» Crystal (p174)

» Lava Falls (p174)

Why Go?

Rafting the Colorado is a virtual all-access pass to the Grand Canyon, in all its wildness, peace and ancient, mighty glory. You'll experience the rush of running world-class rapids with spectacular canyon walls yawning above. As you float down sections of smooth water, chirps of canyon wrens will lilt against the sounds of the river and oar, as you look for ravens and bighorn sheep picking their way along the shore. You'll explore beautiful side canyons (many accessible only from the river), hike to hidden waterfalls and find petroglyphs and ruins, traces of people who came long before. After evening tales of intrepid explorers who ran the river when the gorge was still uncharted, you'll sleep under the stars on sandy beaches while the river whispers you into slumber. Here at the bottom of the Grand Canyon, its depth will take your breath away.

When to Go
Colorado River

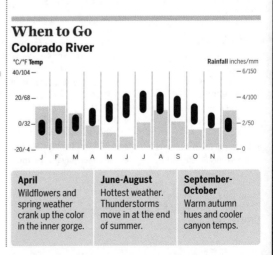

April
Wildflowers and spring weather crank up the color in the inner gorge.

June-August
Hottest weather. Thunderstorms move in at the end of summer.

September-October
Warm autumn hues and cooler canyon temps.

PLANNING TIP

Spring and fall river trips bring pleasantly milder ambient temperatures. But bring warm and waterproof gear, because when you get splashed on the river, that cold water bites.

Fast Facts: Colorado River (Lees Ferry to Lake Mead)

» River miles: 277
» Major rapids: 160
» River drop: 1900ft
» Phantom Ranch elevation: 2400ft

Private Trip Permits

Apply for a permit through the **Grand Canyon River Permits Office** (☑928-638-7843, 800-959-9164; https://npspermits.us; application fee $25). Winners are charged an automatic, non-refundable $400 deposit to reserve a spot.

Resources

» National Park Service (www.nps.gov/grca/park mgmt/crmp_nc-trip -planning.htm)

» Grand Canyon River Outfitters Association: www. gcroa.org

» Hualapai River Runners (www.grandcanyonwest. com/rafting.php) is the only company running one-day motorized trips on the Colorado, based at Grand Canyon West.

Put-in & Takeout Points

Though boats must ply the full course, rafters may join, leave or rejoin a river excursion at several points.

» Put-in at Lees Ferry (river mile 0), 15 miles below Glen Canyon Dam.

» Rafters can take out at Phantom Ranch (mile 87.5) and hike up to the South Rim on the Bright Angel Trail.

» Rafters can also takeout at Whitmore Wash (mile 187.5), fly to the rim via helicopter and transfer to a plane bound for Las Vegas.

» The last takeout points are at Diamond Creek (mile 226), or Pearce Ferry (mile 279.5) or South Cove (mile 296.5), both on Lake Mead.

DON'T MISS

You won't miss any good rapids unless you happen to be unconscious, but the river isn't the only attraction on this ride. One of the great rewards of floating the river is the opportunity to hike to places that are difficult to access from the rim – like the ancient Puebloan granaries at **Nankoweap**, where you'll also discover gorgeous views of river and inner gorge. Side canyons reveal cool, verdant grottos like **Elves Chasm** and swirling rock formations as in **North Canyon**. Set aside your pride and strap your PFD to your bum to bump down the warm, turquoise waters of the **Little Colorado**, a tributary sourced from mineral springs.

Be sure to stop for a cold lemonade and scribble a postcard at **Phantom Ranch**, your one brush with civilization. And don't miss the otherworldly blue-green waters of **Havasu Creek**.

Boat Options

» Most commonly used boats are 18ft neoprene rafts seating three to five passengers, with a guide rowing wooden oars. High center of gravity provides greater stability while giving the guide more power down big rapids.

» Dories – 17ft rigid, flat-bottomed boats – comfortably seat up to four passengers and a guide rowing a set of long wooden oars. Dory trips take one or two days longer than rafting trips.

» Motorized rafts are, typically, inflatable pontoons lashed together to create a 33ft craft. They seat eight to 16 passengers and two or three guides.

» Hard-shell kayaks are most often used on private trips, while some commercial operators provide inflatable kayaks on request.

Planning

The Grand Canyon stretch of the Colorado sees 22,000 annual visitors and is run year-round, though access to some sections is limited under certain conditions. Most commercial trips operate between April and October, with June, July and August being the peak months. Park regulations stipulate that individuals may take only one recreational river trip per calendar year, whether private or commercial.

While summer draws the most traffic, it also brings more afternoon thunderstorms and searing, triple-digit temperatures. The only way to stay cool is to engage in water fights with fellow rafters and take quick dips in the face-numbing water – controlled releases from Glen Canyon Dam keep water temperatures between 48°F and 55°F year-round. Monsoon rains in July and August can also spawn flash floods and increased sediment that turns the water a murky reddish-brown.

COMMERCIAL TRIPS

Given two or three weeks, you can run all 277 river miles through the canyon between Lake Powell and Lake Mead. If that's more vacation than you've got, you can raft one of three shorter sections (each 100 miles or less) in four to nine days, or raft a combination of two shorter sections. Choosing to run the river via motorboat rather than raft shortens the trip by several days.

Most rafters join a commercial outing with one of many accredited outfitters, who offer trips lasting from three to 21 days. Due to their popularity, tours often sell out a year in advance. However, a small percentage of cancellations do occur, so it's sometimes possible to get in on a trip at the last minute.

For those short on time, there are half- and full-day rafting trips, though not necessarily on sections within the Grand Canyon. Operating out of Diamond Creek, about four hours from the South Rim, Hualapai River Runners offers daylong, motorized raft trips in the canyon's west end. Don't want a white-knuckle white-water experience? Wilderness River Adventures runs half-day float trips on the silky-smooth 16-mile stretch of the Colorado that flows between Glen Canyon Dam and Lees Ferry. **Xanterra** (☎303-287-2757, 888-297-2757; www.xanterra.com) offers full-day trips from the South Rim that bus rafters to Page, where they connect with the float trip.

As part of the *Colorado River Management Plan* (CRMP), which serves to protect the river and to preserve a high-quality experience for visitors, the park carefully regulates the number of rafts on the Colorado. Each year, a few hundred noncommercial rafting excursions (also known as private trips) are allowed on the river. If you're planning a private trip, *planning* is the key word. Even before you can begin working out the necessary details, from supplies to waste management to emergency options, you need to score a permit and will be required to have at least one member of your party with the technical rafting experience to run the Colorado.

There are no developed campsites or facilities anywhere along the Colorado. Because this is a wilderness area, where the Leave No Trace ethic applies, visitors are required to make the least impact possible by removing any waste generated and by sticking to established trails to minimize erosion. Groups on the river are self-sufficient, packing in all food and gear and packing out all waste. Rafters camp on pristine, sandy beaches, most of which are fringed with invasive (but lovely) tamarisk stands providing wisps of shade. Usually, only one group will camp on any given beach, affording everyone heaps of privacy.

Orientation

The Colorado River runs 277 miles from Lees Ferry to Lake Mead, with more than 160 sets of rapids keeping things exciting. Unlike most rivers, where the rapids are rated in difficulty as Class I through V on the American white-water rating system, Colorado River rapids are rated from Class 1 through 10 (a Class 10 on the Colorado being about equal to the standard Class V; that is, a King Kong rapid). The biggest single drop (from the top to the base of the rapids) is 37ft, and nearly 20 rapids drop 15ft or more.

The Colorado is a serious river and demands respect – if you do everything your guide tells you and take responsibility for your own safety and that of others, you should have an exciting but safe trip. Be aware that the temperature of the river remains between 48°F and 55°F year-round, and hypothermia can set in quickly. Always check with your guides whether a place is far enough removed from the swift current to be safe for a dip.

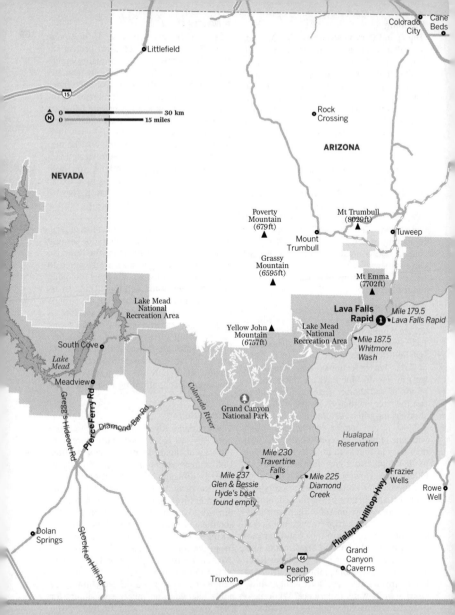

Colorado River Highlights

1 Scout and then slam through formidable **Lava Falls Rapid** (p174)

2 Take in the view of an iconic bend in the river from ancient **Puebloan granaries** (p173)

3 Sidle through a slot canyon and pass pictographs on one of the river's most beautiful hikes, to **Deer Creek Falls** (p175)

4 Hike up Havasu Canyon to the blue-green waters of **Beaver Falls** (p176)

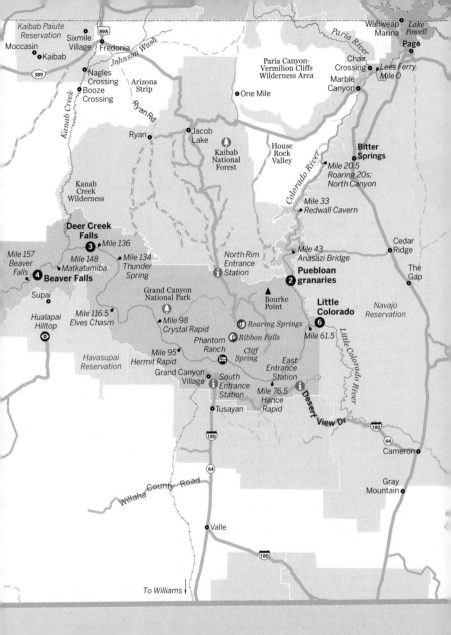

⑤ Wake at a **beach camp** as early-morning light slides across canyon walls

⑥ Bounce down the warm, aquamarine mini-rapids of the **Little Colorado** (boxed text p175)

⑦ Float down **smooth water** and marvel at the multicolored, ancient layers of rock rising above

LEAVE NO TRACE

Make a minimal impact on wilderness areas by following these seven principles:

» Plan ahead and prepare

» Travel and camp on durable surfaces

» Dispose of waste properly

» Leave what you find

» Minimize campfire impacts

» Respect wildlife

» Be considerate of other visitors

For more detailed information, check out www.lnt.org/programs/principles.php.

Along the length of the river, the side canyons and tributaries feeding into the Colorado provide a wealth of hidden places to explore. Many of the canyon's waterfalls, slot canyons and inviting pools are difficult to reach unless you start from the river, and most can't be seen from the rim. Visits to these remote spots can be the most rewarding part of a river trek.

Rafting Companies

Most people join a commercial trip, on which operators provide the boat, all rafting and camping gear, cooking equipment and food. Your multitalented guides wear yet another hat as chefs and prepare all meals. Oar-powered rafting trips cost $200 to $300 per day, while trips via motorboat cost $225 to $325 per day. The minimum age ranges from eight to 12, depending on the outfitter and type of trip. The trips are very popular, so make reservations six to 12 months in advance. If you feel overwhelmed with options, contact the Flagstaff-based booking agency **Rivers & Oceans** (📞928-526-4575, 800-473-4576; www.rivers-oceans.com); it works with all of the companies running trips on the Colorado and doesn't charge a booking fee.

Prices listed here are just a sampling of what each company offers. Pre- and post-trip accommodations as well as transport to or from the trip's start/end point may not be included in the river-trip price. Many companies offer special-interest trips for those interested in subjects as diverse as geology, botany, classical music, art and wine.

📷 Arizona Raft Adventures

(📞928-786-7238, 800-786-7238; www.azraft. com; 6-day Upper Canyon hybrid/paddle trips $1940/2040, 10-day Full Canyon motor trips $2830) This multigenerational family-run outfit offers paddle, oar, hybrid (with opportunities for both paddling and floating) and motor trips.

Arizona River Runners

(📞602-867-4866, 800-477-7238; www.raftarizona. com; 6-day Upper Canyon oar trips $1795, 12-day Full Canyon motor trips $2695) Arizona River Runners has been at its game since 1970, offering oar-powered and motorized trips.

📷 Canyon Explorations/Expeditions

(📞928-774-4559, 800-654-0723; www.canyonex plorations.com; 7-day Upper Canyon trips $2110, 14-day Full Canyon trips $3535) It's possible to kayak the full canyon on paddle trips for an extra $200 (kayakers are accompanied by a kayak guide; once in a blue moon it offers trips with a string quartet for evening performances on the beach).

Canyoneers

(📞928-526-0924, 800-525-0924; www.can yoneers.com; 6-day Upper Canyon oar trips $1850, 7-day Full Canyon motor trips $2395) Some oar-powered trips travel with a historic, restored 'cataract boat' originally used in the '40s.

📷 Colorado River & Trail Expeditions

(📞801-261-1789, 800-253-7328; www.crateinc. com; 5-day Upper Canyon oar, paddle or hybrid trips $1857, 9-day motor trips $2752) Offering a range of motorized and oar-powered trips, this outfit also includes transportation to or from Las Vegas.

Grand Canyon Expeditions

(📞435-644-2691, 800-544-2691; www.gcex.com; 8-day Full Canyon motor trips $2550, 14-day Full Canyon dory trips $3700) In addition to oar and motor trips, this company also offers dory trips for traveling down the river the old-fashioned way. Transportation to and from Las Vegas is included (but optional) in all trips.

Grand Canyon Whitewater

(📞928-645-8866, 800-343-3121; www.grandcanyonwhitewater.com; 6-day Upper Canyon oar trips $1600, 8-day Full Canyon motor trips $2355) With a new name, this formerly family-owned business is run by a new team of old hands who have been running the Colorado since the '70s. Offers both oar and motorized trips.

🚣 Hatch River Expeditions

(📞800-856-8966; www.hatchriverexpeditions.com; 4-day Upper Canyon motor trips $1199, 7-day Full Canyon trips $2310) Hatch has been around since 1929, though of course the motorized rafts are a more recent introduction, and is a reliable company for those seeking a faster trip down the river. Also offers a few oar-powered trips.

Moki Mac River Expeditions

(📞801-268-6667, 800-284-7280; www.mokimac.com; 6-day Upper Canyon oar trips $1949, 8-day Full Canyon motor trips $2597) Trips originate in Las Vegas, and prices include transportation to Vegas and back. Moki Mac is another company that offers dories on some trips.

🚣 OARS

(📞209-736-4677, 800-346-6277; www.oars.com; 6-day Upper Canyon oar trips $2608, 15-day Full Canyon dory trips $5010) One of the best outfitters out there, OARS does oar, paddle and dory trips and offers the option of carbon offsetting your trip.

Outdoors Unlimited

(📞928-526-4511, 800-637-7238; www.outdoorsunlimited.com; 5-day Upper Canyon oar trips $1665, 13-day Full Canyon oar trips $3295) Outdoors Unlimited also offers all-paddle expeditions. As with most outfitters, some spring and fall trips stretch one or two days longer to allow more hikes and exploration along the way.

Tour West

(📞801-225-0755, 800-453-9107; www.twriver.com; 9-day Full Canyon motor trips $2605, 13-day Upper & Middle Canyon oar trips $3530) Trips include transportation to Las Vegas at the end of the trip as well as accommodations on the first night. Oar trips take out at Whitmore Wash; helicopter to rim and charter flight to Marble Canyon or Las Vegas are included.

🚣 Western River Expeditions

(📞801-942-6669, 866-904-1160; www.westernriver.com; 7-day Upper & Middle Canyon motor trips $2695) Taking out at Whitmore Wash, these river trips can last for six or seven days; it also offers half-day to two-day paddle or inflatable kayak trips starting and ending in Moab, Utah.

🚣 Wilderness River Adventures

(📞928-645-3296, 800-992-8022; www.riveradventures.com; 6-day Full Canyon motor trips $2135, 12-day Full Canyon oar trips $3520) Wilderness River Adventures also offers hybrid trips giving rafters the chance to paddle or float as they would on an oar-powered trip.

UPPER SECTION: LEES FERRY TO PHANTOM RANCH

MILE 0 TO MILE 87.5

Beginning at Lees Ferry, where it cuts through the top sedimentary layer of the Moenkopi shale, the upper section of the Colorado River then passes through Marble Canyon and Granite Gorge. The walls of **Marble Canyon** rise higher and higher, quickly exposing layers of rock beneath. Once you hit Mile 20.5, you've entered the **Roaring 20s**, a series of rapids (rated up to 8) that begin with North Canyon Rapid.

At Mile 31.9 you'll see, springing forth from the wall on your right, **Vasey's Paradise**, a lush green garden nourished from the water escaping the Redwall limestone. Shortly thereafter, the wide, low mouth of the enormous **Redwall Cavern** (Mile 33) appears ahead.

Around Mile 50, the beautiful dark-green, burgundy and purple layers of Bright Angel shale appear, as do the doorways of ancient **Puebloan granaries** (Mile 52.7) dating to AD 1100, sitting high above the water. The canyon reaches its confluence with the **Little Colorado River** at Mile 61.5.

This stretch features 28 rapids, 17 of which are rated 5 or higher. Nine rapids drop 15ft or more, including **Hance Rapid** (Mile 76.5), which boasts one of the river's largest single drops, a whopping 30ft. Near Mile 77 the appearance of pink Zoroaster granite intrusions into black Vishnu schist marks the start of **Granite Gorge**.

Side Hikes

Short hikes on the Upper Section end up in amazing little places.

🏃 North Canyon

Duration 1½ hours round-trip

Distance 2 miles round-trip

Difficulty Moderate

Start/Finish Mile 20.5, river right

Summary Hike up to a sculptural pool carved by water.

There isn't much elevation gain to this short hike, but it does entail a scramble up a wash to reach the pool. The erosion pattern above the pool has carved its sinuous curves with a design not unlike a three-dimensional topographic map or Georgia O'Keeffe painting.

🏃 Nankoweap to Granaries

Duration 1½ hours round-trip

Distance 1.5 miles round-trip

Difficulty Moderate

Start/Finish Mile 52.7, river right

Summary Steep hike which rewards the effort with an ancestral Native American site and a killer view.

Though short, this steep hike takes you about 700ft above the river to the ancient Puebloan granaries built into the cliff face. The stacked-stone walls with their square openings can be seen from the river. From up on the ledge, those who aren't awed by the well-preserved archaeological site will be struck by the beautiful views downriver.

MIDDLE SECTION: PHANTOM RANCH TO WHITMORE WASH

MILE 87.5 TO MILE 187.5

Rafters hike in from the South Rim to the boat beach near Phantom Ranch to raft **Middle Granite Gorge**, where Tapeats sandstone meets the Vishnu schist.

This section claims the Colorado's biggest white water, where 'Adrenaline Alley' begins with **Horn Creek Rapid** (Mile 90), and burly **Hermit Rapid** (Mile 95). It

offers the most technically challenging rapids: **Crystal Rapid** (Mile 98) and the granddaddy **Lava Falls Rapid** (Mile 179.5) with its gut-in-throat drop of 37ft. From Lava Falls Rapid, the next 80 miles downstream are a geologic marvel. Columnar basalt lines the canyon walls for thousands of vertical feet.

To leave Whitmore Wash, rafters take a helicopter to the Bar 10 Ranch, where they continue on by plane to Marble Canyon or Las Vegas.

The middle section boasts 38 rapids, 23 of which are rated 5 or higher (Crystal and Lava Falls Rapids both rate 10s). Eight rapids drop between 15ft and 18ft. Operators run this stretch between May and July. Between July and September trips continue to **Diamond Creek** (Mile 225). Oar-powered rafts take seven to nine days; motorboats four to five.

Side Hikes

On the Middle Section you can bomb a mossy pool or hike the world's shortest river.

🏃 Elves Chasm

Duration 10 minutes one way

Distance 0.5 miles one way

Difficulty Easy

Start/Finish Mile 116.5, river left

Summary Quick scramble to a pretty grotto.

Ferns, orchids and scarlet monkeyflowers drape the walls of this grotto, where a waterfall tumbles over intricate travertine formations. It takes five minutes to scramble up Royal Arch Creek from the river. Dive into the grotto's pool and swim to the base of the waterfall. Clamber up through the cave to an opening above a moss-draped rocky chute, then jump back into the pool below.

🏃 Tapeats Creek to Thunder Spring

Duration 4½ hours round-trip

Distance 5 miles round-trip

Difficulty Moderate-difficult

Start/Finish Mile 133.7, river right

Summary Hike to one of the world's shortest rivers, then connect with the Deer Creek Trail.

In drier seasons, the Little Colorado flows down from a mineral spring, which gives the water its tropical warmth and turquoise hue. If the water is clear, the confluence with the big Colorado creates a lovely juxtaposition of colors. Hiking about a half-mile up the side canyon will give you the chance to hop in and run the tiny mini-rapids of the Little Colorado. It's easy – strap that personal flotation device (PFD) around your bum, stick your feet in front of you and float on down.

Thunder Spring, the roaring 100ft waterfall that gushes out of the Muav limestone at Thunder Cave, is the source of Thunder River, one of the world's shortest rivers. Over its half-mile course it plunges more than 1200ft to the confluence with Tapeats Creek.

Just before Mile 134, follow the **Thunder River Trail** upstream along cottonwood-shaded **Tapeats Creek**, crossing it twice. You'll reach the first crossing, a thigh-deep ford of rushing water, in about 45 minutes. The second crossing, an hour later, is via a fallen log.

Leaving Tapeats Creek, you'll slowly zig-zag up an open slope for 30 minutes to expanding views of **Tapeats Amphitheater** and **Thunder Spring** (3400ft) – you'll hear the roar before seeing the waterfall. Enjoy a picnic in the shade at the base of the fall before retracing your steps (1400ft elevation change).

You can make this a seven-hour near-loop hike by continuing on the Thunder River Trail beyond the waterfall, traversing Surprise Valley and descending the Deer Creek Trail to the Colorado.

🏃 Deer Creek

Duration 2½ hours one way

Distance 3 miles one way

Difficulty Moderate-difficult

Start/Finish Mile 136.3, river right

Summary One of the inner gorge's finest hikes, with lush waterfalls and pictographs in a curvy slot canyon.

Downstream from Granite Narrows below Mile 136, **Deer Creek Falls** tumbles into the Colorado. From this welcoming trailhead you head 500ft up a steep, bushy slope to a stunning overlook. From here the trail leads into **Deer Creek Narrows**, an impressive slot canyon where the walls bear remarkable pictographs. The narrows end in an inviting cascade. Above, lush vegetation lines the trail as it meanders along the cottonwood-shaded creek.

The trail crosses the creek and ascends open, rocky slopes to **Deer Creek Spring**, the trail's second waterfall. From here retrace your steps back to the river. Despite having to scramble up and down steep slopes over loose rocks and follow narrow, exposed trails, this hike is one of the inner canyon's best.

🏃 Matkatamiba

Duration 20 minutes round-trip

Distance 0.8 mile round-trip

Difficulty Moderate

Start/Finish Mile 148, river left

Summary Pull yourself through the narrows to get to the amphitheater at Matkatamiba.

Matkatamiba, named for a Havasupai family and nicknamed Matkat, is a very narrow Redwall limestone slot canyon that meets the Colorado at Mile 148. So, wet or dry? You must quickly decide how to spend the next 10 minutes heading up to Matkat's acoustically perfect natural **amphitheater**, lined by ferns and wildflowers. On the tricky wet route, you head upstream through the creek – wading when possible, and crawling on all fours and using handholds to pull yourself over slippery boulders.

But hang on, you get wet on the dry route too, since the first 25ft of both routes start by wading through a chest-deep pool, clambering over a boulder as wide as the creek, then wading through yet another pool. Here the dry route leaves the creek and ascends 100ft of steep rock to an exposed trail that overlooks the narrow chasm. At a sculpted curve where the amphitheater emerges, the two routes merge. The wet route is too dangerous to descend, so return via the dry route.

🚶 Beaver Falls

Duration 4 hours round-trip

Distance 8 miles round-trip

Difficulty Easy-moderate

Start/Finish Mile 157, river left

Summary Explore the blue-green waters of Havasu Canyon from the riverside.

The blue-green spring-fed waters of Havasu Creek plunge over a series of four breathtaking waterfalls to the Colorado. Beaver Falls, which tumbles over travertine formations with one prominent fall, is the cascade nearest to the river. Most backpackers hike in only as far as Mooney Falls, so Beaver Falls – 2 miles further – is almost the exclusive domain of rafters.

The slot canyon near Mile 157 doesn't hint at what lies further up **Havasu Canyon**. A few minutes from the Colorado, the rock walls part to reveal wild grapevines, lush ground cover and tall cottonwoods along the level creekside trail. On this gentle hike, you'll spend about 20 minutes in water as you ford Havasu Creek, cross deep pools and wade upstream through knee-deep water. Once through the first and biggest water obstacle – the lovely, chest-deep **Big Kids Pool** – you'll emerge and climb a log staircase through a Muav limestone tunnel. The trail continues upstream to the base of a cliff near the confluence with Beaver Creek. Scramble up the cliff to reach an **overlook**

of Beaver Falls. Retrace your steps, relaxing and swimming in the several pools.

LOWER SECTION: WHITMORE WASH TO SOUTH COVE

MILE 187.5 TO BEYOND MILE 277

Rafters join the river at Whitmore Wash via helicopter from the North Rim. **Lower Granite Gorge**, the third and last of the canyon's sister granite gorges, starts at Mile 215, marked by the appearance of metamorphic and igneous rock. Though it features more flat water than other stretches, this section still boasts great white water, including 11 rapids, seven of which are rated 5 or higher. The two biggest drops are 16ft and 25ft. Oar-powered rafts take four to five days, motorboats three to four days.

In July and August the trip wraps up at **Diamond Creek** (Mile 225). Trips in May and June, however, continue downstream and can catch a glimpse of the water shimmering over the limestone deposits that make **Travertine Falls** (Mile 230) a petrified waterfall.

You might also muse over the unsolved mystery of Glen and Bessie Hyde's disappearance in 1928 at **Mile 237**, where their flat-bottomed boat was found peacefully floating with everything in it but the Hydes. Eventually, the trip continues beyond the canyon's terminus at **Grand Wash Cliffs** to end at South Cove on Lake Mead.

Understand the
❯ Grand Canyon

population per sq mile

| COCONINO COUNTY | ARIZONA | USA |

♦ ≈ 7 people

Grand Canyon Today

In an era of staycations, Grand Canyon National Park continues to be one of the country's most popular national parks for both Americans and foreign visitors.

Vital Stats

» One mile deep

» 18 miles across at its widest

» 277 river miles long

» Located in: Coconino County, Arizona

A Greener Way

No one comes to Grand Canyon National Park for traffic jams and chaotic atmosphere, so what a blessing the Greenway Plan is. The National Park Service (NPS), working in partnership with the National Parks Foundation, Grand Canyon Association and the US Forest Service, has been developing what will eventually be 73 miles of dirt and paved bicycle and pedestrian paths on both rims. Four of the five planned phases of the Greenway Plan have already been implemented, resulting in pedestrian-only and multi-use paths connecting Hermits Rest to the South Kaibab trailhead on the South Rim. On the North Rim, a paved path now connects Bright Angel Point to the North Kaibab Trailhead. *The Guide* map will show the complete sections of the paved Greenway Trail. Plans are also in the works for a path connecting Grand Canyon Village with the town of Tusayan, outside the South Rim Entrance, but for now the park offers a free park-and-ride shuttle service from 8am to 9:30pm, May to September.

Complementing these vehicle-free paths is the convenient shuttle system on the South Rim. Hop on and off and let these natural gas-powered shuttles get you from Hermits Rest in the west to the South Kaibab Trailhead in the east. Or take a spin on a rental bicycle from Bright Angel Bicycle Rentals on the South Rim, and pedal the park in the open air.

Top Books

» **Hiking Grand Canyon National Park** (Ben Adkison; Falcon, 2011) Indispensable hiking guide to the canyon, with detailed descriptions, hypsometric maps and tips for hiking in this unique environment.

» **Over the Edge: Death in the Grand Canyon** (Michael P Ghiglieri & Thomas M Myers; Puma Press, 2001) Morbidly fascinating and informative, if slightly repetitive, survey of death in the canyon.

» **Beyond the Hundredth Meridian: John Wesley Powell and the Second Opening of the West** (Wallace Stegner; Penguin, 1992) An illuminating look at John Wesley Powell and US water policy, by a literary icon of the American West.

seasonal visitation
(% of visitors)

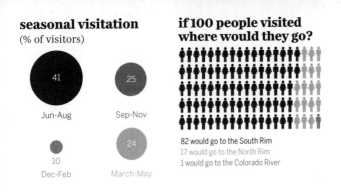

Jun-Aug 41

Sep-Nov 25

Dec-Feb 10

March-May 24

if 100 people visited where would they go?

82 would go to the South Rim
17 would go to the North Rim
1 would go to the Colorado River

Flyovers

With annual visitor numbers to the Grand Canyon nearing five million, helicopter and plane tours do brisk business, buzzing over the canyon at a none-too-quiet volume. For years, environmentalists and the NPS lobbied for the Federal Aviation Administration (FAA) to limit scenic flyovers in order to preserve a sense of serenity for other canyon visitors. In 1988 the FAA implemented flyover restrictions that limited helicopter and airplane traffic to specific corridors away from the most frequently used parts of the canyon. Scenic flyovers are also limited to certain hours of the day, and no flights are allowed below the rim except at Grand Canyon West, on the Hualapai Reservation. As a result, you probably won't notice the distant sounds of most scenic flights, but instead, the natural quiet of canyon breezes and birdsong. Ahhh.

Many scenic flights depart from Las Vegas, fly over Hoover Dam and land inside the canyon on the Hualapai Reservation for a picnic or a short boat ride on the Colorado.

Grand Canyon West & Skywalk

Opened in 2007, the Grand Canyon Skywalk generated a fair amount of controversy for its location, which is considered sacred, and the potential for overdevelopment around the site at Grand Canyon West, on the Hualapai Reservation. The Skywalk, an incongruously oddball glass semicircle hanging over a sheer cliff over the canyon, has proven to be an extremely popular attraction despite its relative remoteness. Bringing in much-needed revenue to the tribe, it hasn't yet resulted in overdevelopment and it has helped fund the paving of one of the reservation's main roads. We definitely wouldn't recommend visiting Grand Canyon West in

Best Maps

» **Trails Illustrated/National Geographic** (2009; 1:35,000 scale) Comprehensive waterproof and tearproof topographic map of Grand Canyon National Park that encompasses both rims, the backcountry and all trails.

» **Sky Terrain** (2009; 1:40,000 scale) Detailing the most popular areas and trails in the Grand Canyon, this waterproof, tearproof topographic map makes an excellent planning tool for backcountry adventures in the canyon.

» **United States Forest Service** (2007; 1:126,720 scale) North Kaibab map covers forest north of the park; Tusayan, Williams & Chalender map covers the south. Both show sights, viewpoints, primitive campsites and forest-service roads.

Adult males make up the largest demographic of those who fall to their deaths at the canyon. (Hint: peeing over the rim isn't as funny as you think it is. Use common sense.)

place of Grand Canyon National Park, but if the Skywalk sounds intriguing to you, chances are you'll find it worth the time and ticket price.

Uranium Mining

It's possible that by the time this book is published, the US government will have placed a 20-year moratorium (the legal limit) on establishing new uranium mining claims outside the borders of Grand Canyon National Park (see p210). However, the moratorium doesn't prevent mining at previously established claims. Even 40 years after the Orphan Mine was closed on the South Rim, it still emits enough radioactive waste that today's backcountry hikers are advised not to drink the water at Horn Creek below.

Grand Canyon on Film

» Koyaanisqatsi (1982)
Among the images in this non-narrative, non-verbal film, the Grand Canyon appears in a time-lapse – clouds passing overhead, transforming features with constantly changing shadow, light and color.

» Thelma & Louise (1991)
Though the dramatic denouement of this women-on-the-run story ended at the Grand Canyon, the final scene was actually shot near Moab, Utah.

» Into the Wild (2007)
This film, based on the true travels of seeker and wanderer Chris McCandless, takes a few liberties for the sake of story, as in the scene where he runs Colorado River rapids.

History

The Grand Canyon's rich history dates back more than 10,000 years, when Paleo-Indian hunters first passed through it in search of Pleistocene megafauna such as mammoth and giant sloth. Native American groups settled and migrated in response to the cycles of climate change, and they left their mark on the canyon, in extensive trail systems, rock art and artifacts hinting at their cultures. Eventually, the fate of modern Native Americans in the Grand Canyon would be determined not by the rhythms of nature but by inexorable European encroachment and ultimately the United States government. As the park was incrementally protected as a game reserve and national monument, it eventually became the country's 17th national park. As its primary administrator, the National Park Service now collaborates with the US Forest Service and neighboring reservations to maintain a sustainable balance between Native American land rights, resource management and future preservation of the park's ecology.

Ancient Cultures of the Grand Canyon

The Archaic Periods

By 9000 years ago, Archaic cultures entered the Grand Canyon region from the Basin and Range Province to the northwest and replaced paleo culture. The Archaic cultures span the period 7000 BC to 1000 BC.

The Early Archaic period, characterized by seasonal habitation, *atlatl* (spear-throwers), woven sandals and groundstone tools, saw an increase in population on the plateaus despite the drier climate and the loss of large Pleistocene game.

About 6000 years ago, a drought that would last on and off for almost 2000 years defined the Middle Archaic period. Conditions became even tougher, and many peoples migrated to more amenable lands. Those

TIMELINE	8000 BC	7000 BC–1000 BC	1000 BC–AD 1300
	Paleo-Indian hunters migrate through the Grand Canyon region in pursuit of Pleistocene megafauna, such as mammoth and giant sloth, which had begun to disappear.	Archaic cultures occupy the canyon, leaving behind evidence of their existence in split-twig figurines and chipped-stone tools that were probably used for hunting.	Basketmaker and ancient Puebloan cultures develop farming communities in and around the canyon, establishing complex trail systems that allowed for outside contact and trade.

Split-twig figurines depicting common prey like bighorn sheep, pronghorn antelope and deer can be viewed at Tusayan Ruins & Museum on the South Rim. Radiocarbon dating tells us that these figurines are estimated to be 3200 to 5000 years old, dating to the Late Archaic period.

Anasazi, the term traditionally used to describe the early Puebloan culture, translates roughly as 'Enemy Ancestors.' Because Hopi and Zuni find this term offensive, contemporary scholars refer to the Anasazi as 'ancestral Puebloans' or 'prehistoric Puebloans.'

who stayed moved between canyons and plateaus, sometimes camping in the caves and leaving evidence of their culture.

As the drought waned, about 4000 years ago (2000 BC), people returned to the region, and the 1000-year Late Archaic period began. Late Archaic evidence at the Grand Canyon includes dozens of elaborate split-twig animal figurines found in Stantons Cave, 50ft above the Colorado River in the Redwall limestone of Marble Canyon. Many are pierced by small twig or cactus thorn, thought to represent arrows, and some were found in shrine-like arrangements. Archeologists believe that nomadic groups used the caves for religious rituals, perhaps as a place to offer gifts to the gods in hopes of luring prey.

Ancestral Puebloans

Puebloan culture blurs with the Basketmaker culture (the canyon's earliest corn-growing people, named for the intricate coiled and watertight baskets they made), and the gradual shift from one period to the other is a result of complicated migrations and developments. Puebloan culture, as defined and explained by archeologists, includes corn-growing cultures that inhabited the southern Colorado Plateau and the Four Corners Region. The word *pueblo* means 'town' and refers to the above-ground adobe or stone structures in which these people lived. Religious ceremonies took place in kivas, circular below-ground buildings reminiscent of pithouses.

Ancestral Puebloan culture is a general term that includes several distinct traditions based on pottery style, geographic location, architecture and social structure; among them are the Chacoan, Mesa Verde, Kayenta, Virgin River, Little Colorado River, Cohonina and Sinagua cultures. By about 700 AD, Basketmaker culture had been completely replaced by Puebloan culture.

Agriculture & Abandonment

From 700 AD to 1000 AD, various strains of early Puebloan culture lived in and around the canyon. On the South Rim, the Cohonina inhabited the canyon west of Desert View (including Havasu Canyon and the Coconino Plateau) and mingled with the Kayenta, living seasonally in the uplands and along the river. Pottery shards found in Chuar Canyon, which were unearthed during a flash flood, suggest that, despite difficult conditions, a farming community thrived in the canyon 1200 years ago.

Paleoclimate research indicates that about 1000 years ago, precipitation increased slightly. For the next 150 years, the Grand Canyon experienced a heyday of farming. Taking advantage of the subtle shift in climate, various bands of ancestral Puebloans spread out, strengthened

» Nampaweap petroglyphs

MARK NEWMAN/LONELY PLANET IMAGES ©

1150–1300

Puebloan tribes abandon their settlements across the Southwest for unknown reasons that might include severe drought, hostile invasions or a combination of both.

1250

The Cerbat/Pai, ancestors of today's Hualapai and Havasupai, migrate from the Mojave Desert to the South Rim, while Southern Paiute migrate from southern Utah to the northern canyon.

1540

Spanish explorer García López de Cárdenas and his party of 12 are led to the South Rim of the Grand Canyon by Hopi guides.

and flourished. While the canyon was by no means lush, the high water table, increased precipitation and wide alluvial terraces made it more agriculturally productive than it would be today.

Then relatively suddenly, between 1150 and 1200, Puebloans abandoned the Grand Canyon. Other centers of Puebloan culture, like Chaco Canyon in northwest New Mexico and Mesa Verde in Southern Colorado, were also abandoned during this period, and scientists cannot agree on exactly why such elaborate and thriving communities would so suddenly leave their homes. Analyses of tree rings, stalagmites and lake pollen suggest that a severe drought descended upon the region at about 1150.

After just a few years of drought, corn reserves dwindled and canyon people were faced with malnutrition and starvation. Though there was no single mass exodus from the canyon, Puebloan peoples drifted away. Cohonina migrated towards Flagstaff; Sinagua drifted to and blended with Hopi mesas to the east. The Kayenta villagers stayed a bit longer than their contemporaries to construct fortlike buildings along the South Rim. According to archeologists, these defensive structures suggest that hostile invasions from migrating tribes further weakened the already vulnerable Puebloan communities and contributed to their withdrawal from the canyon.

Whatever the reason – drought, invasion or a combination of the two – by 1300 the Grand Canyon became merely an echo of the once-thriving agrarian Pueblo culture. Though the evidence suggests that they would return periodically, Puebloans never returned permanently.

Removal of Native Americans

As the farming cultures of the Pueblo people exited the canyon, other cultures moved in. The Cerbat/Pai, ancestors of today's Hualapai and Havasupai, arrived from the Mojave Desert to inhabit the western side of the canyon south of the river. It's not clear when they took up permanent residence – some scholars believe that they came to the region about 100 years after the ancestral Puebloans left, while others believe that it was their arrival that contributed to the Puebloans' departure.

From the early 19th century, US military forces pushed west across the continent, protecting settlers and wresting land from Native Americans, who had little use for European concepts of land ownership. With the 1848 *Treaty of Guadalupe* and the discovery of gold at Sutter's Mill in California, Americans crossed the continent in unprecedented numbers. It wasn't long before they intruded into and permanently transformed the lives and homes of Native Americans who had lived in and around the Grand Canyon for centuries.

Puebloan Ruin Sites

» Phantom Ranch

» Tusayan Ruins & Museum

» Walnut Canyon National Monument

» Wupatki National Monument

The Tusayan Ruin, on the east side of the South Rim, may have been the last Puebloan community in the Grand Canyon region. Archeological records show that it was not built until 1185 and was inhabited by a community of about 30 people for a mere 25 years.

1776	1803	1821	1848
In searching for a path from Santa Fe to present-day Yuma, missionary Francisco Tomás Gárces encounters the Grand Canyon and is the first to call the river the Colorado	The Louisiana Purchase makes the young United States the northeastern neighbor of New Spain, sharing a border at the crestline of the Rocky Mountains and along the Rio Grande.	After over a decade of the Mexican War of Independence, Spain signs the Treaty of Córdoba, securing independence for the Mexican Empire (formerly known as New Spain).	The *Treaty of Guadalupe Hidalgo* ends the Mexican-American War and the United States annexes Mexico's northern territory and Texas, a total of 914,166 sq miles that include Arizona.

EVICTION

As the NPS developed Grand Canyon National Park, Havasupai who had been living around the South Rim and Indian Garden area for generations were compelled to move off of the land. The last Havasupai living at Indian Garden were finally forced out by the NPS in 1928.

Hualapai

After the murder of Hualapai chief Wauba Yuman in 1866, Hualapai chief Sherum engaged American troops in a three-year war. The US Army destroyed their homes, crops and food supplies until the Hualapai surrendered in 1869. They were forced onto a reservation on the lower Colorado and, deprived of rations and unused to the heat of the lower elevations, many died from starvation or illness. The Hualapai escaped the reservation, only to be confined again when President Chester Arthur set aside the current 1,000,000-acre reservation on the south side of the Grand Canyon.

Havasupai

Though the Havasupai escaped the brutality of the Indian Wars, they too were eventually forced to give up their lands and were confined to a reservation as Americans settled in the Grand Canyon region. In 1880 President Rutherford Hayes established an area 5 miles wide and 12 miles long as the Havasupai Reservation, which eventually was expanded to its present-day boundaries. A few years later, the Bureau of Indian Affairs established schools for the Hualapai and Havasupai children to teach them the ways of the white man. Their canyon home was increasingly disturbed by Anglo explorers, prospectors and intrepid tourists as the 19th century drew to a close and the Grand Canyon became a destination for European Americans.

Paiute

Native Americans on the North Rim did not fare any better. US westward expansion brought disease to the Paiute, settlers stole the Paiute's best lands, and by the late 1860s conflict with Anglo pioneers had become common. In the early 20th century only about 100 Kaibab Paiute lived north of the canyon in Moccasin Spring. They were moved onto a reservation in 1907. Today the Kaibab Reservation surrounds Pipe Springs National Monument, in the desert about 80 miles north of the North Rim.

Spanish Explorers & Missionaries

Europeans saw the canyon for the first time in September of 1540. Spanish explorer Francisco Vásquez de Coronado believed that seven cities of gold lay in the northern interior of New Spain, and though several efforts had proved fruitless (he instead found Native American pueblos of stone and mud), he continued to traverse the region in search of gold. Native Americans told him about a great river that would reach riches at the Gulf of California, so he sent García López de Cárdenas and his party of 12 to investigate.

1850-51	1856-58	1858-59	1865
The Territory of New Mexico is formed, which includes the Grand Canyon; military surveyors begin exploring and mapping the country's vast new territories.	Edward Fitzgerald Beale leads a survey mission across the desert with a caravan of camels, establishing the road that later became Route 66 and is now I-40.	First Lieutenant Joseph Christmas Ives and his expedition become the first European Americans to reach the river within the canyon; he declares the region 'altogether valueless'.	The Civil War ends; hundreds of Navajo die on the 'Long Walk' to Fort Sumner after being forced from their traditional lands into an internment camp in eastern New Mexico.

Ancestral Puebloan occupants of the Grand Canyon established an intricate trail system throughout the gorge and side canyons, allowing access all over the canyon and to the river. Spurs in all directions linked canyon communities and facilitated trade with cultures throughout the Southwest. Remnants of these paths can still be seen today; some were modified by prospectors, early tourist entrepreneurs and the National Park Service (NPS) and are still in use. One of the most striking of these ancestral Puebloan trails is a stick footbridge across a gap in the cliffs called the Anasazi Bridge, which can be seen on the north side of the river, upstream from President Harding Rapid.

It is not clear where Cárdenas and his men stood when they first saw the Grand Canyon, but based on his written record historians believe it was somewhere between Moran Point and Desert View, on the South Rim. Though Hopi guides knew of relatively easy paths into the canyon, they didn't share them, and Cárdenas' men managed to descend only about one-third of the way down before turning back. The canyon was too much of an obstacle, and the rewards were too little.

Finding no gold or riches of any sort, Spanish explorers left the canyon country to the Native Americans – who were not, however, left in peace. The Catholic church of Spain, more interested in converting the natives to Christianity than finding gold, spent the next several hundred years building missions in the Southwest and severely punishing resistors.

Despite the unwelcoming conditions, Spanish missionaries traversed the inhospitable terrain of Northern Arizona in search of both converts and routes to Santa Fe. Inevitably, some stumbled upon the canyon. In 1776, about 200 years after Cárdenas tried to reach the river, Francisco Tomás Gárces reached the canyon in an effort to find a path to Santa Fe from what is now Yuma, Arizona. A kind and gentle man who is widely regarded to be the second European visitor to the canyon, Gárces named the river 'Rio Colorado,' meaning 'Red River.' He spent several days with the hospitable Havasupai. Because they had been sheltered in their canyon home, the Havasupai had not yet developed a fear and hatred of Spanish missionaries, and they showered him with feasts and celebration. He marveled at their intricate system of irrigation and treated them with courtesy and respect. He continued east into Hopi country, but they refused to give him shelter or food. Later that year, Silvestre Vélez de Escalante, Francisco Atanasio Domínguez and Captain Bernardo Miera y Pacheco came upon the canyon while trying to find a route from Monterey, California, to Santa Fe.

1866	1868	1869	1869
Hualapai chief Wauba Yuman is murdered, precipitating a three-year war against the US military in which an estimated one-third of the Hualapai population was killed.	The Navajo Reservation is established on 5500 sq miles in the heart of their ancient lands, eventually growing into the largest reservation in the country.	The transcontinental railroad is completed, connecting the existing eastern railroad from Council Bluffs, Iowa to Oakland, California, and speeding the population of the West.	Geologist, naturalist and Civil War veteran John Wesley Powell and his crew of nine become the first people to successfully run the Colorado River.

PADDLING
PIONEERS

Wallace Stegner's
engaging *Beyond
the Hundredth
Meridian: John
Wesley Powell &
the Second Open-
ing of the West*
recalls Powell's
historic first river
trip down the
Colorado within
the context of
developing the
West.

Historians believe that no more than a handful of Europeans visited the canyon from 1540 until the early 19th century, so their influence on the indigenous people and land was minimal during this time.

Birth of the Southwest

In the mid-19th century several events occurred over the course of a few years that would transform the American Southwest within a half-century. With the *Treaty of Guadalupe Hidalgo* in 1848, the Mexican-American War ended, and the United States acquired Mexico's northern territory, which would eventually become Arizona, California, Nevada, Utah, Colorado and New Mexico. This, along with the territories acquired with the Louisiana Purchase only 40 years earlier, more than doubled the size of the US and forced the federal government to grapple with the problem of running a Jeffersonian system of representative government while also maintaining a national identity despite great geographical and cultural distances. That same year, gold was discovered at Sutter's Mill in California. In 1850 the territory of New Mexico, including Arizona and the Grand Canyon, was created.

Forty-niners rushing toward gold in California, and pioneers hoping to build homes in the new West, needed wagon roads. Moreover, if the US was to retain control over the vast wilderness they had just acquired, it needed to know exactly what it was. And so the government sent military men to identify and map its new territory in the 1850s. Edward Fitzgerald Beale took a caravan of camels across the desert in the late 1850s, creating the road that would eventually become Route 66 (now replaced by the I-40).

In 1858 First Lieutenant Joseph Christmas Ives was appointed to explore the still-mysterious 'big canyon' region. Directed to find an inland waterway, Ives set off on the steamboat *The Explorer* on December 31, 1858, from the Gulf of Mexico. He traveled upriver for two months but crashed into a boulder in Black Canyon (near today's Hoover Dam) before ever making it into the canyon. He abandoned his river efforts and set off on Beale's road, along with artists Heinrich Baldwin Mollhausen and Baron Friedrich W Von Egloffstein, a geologist, various Native American guides, soldiers, packers, trail builders and about 150 mules. After about a month, they scrambled down a side canyon north of Peach Springs and became what historians believe to be the first European Americans known to reach the river within the canyon. Mollhausen and von Egloffstein are credited with creating the first visual representations of the Grand Canyon.

Frustrated with the difficulty of the terrain and the lack of water, Ives cut south to Beale's road west of Havasu Falls, and eventually returned east to organize the expedition's maps, landscape etchings and

1870-90	1880	1883	1884
Ranchers and settlers arrive in the Grand Canyon region; by 1890, the non-Native American population of the Arizona Territory reaches more than 88,000.	President Rutherford Hayes establishes the Havasupai Reservation on a mere 518 acres along Havasu Creek; the Havasupai accept this without opposition, for fear of expulsion from their ancestral land.	President Chester Arthur establishes the Hualapai Reservation on one million acres of land, part of which comprises ancestral lands of the Hualapai Nation.	Prospector John Hance, having given up on mining yields, takes the first tourists into the canyon on his mining trails and charges them $1 for dinner and lodging.

lithographs into a cohesive report on the 'big canyon.' While acknowledging its sublime beauty (perhaps the first to do so), Ives concluded that the region was 'altogether valueless... Ours has been the first and will doubtless be the last party of whites to visit this profitless locality... It seems intended by nature that the Colorado River, along with the greater portion of its lonely and majestic way, shall be forever unvisited and undisturbed.' Within 130 years of this statement, over 5 million people were visiting the Grand Canyon National Park per annum, but the idea of nature as a destination in itself, as something to be preserved as an American treasure, did not become a popular notion until the late 19th century. Until that point Americans were interested in nature only in as much as it could be exploited for material gain.

John Wesley Powell

Fascinated by the reports of initial surveys of the Grand Canyon, John Wesley Powell cobbled together a makeshift team of volunteers and private funding to finance an expedition to the Colorado River. The work of this one-armed Civil War veteran and professor of geology would set the stage for the canyon's transformation from a hurdle to a destination.

In May of 1869, Powell and his crew of nine launched four wooden boats, laden with thousands of pounds of scientific equipment and supplies, from Green River, Wyoming. They floated peacefully until one of the boats, the *No Name*, smashed into rocks at rapids that Powell named Disaster Falls. Despite this and the loss of supplies, they continued down the Green River, joined the Colorado River on July 17 and floated through Glen Canyon without further mishap. The waters of the Colorado in the 'big canyon,' however, were not so kind. They portaged their heavy boats around rapids and ran others, baked under the hot sun, repaired leaks and sustained themselves on meager rations of flour, coffee and dried apples. Powell took notes on the geology and natural history, and they spent time scrambling over cliffs, taking measurements and examining rocks, canyons and streams in what Powell called their 'granite prison.'

On August 27 they came to a particularly wild rapid that Powell named Separation Rapid. Here, three men – Bill Dunn and brothers Seneca and Oramel Howland, who were exhausted, fed up with their wilderness conditions and convinced that they would never make it through alive – abandoned Powell and hiked north out of the canyon in hopes of finding civilization. Instead, it is believed that they were attacked and killed by Shivwits Paiute men who mistook them for prospectors who had murdered a Paiute woman. The Powell expedition made it through the wild water, as well as through several other rough rapids, and emerged three days later close to what is now Lake Mead. After 14 weeks on the river,

HISTORY JOHN WESLEY POWELL

Thomas Moran's painting *The Grand Chasm of the Colorado*, purchased by Congress in 1874 for $10,000, hung in the National Capitol building and would be influential in securing national-park status for the Grand Canyon.

Upon first viewing the below, García López de Cárdenas and his exploratory party believed it to be about 6 ft wide. After several days spent attempting to find a route to the river and discovering that they had grossly underestimated its scale, the effort was abandoned.

1890

William Wallace Bass sets up a dude ranch on the South Rim and takes tourists into Havasu Canyon, befriending the Havasupai and facilitating cross-cultural exchange with the tribe.

1890s

A stagecoach line runs from Flagstaff to the South Rim, ferrying hardy tourists over bumpy, dusty roads on a journey that lasted one to two days.

RALPH HOPKINS/LONELY PLANET IMAGES ©

» Historic cabin on the Bass Trail, North Rim

INDESCRIBABLE
WONDERS

Powell and his crew became the first known people to travel the length of the Colorado River through what Powell named the Grand Canyon.

Powell returned to the Colorado River in 1871 for a second expedition, this time with photographer EO Beaman, who produced about 350 images of the Grand Canyon, and artist Frederick Samuel Dellenbaugh. In 1873 Thomas Moran, the landscape painter who would become the artist most associated with the Grand Canyon, and photographer John Hiller visited the rim country with Powell. Powell's 1875 report, entitled 'The Exploration of the Colorado River of the West,' as well as newspaper and magazine articles – and in particular the visual representations by Moran and Hiller that accompanied these written accounts – planted the seeds for the canyon as a tourist destination. For the first time, the general public saw spectacular images of the Grand Canyon, sparking their desire to see its grandeur for themselves. Within a quarter of a century, through the combined forces of the prospectors-turned-tourist guides, the railroad and the Fred Harvey Company, the Grand Canyon would become an iconic American treasure.

Tourists Arrive

Railroad to the Canyon

With the arrival of the Atlantic and Pacific Railroad to Flagstaff and Williams in the early 1880s, tourists trickled to the canyon's South Rim. In 1883 a total of 67 hardy tourists made the 20-mile trek from Peach Springs (the nearest train line to the Grand Canyon) to Diamond Creek. From there, they descended another two miles along Diamond Creek Wash to the Colorado River. In 1884 JH Farlee eked out the Grand Canyon's first wagon trail to Diamond Creek and built the canyon's first hotel at the end of the line.

When the railroad to the South Rim was completed in 1901, tourism at the canyon accelerated. Instead of paying $20 and enduring a teeth-rattling 12-hour stagecoach ride, visitors could pay $3.95 and reach the rim from Williams in three hours.

In 1902 brothers Ellsworth and Emery Kolb came to the canyon, and within a few years they set up a photography studio on the rim. Tourists could ride a mule into the canyon in the morning and have a photo of their journey by the next day. Fred Harvey, who joined the Santa Fe Railroad in 1876 to provide hotels and services to its passengers, earned a reputation for luxurious trackside accommodation, fine dining and impeccable service. In 1905, only four years after the train's arrival at the rim, his Fred Harvey Company built El Tovar, an elegant hotel, and established Hopi House. Fred Harvey hired Hopi to live there, demonstrate their crafts, wear native costumes and perform dances for the tourists.

Of the canyon, John Wesley Powell wrote: 'The wonders of the Grand Canyon cannot be adequately represented in symbols of speech, nor by speech itself. The resources of the graphic art are taxed beyond their powers in attempting to portray its features. Language and illustration combined must fail.'

1893	1896	1901	1902
President Benjamin Harrison proclaims the Grand Canyon a National Forest Preserve, a designation that offers some environmental protection but still allows mining and logging.	On the site where today's Bright Angel Lodge sits, the Bright Angel Hotel was originally established by James Thurber (not that James Thurber), who ran a stagecoach line from Flagstaff.	The Atchison, Topeka and Santa Fe Railway completes a spur line to the South Rim and begins running from Williams directly to the Grand Canyon.	A survey crew caught in North Rim winter weather determined that Bright Angel Canyon was the best route to the river; this became the North Kaibab Trail.

While tourism on the rims and on inner-canyon trails developed feverishly at the beginning of the 20th century, the idea of rafting on the 277 miles of the Colorado River through the canyon attracted only a few intrepid adventurers. One of the earliest of these was Robert Brewster Stanton, who went down the river in 1889 to survey it for a rail line. He lost several men, and the idea of a rail line along the river was wisely abandoned. After 1900, several prospectors survived the trip, and in 1911 the Kolb brothers filmed their river expedition and began screening it to tourists.

Of the many early tourists who tried to raft the river but never finished, honeymooners Glen and Bessie Hyde would become the most famous. They set out in 1928, without lifejackets, to be the first man and woman pair to run the Colorado through the canyon. They ran the 424 miles from Green River, Utah, to Bright Angel Creek (including the rapids at Cataract Canyon) in 26 days and hiked up to Bright Angel Lodge for a rest, publicity photographs and interviews. Though witnesses say Glen seemed excited to continue, and loved the media attention, Bessie hinted at being less than thrilled to return to the river. As Emory Kolb and his daughter Edith walked them to the trailhead, Bessie noticed Edith's shoes and, looking at her own hiking boots, commented rather sadly, 'I wonder if I shall ever wear pretty shoes again.' As fate would have it, she never would. The honeymooners never emerged from the canyon, and their disappearance remains one of the park's greatest mysteries.

In 1938 Norman Nevills started the first commercial river-running business, but by 1949 still only 100 people had run the Colorado through the Grand Canyon.

Now that the Native Americans had been confined to reservations and the wilderness had been tamed, Americans began to see an innocence and authenticity in Native American culture and in the natural landscape that was lacking in industrialized life. No longer a threat, Native Americans and their crafts and lifestyle became a subject for the tourist gaze.

The Grand Canyon, with its proximity to the Native Americans of the Southwest and its spectacular wilderness scenery that could be enjoyed from the comfort of rimside hotels, offered Americans a safe opportunity to return to a romanticized past. Furthermore, the magnificent landscape of the American West, unique in its geologic features, gave a young country looking for a history and a unifying sense of nationality something to claim. The American West gave the country a unique identity, and tourists flocked to the Grand Canyon.

1905	**1906**	**1907**	**1907**
The Fred Harvey Company, in partnership with the Atchison, Topeka and Santa Fe Railway, opens El Tovar on the South Rim, designed by Mary Colter.	Grand Canyon Game Preserve is set aside on the North Rim; it limits livestock grazing but also results in the hunting and eventual disappearance of indigenous wolves and mountain lions.	Tourists cross the Colorado River in a cage strung on a cable built by David Rust, who ran a tourist camp at the bottom of the canyon.	Kaibab Paiute are moved to a reservation encompassing fewer than 200 sq miles that do not border Grand Canyon National Park and comprise a fraction of their ancestral lands.

Tourism on the North Rim

Because of its isolation, tourism on the North Rim developed more slowly, and even today it only receives 10% of the park's visitors. The Arizona Strip, the remote desert country north of the rim, was originally settled in the mid-19th century by Mormons, who were trying to escape increasingly strict laws against polygamy.

Most visitors to the Kaibab Plateau went for sport hunting. In June 1906 Teddy Roosevelt created Grand Canyon Game Preserve. The United States Forest Service prohibited deer hunting in the preserve and set about eliminating all of the animal's predators. James T 'Uncle Jim' Owens, in his capacity as the reserve's first game warden, guided hunting trips and oversaw the killing of hundreds upon hundreds of badgers, coyotes, wolverines, cougars and grizzly bears.

Following the arrival of the first car to the North Rim in 1909, the forest service began advertising scenic attractions on the Kaibab Plateau. In 1913 the forest service built the 56-mile Grand Canyon Hwy to the Bright Angel Ranger Station, at Harvey Meadow. Aldus Jensen and his wife ran a small tourist service with tent accommodation. They led guests along the Rust Trail to the river, where they would connect with Fred Harvey wranglers. In 1917 Wylie's Way Camp opened near the fire tower at Bright Angel Point, and Jensen closed down his services. A step above tents, Wylie's Way Camp could accommodate up to 25 guests and offered tent cabins; guided tours to Cape Royal, Point Sublime and other destinations; mule trips; and a central dining room.

Visitors arriving at the North Rim from the north had to take the 135-mile stagecoach from Marysvale, Utah, to Kanab and then travel the 80 miles or so to the rim by whatever means they could find. Alternatively, beginning in 1907, they could hike into the canyon from the South Rim, cross the Colorado River in a cage strung on a cable, and hike up to the North Rim on the North Kaibab Trail (constructed in 1903). On the canyon's bottom, visitors stayed in a tourist camp at the mouth of Bright Angel Creek, the predecessor to Colter's 1922 Phantom Ranch.

Also in 1922, Gronway and Chauncey Parry began automobile tours to the North Rim, and Will S Rust opened a tourist camp north of the park. In 1919 a rough dirt road from Kanab to the North Rim was completed, and by 1925 more than 7000 visitors arrived at Bright Angel Point. In 1928 Union Pacific architect GS Underwood designed the original Grand Canyon Lodge, and a suspension bridge was built across the river to connect the South and North Kaibab Trails. Though a fire on September 1, 1932, destroyed the main lodge on the North Rim, it was rebuilt in 1937, and the guest cabins, still used today, were left unharmed.

The Grand Canyon Historical Society publishes *The Ol' Pioneer*, a quarterly magazine profiling historical characters and events at the canyon. Become a member to get a subscription to *The Ol' Pioneer*; selected archives are available for downloading at www.grandcanyonhistory.org.

1908	1919	1922	1928
President Teddy Roosevelt creates Grand Canyon National Monument, one of the acts for which he became known as a pioneering conservationist in the United States.	The Grand Canyon finally earns a national park designation, becoming the United States' 17th national park; during this year, the Grand Canyon receives 44,000 visitors.	The Fred Harvey Company builds Phantom Ranch, designed by Mary Colter, along the Colorado River at the confluence of Bright Angel Creek and Phantom Creek.	Designed by Gilbert Stanley Underwood, the Grand Canyon Lodge is built on the North Rim; the main lodge and over 100 cabins feature stonework that blends with the landscape.

Evolution of a Park

In 1908 President Theodore Roosevelt created the Grand Canyon National Monument, and in 1919 President Woodrow Wilson made Grand Canyon the 17th national park in the US. Over 44,000 people visited the park that year. By 1956 more than one million people would visit the Grand Canyon annually.

The Great Depression slowed the frenzy of park development, and from 1933 to 1942 the Civilian Corps Conservation, the Public Works Administration and the Works Progress Administration did everything

MARY COLTER'S GRAND VISION

Mary Colter's buildings blend so seamlessly into the landscape that, were it not for the tourists strolling around them, you could conceivably not even notice the structures. Indeed, Colter's buildings add to the beauty of Grand Canyon National Park because they succeed so magnificently in adding nothing at all.

In 1883 at the age of 14, Mary Colter (1869–1958) graduated from high school in St Paul, Minnesota. She studied art in San Francisco and spent her entire career designing hotels, shops, restaurants and train stations for the Fred Harvey Company and the Santa Fe Railway. Beginning in the late 1870s, these two companies worked as a team to transform the American West into a tourist destination.

Colter's work follows the sensibility of the Arts and Crafts Movement. In keeping with the nationalist spirit of the late 19th century, and reacting against industrialized society, the Arts and Crafts aesthetic (or Craftsman style) looked toward American models, rather than European traditions, for inspiration. The movement revered handcrafted objects, clean and simple lines and the incorporation of indigenous material. For an excellent example of well-preserved, classic Arts and Crafts design, stop by the Riordan Mansion in Flagstaff.

Colter spent a great deal of time researching all her buildings, exploring ancient Hopi villages, studying Native American culture and taking careful notes. The Colter buildings in Grand Canyon National Park use local material such as Kaibab limestone and pine, and incorporate stone, wood, iron, glass and brick. They embrace Native American crafts like woven textile and geometric design, and echo Indian architecture with kiva fireplaces and vigas (rafters) on the ceiling.

The conundrum of preserving expanses of Western land as sacred American wilderness while at the same time developing them for tourists was solved in part by Colter's brilliant designs. Her buildings, known as 'National Park Service rustic,' stand in harmony with their natural environment and served as models and inspiration for subsequent tourist services in national parks throughout the country.

Arnold Berke's *Mary Colter: Architect of the Southwest* is a beautifully illustrated and well-written examination of the life and work of Mary Colter.

1928	1936	1956
Construction of the Kaibab Suspension Bridge (the Black Bridge), a rigid suspension span, replaces the old swinging bridge and completes the cross-canyon Kaibab Trail.	Hoover Dam (formerly known as Boulder Dam), a feat of engineering, is built on the Colorado River west of the canyon, creating Lake Mead.	Two airplanes on eastward flights from Los Angeles collide mid-air over the canyon, resulting in the establishment of a national air-traffic control system.

LEE FOSTER/ LONELY PLANET IMAGES ©

» Hoover Dam

CONTROVERSY

from touching up buildings to creating trails and cleaning ditches. Fewer tourists visited during this period, giving rangers breathing room to develop interpretive programs – the predecessors of today's ranger talks.

The dearth of visitors from the Depression through the end of WWII resulted in a quieter, more relaxed Grand Canyon National Park. However, as soon as the war ended, Americans – in love with their cars and eager to explore and celebrate their country – inundated the national parks. The flood prompted another flurry of construction, and from 1953 to 1968 the park built more trails, enhanced existing trails, improved roads and built Maswik, Kachina and Thunderbird Lodges. Steel and concrete buildings joined the classic rustic style of El Tovar and Mary Colter's architecture.

In 1975, President Gerald Ford signed the *Grand Canyon National Park Enlargement Act*, doubling the size of the park by integrating it with Grand Canyon National Monument and Marble Canyon National Monument. This same act returned land to the Havasupai. The following year, the park received three million visitors. In 1979 Grand Canyon National Park was designated a Unesco World Heritage site.

Over at the West Rim, the Hualapai Nation opened Grand Canyon Skywalk in 2007. This horseshoe-shaped glass platform, cantilevered 4000ft above the canyon floor, brought with it a flood of tourism and controversy over the sustainability of more development in this fragile environment. Fortunately for the tribe, the Skywalk is a wildly popular attraction despite its relative isolation, bringing much-needed revenue to the Hualapai. As in the national park and Havasu Canyon, the constant challenge of balancing tourism with environmental stewardship continues.

Proposed construction of two gigantic dams on the Colorado in the mid-60s was famously quashed by public protest after the Sierra Club published full-page ads in major newspapers asking, 'Should we also flood the Sistine Chapel so tourists can get nearer the ceiling?'

1963	1964-67	1979	2007
Controversial Glen Canyon Dam is built on the Colorado River east of the canyon, flooding and thus destroying Glen Canyon to create what is now Lake Powell.	Dams at Marble Gorge and Bridge Canyon are proposed for the Colorado River, but massive public outrage quashes the proposal, in large part due to the Glen Canyon Dam outcome.	Grand Canyon National Park is designated a Unesco World Heritage site, recognized not only for its extraordinary beauty but also for its geologic and ecological significance.	The Hualapai Nation opens the controversial glass Skywalk at Grand Canyon West, bringing droves of tourist traffic to the relatively remote West Rim.

Grand Geology

While neither the longest nor the deepest canyon in the world, the Grand Canyon is certainly one of the most awe-inspiring. For geologists, the canyon showcases a remarkably well-preserved, two-billion-year-old slice of geologic history. In these exposed layers, half of the Earth's life span is revealed, serving as a window into our planet's past.

The Story in the Rocks
Vishnu Schist & Zoroaster Granite

The story begins in the canyon's innermost recesses, where the Colorado River continues to carve a deep channel into progressively older rock. The bottommost layer, Vishnu schist, is dark and fine-grained, with vertical or diagonal bands that contrast with the canyon's horizontal upper layers. Down around Phantom Ranch, look for intruding bands of pinkish Zoroaster granite, in gorgeous contrast. Together, these are among the oldest exposed rocks on Earth's surface.

The schist offers evidence that two billion years ago the canyon region lay beneath an ancient sea. For tens of millions of years, silt and clay eroded into the water from adjacent landmasses, settling to the seafloor. These sediments, along with occasional dustings of lava and ash, accumulated to a thickness of 5 miles and were later buried beneath another 10 miles of additional sediment. By 1.7 billion years ago these layers had buckled and uplifted into a mighty mountain range that rose above the water. In the process, intense heat and pressure transformed the sedimentary layers into metamorphic schist and gneiss.

Stromatolites

At the time, the region lay near the equator, but the uplifted landmass soon began a northward migration while undergoing a long spell of erosion. So much of the uplifted material eroded away that it left a significant gap (or unconformity) in the geologic record – from 1.7 billion to 1.2 billion years ago. Lost with hardly a trace was the mountain range itself, which finally wore down into a low coastal plain. Gradually the landmass sank back into the sea, providing a platform for marine algae, which secreted the Bass limestone that now sits atop the Vishnu schist. Marine fossils in the Bass limestone include such primitive life forms as cabbage-like stromatolites.

The Precambrian Era & the Great Unconformity

In the late Precambrian era (1.2 billion to 570 million years ago) the region alternated between marine and coastal environments as the ocean repeatedly advanced and retreated, each time leaving distinctive layers of sediment and structural features. Pockmarks from raindrops, cracks in drying mud and ripple marks in sand have all been preserved in one form or another, alongside countless other clues. Much of this evidence

INTERACTIVE

The Yavapai Geology Museum & Observation Station on the South Rim, aside from having fantastic canyon views, features kid-friendly interactive exhibits explaining the geology of the canyon from various angles, and binoculars to check out the main exhibit. Rangers give daily geology talks here; check *The Guide* for current info.

was lost as erosional forces scraped the land back down to Vishnu schist. The resulting gap in the geologic record is called the Great Unconformity, where older rocks abut against much newer rocks with no intervening layers. Fortunately, pockets of ancient rock that once perched atop the Vishnu schist still remain and lie exposed along the North and South Kaibab Trails, among other places.

The Paleozoic Era

The Precambrian era came to an end about 570 million years ago. The subsequent Paleozoic era (570 to 245 million years ago) spawned nearly all of the rock formations visitors see today. The Paleozoic also ushered in the dramatic transition from primitive organisms to an explosion of complex life forms that spread into every available aquatic and terrestrial niche – the beginning of life as we know it. The canyon walls contain an abundant fossil record of these ancient animals, including shells like cephalopods and brachiopods, trilobites, and the tracks of reptiles and amphibians.

The Paleozoic record is particularly well preserved in the layers cut by the Colorado, as the region has been little altered by geologic events such as earthquakes, faulting or volcanic activity. Every advance and retreat of the ancient ocean laid down a characteristic layer that documents

A ROCK PRIMER

Rocks are divided into three large classes – sedimentary, igneous and metamorphic – each well represented in the Grand Canyon.

Sedimentary

Sedimentary rock originates as accumulations of sediments and particles that cement together over time. Borne by water or the wind, the sediments generally settle in horizontal layers that preserve many features, suggesting how they formed. Three types of sedimentary rock are present in the canyon:

Limestone Comprises little more than calcium carbonate, a strong cement that softens and easily erodes when wet.

Sandstone Consists of sand particles that stack poorly, leaving lots of room for the calcium carbonate cement to penetrate, making this a very hard and durable rock.

Mudstone (including shale) At the opposite end of the spectrum from limestone, mudstone consists of flaky particles that stack so closely together there's little room for the binding cement, thus mudstone is often very soft and breakable.

Igneous

Igneous rock originates as molten magma, which cools either deep underground or after erupting to the surface as lava or volcanic ash. Volcanic rocks are common west of Toroweap Valley, where they form such prominent features as Vulcans Throne and Lava Falls. Granite that cooled deep inside the earth lies exposed along the inner gorge – in fact, canyon explorer John Wesley Powell originally named the river corridor Granite Gorge.

Metamorphic

Metamorphic rock starts out as either sedimentary or igneous, then transforms into other kinds of rock following exposure to intense heat or pressure, especially where the Earth's crust buckles and folds into mountain ranges. Metamorphic rock usually remains hidden deep underground. Two types of metamorphic rock are common in the canyon:

Schist Deriving from shale, sandstone or volcanic rock, schist lines the inner gorge and is distinguished by narrow, wavy bands of shiny mica flakes.

Gneiss Forming light-colored intrusions within the schist, gneiss is characterized by its coarse texture and the presence of quartz and feldspar.

Geology of the Grand Canyon

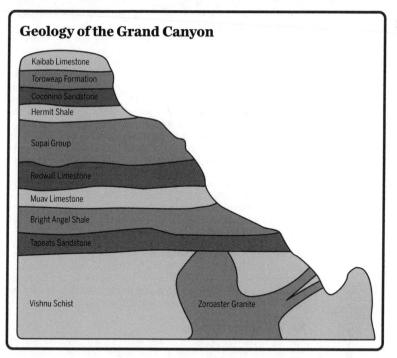

Kaibab Limestone
Toroweap Formation
Coconino Sandstone
Hermit Shale
Supai Group
Redwall Limestone
Muav Limestone
Bright Angel Shale
Tapeats Sandstone
Vishnu Schist
Zoroaster Granite

whether it was a time of deep oceans, shallow bays, active coastline, mudflats or elevated landscape. Geologists have learned to read these strata and to estimate climatic conditions during each episode.

The science of stratigraphy (the reading of rock layers) stemmed from work at the canyon, at a time when American geology was in its infancy and considered vastly inferior by European geologists.

The Mesozoic Period & the Kaibab Uplift

Considering the detailed Paleozoic record, it's puzzling that evidence of the following Mesozoic period (245 to 70 million years ago) is entirely absent at the canyon, even though its elaborate layers are well represented just miles away on the Colorado Plateau and in nearby Zion, Bryce and Arches National Parks. Towering over the landscape just south of the South Rim, Red Butte is a dramatic reminder of how many thousands of feet of Mesozoic sediments once covered the canyon 70 million years ago. So what happened to all of this rock, which vanished before the river even started shaping the canyon? About 70 million years ago the same events that gave rise to the Rocky Mountains created a buckle in the earth known as the Kaibab Uplift, a broad dome that rose several thousand feet above the surrounding region. Higher and more exposed, the upper layers of this dome eroded quickly and completely.

Evidence from the past 70 million years is equally scarce at the canyon, as the movement of materials has been away from the canyon rather than into it. Volcanism has added a few layers of rock in parts of the west canyon, where lava flows created temporary dams across the canyon or simply flowed over the rim in spectacular lava waterfalls, the latter now frozen in time in places such as Lava Falls. The stretching of

Earth's crust also tilted the region to the southwest, shifting drainage patterns accordingly.

But the story that interests visitors most, namely how the canyon has changed in the past five million years, is perhaps the most ambiguous chapter of all. Geologists have several competing theories but few clues. One intriguing characteristic is that the canyon's east end is much older than the western portion, suggesting that two separate rivers carved the canyon. This fits into the oft-repeated 'stream piracy' theory that the Kaibab Uplift initially served as a barrier between two major river drainage systems. The theory assumes that the western drainage system eroded quickly into the soft sediments and carved eastward into the up-lift, eventually breaking through the barrier and 'capturing' the flow of the ancient Colorado River, which then shifted course down this newly opened route.

Alternate theories assume other river routes or different timing of the erosion, placing it either before or after the uplift. Until more evidence is uncovered, visitors will have to simply marvel at the canyon and formulate their own theories about how this mighty river cut through a giant bulge in Earth's crust millions of years ago.

Reading the Formations

After the initial awe has worn off, many visitors are eager to learn how to identify the formations that so neatly layer the canyon. The distinctive sequence of color and texture is worth learning, as you'll see it over and over again on each rim, from each viewpoint and along each trail.

Kaibab Limestone

Starting at the top, a layer of creamy white Kaibab limestone caps the rim on both sides of the canyon. This formation is about 300ft thick and erodes to form blocky cliffs. Limestone surfaces are pitted and pock-marked, and rainwater quickly seeps into the rock to form sinkholes and underground passages. Fossils include brachiopods, sponges and corals.

Toroweap Formation

The Toroweap Formation is the vegetated slope between the cliffs of Kaibab limestone above and massive Coconino cliffs below. Similar in composition to the Kaibab, the Toroweap is a pale yellow to gray crumbly limestone that also contains marine fossils.

Coconino Sandstone

It's quickly evident how sandstone erodes differently from limestone when you descend past Coconino sandstone along the Bright Angel Trail, one of the few places a trail can negotiate these sheer 350ft cliffs. Inspect the rock face closely to spot fine crosshatches, evidence of windblown ripples that once crisscrossed huge sand dunes. Even more fascinating is the wealth of fossilized millipede, spider, scorpion and lizard tracks found in this formation.

To identify what geologic layers you're gaping at as you hike the Bright Angel, pocket the fabulous laminated *Field Guide to Geology along the Bright Angel Trail* by Dave Thayer. Containing basic explanations and illustrations about canyon geology, it's a handy little reference guide that weighs next to nothing.

Memorize the catchphrase 'Know The Canyon's History, See Rocks Made By Time,' in which the capital letters represent the formations from rim to canyon floor (eg, K for Kaibab limestone). The formations are described in that order in this chapter.

GEOLOGIC WONDERS

Vulcans Throne (boxed text p138) The park's most impressive cinder cone.
Bright Angel Canyon (p136) An excellent example of how creeks follow fault lines across the landscape.
Havasu Creek (p176) Stupendous travertine formations and beautiful waterfalls.
Toroweap Overlook (boxed text p138) The canyon's most dramatic viewpoint.
Vishnu Temple (p137) One of the canyon's most prominent temples.

Hermit Shale

Below these mighty cliffs lies a slope of crumbly red Hermit shale. This fine-grained shale formed under shallow tidal conditions and contains fossilized mud cracks, ripple marks and the footprints of reptiles and amphibians. Today it supports a distinctive band of shrubs and trees including oak, hop tree and serviceberry. Hermit shale is so soft that in the western canyon it has eroded completely, leaving a broad terrace of Esplanade sandstone.

Supai Group

Just below the Hermit shale are the red cliffs and ledges of the Supai Group, similar in composition and color but differing in hardness. This is a set of shale, limestone and sandstone layers, and each dominates different portions of the canyon. All formed under similar swampy coastal conditions, where shallow waters mingled with sand dunes. Deposited some 300 million years ago when amphibians first evolved, these formations preserve early footprints of these new animals. Supai cliffs can be stained red by iron oxides or black from iron or manganese.

Redwall Limestone

Next is the famous Redwall limestone, one of the canyon's most prominent features. Viewed from the rim, the Redwall is a huge red cliff that towers 500ft to 800ft over the broad Tonto Platform. The Redwall also forms a dividing line between forest habitats above and desert habitats below. The rock is actually light-gray limestone that has been stained red by iron oxides washed down from layers above. This formation is pitted with many caves and alcoves and contains abundant marine fossils, including trilobites, snails, clams and fish.

Muav Limestone

Muav limestone is a small slope of varying thickness that marks the junction of Redwall sandstone and the Tonto Platform. This marine formation contains few fossils but features many eroded cavities and passages.

Bright Angel Shale

Perched just above the dark inner gorge, the broad, gently sloping Tonto Platform is the only break in a long jumble of cliffs and ledges. The platform is not a formation at all but rather the absence of one, where soft greenish Bright Angel shale has been largely stripped away to reveal the hard Tapeats sandstone beneath. These slopes of grayish-green shale can be seen on the South Kaibab Trail, but seen from the river, its intact layers of green and purple are remarkably colorful.

Tapeats Sandstone

The last and oldest Paleozoic sedimentary layer is the Tapeats sandstone, below which lies the huge gap (the Great Unconformity) that separates the sedimentary layers of the canyon from the ancient Vishnu schist of the inner gorge. Collectively referred to as the Tonto Group, Tapeats, Bright Angel and Muav all formed along the same ocean shoreline. Tapeats originated with coarse cobbles along an ancient beach, Bright Angel shale comprises fine mud deposits that collected just offshore from the beach, and Muav limestone consists of calcium carbonate that fused in deep water.

GRAND GEOLOGY

The steep Hermit Trail offers excellent opportunities to see various types of fossils. Near the trailhead, the Kaibab limestone holds marine fossils. About a mile down the trail, fossilized reptile tracks appear in Coconino sandstone, and not quite 2 miles down you can find fossils of ferns.

FOSSILS

On the South Rim, rangers lead daily fossil walks; these easy walks examine marine fossils along a half-mile stretch along the rim.

TRAIL OF TIME

As you walk the Rim Trail on the South Rim, you'll notice the Trail of Time exhibit, which debuted in 2010. Each one million years is represented by one meter (3.3ft) along the way, marked by bronze signs embedded in the trail. Alongside the trail are beautiful, polished examples of stone from geologic layers deep within the canyon that correspond with the time period on the trail. Interpretive signs and viewing spots dot the gentle trail, which you can follow for about two miles from Yavapai Geology Museum & Observation Station back to the Bright Angel Lodge area.

Geology 101 on the South Rim

» Trail of Time on the Rim Trail

» Yavapai Geology Museum & Observation Station

Interested in geology? Consider the comprehensive, authoritative, informative (and rather technical) *Grand Canyon Geology*, edited by Stanley Beus and Michael Morales.

Forces at Work

What's truly remarkable about the Grand Canyon is not how big it is, but how small it is. In terms of sheer volume, much more material has been removed from the Grand Wash Trough just below the canyon or other stretches where the river meanders across vast floodplains. But the canyon's narrow scale continues to concentrate erosive forces in dramatic fashion.

Obviously foremost among the erosive forces is water, which chisels virtually every inch of the landscape. Its differing effect on various rock types is readily apparent in the canyon's stair-step profile – the softer rock formations crumbling into gentle slopes at the foot of sheer hard cliffs.

On a subtle level, water may simply seep deeply into the rock. The water gradually weakens the rock matrix, causing large or small bits of rock to break free in the form of landslides.

A weathering effect known as frost riving occurs when water works down into cracks and freezes. Freezing water exerts a tremendous outward force (20,000lb per square inch), which wedges into these crevices, prying loose blocks of rock from the canyon cliffs.

Streams have gradually eroded defined side canyons on both rims, cutting back ever deeper into their headwalls. This effect is especially pronounced on the higher-altitude North Rim, as it catches more runoff from passing storm systems. This rim angles to the south, pouring its runoff into the canyon. As the South Rim likewise slopes to the south, its waters flow away from the canyon.

As parallel side canyons cut back toward their headwalls, they create the canyon's distinctive temples and amphitheaters. Neighboring streams erode either side of a long promontory or finger of rock, then carve the base of the promontory, leaving the tip stranded in open space. Over time these isolated islands of elevated rock weather into rugged spires called temples, while the headwalls of the side canyons become amphitheaters.

Water is not always as patient and imperceptible. Late-summer thunderstorms cause flash floods that resculpt the landscape in minutes. A tiny trickling brook carrying grains of sand can quickly explode into a torrent that tosses house-sized boulders with ease.

Although the Colorado cut through the soft sedimentary layers at lightning speed, the river has now reached extremely hard Vishnu schist, and erosion has slowed dramatically. As the river approaches sea level, downward erosion will cease altogether, even as the canyon continues to widen. This lateral (sideways) erosion proceeds 10 times faster than downward cutting. Thus, far in the future, the Grand Canyon may be referred to as the Grand Valley.

Wildlife of the Grand Canyon

Wildlife in the park ranges from secretive bighorn sheep and prehistoric condors to scampering lizards and nosy ringtail cats, all scattered across a vast region. For some species the Grand Canyon presents an insurmountable obstacle, while for others it's a life-sustaining corridor through a forbidding desert. If you remain patient and alert, you'll spot some of these canyon denizens, but while you wait for an appearance, it doesn't hurt to learn about their background and habitat.

Animals

Grand Canyon National Park is home to 316 bird species, 89 mammal species, 56 reptile and amphibian species and 17 fish species.

Large Mammals

Mountain Lions

Even veteran biologists rarely see the mountain lion. But a large population does live here, and the canyon rates among the best places in North America to spot this elusive cat. While mountain lions roam throughout the park, they gravitate to forests along the North Rim in pursuit of their favorite food, mule deer. Reaching up to 8ft in length and weighing as much as 160lb, this solitary animal is a formidable predator that rarely bothers humans.

Mule Deer

Rim forests and meadows are the favored haunts of mule deer, which commonly graze at dusk in groups of a dozen or more. After their predators were systematically hunted out of the park in the early 1900s (even Teddy Roosevelt came to the canyon to hunt mountain lions), the deer experienced a massive population explosion. Less common on the South Rim and within the canyon, deer move seasonally to find water and avoid deep snows.

Bighorn Sheep

Like solemn statues, bighorn sheep often stand motionless on inaccessible cliff faces or ridgelines and are readily identified by their distinctive curled horns. During breeding season, males charge each other at 20mph and ram horns so loudly the sound travels for miles. Look for bighorns in side canyons along the Tonto Platform beneath the South Rim. Bring binoculars, as hikers seldom encounter this animal at close range.

Celebrate Wildlife Day takes place on the South Rim in April or May each year. It features family-friendly activities, presentations, a live animal open house and indoor and outdoor educational programs.

Small herds of elk are commonly spotted around the park. They can often be seen grazing along the entrance roads to the South and North Rims, and even in the developed areas of Grand Canyon Village. Keep an eye out and slow down for roaming elk, especially around dusk.

Coyotes & Foxes

Wild members of the dog family include the ubiquitous coyote and its much smaller cousin, the gray fox. Both share the same grayish-brown coat, and each has adapted to human activity, growing increasingly comfortable around roads, buildings and (of course) any unattended food. You stand a good chance of seeing coyotes in the daytime, especially around meadows, where they hunt for rodents. Foxes often emerge at night, when you might spy one crossing a trail or road.

Small Mammals
Chipmunks & Squirrels

While similar in appearance, the region's three chipmunk species do bear subtle differences. The South Rim is the exclusive domain of the gray cliff chipmunk, an extremely vocal species that can bark an estimated 5800 times in a half-hour, twitching its tail with each call. This species shares the North Rim with least chipmunks and Uinta chipmunks, although cliff chipmunks are relegated to rocky ledges and cliffs. Least chipmunks inhabit open areas, while Uinta chipmunks live in forests and are abundant around North Rim campgrounds and picnic sites.

The most conspicuous members of the squirrel family are speckled gray rock squirrels, which scoot fearlessly amid visitors' feet along rim trails and viewpoints. Hoping for handouts (strictly forbidden), these large squirrels will boldly explore unattended gear or sidle up to resting hikers. True to its name, this species nearly always inhabits rocky areas.

Living on opposite rims, Abert's and Kaibab squirrels demonstrate how the canyon divided populations into distinct subspecies. These long-eared squirrels were a single population only 20,000 years ago, when forests grew in the canyon. The squirrels split into two populations when the climate warmed and dried and the canyon was transformed into desert habitat. Today, the dark-bellied, white-tailed Kaibab squirrel of the North Rim is considered a subspecies of the Abert's squirrel of the South

Those cheeky little rock squirrels sure are adorable, creeping along on their bellies to investigate the sandwich you're eating. Just keep in mind that squirrel bites are one of the most common injuries at the South Rim. Squirrels can also carry hantavirus, rabies and the plague.

THE MEXICAN WOLF

In 1998, an endemic Southwestern predator took its first tentative steps back to the wild. Eleven captive-bred Mexican wolves, a subspecies of the gray wolf, were released in east-central Arizona in a project aimed at reintroducing 100 wolves into a 7000-sq-mile area over 10 years. The current population stands at about 50 individuals.

The Mexican wolf traditionally ranged in 'sky islands' (high-elevation areas) as far south as central Mexico and as far north as southern Colorado. They are the smallest, most genetically distinct subspecies of gray wolf in North America. But government campaigns to eradicate predators resulted in the wild US population of Mexican wolves going extinct by the 1950s. In 1976 they were declared an endangered species, a designation that remains in place today.

Gray wolves have been reintroduced successfully in the northern Rockies, where the landscape actually rebounded as a result. Aspen groves became healthier as they were no longer overgrazed by elk and mule deer. Of course, wary local residents and ranchers who lose livestock oppose the addition of Mexican wolves to the ecosystem. As with any top-tier predator, on-the-ground issues of reintroduction are quite complex.

The US Fish and Wildlife Service, in collaboration with state and Native American agencies, oversees the reintroduction program and is currently investigating further action to create a wild, healthy, sustainable population of Mexican wolves. One idea is to reintroduce the wolves in a range near the North Rim of the Grand Canyon, where human population, cattle ranching and road density are low but where mule deer and elk are plentiful. But at the moment, the continued existence of the wild Mexican wolf remains tenuous.

Rim. Both depend on ponderosa pine forests for their livelihood, rarely wandering more than 20yd from these trees. Each species is common on its respective rim; in their winter coats, they look especially jaunty with furry tassels adorning their ears.

Ringtail

One of the area's most intriguing creatures is the nocturnal ringtail, which looks like a wide-eyed housecat with a raccoon's tail. Once common around park campsites, where they would emerge at night to raid campers' food supplies, ringtails have been discouraged by modern food-storage techniques, though they are still observed along the rims and river corridors.

Birds
Small Birds

A harbinger of spring, the broad-tailed hummingbird zips energetically about the park from May through August. Males bear a notch in their wing feathers that creates a distinctive whirring sound in flight, making this diminutive bird sound impressively big, thus attracting mates. They are common in wildflower-filled forest glades on both rims.

Forests and campgrounds on both rims host large numbers of the sparrow-sized dark-eyed junco. Hopping about the forest floor in search of seeds and insects, this bird is conspicuous for its black hood and its habit of nervously flicking its tail outward to flash white outer tail feathers. Similar in appearance but restricted to trees is the mountain chickadee, a perennial favorite with children because its merry song sounds like *cheese-bur-ger*. Both species are hardy and number among the handful of birds that remain in the park year-round.

The first birds many visitors encounter are white-throated swifts, which swoop and dive over towering cliff faces at rim viewpoints. Designed like sleek bullets, these sporty 'tuxedoed' birds seem to delight in riding every wind current and chasing each other in playful pursuit. Flying alongside the swifts are slightly less agile violet-green swallows, which are a familiar sight around campgrounds and park buildings.

Only hikers that descend to the sparsely vegetated Tonto Platform will spot the beautiful black-throated sparrow, one of the few species able to survive in this scorching desert habitat. Sporting a jaunty black bib and crisp white facial stripes, this bird brightens scrubby slopes with its sweet *chit-chit-cheee* song.

The stirring song of the canyon wren is for many people the most evocative sound in the park. So haunting is this song, it hardly seems possible that this tiny reddish rock-dweller could produce such music. Starting out as a fast series of sweet tinkling notes, the song fades gracefully into a rhythmic cadence.

Underscoring the importance of water in this desert landscape, it comes as a shock to find American dippers (formerly known as water ouzels) beside streams deep within the canyon. These energetic bundles of gray feathers rarely leave the cascading streams, where they dive beneath the cold water to capture insects and larvae. Look closely to spot the flash of this bird's whitish, translucent eyelids, which allow it to see underwater.

Birds of Prey

Of the six owl species occurring regularly in the park, none is as familiar as the common and highly vocal great horned owl, which regularly fills the echoing canyons with its booming hoots. This is among the largest and most fearsome of all the region's raptors, and when one moves into

WILDLIFE OF THE GRAND CANYON ANIMALS

Whether you enjoy the aerial acrobatics of swifts and swallows atop rimside cliffs or the bright songs of warblers among riverside thickets, there's no question that the canyon's 373 bird species are among the region's premier highlights.

CONDOR

The last wild condor to soar over the Grand Canyon was spotted in 1924...until the US Fish and Wildlife Service released six endangered California condors in northern Arizona in 1996, the happy result of a captive breeding program.

the neighborhood, other owls and hawks hurry on to more favorable hunting grounds or run the risk of being hunted down as prey themselves. Hikers may be startled to glance up and spot this bird's huge glaring face and prominent 'horns' (actually long erect feathers) as it peers down at them from a crevice along the rim.

Commanding vast hunting territories of some 50 sq miles, powerful golden eagles may be observed as they travel widely in search of jackrabbits and other prey. Boasting 7ft wingspans, they are among the canyon's largest birds, second in size only to recently arrived California condors. Watch for the characteristic golden tint on the eagle's shoulders and neck.

Given their endangered status in recent decades, peregrine falcons are surprisingly common throughout the park. Here they find plenty of secluded, cliffside nesting sites, as well as one of their favorite food items, white-throated swifts, which they seize in midair. Look for the falcon's long, slender wings and dark 'moustache.'

> If you spend a night below the rim – at Indian Garden or in Havasu Canyon, for example – you may be treated to an incredible chorus of frogs and toads croaking en masse, the barbaric yawps echoing off canyon walls like some Godzilla-sized canyon creature.

Amphibians & Reptiles
Frogs & Toads

The bleating choruses of common canyon tree frogs float up from boulder-strewn canyon streams each night. Gray-brown and speckled like stone, these tiny frogs dwell in damp crevices by day, emerging at night beside rocky pools.

Occupying similar habitat (because water occurs in limited patches) is the aptly named red-spotted toad, a small species with (you guessed it) red-tipped warts covering its body. Its nighttime song around breeding pools is a high musical trill.

CONDORS

When critically endangered California condors were released at the nearby Vermilion Cliffs in 1996, the canyon experience was forever and profoundly altered. As was the case when wolves were reintroduced to Yellowstone National Park, visitors seem utterly fascinated by the condors. With 9ft wingspans and bare, featherless heads, these birds are an unforgettable sight.

It's a miracle condors are around at all, seeing as their world population declined to less than two dozen birds in the 1980s. Many assumed these gigantic prehistoric holdovers were on the brink of extinction. Following a concerted captive breeding effort, however, there are now more than 70 condors flying around the park and nearby areas.

Fortunately for park visitors, condors have a strong affinity for large crowds of people. This is an evolutionary trait, as condors are carrion feeders, and crowds of large mammals like humans are more likely to produce potential food. As a result, condors often hang around popular rim viewpoints like Grand Canyon Lodge on the North Rim and Grand Canyon Village on the South Rim.

Condor populations are far from secure, however, even in the park, where they seem to have plenty of food and room to roam. The true test will be whether the species can continue to reproduce successfully. Pairs laid their first egg in 2001 and a total of 13 chicks have been born in the wild since reintroduction began. The canyon birds are all still young and inexperienced, so biologists hope that as the birds mature, more pairs will form and try to breed. Given that condors live about 50 years, there's plenty of time for these birds to settle down in their new home.

How can you tell you're looking at a California condor and not a common turkey vulture? Condors have a wingspan of about 9ft, while those of turkey vultures are about 6ft. Turkey vultures tend to rock slightly in the wind and flap more often than condors, who soar more smoothly.

Lizards

Perhaps the most abundant and widespread reptile in the park is the eastern fence lizard, a creature 5in to 6in long that you'll likely see perched atop rocks and logs or scampering across the trail. During breeding season, males bob enthusiastically while conspicuously displaying their shiny blue throats and bellies. Females have dark, wavy crossbars on their backs and only a pale bluish wash underneath.

As delicate in appearance as a fragile alabaster vase, the banded gecko has thin, practically translucent velvety skin. Emerging at night to hunt small insects, this lizard is not readily found unless you're hiking the desert slopes at night with a flashlight.

The strangest reptile in the park is the rarely seen Gila monster, which looks like a 2ft-long orange-and-black sequined sausage. Mostly placid, it's capable of quick lunges and powerful bites with its massive black-rimmed jaws. The lizard holds on tenaciously as its venomous saliva enters bite wounds. No human deaths have been attributed to this species, but the venom is a potent neurotoxin and victims should seek immediate medical care. Though encounters are rare, this lizard is best left alone.

Snakes

Home to some 20 snake species, the park is a great place to learn about these misunderstood animals. Commonly encountered in a range of habitats is the gopher snake, often mistaken for a rattlesnake because it vibrates its tail in dry leaves when cornered or upset. Sporting an attractive tan body with dark-brown saddles, this lithe constrictor preys on rodents and small birds.

The snakes that elicit the most interest are the six resident species of rattlesnake. The southwestern speckled and the northern black-tailed rattlesnake are the rarest, while the other four are subspecies of the western diamondback rattlesnake family: the Great Basin, the Mojave, the Hopi and the most common of all, the Grand Canyon pink rattlesnake. Nothing quite approaches the jolt of terror and adrenaline prompted by the angry buzz of a rattlesnake. Humans and wild animals both react with instinctive fear, although rattlesnakes rarely strike unless provoked.

Insects

Summer visitors will likely hear desert cicadas, whose ceaseless rasping and clicking is produced by vibrating membranes stretched over resonating sound chambers. Finding one of these inch-long insects is another matter altogether, as they are masters of camouflage – one reason they're able to screech all day and still avoid predators.

Also notable are inch-long, shiny metallic-blue carpenter bees, which tunnel through dead wood in dry forested areas. Unlike colonial hive-making bees, carpenter bees lead solitary lives and spend much of their time chasing away interlopers who might move into their tunnels.

The canyon's many butterfly species are highlighted by the distinctive orange-and-black monarch butterfly, which flutters through the park in large numbers in late summer, en route to Mexican wintering grounds. This large, showy butterfly avoids predation because as a larva it feeds on milkweed plants that contain noxious alkaloids – animals that try to eat monarchs suffer a severe reaction to these plant compounds.

Plants

The park supports a fantastic mix of plant communities and is home to more than 1400 species from four of North America's major biological provinces – the Rocky Mountains and the Mojave, Sonoran and Great Basin Deserts. Each province contributes unique species to the mix.

WILDLIFE OF THE GRAND CANYON ANIMALS

Of the six rattlesnake species found in the canyon, the most common is the Grand Canyon pink rattlesnake, a subspecies of the Western Diamondback that evolved to blend in with the warm tints of the canyon's geologic layers.

RATTLESNAKES

Plants of the Rocky Mountain province are found on both rims, especially the North Rim, where Engelmann spruce and quaking aspen form distinctive moist forests. Plants of the desert provinces occupy the inner canyon, where the climate is much hotter and drier. Mojave plants are found from downriver up to Hundred and Fifty Mile Canyon, Sonoran plants (including ocotillo and mesquite) dominate the central canyon, while Great Basin plants (such as rabbitbrush and sagebrush) take over from lower Marble Canyon to Lees Ferry.

Botany enthusiasts will appreciate *A Field Guide to the Plants of Arizona*, by Anne Epple, while those interested in how regional plants can be used will enjoy *Wild Plants & Native People of the Four Corners*, by William Dunmire and Gail Tierney.

Trees

Pine, Spruce & Aspen

Due to their prominence and longevity, trees serve as excellent indicators of different life zones and local environmental conditions. The stately ponderosa pine, for example, defines the distinctive forested belt between 6000ft and 8000ft. In many places along the North Rim and on the highest points of the South Rim this species forms nearly pure stands that cover many acres. To identify this species, look for large spiny cones, long needles in clusters of three, and yellowish bark that smells like butterscotch.

At higher elevations ponderosa pines mingle with two other species that characterize the Rocky Mountain boreal forest. Engelmann spruce has a curious bluish tinge to its needles and inch-long cylindrical cones with paper-thin scales. To confirm its identity, grasp a branch and feel for sharp spiny-tipped needles that prick your hand. Young Engelmann spruce are a favorite choice for Christmas trees because they flaunt such perfect shapes. Quaking aspen is immediately recognizable for its smooth, white bark and circular leaves. Every gust of wind sets these leaves quivering on their flattened stems, an adaptation for shaking off late snowfalls that would otherwise damage fragile leaves. Aspen groves comprise genetically identical trunks sprouting from a common root system that may grow to more than a hundred acres in size. By budding repeatedly from these root systems, aspens have what has been called 'theoretical immortality' – some aspen roots are thought to be more than a million years old.

Piñon-Juniper Woodlands

A ponderosa pine will turn anyone into a tree-hugger. Look for one with gold-colored bark, and commune with it for a moment. Don't be shy – really get your nose up against that sweet tree and take a deep breath – the scent is redolent of vanilla, maple syrup, butterscotch, or...?

Habitats at the lower edge of the ponderosa pine belt are increasingly arid, but two trees do particularly well along this desert fringe. Piñon pines are well known for their highly nutritious and flavorful seeds, sold as 'pine nuts' in grocery stores. These same seeds have been a staple for Native Americans wherever the trees grow, and many animals feast on the seeds when they ripen in the fall. Piñons have stout rounded cones and short paired needles. Together with Utah junipers, piñon pines form a distinctive community that covers millions of acres in the Southwest. Such 'PJ woodlands' dominate broad swathes of the South Rim and canyon walls down to 4000ft. Blue, berrylike cones and diminutive scalelike needles distinguish junipers from other trees. Birds feed extensively on juniper 'berries,' prompting the seeds to sprout by removing their fleshy coverings.

Oaks

Consorting with piñons, junipers and ponderosas is the beautiful little Gambel oak, whose dark-green leaves turn shades of yellow and red in autumn and add a classy palette of color to an already stunning landscape. Often occurring in dense thickets, oaks produce copious quantities of nutritious, tasty acorns long favored by Native Americans and used to make breads, pancakes, soups and ground meal.

Cottonwood

Rivers and watercourses in this harsh desert landscape are lined with thin ribbons of water-loving plants that can't survive elsewhere. Towering prominently above all others is the showy Fremont cottonwood, whose large, vaguely heart-shaped leaves rustle wildly in any wind. Hikers in the canyon's scorching depths find welcome respite in the shade of this tree. In spring, cottonwoods produce vast quantities of cottony seed packets that fill the air and collect in every crack and crevice.

Tamarisk

Since construction of upstream dams, aggressive weedy tamarisk has replaced ancestral communities of willows and other native plants. Though this delicately leaved plant from Eurasia sports a handsome coat of soft pink flowers through summer, its charms end there, for this plant robs water from the soil and completely overwhelms native plant communities. Producing a billion seeds per plant and spreading quickly, this species now dominates virtually every water source in the Southwest deserts.

Shrubs
Acacia & Mesquite

Despite the prevalence of tamarisk along stream banks, a few native plants manage to hold on. Easily recognized are catclaw acacia and honey mesquite, thorny members of the pea family that produce seeds in elongated, brown peapods. Each species features delicate leaflets arranged in featherlike sprays. Mesquite was a staple among Southwest Indians, providing food, fuel, building materials and medicines. Charcoal from this tree is prized today for the unique flavor it lends to barbecues.

Fendlerbush

Many shrub species cloak the canyon walls above the Tonto Platform. Here the steep slopes offer a variety of shaded niches, seeps and springs where shrubs form thickets. In spring and early summer these sweet-scented thickets fairly hum with bees, butterflies and birds at work among the abundant blossoms. While blooming, the white-flowered fendlerbush is a powerful magnet for such butterflies as admirals and painted ladies. This 9ft-high shrub sports curious flowers with four widely separated, spoon-shaped petals.

Big Sagebrush

Abundant on both rims is the distinctive big sagebrush, a plant that dominates millions of acres of dry desert habitat from northern Arizona to Canada. Tolerant of cold and rain to a degree not found in other desert species, sagebrush ranges from valley floors to high desert peaks across the West. Three-lobed leaves and an aromatic scent make identification of this species a cinch.

Wildflowers

The park's dazzling variety of wildflowers put on an extravagant show – and because habitats range from arid desert to snowy heights there are always flowers blooming somewhere from early spring on. Even in midsummer, pockets of water foster lush wildflower gardens in shaded recesses within the canyon, while sudden thunderstorms trigger brief floral displays.

Raising eyebrows whenever encountered by hikers, the oddly inflated desert trumpet presents its loose arrangement of tiny yellow flowers any

Removal of invasive tamarisk is an ongoing task in the riparian areas in and around the Grand Canyon. You can often find excellent short-term volunteer opportunities through Grand Canyon Trust Volunteers, who work in conjunction with the National Park Service to remove tamarisk and other non-native plants.

time between March and October. Just below the flowers, the stem balloons out like a long slender lozenge. Old stems maintain this shape and are just as curious as the living plant. Sometimes wasps drill into the plant and fill its hollow stems with captured insects as food for developing larvae.

One of the more conspicuous desert flowers, especially along roadsides, is the abundant peachy-pink globe mallow. Shooting forth as many as 100 stems from a single root system, they can tint the desert with their distinctive color. At least 10 mallow species live within the park.

Seeps, springs and stream banks are fantastic places to search for some of the most dramatic flower displays. The brilliant flash of crimson monkeyflowers amid lush greenery comes as something of a shock for hikers who've trudged across miles of searing baked rock. Apparently, someone once saw enough of a monkey likeness to name this wildflower, but you're more likely to notice the 'lips' that extend above and below the flower.

Columbines are also common at these seeps and springs, though some species range upward into moist forested areas of the park. The gorgeous golden columbine is most common in wet, shaded recesses of the inner canyon. Red columbine is a rare find in a wide range of forests and shaded canyons, while the blue-and-white Colorado columbine is a resident of Rocky Mountain spruce-fir forests along the North Rim. The long spurs of columbine flowers hold pockets of nectar that attract large numbers of butterflies and hummingbirds.

Though this hardly seems the place to find orchids, the beautiful giant helleborine is in fact common at seeps and springs within the canyon. The distinctly orchid-like flowers are a medley of green and yellow petals with purple veins. Though it goes without saying that you should never pick flowers in a national park, it's especially important that these precious orchids be admired and left undisturbed.

Cacti

Although they could be classified with wildflowers, the park's two dozen cacti are a group of plants unique unto themselves. Foremost among the cacti are the 11 members of the prickly pear group, familiar for their paddle-shaped pads that resemble beaver tails. In fact, one of the most common species is called beavertail cacti, while a rarer species is known as pancake pear. Both the pads and fruit are commonly eaten after proper preparation. Be aware that the spines (glochids) detach easily on contact and are highly irritating.

Often dubbed the classic beautiful cacti, stunning claret cup hedgehog cacti shine like iridescent jewels in the dusty desert landscape, where

HANGING GARDENS

Even though much of the Grand Canyon region appears arid, there is in fact water locked up inside the layers of porous sandstone – the byproduct of countless torrential rainstorms, which pour down onto the surface and percolate deep into the stone. Over time this water flows laterally and emerges from cliff faces as various seeps and springs. Flowing waters erode soft sandstone, causing the rock to collapse and form cool, shady overhangs. The constant water supply then fosters a rich community of algae on vertical surfaces and, below that, lush gardens of delicate flowering plants and ferns known as hanging gardens. These gardens of lacy and delicate maidenhair ferns, columbines, orchids, monkeyflowers and primroses are a welcome sight to parched desert travelers. Botanists also treasure these alcoves, as many of the plants are unique to the Colorado Plateau, occurring nowhere else but in these hanging gardens.

» In front of Bright Angel Lodge at the South Rim, look for **California condors** hanging out on ledges below. From any viewpoint on either rim, you will often see them wheeling around on thermals.

» It's not uncommon to encounter roaming **elk** and **mule deer** in wooded areas on both rims, even in the middle of the day. Show up in the early morning around El Tovar, or around dusk.

» **Bighorn sheep** are more elusive, but we've encountered one grazing placidly in a drainage off of the heavily trafficked Bright Angel Trail. You'll have a better chance of spotting them from a river vantage point.

» If you are lucky enough to sight a **mountain lion**, buy yourself a lottery ticket immediately.

they are the first to bloom in spring. Their deep scarlet flowers burst forth from as many as 50 stems per clump, blooming simultaneously for a period of several days.

Life Zones

Boreal Forest

On the highest peaks of the North Rim perches boreal forest, an offshoot of the Rocky Mountains and home to many of the same plants and animals. Unlike other canyon habitats, this is a land of cool, moist forests and lush meadows. Snowfall may exceed 150in and persist for six to seven months of the year, conditions that favor trees like the Engelmann spruce, Douglas fir and quaking aspen and animals like red squirrels, blue grouse and broad-tailed hummingbirds.

Ponderosa Pine Forest

Broad, flat plateaus on both rims are dominated by ponderosa pine forest. This species forms nearly pure stands of stately, fragrant trees at around 7000ft, where temperatures are moderate and rainfall averages about 20in a year. Characteristic species populating these forests include the unique Abert's and Kaibab squirrels, as well as a variety of bird species, ranging from American robins to northern flickers.

Piñon-Juniper Woodlands

Sharing the rim with ponderosa pines and cloaking the canyon walls down to about 4000ft are piñon-juniper woodlands. These forests of piñon pines and Utah junipers signal desertlike conditions, where snow scarcely ever falls and annual rainfall hardly exceeds 10in. Shrubs such as cliff rose, sagebrush and Mormon tea thrive here. Animals include rock squirrels, cliff chipmunks, and scrub and piñon jays.

Desert Scrub Community

Between the canyon's inner gorge and the great cliffs above there is a broad apron known as the Tonto Platform. Here, in a zone of blazing summer heat and little rain at 3000ft to 4000ft, clings the desert scrub community. Dominating the platform is low-growing blackbrush, along with a handful of other hardy species such as prickly-pear cacti. Visitors will spot few birds and only the occasional black-tailed jackrabbit or white-tailed antelope squirrel.

Amateur naturalists should track down *A Field Guide to the Grand Canyon* by Stephen Whitney (also available in e-book version) or *A Naturalist's Guide to Canyon Country* by David Williams, both of which cover the region's common plants and animals.

Want to know how things are looking in the canyon today? Visit Yavapai Point on the South Rim vicariously via the webcam at www .explorethe canyon.com/ grand-canyon-webcam. The image is refreshed every half hour.

Riparian zone

Lining every waterway in the area is a separate and distinct habitat known as the riparian zone. The presence of precious water draws many plants and animals to this zone. Crimson monkeyflowers and maidenhair ferns mark the scattered seeps and springs, while stream banks near the river are choked by tamarisk, an aggressive introduced plant. Red-spotted toads and beavers share these waters with ducks, herons and other birds that come to drink.

Life Through the Seasons

The canyon encompasses such a wide variety of climatic extremes that the seasons are as complex as the landscape. While one rim celebrates spring, the other rim may still languish in the grip of winter, and in the depths of winter the canyon floor can experience hotter temperatures than in summer elsewhere in the country.

April ushers in the first long spells of fair weather, interrupted by lingering wet winter storms. Even as golden eagles and peregrine falcons nest along the river, the North Rim may remain under many feet of snow. Migrant birds arrive in numbers through May. Along the South Rim and within the canyon itself, wrens, phoebes and warblers fill the air with song and activity. Mammals likewise take advantage of the short season between winter cold and summer heat.

By June, however, temperatures begin to soar, and animal activity slows to a trickle. Daytime temperatures in excess of 100°F are the norm through August. Torrential afternoon thunderstorms alleviate the agony for a few hours each day. June through August is usually the best time to observe wildflowers along the North Rim.

Clear, cool days make autumn the ideal time for visits to the park, though wildflowers have gone to seed and many birds have already made the journey south. Remaining behind are the resident animals – mammals fattening up for hibernation and a handful of birds that feast on the plentiful seeds. Other animals remain active through winter, especially on the canyon floor, where temperatures remain moderate and snow rarely falls.

Canyon Conservation

Sprawling across 1.2 million acres, Grand Canyon National Park protects a sizable portion of the Colorado Plateau, as well as 277 free-flowing miles of the Colorado River. The fact that nearly 5 million people a year visit this fragile desert landscape means that tourism and development have a lasting impact. Even an action as simple as walking off the trail is detrimental when multiplied many times over by a steady stream of visitors, most of whom drive to the park in private vehicles. Of course, the National Park Service is acutely aware of these and other environmental impacts, and works to mitigate these impacts wherever possible, often in conjunction with other agencies. Although the environmental issues change, the commitment to protecting this natural wonder remains the same.

'Leave it as it is. You cannot improve upon it. The ages have been at work on it and man can only mar it. What you can do is to keep it for your children, your children's children, and for all who come after you...' – President Theodore Roosevelt

Damming Consequences

Locked in by Glen Canyon Dam at its eastern end and Hoover Dam to the west, the once mighty Colorado River has undergone profound changes, with significant impacts on the many plants and animals that depend on the river and its natural cycles.

No group of animals has suffered more than the handful of native fish that once thrived in the warm, sediment-laden waters of the Colorado. Upstream from the canyon, Glen Canyon Dam now captures nearly all of the 380,000 tons of sediment that once flowed annually through the canyon. The dam instead releases clear cold water in a steady year-round flow that hardly resembles the ancestral seasonal flood cycle. Under this managed regime, unique fish like the Colorado squawfish, razorback sucker and prehistoric-looking humpback chub have been almost entirely displaced by introduced trout, carp and catfish that flourish in the current conditions.

Another change has been the gradual loss of riverside beaches, as the river no longer deposits sediments in backwater stretches. Beaches have also become overgrown, since the river no longer floods away seedlings that take root on open sand; many former sandbanks are now densely vegetated with thickets of highly invasive tamarisk. Additionally, algal growth has skyrocketed due to sunlight penetrating clear water that was once murky; the algae then supports a food chain benefiting non-native rainbow trout. Algae also soak up phosphorus, a critical nutrient that otherwise fuels aquatic diversity.

Efforts to alleviate this damage include a series of experimental, high-volume releases of water from the Glen Canyon Dam that have helped rebuild beaches and stabilize humpback chub populations. Even better news for these native fish is that several populations of juvenile humpback chub have been translocated successfully to Shinumo Creek and

CRYPTOBIOTIC CRUSTS

One of the Grand Canyon's most fascinating features is also one of its least visible and most fragile. These living crusts cover and protect desert soils, literally gluing sand particles together so they don't blow away. Cyanobacteria, among Earth's oldest life forms, start the process by extending mucous-covered filaments that wind through the dry soil. Over time these filaments and the sand particles adhering to them form a thin crust that is colonized by microscopic algae, lichens, fungi and mosses. This crust absorbs tremendous amounts of rainwater, reducing runoff and minimizing erosion.

Unfortunately, this thin crust is quickly fragmented under the impact of heavy-soled boots, not to mention bicycle, motorcycle and car tires. Once broken, the crust takes 50 to 250 years to repair itself. In its absence, the wind and rains erode desert soils, and much of the water that would otherwise nourish desert plants is lost.

Visitors to the canyon and other sites in the Southwest bear the responsibility to protect cryptobiotic crusts by staying on established trails. Literally look before you leap – intact crusts form a glaze atop the soil, while fragmented crusts bear sharp edges.

Havasu Creek, which bodes well for their reintroduction to their natural habitat.

Water Conservation

Combining powerful advocacy with a passion for the landscape, the Glen Canyon Institute (www .glencanyon .org) is dedicated to restoring a healthy Colorado River system.

Water remains a critical issue because it is gathered from wells and seeps on the Coconino Plateau, and nearby developments threaten to strain the limits of the supply. Because water use in the region is expected to double over the next 50 years, there is growing uncertainty about whether the area's natural seeps and springs will start drying up as the aquifer is drawn down.

Air Pollution

It's a grim reminder of modern life that a pall of air pollution frequently hovers over the canyon, in both summer and winter. Unfortunately, the haze comes from sources as far away as Los Angeles, and not much can be done locally to remedy incoming pollution.

Inside the park, however, the South Rim has been developing an effective public transit system, and a growing network of pedestrian and bicycle trails on both rims (see p178), as a way of reducing traffic congestion and air pollution.

Uranium Mining

Visiting Grand Canyon National Park means taking the 'stay hydrated!' message to heart and drinking plenty of water. We also (arguably) need to shower after logging miles on dusty trails, but we can easily lessen our impact on this desert environment with simple measures like taking shorter showers.

The park is also threatened by a modern-day Gold Rush taking place right on its borders. More than 1100 uranium mining claims have been staked within 5 miles of the park since 2003, and there is considerable evidence that mining activity on this scale could severely and adversely impact the precious water supply and air quality. Exposure to uranium increases the risk of lung and bone cancer.

While government-run uranium-mining operations from decades ago certainly aren't indicative of future outcomes, it must be pointed out that abandoned mines in the Navajo Nation were never properly closed. The Environmental Protection Agency is currently assessing these mines and the health of the Navajo people living near them.

At the time of writing, the US Secretary of the Interior had temporarily extended a moratorium on new uranium mining claims. Whether this will result in the optimal 20-year protection (the legal limit) of a million-acre buffer zone around already protected lands near the park is pending.

Native Americans of the Grand Canyon

Human habitation of the Grand Canyon region dates back at least 4000 years – according to carbon-dating of split-twig animal figurines – and continues to the present day. Tribes whose reservations now border Grand Canyon National Park and who reside on the land surrounding the park include the Hualapai, Havasupai, Navajo, Hopi and Paiute peoples.

To varying degrees, these local tribes rely on tourism coming through the Grand Canyon region. You'll be contributing to the tribes' economies if you take tribal-run tours, stay at campsites or lodges on the reservations or purchase handicrafts and art directly from tribal members.

When visiting reservations, keep in mind that they are sovereign nations within the US and that tribal laws may apply (though federal laws supersede them).

The Havasupai (Havsuw 'Baaja)

Well known for their beadwork and basketry, the Havasupai (whose name translates as 'people of the blue-green waters') share the Yuman language with the Hualapai. Both tribes are together referred to as Northeastern Pai. Their legends tell them that mankind originated on a mountain near the Colorado River. They left their Mojave relatives behind and headed to Meriwitica, near Spencer Canyon (a tributary of Grand Canyon). The Hualapai stayed near Meriwitica, but one story explains that a frog, enticed by the stream and lush vegetation, led the Havasupai east to Havasu Canyon. Archaeological records indicate that the Northeastern Pai arrived at the Grand Canyon around AD 1150, and the Havasupai have occupied Havasu Canyon since about that time.

Today over 30,000 tourists visit Havasu Canyon every year, and the Havasupai's lives and economic survival are integrally related to the tourist industry that has developed in and around Grand Canyon National Park. They, along with the Hualapai, do not participate in the gaming industry. In Supai, the village at the bottom of the canyon, the Havasupai run a lodge and campground, as well as a small village store, serving the tourist industry. The village's isolation probably magnifies the tension created by the outside influence of mainstream American culture on the younger generation of Havasupai. The traditional structure of Havasupai society, based on respect for tribal elders and the tribal council, remains in place despite such outside pressures – but as with much of life for many Native Americans, this continues to be a struggle.

The Hualapai (Hwal' bay)

The Hualapai trace their origins to Kathat Kanave, an old man who sometimes took the form of a coyote and lived in Mada Widita Canyon (also known as Meriwitica), on the canyon's westernmost edge. He taught the Pai (literally 'The People') how to live in the canyon, explaining what herbs cured which ailments and how and what to plant. The Hualapai and Havasupai developed complex systems of irrigation and spent summers farming within the canyon, at places like Havasu Canyon and Indian Garden. During the winter, they hunted on the plateau. Through trade with other tribes, they acquired peaches, figs, wheat, melons, cattle and horses.

Nowadays the Hualapai Reservation, bordering a large section of the Grand Canyon's South Rim, stretches as far south as Route 66. The Hualapai (meaning 'people of the pine trees') counts itself among the few tribes in the Southwest that do not generate revenue from gambling; instead, they've tried their hand at tourism, most successfully through motorized rafting tours on this section of the Colorado River, and through tourism on the scenic West Rim (known as Grand Canyon West). If you plan to travel off Route 66 on the Hualapai Reservation, you must purchase a permit in tiny Peach Springs.

Like the Havasupai, the Hualapai are renowned for their basketry.

At the bottom of Havasu Canyon, two Supai sandstone rock spires stand over the village of Supai. Known as Wii Gl'iiva, the spires – one male, one female – are believed to be guardian spirits watching over the Havasupai.

The Navajo (Diné)

The Navajo people comprise one of the largest tribes in North America; about one of every seven Native Americans are Navajo. Bordering the

RESERVATION ETIQUETTE

Visitors are usually welcome on Native American reservations, as long as they behave in an appropriately courteous and respectful manner. Tribal rules are often clearly posted at the entrance to each reservation, but here are some general guidelines.

» **Alcohol** Most reservations ban the sale or use of alcohol.

» **Ceremonials and powwows** These are either open to the public or exclusively for tribal members. Ceremonials are religious events, and applauding, chatting, asking questions or trying to talk to the performers is rude. Photography and other forms of recording are rarely permitted. While powwows also hold spiritual significance, they are usually more informal.

» **Clothing** Modest dress is customary. Especially when watching ceremonials, you should dress conservatively; tank tops and short shorts are inappropriate.

» **Photography and other recording** Many tribes ban all forms of recording, be it photography, videotaping, audiotaping or drawing. Others permit these activities in certain areas only if you pay the appropriate fee (usually $5 to $10). If you wish to photograph a person, do so only after obtaining his or her permission. A posing tip is usually expected. Photographers who disregard these rules can expect tribal police officers to confiscate their cameras and then escort them off the reservation.

» **Private property** Use common sense here – don't trespass on private property unless invited. Don't climb on ruins or remove any kind of artifact from a reservation. *Kivas* (ceremonial chambers) are always off-limits to visitors. Off-road travel is not allowed without a permit.

» **Recreation** Activities such as backpacking, camping, fishing and hunting require tribal permits. On Native American lands, state fishing or hunting licenses are not valid.

» **Verbal communication** It is considered polite to listen without comment, particularly when an elder is speaking. Be prepared for long silences in the middle of conversations; such silences often indicate that a topic is under serious consideration.

eastern edge of the national park, the 27,000-sq-mile **Navajo Reservation** (☑928-871-6436) is the biggest in the US. If you enter the park through the East Entrance, you'll pass through the Navajo Reservation; the tiny outpost of Cameron, also on the reservation, marks the intersection of Hwys 89 and 64, which leads to the East Entrance.

The Navajo Nation (also known as the Diné) has historically been adaptable to the ways of other tribes and cultures, which perhaps has contributed to the nation's strength and size. But the Navajo people have certainly not been exempted from the poverty and historical struggle of all Native American tribes.

The Navajo are renowned not only for their jewelry, pottery and sand paintings, but most famously for their weaving. Sought-after Navajo rugs, which can take months to complete, can be found for sale throughout the region, from Sedona to the South Rim. Most of the processes are still done by hand: carding the wool, spinning the thread, dying the threads with natural concoctions, and hand-weaving the designs themselves. You can find some examples at reputable dealers like Hopi House in Grand Canyon Village or the excellent Garland's Navajo Rugs in Sedona.

Between Cameron and the East Entrance of the park, Navajo stalls along the side of the highway sell jewelry and handicrafts. Some are preceded by hand-painted signs announcing, 'Friendly Indians Ahead!' These are great opportunities to buy locally, and often directly, from the artisans.

The Hopi

East of the Grand Canyon lies the 2410-sq-mile **Hopi Reservation** (☑928-734-3283), which is completely surrounded by the Navajo Reservation. The Hopi are Arizona's oldest tribe and are probably best known for their unusual, often haunting kachina dolls.

According to Hopi religion, kachinas (*katsinam* in Hopi) are several hundred sacred spirits that live in the San Francisco Peaks north of Flagstaff. At prescribed intervals during the year, they come to the Hopi Reservation and dance in a precise and ritualized fashion. These dances maintain harmony among all living things and are especially important for rainfall and fertility. Kachina dolls, elaborate in design and color and traditionally carved from the dried root of the cottonwood tree, represent these sacred spirits.

While some kachina dolls are considered too sacred for public display or trade, Hopi artisans carve kachina dolls specifically to be sold to the general public. You can buy these, as well as pottery, basketwork and jewelry at Hopi House in Grand Canyon Village, at the Watchtower at Desert View, at the Cameron Trading Post and in the trading companies of Flagstaff.

The Paiute (Nuwuvi)

The Southern Paiute people occupy land north of the Colorado River in what is known as the Arizona Strip, and have traditionally used the canyon for hundreds of years. After contact and conflict with Navajo and Ute slavers, Spanish explorers, Mormon settlers and the US government, the Southern Paiute now live in scattered settlements and reservations in California, Utah, Nevada and Arizona.

One branch of this tribe, the Kaibab Paiute, occupies a reservation in northern Arizona, just west of Fredonia and south of Kanab, Utah. The tribe is largely involved in both agriculture and tourism and runs a visitor center and campground at Pipe Spring National Monument.

Wade deeper into the background of the Havasupai with the ethnography *I Am the Grand Canyon: The Story of the Havasupai People*, by Stephen Hirst, told largely in their own words.

On the Hopi Reservation, Old Oraibi is one of the oldest continuously inhabited villages in the US. There is no official census data for the village, nor contemporary photographs, as photos and drawings are not allowed here, site of the tribe's most sacred traditions.

Survival Guide

>

Directory A-Z

Accommodations

Accommodations in the park range from historic lodges, with dark beams and overstuffed chairs, to rustic cabins and standard motel rooms. Be sure to book early, particularly if you have a specific lodging in mind (perhaps a rimside cabin on the North Rim or the wonderful Buckey O'Neill Cabin on the South Rim).

The South Rim boasts the majority of accommodations, while the North Rim offers just one lodge and one campground. Inside the canyon, there's a lodge and several backcountry campgrounds.

Some hotels, such as the South Rim lodges, maintain the same rates year-round. However, in the region room rates drop drastically in the winter. During holidays, spe-cial events and weekends, rates may be higher.

Chain hotels, as well as more atmospheric inns and B&Bs, often have great on-line deals, so it's worth shopping around if you can. For last-minute deals outside the park, check www.expedia .com, www.travelocity.com, www.orbitz.com, www.price line.com, www.hotwire.com and www.hotels.com.

B&Bs

In the South Rim region, Williams, Sedona and Flagstaff have several excellent B&Bs, all of which have their own unique feel. B&B hosts tend to be knowledgeable about the area and offer great advice on things to see and do in their hometowns and at the canyon.

Camping

Free dispersed camping (independent camping at nonestablished sites) is allowed in Kaibab National Forest, which borders both rims. Don't camp within a quarter-mile of the highway or any surface water, within a half-mile of any developed campground, or in meadows. Fires are not permitted, and campers are expected to leave no trace (see p35). See the camping chart on p82 for a quick overview of campsites on the South Rim; on the North Rim, see p144. Women who are camping solo should also take commonsense precautions and consider avoiding isolated campsites.

Hostels

Hostels in the Grand Canyon region are few and far between, but they all promise a quality experience. Look for the two lovely sister hostels in Flagstaff and the Grand Canyon Hotel in Williams, which offers hostel-style accommodations in addition to private rooms.

Hotels & Motels

This being Route 66 territory, some local roadside motels have historical charm emanating from the walls. Others may emanate less pleasant stuff. But generally, motels round these parts can be anything from the tiny, run-down variety to restored, upscale places that stray out of the budget range.

Chain hotels provide the generic but consistent level of quality you would expect, but there are also some great family-run inns and hotels throughout the area.

Lodges

Inside the park, lodges are basically the park's hotels, where the rooms are comfortable enough but don't necessarily have the rough-hewn exposed beams and crackling fireplaces the word 'lodge' connotes. However, some lodges do have more rustic charm than others – El Tovar (South Rim) and

ACCOMMODATION PRICING

Budget	up to $100	Options range from campgrounds to hostels and roadside motels, denoted by a $ symbol throughout this book. Quality and facilities vary widely – some campgrounds offer merely a site to lay your head, while motels might include amenities like a complimentary continental breakfast.
Midrange	$100–200	Marked with a $$ symbol throughout the book. Midrange options typically occupy a place on the hotel or lodge spectrum. Most midrange places have private bathrooms, air-conditioned rooms, TVs, telephones and parking, but of course some have more character than others.
Top End	$200 and over	Top-end accommodations are designated with the $$$ symbol. Top-end accommodations in the region tend to be B&Bs, upscale inns or resorts, all of which will vary in style and in the luxuries they offer.

Grand Canyon Lodge (North Rim) leap to mind.

Business Hours

Generally speaking, business hours are from 9am to 5pm. In the bigger towns, supermarkets are open 24 hours a day. Unless there are variances of more than half an hour in either direction, the following serve as regular opening hours throughout this book.

Banks 10am-5pm Mon-Fri
Bars 5pm-2am
Restaurants breakfast 7am-10:30am, lunch 11am-2:30pm, dinner 5-9pm
Shops 9:30am-5:30pm

Courses

The Grand Canyon's rich natural and cultural history provides endless material for discussion and discovery. Several organizations offer year-round classes on a variety of subjects, from one-day classes to extended learning vacations. While most require advance reservations, programs like the regularly scheduled ranger talks are open on a drop-in basis. Check *The Guide* for details on current classes and workshops.

The **environmental education office** (☑928-638-7662; www.nps.gov/grca/forteachers) offers ranger-led curriculum-based, field trips for children in grades four through six that focus on the canyon's ecology, geology and history. Workshops and educational materials are also available for teachers who would like to incorporate the lessons into their curriculum. Classes are free, but advance reservations are required.

Grand Canyon Field Institute (☑866-471-4435, 928-638-2485; www.grandcanyon.org/fieldinstitute) Run by the Grand Canyon Association (official nonprofit partner of the park), the field institute offers more than 100 classes annually. Subjects include natural history, wilderness studies, backcountry medicine and photography. Most instructors have advanced degrees in their field of study and have led canyon trips for several years.

Museum of Northern Arizona (☑928-774-5211; www.mnaventures.org) Organizes an array of customized, small-group educational tours led by scientists, writers and artists through its MNA Ventures program. Options include hiking, backpacking, river rafting, horseback riding, van tours and hotel-based trips throughout the Southwest.

Northern Arizona University's Grand Canyon Semester (☑928-523-9333; www.grandcanyonsemester.nau.edu) Three-month interdisciplinary semester, (comparable to a semester abroad), examining the region's geology, history, ecology, geography and politics, among other topics. While most participants are college-age students, the course is open to anyone.

Discount Cards

American Automobile Association (AAA) members can get hotel, rental-car and National Park Pass discounts by showing their cards where such offers are advertised. Backpackers who plan on doing more than one backcountry trek within the space of a year can save on permit fees with a Frequent Hiker Membership (see p34).

Park Passes

If you plan to stay at the park for longer than a week, or to make a return visit within the year, consider purchasing a $50 **Grand Canyon Annual Pass**, which allows unlimited visits for 12 months. Better yet, an annual $80 **America the Beautiful Annual Pass** grants the holder and any accompanying passengers in a private vehicle free admission to any National Park Service (NPS) site in the US, as well as all sites administered by the US Fish & Wildlife Service (USFW), the US Forest Service (USFS) and the Bureau of Land Management (BLM).

If you're 62 or older, purchase the $10 **America the Beautiful Senior Pass**, which grants access to all NPS, USFW, USFS and BLM sites and is good for the holder's lifetime. An **America the Beautiful Access Pass** is free to US residents who are permanently disabled, and offers the same benefits as the Senior Pass; you must offer medical proof of your disability to be eligible.

All passes are available at the park entrance stations. The Senior and Access Passes must be purchased in person at a park, but you can get an America the Beautiful Pass in advance with a credit card (☑888-275-8747; http://store.usgs.gov/pass/). It takes up to two weeks to receive and there's an additional cost for shipping; priority shipping (five business days) is also available.

Senior Cards

Travelers aged 50 and older can receive rate cuts and benefits in many places. Inquire about discounts at hotels, museums and restaurants before you make reservations or purchase tickets. With an America the Beautiful Senior Pass, US citizens aged 62 or over

receive free admission to national parks and a 50% discount on camping fees (reserve at www.recreation.gov). Discounts may also be available to over-50s holding membership cards with the **American Association of Retired Persons** (AARP; ☑888-687-2277; www.aarp.org; 601 E St NW, Washington, DC 20049; annual membership for individual plus spouse $16).

Student & Youth Cards

Museums and theaters often give discounts if you flash a student ID. Some tour operators in the area also give student discounts.

Food

Prices listed throughout the book are for dinner – expect lower prices for breakfast and lunch. Eating listings are detailed in order of ascending price ranges, thus:

Budget Mains less than $10

Midrange Mains from $10 to $20

Top End Mains $20 or more

LAST-MINUTE ACCOMMODATIONS

It is possible to get last-minute accommodations at the Grand Canyon, even along the South Rim during summer peak season. Your first step should be to call **Xanterra** (☑888-297-2757), the official park concessionaire. Reservations may be canceled up to 48 hours in advance, so you never know when a room may be available. If you're looking for same-day accommodations, call the lodges directly through the **North Rim switchboard** (☑928-638-2612) or **South Rim switchboard** (☑928-638-2631). There's no waiting list, so keep trying. If all else fails, you can camp for free just about anywhere in Kaibab National Forest (see p215) on either rim.

South Rim

» If you don't find a room on the South Rim, check motels in Tusayan, only 7 miles from the South Entrance, or the motel in Valle, about 15 miles further south.

» In Cameron, 32 miles east of the East Entrance along Hwy 64 (but otherwise in the middle of nowhere), is the pleasant Cameron Trading Post & Motel, which often has vacancies.

» Safest bets are further away in Williams, 59 miles south of the park, and Flagstaff, 80 miles south, both of which offer plenty of accommodation options.

North Rim

» The closest places to stay outside the North Rim are Kaibab Lodge, 5 miles from the park entrance, or Jacob Lake Inn, 30 miles north.

» DeMotte Campground, across from Kaibab Lodge, is arguably the nicest campground in the region and there's also a campground in Jacob Lake.

» If everything is booked, you'll have to head to Kanab, a pleasant town about 85 miles north, where you'll find a hostel and several motels with rates from $70 to $100.

Picnicking is a great way to not only save money, but also enjoy some quiet moments. If you're visiting the park for more than a day, buy a small cooler to stow picnic supplies and keep drinks cold; consider a backpack-style cooler so you can easily carry it with you.

In-room refrigerators are a rarity in park lodges, but you can get ice at Canyon Village Marketplace on the South Rim, Desert View Marketplace at the East Entrance near Desert View Campground, and the North Rim General Store.

Canyon Village Marketplace (South Rim) is the park's only full-size grocery. Desert View Marketplace sells a few basic grocery items like canned goods, milk and beer. You're best off buying groceries in Flagstaff or Williams before arriving at the park, where prices are much higher.

The North Rim General Store offers a small but thorough selection of groceries, such as steak, frozen meat, eggs, cheese, diapers, beer, wine and firewood. The closest full grocery store is in Kanab, a 90-minute drive north.

Insurance

The US is an expensive country in which to get sick, crash your car or be robbed, so protect yourself. For car insurance, see p225; for health insurance, see p228. To insure yourself from theft from your car, consult your homeowner's (or renter's) insurance policy before leaving home.

Worldwide travel insurance is available at www .lonelyplanet.com/travel_ services. You can buy, extend and claim online any time – even if you're already on the road traveling.

Internet Access

Midrange and top-end hotel rooms usually have high-speed cable, DSL or wireless internet access. Nowadays, many lower-end motels and lodges offer free wi-fi. If you aren't traveling with your own computer, common places to find internet access are public libraries (where access is usually limited but free) or at local cafes for a small fee. In places where internet access is available at guest terminals, we've used the @symbol. Where wi-fi is available, look for the 🛜symbol.

Public Holidays

During the winter holiday season (December 24 through January 2), accommodations can get extremely tight at the canyon. Things can also get hectic during the summer high season between Memorial Day and Labor Day. Traffic gets worse around the South Rim on holidays, and people should make reservations for special transportation options like the Grand Canyon Railway trains. Refer to p18 for more seasonal information.

New Year's Day January 1

Martin Luther King, Jr Day 3rd Monday in January

Presidents Day 3rd Monday in February

Easter Late March or early April

Memorial Day Last Monday in May

Independence Day July 4

Labor Day 1st Monday in September

Columbus Day 2nd Monday in October

Veterans Day November 11

Thanksgiving Day 4th Thursday in November

Christmas Day December 25

Showers & Laundry

Camper Services Building (⊘8am-6pm) Near Mather Campground on the South Rim; provides coin laundry and pay showers. Last laundry load must go in by 4:45pm.

North Rim Campground (⊘7am-10pm) Pay shower and laundry facilities on access road leading to campground. Water must be pumped up more than 3000ft from Roaring Springs, so use these services sparingly.

PRACTICALITIES

» Major local papers include the *Arizona Daily Sun* (www.azdailysun.com), *Salt Lake Tribune* (www.sltrib. com), *Deseret News* (www.deseretnews.com), *Las Vegas Review Journal* (www.lvrj.com) and *Las Vegas Sun* (www.lasvegassun.com).

» Broadcast out of Northern Arizona University, local NPR stations include KNAD (91.7 in Page), KNAG (90.3 at the Grand Canyon) and KNAU (88.7 in Flagstaff).

» The imperial system is used for weights and measures.

» Voltage is 110/120V, 60 cycles.

» Videos are on the NTSC system, which is incompatible with the PAL system.

Tours

Among the best organized tours are those offered via the Grand Canyon Field Institute and the Museum of Northern Arizona (see p216). See also the Activities chapter (p29), which lists the best companies that provide activity-based tours in the region.

The following tours of the South Rim stop at viewpoints and selected sights; most include time for a walk along the rim. Airlines in Tusayan offer scenic canyon tours (see p38). For details on guided rafting trips, see p172 and p96.

From Flagstaff & Williams

American Dream Tours (☎928-527-3369, 888-203-1212; www.americandream tours.com; day tours adult/child $98/69) Departing from Flagstaff, Williams and Tusayan, each tour takes no more than 14 people per van on all-inclusive one-day trips around the South Rim.

Grand Canyon Jeep Tours (☎928-716-9389; www .grandcanyonjeeps.com) One-day and multiday tours to the canyon, with options to add on river floats or take a half-day excursion. Departing from Flagstaff, Williams or Tusayan.

Grand Canyon Railway Does unique train rides to the South Rim, as well as combination train/bus tours. See the boxed text p226.

Marvelous Marv's (☎928-707-0291; www.marvelousmarv .com; per person $85) The best personalized tours around are run by this quirky local. He'll pick you up from your hotel or campground in or around Williams to take you for a full-day tour at the South Rim in his 15-passenger, air-conditioned van. Cash, travelers checks or personal US checks only.

Open Road Tours (☎855-563-8830, 602-997-6474; www .openroadtours.com; day tours adult/child $95/55) From Flagstaff, Open Road offers a one-day tour of the park and Navajo Reservation, including a stop at the Cameron Trading Post.

From Las Vegas

Air packages are a popular way to do day tours of the canyon from Las Vegas. For helicopter or plane tours of the canyon, see p38.

Grand Canyon Tour Company (☎800-222-6966, 702-655-6060; www.grand canyontourcompany.com) Go with a one-day bus trip to the South Rim ($170 for two if booked online), or an air/bus combo tour ($440 for two if booked online); a wide variety of tours are offered on its website.

Sundance Helicopters (☎800-653-1881; www .helicoptour.com) Offers trips further west to the Hualapai Reservation, which isn't subject to the same air regulations enforced elsewhere in the canyon. Among tour offerings are a flight to the Skywalk ($487) or a quick pontoon-boat ride on the Colorado with a riverside champagne picnic ($521).

From Kanab

Allen's Guided Tours (p147) Leads horseback riding tours in Kaibab National Park (North Rim).

Terry's Camera Trading Co (☎435-644-5981; 19 W Center St; ⊗8am-6pm Mon-Sat) Terry has been exploring and photographing the canyon and the surrounding desert and plateau country for more than 25 years; he offers customized 4WD photography tours of remote North Rim spots.

Travelers with Disabilities

Grand Canyon National Park offers many attractions and services for travelers with disabilities. Ask for an updated *Accessibility Guide* when you enter the park, which clearly maps out all the accessible bathrooms, showers, campsites, guestrooms and parking lots, describes accessibility at overlooks,

---

LOCAL LIQUOR LAWS

In Utah, though you'll encounter some of the most conservative liquor laws in the country, the state has significantly toned down the weirdness factor. As everywhere in the US, you must be aged 21 to drink legally. Grocery stores sell near-beer (which doesn't exceed 3.2% alcohol content) seven days a week, but state-run liquor stores sell full-strength beer, wine and spirits Monday through Saturday.

Utah bars used to have to call themselves 'private clubs' and charge nominal membership fees to get around arcane liquor laws, but this confusing rigmarole was eliminated in 2009. Now, all you need in order to enter a bar is valid identification showing that you're 21 or over – hallelujah! Drinks are still strictly portioned; for example, you can't order a double shot of anything and can only order one drink at a time. Clever imbibers will find ways to get around this.

Note also that alcohol is prohibited on all Native American reservations and cannot be transported on or through the reservations.

Entering the Region

» For the most up-to-date visa and immigration information, check with the **US Department of State** (☎202-663-1225; www.travel.state.gov).

» Most foreign visitors to the US need a visa, but a visa waiver program (VWP) allows citizens of 36 countries to enter the US for stays of 90 days or less without first obtaining a visa.

» Visitors eligible for the VWP must apply for entry approval via the Electronic System for Travel Authorization (ESTA), at least 72 hours before travel. Apply through the **Department of Homeland Security** (www.esta.cbp.dhs.gov/esta; fee $14).

» Your passport should be valid for at least another six months after you leave the US.

Embassies & Consulates

Australia (Los Angeles; ☎310-229-2300; www.usa.embassy.gov.au)
Canada (Phoenix; ☎602-508-3577; www.canadainternational.gc.ca)
France (Los Angeles; ☎310-235-3200; www.ambafrance-us.org)
Germany (Los Angeles; ☎323-930-2703; www.germany.info)
Japan (Los Angeles; ☎213-617-6700; www.us.emb-japan.go.jp)
New Zealand (Los Angeles; ☎310-566-6555; www.nzembassy.com/usa)
UK (Los Angeles; ☎310-481-0031; www.ukinusa.fco.gov.uk)

Money

» ATMs are available 24 hours at most banks, shopping malls, grocery and convenience stores. Bank surcharges often apply in addition to fees charged by your own bank.

» Most ATMs are affiliated with international networks and offer reasonable exchange rates.

» Most hotels, restaurants and shops accept cash and credit cards.

» It's customary to tip restaurant waitstaff 15% to 20% of the pretax bill, and tip bartenders $1 per drink. Tips make up a significant part of food-service workers' income.

» Prices in this book are quoted in the local currency, US dollars ($), unless otherwise stated.

Post

The **US Postal Service** (USPS; ☎800-275-8777; www.usps.com) is inexpensive and reliable. At the time of research, standard letters up to 1oz (about 28g) cost $0.44 within the US;

and identifies 'windshield view' spots along the South Rim. You can also download a PDF version of the *Accessibility Guide* from the park website (go to www.nps.gov/grca and click through the Plan Your Visit link to Things to Know Before You Come, then Accessibility). You can also obtain an Accessibility Permit for designated parking at either entrance station.

Around the Southwest, public buildings are required to be wheelchair accessible and to have appropriate restroom facilities. Public transportation must be accessible to all, and most chain hotels have rooms or suites for disabled travelers. Telephone companies provide relay operators for the hearing impaired. Many banks provide ATM instructions in Braille, curb ramps are common and many busy intersections have audible crossing signals.

Useful organizations for disabled travelers include the following:

Mobility International USA (☎541-343-1284; www.miusa.org; 132 E Broadway, Suite 343, Eugene, OR 97401) Advises disabled travelers on mobility issues.

Society for Accessible Travel & Hospitality (☎212-447-7284; www.sath.org; 347 Fifth Ave, Suite 605, New York, NY 10016) Publishes a quarterly magazine and provides information on travel for the disabled.

Activities

Mule rides are provisionally accessible with advance notice. Contact the **South Rim switchboard** (☎928-638-2631), and they'll connect you with the barn to discuss your needs with the head wrangler.

To secure a bus tour, call at least one week in advance

postcards and letters cost $0.80 to both Canada and Mexico and $0.98 to all other countries. Postage rates increase by a cent or two every few years.

Telephone

CELL (MOBILE) PHONES

You'll need a multiband GSM phone to make calls in the US. Installing a US prepaid rechargeable SIM card is usually cheaper than using your own network. They're available at major telecommunications or electronics stores. If your phone doesn't work in the US, these stores also sell inexpensive prepaid phones.

Cell-phone reception in the park can be sketchy, depending on your provider network. No one gets reception below the rim, where satellite phones are the only way to call out of the canyon.

DIALING CODES

» US phone numbers begin with a three-digit area code, followed by a seven-digit local number.

» When dialing a number within the same area code, simply dial the seven-digit number; for long-distance calls, dial the entire ten-digit number preceded by ☏1.

» Toll-free numbers begin with ☏800, ☏866, ☏877 or ☏888 and must be preceded by ☏1.

» For direct international calls, dial ☏011 plus the country code plus the area code plus the local number.

» If you're calling from abroad, the US country code is ☏1.

Time

» Arizona is on Mountain Standard Time (MST) but does not observe Daylight Savings Time (DST).

» The Navajo Reservation *does* observe Mountain Daylight Savings Time during the summer, putting it one hour ahead of Arizona and on the same time as Utah and New Mexico.

» DST starts on the second Sunday in March (clocks are set ahead one hour) and ends on the second Sunday in November (clocks are set back one hour).

» When it's noon in June in Arizona, it's noon in San Francisco, 2pm in Chicago, 3pm in New York, 8pm in London and 5am the next day in Sydney.

---

to reserve a seat. The wheelchair-accessible bus has only 30 seats and the standard buses about 56; if a wheelchair user books a tour, the concessionaire can limit the number of reservations.

River concessionaires can in many cases accommodate people with disabilities, even on multiday white-water trips. Call **Grand Canyon River Trip Information** (☏800-959-9164) for info. If you're not ready for rapids, **Xanterra** (☏888-297-2757) offers a bus trip to Page, where rafters can do a half-day float from Glen Canyon to Lees Ferry. Accessible accommodations can be arranged in advance.

Getting Around

Free loaner wheelchairs are usually available at the Grand Canyon Visitor Center on the South Rim, and at the visitor center or Grand Canyon Lodge on the North Rim.

Many sites along the South Rim are readily accessible. The 2-mile stretch from Mather Point to Bright Angel Lodge is easiest for those who have difficulty walking or use a wheelchair, and a golf cart runs regularly between the information plaza and Mather Point (about 200yd).

The Powell, Hopi and Pima Overlooks on Hermit Rd and the Yaki, Grandview, Moran and Desert View Overlooks on Desert View Dr all offer wheelchair access. See p59 for more about these overlooks.

Hopi House is accessible only through a 29in-wide door, while steps and small doors at Kolb and Lookout Studios are more problematic. At the Tusayan Ruins & Museum, a level, paved trail leads into the museum and around the pueblo dwelling. All lodges except Bright Angel offer accessible guestrooms, and Mather, Desert

LOST & FOUND

If you lose something in or near the lodges or restaurants on the South Rim, call the **main switchboard** (☏928-638-2631) and ask to be connected to the place where you last had the item. Otherwise, ask to be connected to the **Lost and Found Office** (☏928-638-7798), where found items are eventually returned. The park asks that you turn in found items to Grand Canyon Visitor Center.

If you lose an item anywhere on the North Rim, contact the **visitor center** (☏928-638-7864) or **Grand Canyon Lodge** (☏928-638-2612).

View and Trailer Village Campgrounds include a few accessible campsites.

Descending into the canyon is a different story. The Bright Angel (South Rim) and North Kaibab (North Rim) trails are the least rocky, but still pose a challenge. Use extreme caution. To take a certified service dog below the rim, you must first check in at the Backcountry Information Center on either rim.

On the North Rim, the best overlook is Cape Royal, where a fairly level, 0.6-mile paved trail leads to several canyon viewpoints. There's a wheelchair-accessible viewing platform at Point Imperial. Public spaces at Grand Canyon Lodge are easily negotiable by people with limited mobility, and four guestrooms have been specially modified. The North Rim Campground provides two accessible sites with picnic tables and one bathroom.

All shuttles are wheelchair accessible. Accessibility permits (available at entrance stations, Grand Canyon Visitor Center and elsewhere) also grant private vehicle access into shuttle-only areas.

Volunteering

There are loads of opportunities to volunteer at and around Grand Canyon National Park, for one-day projects or longer-term endeavors. Volunteers can work on trail maintenance, restore grasslands, pull invasive plants from the inner gorge, train to be an interpretive ranger or work with youth organizations.

American Conservation Experience (☏928-226-6960; www.usaconservation.org) Restoration and conservation work opportunities in and around the park, for American and international youth. In exchange for 40 hours' work a week, volunteers are housed and fed.

Grand Canyon Trust Volunteers (☏928-774-7488; www.grandcanyontrust.org, www.gcvolunteers.org) The volunteer arm of the nonprofit Grand Canyon Trust offers opportunities to participate in its Grand Canyon Volunteers projects. These range from assisting graduate students with research at Northern Arizona University in Flagstaff to week-long tamarisk-removal trips in the backcountry.

National Park Service (www.volunteer.gov/gov) Lists available volunteer positions in the park, including year-round openings for revegetation volunteers. Duties include seed collection, plant propagation and non-native plant removal. Limited free camping may be available. Find job details and apply in advance by searching for Grand Canyon openings.

Sierra Club, Grand Canyon Chapter (☏602-253-8633; www.arizona.sierraclub.org; 202 E McDowell Rd, Suite 277, Phoenix, AZ 85004) The Grand Canyon chapter publishes the local newsletter *Canyon Echo* and offers occasional opportunities to volunteer in the area.

Student Conservation Association (☏510-832-1966; www.thesca.org) Excellent volunteer opportunities for high school and college-aged students interested in hands-on conservation work.

Work

Seasonal work at the park tends to be low-paying service jobs that are mostly filled by young people. For the best shot at seasonal employment, apply well ahead of time through the **US Federal Government website** (www.usajobs.com). Planning ahead is essential, whether you are applying for NPS or park concessionaire jobs – applications for summer jobs are typically due during December and January. **Cool Works** (www.coolworks.com) is a good place to look for non-NPS jobs and volunteer opportunities.

Non US citizens must apply for a work visa from the US embassy in their home country before leaving. Visas vary, depending on how long you're staying and the kind of work you plan to do. Generally, you need a J-1 visa, which you can obtain by joining a visitor-exchange program (issued mostly to students for work in summer camps), an H-1B visa for skilled professionals or an H-2B visa, when you are sponsored by a US employer. The latter two may require evidence of a job offer from an employer who considers your qualifications unique and not readily available in the US.

Transportion

GETTING THERE & AWAY

Travelers to the Grand Canyon usually fly or drive to a gateway city before continuing to the national park via train, car or bus.

Air

Airports

Main air hubs to the park are Las Vegas, Nevada; Phoenix, Arizona; Salt Lake City, Utah; and Albuquerque, New Mexico.

McCarran International Airport (LAS; ☎702-261-5211; www.mccarran.com) Sixth-busiest airport in the US, but also one of the country's more efficient airports. Advantages to flying into Vegas include its proximity to the North Rim and year-round cheap flights and city packages. Driving to the park from Vegas is also easy, with minimal traffic to either rim.

Sky Harbor International Airport (PSH; ☎602-273-3300; www.phxskyharbor.com) Phoenix offers more connecting airlines and routes, but you risk getting caught in traffic. Once you do escape the city, the drive north on Hwys 89 and Alt 89 to Flagstaff is beautiful, passing through several mountain towns and Sedona's celebrated red-rock country. For a faster option, America West Express offers several flights a day from Phoenix to Flagstaff, 80 miles south of the South Rim.

Salt Lake City International Airport (SLC; ☎801-575-2400; www.slcairport.com) A great place to fly into if you're headed for the North Rim. SLC has a reputation for being one of the more low-stress airports of its size in the US.

Albuquerque International Sunport (ABQ; ☎505-244-7700; www.cabq.gov/airport) Of the four airports in the region, this is the least convenient to the Grand Canyon but is a good option for those planning on spending time in this part of the Southwest.

Airlines

Domestic and Canadian airlines:

Air Canada (☎888-247-2262; www.aircanada.com)
Alaska Airlines (☎800-252-7522; www.alaskaair.com)
American Airlines (☎800-433-7300; www.aa.com)
Delta (☎800-221-1212; www.delta.com)
Frontier Airlines (☎800-432-1359; www.frontierairlines.com)
JetBlue (☎800-538-2583; www.jetblue.com)
Southwest Airlines (☎800-435-9792; www.southwest.com)
United Airlines (☎800-864-8331; www.united.com)
US Airways (☎800-428-4322; www.usairways.com)

Airlines flying from the UK, Ireland and Europe include **Aer Lingus** (☎516-622-4222; www.aerlingus.com), **British Airways** (☎800-247-9297; www.britishairways.com), **Virgin Atlantic** (☎800-862-8621; www.virgin-atlantic.com) and **XL Airways France** (☎877-496-9889; www.xlairways.com). From Australia and New Zealand there's **Air New Zealand** (☎800-262-1234; www.airnewzealand.com) and **Qantas** (☎800-227-4500; www.qantas.com.au).

Land

Bus

Arizona Shuttle (☎928-226-8060, 877-226-8060; www.arizonashuttle.com) Shuttles to the park ($25) depart three times daily from the Flagstaff train depot. Other routes include Flagstaff to Williams ($19) and Phoenix Sky Harbor to Flagstaff ($38).

Greyhound (☎928-774-4573, 800-231-2222; www.greyhound.com) Flagstaff to Albuquerque ($57, six hours), Las Vegas ($59 Monday to Friday, $71 Saturday and Sunday, 5½ hours), Los Angeles ($70, 13 hours) and Phoenix ($32, three hours).

Trans-Canyon Shuttle (☎928-638-2820; www.transcanyonshuttle.com; PO Box 348, Grand Canyon, AZ 86023) Runs the crucial route between the North and South Rims, from mid-May to

CLIMATE CHANGE & TRAVEL

Every form of transport that relies on carbon-based fuel generates CO_2, the main cause of human-induced climate change. Modern travel is dependent on aeroplanes, which might use less fuel per kilometer per person than most cars but travel much greater distances. The altitude at which aircraft emit gases (including CO_2) and particles also contributes to their climate change impact. Many websites offer 'carbon calculators' that allow people to estimate the carbon emissions generated by their journey and, for those who wish to do so, to offset the impact of the greenhouse gases emitted with contributions to portfolios of climate-friendly initiatives throughout the world. Lonely Planet offsets the carbon footprint of all staff and author travel.

mid-October. A godsend for rim-to-rim hikers, the shuttle is also a good option for those who want to see both rims and don't want to bother with a car. Makes one daily trip in each direction ($80, 4½ hours; $150 round-trip). Reservations are required, Payment is by check (credit cards not accepted). Infant car seats not provided.

Car & Motorcycle

From Las Vegas, it's an easy drive to either rim. To get to the North Rim, head north on I-15 into Utah. Just past St George, take Hwy 9 east to Hurricane. You can either continue on Hwy 9 through Zion National Park, then connect with Hwy 89 down through Kanab to Fredonia, or take Hwy 59/389 southeast to Fredonia and connect with Alt 89. Alt 89 heads southeast to Jacob Lake, where Hwy 67 leads 30 miles to the park entrance station. The most direct route to the South Rim is Hwy 93 south to I-40, then east to Williams, where you'll turn north on Hwy 64 to Valle, then follow Hwy 180 into the park.

From Phoenix, take I-17 north to Flagstaff and continue on Hwy 180 north to the South Rim. Another option is to take Hwy 60 northwest to Hwy 89 through Prescott, then connect with Alt 89, which winds northeast through forested mountains to Sedona. From there it's a short jaunt north through Oak Creek Canyon to Flag-

staff. It is a beautiful drive, but traffic can be brutal in summer, particularly around Sedona. If you're continuing to the North Rim from Flagstaff, take Hwy 89 north. (At Cameron, Hwy 64 leads 32 miles west to the South Rim's East Entrance.) About 60 miles north of Cameron, Alt 89 turns east through Lees Ferry and Marble Canyon to Jacob Lake.

AUTOMOBILE ASSOCIATIONS

American Automobile Association (AAA; ☎800-564-6222; www.aaa.com; basic annual membership $65) Along with maps and trip-planning information, AAA members also receive discounts on car rentals, air tickets, hotels and attractions, plus emergency roadside service and towing (☎800-222-4357). Has reciprocal agreements with international automobile associations such as CAA in Canada; be sure to bring your membership card from your country of origin.

Better World Club (☎866-238-1137; www.better worldclub.com) This eco-friendly auto club supports environmental causes in addition to offering emergency roadside assistance for drivers and cyclists, discounts on vehicle rentals (including hybrids and biodiesels) and auto insurance.

DRIVER'S LICENSE

You will need your vehicle's registration papers, liability insurance and an Interna-

tional Driving Permit (IDP) in addition to your domestic license. Contact your local automobile association for details about required documentation. An international driver's license, obtained in your home country, is only necessary if your country of origin is a non-English-speaking one.

ROAD DISTANCES (MILES)

Albuquerque to South Rim	400
Las Vegas to South Rim	277
Las Vegas to North Rim	268
Phoenix to South Rim	223
Salt Lake City to North Rim	392
Los Angeles to South Rim	490

RENTAL

Most car-rental agencies require renters to be at least 25 years old, and some have an upper age limit as well. When shopping around, always check with the agency itself. It's illegal to drive without automobile insurance, so consult your policy from your home country before leaving. See p225 for more information on insurance.

The following major car-rental agencies operate out of the airports in Las Vegas and Phoenix. You can also rent cars in Flagstaff, though rates are higher than in Phoenix or Las Vegas.

Avis (☎800-331-1212; www
.avis.com)
Budget (☎800-527-0700;
www.budget.com)
Enterprise (☎800-261-7331;
www.enterprise.com)
Hertz (☎800-654-3131; www
.hertz.com)
National (☎877-222-9058;
www.nationalcar.com)
Thrifty (☎800-847-4389;
www.thrifty.com)

INSURANCE
Liability insurance covers
people and property that
you might hit. For damage to
the rental vehicle, a collision
damage waiver is available
for about $15 per day. Colli-
sion coverage on your vehicle
at home may also cover damage to rental cars; check your
policy before leaving home.

Some credit cards offer
reimbursement coverage for
collision damage if you rent
the car with that credit card,
although most do not cover
rentals of more than 15 days
or exotic models, vans and
4WD vehicles.

Most rental companies
stipulate that damage a car
sustains while driven on
unpaved roads is not covered
by the insurance they offer.
Check with the agent when
you make your reservation.

ROAD RULES
Throughout the US, cars
drive on the right side of the
road. Apart from that, road
rules differ slightly from state
to state, but all require the
use of safety belts as well as
the proper use of child safety
seats for children under the
age of five.

» Speed limits vary; on rural
interstates the speed limit is
75mph, but this drops down
to 65mph in urban areas
(55mph in Arizona).

» Pay attention to livestock-
or deer-crossing signs –
tangle with a deer, cow or elk
and you'll total your car in
addition to killing the critter.

» You can incur stiff fines,
jail time and other penalties
if caught driving under the
influence of alcohol. The legal
limit for blood alcohol level is
0.08% in Arizona and most
other states.

Train
Operated by **Amtrak** (☎800-
872-7245; www.amtrak.com),
the *Southwest Chief* makes
a daily run between Chicago
and Los Angeles, with stops
at Flagstaff and Williams. In
Williams you can connect
with the historic Grand Canyon Railway (see boxed text,
p226), with original 1923 Pull-
man cars chugging the scenic
65 miles to the South Rim.

GETTING AROUND
On the South Rim, the most
hassle-free way to get around
is to drive into the park,
park your car and use the
convenient shuttles and your
own pedestrian power. On
the North Rim, unless you're
taking the Trans-Canyon
Shuttle, you'll have to drive
in yourself, as there are few
services on this rim (none
during the winter).

Bicycle
Inside the Park
Because roads on the South
Rim are so heavily trafficked,
a great alternative is to get
around by bicycle. As more
sections of the Greenway

Trail (see p178) are completed, pedaling through the park
has become an ever more
refreshing way to get around.
Bikes are allowed on all roads
but none of the trails (except
the Greenway Trail) on the
South Rim. Rent 'comfort
cruiser' bikes at **Bright Angel Bicycles** (p86).

On the North Rim, you can
rent mountain bikes at the
gas station (⊙7am-7pm) at
the North Rim Campground
entrance. You can fashion
a terrific extended ride out
to Point Imperial and on
to Cape Royal, about 45
miles each way from Grand
Canyon Lodge. The park's
35mph speed limit ensures
slow traffic, and the pine-
fringed road offers a good
riding surface.

For a short, sweet North
Rim ride that's well suited
to families, take the Bridle
Trail, which leads from the
North Kaibab Trailhead to the
campground (0.5 miles) and
lodge (1.5 miles). Mountain
bikes are allowed on blacktop
roads only, except for the 17-
mile dirt road to Point Sublime, and the Bridle Trail from
the campground to the lodge.

See p233 for more infor-
mation on bike safety within
the park.

Beyond the Park
Check out Sarah Alley's
detailed book *The Mountain
Biker's Guide to Arizona* for

RV RENTAL

Recreational vehicles are a great way to travel the
Grand Canyon region, where campgrounds are plentiful. If you need to rent a vehicle anyway, renting an RV
can save money on accommodations. RV rental rates
vary by vehicle size, model and mileage; expect to pay
at least $100 per day.
Apollo (☎800-370-1262; www.apollorv.com) With a
branch in Las Vegas, Apollo rents everything from cozy
campervans for two, to family-size motorhomes.
Cruise America (☎800-672-8042, www.cruiseamerica
.com) Renting nationwide, company offices include
Phoenix, Flagstaff and Las Vegas. Website features the
Renters Assistance Guide, with RV operating tips.

RIDING THE RAILS

On September 17, 1901, the first Grand Canyon Railway train departed Williams to carry its pioneering passengers to the South Rim – and so began the modern era of the canyon as tourist destination. Instead of the hurdle of a long and arduous stagecoach ride, tourists could now travel to the canyon in relative comfort. By 1968, car travel had made the train obsolete. Only three passengers were on that year's final trip to the rim.

In 1989, Max and Thelma Biegert bought and lovingly restored the train, resuming passenger service after a 21-year absence. The Biegerts sold the company in 2007 to Xanterra Parks and Resorts, the concessionaire at the South Rim.

Today, diesel locomotives make the daily journey to Grand Canyon Village. On a few select days each year, the railway runs a steam locomotive with engines powered by waste vegetable oil.

Passengers can choose from four classes of service:

Coach Class (adult/child $70/40 round-trip) Features 1950s-style cars with large windows and room for roving musicians and marauders.

First Class (adult/child $140/110) Has air-conditioning, spacious reclining seats, and snacks and beverages on offer in both directions.

Observation Dome ($170) With upper-level seating in a glass-enclosed dome, featuring snacks, beverages and a champagne toast on the return trip; not open to children under 16.

Luxury Parlor Class ($190) Incredibly comfortable cushioned window seats and an open-air rear platform; not open to children under 16.

A 1952 parlor car doubles as a cafe, selling coffee, candy, box lunches, sunscreen, water and film.

Even if you're not a train buff, or if you generally shrink from traveling en masse, the train can be a lot of fun if you get into the spirit. A banjo player or other musician wanders the aisles, joking with passengers and strumming such folk classics as 'I've Been Working on the Railroad.' Something about riding the rails, waving your arms out the window or pretending to be FDR stumping on the rear platform brings the kid out in people. A mock horseback chase and train robbery enliven the return trip.

The train departs the 1908 Grand Canyon Railway Depot in Williams at 9:30am, following a 9am Wild West shoot-out by the tracks (a slapstick performance to put you in the mood). You'll arrive at Grand Canyon Depot at 11:45am. The return train pulls out at 3:30pm, arriving back in Williams at 5:45pm. Most people approach it as a day trip, but you can purchase a one-way ticket or spend a few days in the park and return on a later train. Packages are available through the Grand Canyon Railway Hotel in Williams, and lodgings at the rim. For reservations and details, contact **Grand Canyon Railway** (☎800-843-8724; www.thetrain.com).

more information on self-guided biking around the Grand Canyon.

Outside the South Rim, great mountain-biking trails in Kaibab National Forest include a 16-mile trail running from the Tusayan Trailhead to the Grandview Lookout Tower. For more information, see p87). Stop at the **Tusayan Ranger Station** (☎928-638-2443; ⊙8am-5pm) for trail maps and directions.

See the South Rim chapter for more on cycling

around Flagstaff (p101) and Sedona (p111).

Outside the park beyond the North Rim, there's plenty of good single-track for mountain bikers in Kaibab National Forest (p147), teeming with old-growth ponderosa pines, steepsided canyons, aspen groves and velvety meadows. The 18-mile Rainbow Rim Trail winds along the rim through aspen and ponderosa, passing five viewpoints with gorgeous panoramas. Pick up a map and information at the Kai-

bab Plateau Visitor Center in Jacob Lake.

Car & Motorcycle

RV traffic is commonplace in this region, so you won't have any problems finding pull-through campsites and dump stations.

There's a **gas station** (⊙7am-7pm) on the access road to North Rim Campground, where basic repairs can be completed. At the South Rim, nearest gas stations are in the town of

Tusayan and inside the park at **Desert View Chevron** (☏928-638-2365; ◷24hr Mar-Sep), near the East Entrance. The **garage** (◷8am-5pm Mon-Fri) in Grand Canyon Village also offers limited service and repairs. Call ☏928-638-2631 for 24-hour emergency towing.

Road Conditions & Hazard

Check road conditions within the park by calling the automated information line at ☏928-638-7888. For conditions in Kaibab National Forest (South Rim), call the **Tusayan Ranger Station** (☏928-638-2443); for conditions in Kaibab National Forest (North Rim), call the **Kaibab Plateau Visitor Center** (☏928-643-7298).

Ranging between 6500ft and 7500ft in elevation, roads in Flagstaff and environs may experience snow and ice from October through April. At elevations approaching 9000ft, roads along the North Rim are even more susceptible to weather. The drive up from deserts north and east of the park climbs about 4000ft, and conditions change rapidly – you may start out in sunny, dry weather in Kanab or Lees Ferry and wind up

battling rain, hail or snow in Jacob Lake. The forest service's dirt roads, particularly those in Kaibab National Forest, may be impassable after even a light rain. Always check with a ranger before heading out.

You'll need a high-clearance 4WD vehicle to tackle both the 17-mile road to Point Sublime (a minimum two-hour round-trip) and the 60-mile dirt road to Toroweap. Absolutely do not attempt these drives without first telling someone where you're going, and bring plenty of water.

If driving to Grand Canyon West on the Hualapai Reservation, be aware that nine of the 21 miles of Diamond Bar Rd are regularly graded but unpaved road. In wet weather, a 4WD vehicle is advisable. Be sure to start out with a full tank of gas and a good supply of water. Also on the Hualapai Reservation, Diamond Creek Rd is best traveled by 4WD with a plentiful supply of water. Even in the best of circumstances, this rough road leading directly to the Colorado River necessitates at least two creek crossings.

The main hazard to look out for is wildlife in and around the parks, or livestock

in rural areas surrounding the park.

Shuttle

Free shuttle buses operate every 10 to 15 minutes along three connecting routes on the South Rim. Except for an early-morning shuttle to the North Kaibab Trailhead, the only way to explore the North Rim is by car, bicycle or foot.

Hermits Rest Route Accesses the 8-mile stretch of rim road west of Grand Canyon Village. This road is closed to private vehicles from March through November; the only way to see the overlooks then is via shuttle, bicycle or on foot.

Village Route You can drive to most facilities in the village, but it's easier to park your car and take one of the shuttles.

Kaibab/Rim Route Stops at Pipe Creek Vista, South Kaibab Trailhead and Yaki Point, the last of which is closed to private vehicles year-round.

Health & Safety

Educating yourself on the Grand Canyon's unique environment and hazards will go a long way toward making your visit a safe and healthy one.

BEFORE YOU GO
Even strolling the scenic viewpoints around the Grand Canyon will be easier and more enjoyable if you're somewhat physically fit. If you're not in decent shape and you plan on doing any hiking, start getting regular, vigorous physical exercise at least three weeks prior to your trip.

When possible, visitors from lower elevations and cooler climes should allow several days to acclimatize before undertaking any strenuous activity at the Grand Canyon.

Insurance
Review the terms of your health-insurance policy before going on a trip; some policies don't cover injuries sustained as a result of dangerous activities, which can include such pursuits as rock climbing or mountaineering. Double-check that emergency medical care, and emergency evacuation to your home country (if you're not from the US), is covered by your policy.

Medical Checklist
Your first-aid kit should include:
» adhesive tape
» bandages and safety pins
» elasticized support bandage for knees, ankles etc
» gauze swabs
» nonadhesive dressings
» paper stitches
» small pair of scissors
» sterile alcohol wipes
» thermometer (note that mercury thermometers are prohibited by airlines)
» tweezers

Medications & Miscellany
In addition to regular medications you need, consider including some of these over-the-counter meds:
» antidiarrhea and antinausea drugs
» antifungal cream or powder
» antihistamines
» antiseptic
» calamine lotion, sting-relief spray or aloe vera
» cold and influenza tablets, throat lozenges and nasal decongestant
» eye drops
» insect repellent
» multivitamins – especially for longer hikes, when dietary vitamin intake may be inadequate
» painkillers (such as aspirin, acetaminophen or ibuprofen)
» rehydration mixture – particularly important when traveling with children
» sunscreen and lip balm
» water-purification tablets or iodine

Further Reading
Backcountry First Aid and Extended Care by Buck Tilton (Falcon, 2007) is a useful pocket-size guide. *Medicine for the Outdoors* by Paul S Auerbach (Mosby, 2009) gives brief explanations of myriad medical problems and practical treatment options, and *Wilderness 911* by Eric A Weiss (The Mountaineers Books, 2007) is a step-by-step guide to first aid and advanced care in remote areas.

IN THE PARK
For the casual visitor to the park, health and safety usually requires little effort apart from keeping sufficiently hydrated and not goofing off on the rim. However, for those heading below the rim, preparation and responsibility for one's own safety are key to a safe adventure. Many emergencies below the rim occur because visitors overestimate their abilities and come underprepared to deal with the consequences.

Always lock your car and put valuables in the trunk, particularly if you park at a trailhead. Physical assault is rare in the park, but use caution when hiking alone.

Medical Assistance

In an emergency on either rim, dial ☑911; from your lodge or cabin, dial ☑9-911.

Those seeking a higher level of self-reliance might be interested in taking a wilderness first-aid course or getting certified as a Wilderness First Responder.

Wilderness Medicine Institute (WMI; www.nols.edu/wmi)

Wilderness Medicine Training Center (WMTC; www.wildmedcenter.com)

South Rim

At Grand Canyon Village, **North County Community Health Center** (☑928-638-2551; www.northcountrychc.org; 1 Clinic Rd; ☺8am-6pm mid-Oct to mid-May) offers walk-in medical care. The nearest pharmacy is 60 miles south at the **Safeway** (☑pharmacy 928-635-5977; 637 W Route 66; ☺5am-10pm) in Williams. The nearest hospitals to the South Rim are 80 miles south in Flagstaff, including the top-notch **Flagstaff Medical Center** (☑928-779-3366; www.flagstaffmedical center.com; 1200 N Beaver St).

North Rim

Rangers provide emergency medical care within the park; the nearest hospital, **Kane County Hospital** (☑435-644-5811; www.kchosp.net; 355 N Main St), is 80 miles north in Kanab, Utah. Also in Kanab is the nearest pharmacy, **Zion Pharmacy** (☑435-644-2702; 14 E Center St; ☺9am-6pm Mon-Fri, to noon Sat).

Page Hospital (☑928-645-2424; www.bannerhealth .com; 501 N Navajo Dr) is 114 miles from the North Rim in Page, Arizona. Page also has a pharmacy in the local **Safeway** (☑928-645-8155; 650 Elm St; ☺9am-8pm Mon-Fri, 9am-6pm Sat, 10am-4pm Sun).

Common Ailments

Plaguing hikers in the Grand Canyon and beyond, these common ailments may strike your hike.

Blisters

To avoid blisters, make sure your walking boots or shoes are well worn in before you hit the trail. Boots should fit comfortably with enough room to move your toes. Socks should fit properly and be specialized for walkers; be sure there are no seams across the widest part of your foot. Wet and muddy socks can also cause blisters, so pack a spare pair. Keep your toenails clipped, but not too short. If you feel a blister coming on, treat it sooner rather then later by applying a bit of moleskin or duct tape.

Fatigue

More injuries happen toward the end of the day than earlier, when you're fresher. Although tiredness can simply be a nuisance on an easy hike, it can be life-threatening on narrow exposed ridges or in bad weather. Never set out on a hike that is beyond your capabilities on the day. If you feel below par, have a day off.

Don't push yourself too hard – take rests every hour or two and build in a good half-hour lunch break. Toward the end of the day, take down the pace and increase your concentration. Eat properly throughout the day – nuts, dried fruit and chocolate are all good energy-rich snacks.

Giardiasis

This parasitic infection of the small intestine, commonly called giardia, occurs throughout North America and the world. Symptoms may include nausea, bloating, cramps and diarrhea, and may last for weeks. Giardia is easily diagnosed by a stool test and readily treated with antibiotics.

To protect yourself from giardia, avoid drinking directly from lakes, ponds, streams and rivers, which may be contaminated by animal or human feces. Giardia can also be transmitted from person to person if proper hand washing is not performed.

Knee Strain

Many hikers feel the burn on long, steep descents. Although you can't eliminate strain on the knee joints when dropping steeply, you can reduce it by taking shorter steps that leave your legs slightly bent and ensuring that your heel hits the ground before the rest of your foot. Some walkers find that compression bandages help, and trekking poles are very effective in taking some of the weight off the knees.

Travelers' Diarrhea

Serious diarrhea caused by contaminated water is an increasing problem in heavily used backcountry areas. If diarrhea does hit you, fluid replacement is the mainstay of management. Drink weak black tea with a little sugar, soda water or flat soft drinks diluted with 50% water.

For severe diarrhea, a rehydrating solution is necessary to replace minerals and salts. Commercially available oral rehydration salts (ORS) are very useful. Stick to a bland diet as you recover. Gut-paralyzing drugs such as diphenoxylate or loperamide can relieve symptoms but don't cure the problem.

Environmental Hazards

Altitude

As the South Rim is more than 7000ft above sea level and the North Rim 8801ft at its highest point, altitude sickness is fairly common. Characterized by shortness of breath, fatigue and headaches, it can be avoided by drinking plenty of water and taking a day or two to acclimatize before attempting any long hikes.

Bites & Stings

Commonsense approaches to these concerns are the most effective. Wear boots when hiking to protect from snakes; wear long sleeves and pants to prevent tick and mosquito bites.

SCORPIONS

Commonly found in Arizona, the bark scorpion is the only dangerous species of scorpion in the US. To prevent scorpion stings, inspect and shake out clothing, shoes and sleeping bags before use. If stung, immediately apply ice or cold packs, immobilize the affected body part and go to the nearest emergency room.

SNAKES

Several species of rattlesnake are found in the Grand Canyon. Most snakebites can be prevented by respecting the snake's space – if you encounter one, move away slowly. Those bitten will experience rapid swelling, severe pain and possibly temporary paralysis. Death is rare, but children are at higher risk.

To treat snakebite, place a light constricting bandage over the bite, keep the wounded part below the level of the heart and move it as little as possible. Attempting to suck out the venom is not considered an effective strategy. Stay calm and get to a medical facility for antivenin treatment as soon as possible.

TICKS

Always check your body for ticks after walking through high grass or thickly forested areas. If ticks are found unattached, they can simply be brushed off. If a tick is found attached, press down around the tick's head with tweezers, grab the head and gently pull upwards – do not twist it. (If no tweezers are available, use your fingers, but protect them from contamination with a piece of tissue or paper.)

Do not douse an attached tick with oil, alcohol or petroleum jelly. Transmitted by ticks, Lyme disease is uncommon in Arizona, but you should consult a doctor if you get sick in the weeks after your trip.

Cold

HYPOTHERMIA

This life-threatening condition occurs when prolonged exposure to cold thwarts the body's ability to maintain its core temperature. Hypothermia is a real danger for winter hikers. Remember to dress in layers and wear a windproof outer jacket. If possible, bring a Thermos containing a hot (nonalcoholic) beverage.

Hypothermia doesn't just occur in cold weather – dehydration and certain medications can predispose people to hypothermia, especially when they're wet, and even in relatively warm weather. Symptoms include uncontrolled shivering, poor muscle control and a careless attitude. Treat symptoms by putting on dry clothing, giving warm fluids and warming the victim through direct body contact with another person.

Heat

DEHYDRATION & HEAT EXHAUSTION

The canyon is a dry, hot place, and even if you're just walking along the rim, lack of water can cause dehydration, which in turn can lead to heat exhaustion. To prevent dehydration, take time to acclimatize to high temperatures, wear a wide-brimmed hat and make sure to drink plenty of fluids. Hikers should drink a gallon of water per day. It's also wise to carry water in your car in case it breaks down.

Characterized by fatigue, nausea, headaches, cramps and cool, clammy skin, heat exhaustion should be treated by drinking water, eating high-energy foods, resting in the shade and cooling the skin with a wet cloth. Heat exhaustion can lead to heatstroke if not addressed promptly.

HEATSTROKE

Long, continuous exposure to high temperatures can lead to heatstroke, a serious, sometimes fatal condition that occurs when the body's heat-regulating mechanism breaks down and one's body temperature rises to dangerous levels.

Symptoms of heatstroke include flushed, dry skin, a weak and rapid pulse, poor judgment, inability to focus and delirium. Move the victim to shade, remove clothing, cover them with a wet sheet or towel and fan them continually. Hospitalization is essential for heatstroke.

HYPONATREMIA

While drinking plenty of water is crucial, it's also important to supplement water intake with salty snacks and electrolyte drinks to avoid hyponatremia (a dangerously low sodium level in the blood). In the dry heat of the canyon, sweat can evaporate off of your skin so quickly that you may not notice how much you've perspired. Salt lost through sweating must be replaced in order to keep a balanced sodium level in the blood.

Symptoms of hyponatremia are similar to early signs of heat exhaustion: nausea, vomiting and an altered mental state. Give the victim salty foods and seek immediate help if their mental alertness diminishes.

Sunburn

In the desert and at high altitude you can sunburn in less than an hour, even through cloud cover. Use lots of sunscreen (minimum SPF 15, ideally SPF 45), especially on skin not typically exposed to sun. Be sure to apply sunscreen to young children, particularly babies, and wear wide-brimmed hats.

Weather & Flash Floods

Even if the sky overhead is clear, distant rainstorms can send walls of water, debris and mud roaring through side canyons without warning. Such flash floods have killed people caught in creeks and dry riverbeds. Never camp in dry washes, and be sure to check weather reports for the entire region before venturing into the canyon. This is crucial if you're planning on hiking through any slot canyons. Flash floods are most common during summer storms in July, August and September.

Don't underestimate the summer heat – temperatures routinely soar past 100°F in the canyon. In winter months, snow and ice can make trails slick and dangerous. Ask a ranger about conditions before heading out.

Wildlife

For their own safety and yours, it's illegal to approach or feed any wildlife – from those chubby South Rim squirrels (who bite!) to seemingly placid elk. In the canyon, always shake out shoes and sleeping bags to dislodge hiding scorpions. Also keep an ear out for rattlesnakes, whose rattle is a warning signal.

Safe Hiking

It's easy to become complacent when hiking in the Grand Canyon, given the clearly marked trails and

PREHYDRATION

Since your body can only absorb about a quart of water per hour, it's highly beneficial to prehydrate before embarking on a long hike. To get a head start on hydration, drink plenty of water the day and evening before your hike, and avoid diuretics like caffeine and alcohol.

ease of descent. But hiking here can be serious business. On average, there are 400 medical emergencies each year on canyon trails, and more than 250 hikers need to be rescued at their own hefty expense. Several have died.

Time and again, hikers who have been rescued from the canyon say that their biggest mistake was underestimating how hot the canyon can be. The best way of ensuring a rewarding hike is proper planning. Learn about the trails, honestly assess your limitations and respect them.

Take note if you haven't had to pee as often as usual, or if your urine is dark yellow or amber-colored. These are indicators of dehydration, which can rapidly spiral into more dire health concerns. Loss of appetite and thirst may be early symptoms of heat exhaustion, so even if you don't feel thirsty, drink water often and have a salty snack while you're at it. Add a little electrolyte replacement powder (like Gatorade) to your water. Err on the side of caution and bring more water and food than you think you'll need – even if it turns out you don't need it, it could save someone else's life.

Falls

Almost every year people fall to their death at the Grand Canyon. Stay on the trails, refrain from stepping over guardrails, and absolutely do not allow children to run along the rim. There isn't as much railing as you may expect. Jokingly posing for 'look, I'm falling over the rim!' photographs is ill-advised, as several unfortunate souls have had vertigo attacks or

loose rocks have actually sent them over the edge.

Parents should consider carrying toddlers in baby backpacks along and below the rim. When hiking below the rim, wear sturdy shoes or boots.

Getting Lost

The park comprises 1904 sq miles of desert terrain, making it too easy to lose your way in its labyrinth of side canyons and sheer cliffs. It is imperative that you plan any hike carefully and appropriately. Whether backcountry hiking or driving in remote areas, always carry an adequate map and supply of drinking water.

Leave a detailed itinerary with a friend, listing routes and dates, as well as identifying details of your car. Cell phones won't get a signal inside the canyon. For backcountry hikes, bring a topo map, know how to read it and never stray from trails under any circumstances.

If you do get lost, search-and-rescue operations may take days to find you. Stay calm and stay put, making your location as visible as possible by spreading out colorful clothing or equipment in an exposed place. Use a signal mirror (an old CD is a good lightweight substitute) and ration food and water. Do not attempt to blaze a shortcut to the river; people have died from falls, exposure or dehydration after stranding themselves on steep, dead-end ledges or ridges.

Lightning

Being below the rim does not protect you from lightning

SAFETY TIPS FOR HIKING SMART

Nuts and bolts for safe hiking in the Grand Canyon:

» **Down = 2x up** Make this formula your hiking mantra. Generally speaking, it takes twice as long to wheeze back up the canyon as it does to breeze down. So if you'd like to hike for six hours, turn around after two. Most first-time canyon hikers slog uphill at about 1mph.

» **Never leave the trail** Stay on marked trails, both for safety and erosion control. Nowhere is this more important than in the Grand Canyon, where hazards include stupefying drop-offs. It's also extremely difficult for rescuers to find a hiker who has wandered off-trail.

» **Don't hike alone** Most of those who get in trouble in the canyon are solo hikers, for whom the risks are multiplied. Backcountry hikes are safer (and more enjoyable) with a companion.

» **Take your time** Given the altitude and extreme aridity, go slow to avoid overexertion. Ideally, you should be able to speak easily while hiking, regardless of the grade. Be sure to take a five- to 10-minute break every hour to recharge, in the shade if possible.

» **Eat and drink often** Pay close attention to your intake of food and fluids to prevent dehydration and hyponatremia (low blood sodium level). One good strategy is to have a salty snack and a long drink of water every 20 to 30 minutes. In summer months each hiker should drink about a gallon of water per day. Eat before you're hungry and drink before you're thirsty. Prior to a major hike, eat a healthy breakfast and drink lots of water; afterward, replenish with more water and treat yourself to a big dinner.

» **Take care of your feet** In addition to sturdy, comfortable, broken-in boots and medium-weight socks, bring moleskin for blisters and make sure your toenails are trimmed. On long hikes, soak your feet in streams to reduce inflammation and safe-guard against blisters (just be sure to dry them thoroughly before replacing your socks). After hiking, elevate your feet.

» **Don't be overly ambitious** Particularly for novice hikers, it's a good idea to spend the first day or two gauging your ability and response to the climate and terrain. If you're planning long hikes, test your desert legs on a more level hike or a short round-trip of 2 to 4 miles, then work your way up to more difficult trails.

» **Stay cool** Hike during the cooler early-morning and late-afternoon hours – this goes double in summer, when rim temperatures heat up past the 90°F mark and the canyon floor often exceeds 110°F. Splash water on your face and head at streams and water sources, and soak your shirt or bandana to produce an evaporative cooling effect.

strikes. If a thunderstorm catches you on an exposed ridge or summit, look for a concave rock formation to shelter in, but avoid touching the rock itself. Never seek shelter under objects that are isolated or higher than their surroundings.

In open areas where there's no shelter, find a depression in the ground and take up a crouched-squatting position with your feet together; do not lie on the ground. Avoid contact with metallic objects such as pack frames or hiking poles. Should anyone be struck by lightning, immediately begin first-aid measures such

as checking their airway, breathing and pulse, and starting burn treatment. Get the patient to a doctor as quickly as possible.

Rescue & Evacuation

Hikers should take responsibility for their own safety and aim to prevent emergency situations, but even the most safety-conscious hiker may have a serious accident requiring urgent medical attention. In case of accidents, self-rescue should be your first consideration, as search-and-rescue operations into the canyon are very expensive and require emer-

gency personnel to put their own safety at risk.

If a person in your group is injured, leave someone with them while others seek help. If there are only two of you, leave the injured person with as much warm clothing, food and water as it's sensible to spare, plus a whistle and flashlight. Mark their position with something conspicuous.

Rockfall

Always be alert to the danger of rockfall, especially after heavy rains. If you accidentally loosen a rock, loudly warn other hikers below. Bighorn sheep sometimes dislodge rocks, so animal-watchers should be especially vigilant.

Traumatic Injuries

Detailed first-aid instruction is outside the scope of this book, but here are some basic tips and advice. If the victim is unconscious, immediately check if they are breathing. Clear their airway if it's blocked, and check for a pulse – feel the side of the neck rather than the wrist. Check for wounds and broken bones – ask the person where they have pain if they are conscious; otherwise, gently inspect them all over (including their back and the back of their head), moving them as little as possible in case they've sustained a neck or back injury.

Control any bleeding by applying firm pressure to the wound. Bleeding from the nose or ear may indicate a fractured skull. Don't give the person anything by mouth. Manage the person for shock. Raise their legs above heart level (unless their legs are fractured or they've suffered a venomous bite); dress any wounds and immobilize any fractures; loosen tight clothing; keep the person warm by covering them with a blanket or other dry clothing; insulate them from the ground if possible.

Most cases of brief unconsciousness are not associated with serious brain injury, but as a general rule, any person who has been knocked unconscious should be watched for deterioration. If they do deteriorate, go and seek medical attention immediately.

FRACTURES

Indications of a fracture are pain (tenderness of the affected area), swelling and discoloration, loss of function or deformity of a limb. Unless you know what you're doing, don't try to straighten an obviously displaced broken bone. To protect from further injury, immobilize a non-displaced fracture (where the broken bones are in alignment) by splinting it, usually in the position found, which will probably be the most comfortable position. If you do have to splint a broken bone, remember to check regularly that the splint is not cutting off the circulation to the hand or foot.

Compound fractures (or open fractures, in which the bone protrudes from the skin) require urgent treatment, as there is a risk of infection. Fractures of the thigh bone also require urgent treatment as they involve massive blood loss and pain. Seek help and treat the patient for shock. Dislocations, where the bone has come out of the joint, are very painful and should be set as soon as possible.

Broken ribs are painful but usually heal by themselves and do not need splinting. If breathing difficulties occur, or the person coughs up blood, medical attention should be sought urgently, as this may indicate a punctured lung.

INTERNAL INJURIES

These are more difficult to detect and cannot usually be treated in the field. Watch for shock, which is a specific medical condition associated with a failure to maintain circulating blood volume. Signs include a rapid pulse and cold, clammy extremities. A person in shock requires urgent medical attention.

SPRAINS

Ankle and knee sprains are common injuries among hikers, particularly when crossing rugged terrain. To help prevent ankle sprains, wear boots that have adequate ankle support. If you suffer a sprain, immobilize the joint with a firm bandage, and if possible, immerse the foot in cold water. Relieve pain and swelling by resting and icing the joint, and keeping it elevated as much as possible for the first 24 hours. Take over-the-counter painkillers to ease discomfort. If the sprain is mild, you may be able to continue your hike after a couple of days.

For more severe sprains, seek medical attention as an X-ray may be needed to find out if a bone has been broken.

Safe Cycling

On the South Rim, cycling is permitted on the Greenway Trail (see boxed text, p225), as well as on all paved and unpaved roads. Cyclists must adhere to traffic regulations and should use caution along the heavily trafficked roads, especially during the busy summer season. On Hermit Rd, bicyclists are required to pull off the road to allow vehicles to pass. Always wear a helmet and bright colors to improve your visibility to drivers.

Cycling around the North Rim is a whole other animal. Single-track trails and forest roads abound in the Kaibab National Forest for mountain bikers. Because the area is so remote compared with the developed South Rim, cyclists should wear helmets and come supplied with water, food and first aid. For more information on biking the North Rim, see (p143).

Clothing & Equipment

Arriving outfitted with the proper clothing and equipment will keep you comfortable and safe on your adventures. Much of what is appropriate to bring depends on the season you're visiting and what activities you plan to pursue.

Plan carefully for the season, particularly if you're planning to explore the backcountry for the first time. Many first-time visitors are surprised by the weather, especially the extreme heat of summer and the high-country cold of the North Rim. Below the rim, you'll have to be self-sufficient.

We've covered most of the basic equipment and attire here, with tips on what to look for.

Clothing

Modern outdoor garments made from synthetic fabrics (which are breathable and actively wick moisture away from your skin) are better for hiking than anything made of cotton or wool. The exception to this is if you're hiking out of the canyon in midsummer, when cotton is a godsend. Soak cotton shirts or bandanas with water at every opportunity, and allow the evaporative cooling effect to ease your journey.

Layering

To cope with changing temperatures and exertion, layering your clothing is a good way to regulate your body temperature.

» Upper body: start with a base layer made of synthetic thermal fabric (eg Polartec); second layer is a long-sleeved shirt; third layer can be a fleece sweater or pile jacket that wicks away moisture. Outer shell consists of a weatherproof jacket.

» Lower body: shorts will be most comfortable in midsummer, although some prefer long pants – light, quick-drying fabric (no more than 30% cotton) is best. Convertible pants with zip-off legs are good for temperature regulation. Waterproof overpants form the outer layer.

Waterproof Shells

» Grand Canyon hikers should always carry a windproof and waterproof rain jacket and pants. Gore-Tex or similar breathable fabrics work best; waterproof shells should be properly seam-sealed.

» The jacket should have a hood that accommodates headwear and allows peripheral vision. Ideally it will have a spacious map pocket and a heavy-gauge zip protected by a storm flap.

ROUTE FINDING

While accurate, our maps are not perfect. Inaccuracies in altitudes are commonly caused by air-temperature anomalies. Natural features such as river confluences and mountain peaks are in their true position, but sometimes the location of villages and trails is not always so (this may be because a village is spread over a hillside, or the size of the map does not allow for detail of the trail's twists and turns). However, by using several basic route-finding techniques, you will have few problems following our descriptions:

» Be aware of whether the trail should be climbing or descending.

» Check the north-point arrow on the map and determine the general direction of the trail.

» Time your progress over a known distance and calculate the speed at which you travel in the given terrain. From then on, you can determine with reasonable accuracy how far you have traveled.

» Watch the path – look for boot prints and other signs of previous passage.

» When looking for pants, choose a pair with slits for pocket access and long leg zips so that you can pull them on and off over boots.

Footwear, Socks & Gaiters

» It is vital that your boots are properly worn in before you begin any serious hiking.

» Some hikers prefer the greater agility that lightweight boots allow, while others insist on heavier designs that give firm ankle support and protect feet in rough terrain. Either way, hiking boots should have a flexible (preferably polyurethane) midsole and an insole that supports the arch and heel. Nonslip soles (such as Vibram) provide the best grip.

» Try on hiking boots in warm weather, preferably in the afternoon or evening, to accommodate for foot swell. Try boots on with thick hiking socks; they should still offer plenty of toe room.

» Most hikers carry a pair of river sandals or flip-flops to wear around camp. River sandals are also useful when fording waterways.

» Synthetic socks that draw moisture away from your feet are another must.

» If you're hiking in wet conditions, gaiters will help keep water, mud or snow from running down your waterproof pants into your shoes.

Navigation

Maps & Compass

You should always carry a good map of the area you are hiking in, and know how to read it. Before setting off on your trek, ensure that you understand the contours and the map symbols, plus the main ridge and river systems in the area. Also familiarize yourself with the true north–south directions and the general direction in which you are heading. On the trail, try to identify major landmarks such as mountain ranges and gorges, and locate them on your map. This will give you a better understanding of the region's geography.

Buy a compass and learn how to use it. The attraction of magnetic north varies in different parts of the world, so compasses need to be balanced accordingly.

Compass manufacturers have divided the world into five zones. Make sure your compass is balanced for your destination zone. There are also 'universal' compasses on the market that can be used anywhere in the world.

This is a very basic introduction to using a compass and will only be of assistance if you are proficient in map reading. For simplicity, it doesn't take magnetic variation into account. Before using a compass we recommend you obtain further instruction.

READING A COMPASS

Hold the compass flat in the palm of your hand. Rotate the bezel so the red end of the needle points to the N on the bezel. The bearing is read from the dash under the bezel.

ORIENTING THE MAP

To orient the map so that it aligns with the ground, place the compass flat on the map. Rotate the map until the needle is parallel with the map's north–south grid lines and the red end is pointing to north on the map. You can now identify features around you by aligning them with labeled features on the map.

TAKING A BEARING FROM THE MAP

Draw a line on the map between your starting point and your destination. Place the edge of the compass on this line with the direction-of-travel arrow pointing towards your destination. Rotate the bezel until the meridian lines are parallel with the north–south grid lines on the map and the N points to north on the map. Read the bearing from the dash.

FOLLOWING A BEARING

Rotate the bezel so that the intended bearing is in line with the dash. Place the compass flat in the palm of your hand and rotate the base plate until the red end points to N on the bezel. The direction-of-travel arrow will now point in the direction you need to walk.

DETERMINING YOUR BEARING

Rotate the bezel so the red end points to the N. Place the compass flat in the palm of your hand and rotate the base plate until the direction of travel arrow points in the direction in which you have been trekking. Read your bearing from the dash.

GPS

Originally developed by the US Department of Defense, the Global Positioning System (GPS) is a network of more than 20 earth-orbiting satellites that continually beam encoded signals back to earth. Small computer-driven devices (GPS receivers) can decode these signals to give users an extremely accurate reading of their location – to within 30m, anywhere on the planet, at any time of day, in almost any weather.

The cheapest hand-held GPS receivers now cost less than US$100 (although these may not have a built-in averaging system that minimizes signal errors). Other important factors to consider when buying a GPS receiver are its weight and battery life.

Remember that a GPS receiver is of little use to trekkers unless used with an accurate topographical map. The receiver simply gives your position, which you must then locate on the local map.

EQUIPMENT CHECKLIST

Though it's tempting to simply toss everything into the car at the last minute, taking time to think things through as you pack can save you a lot of headaches down the road. Your list will vary, depending on your travel circumstances.

CLOTHING

» broad-brimmed hat (one that ties under the chin is required for all mule trips) in summer
» hiking boots, or sturdy trail-running shoes, and spare laces
» river sandals or flip-flops
» shorts and lightweight trousers or skirt
» socks and underwear
» sweater or fleece
» thermal underwear
» T-shirt and long-sleeved shirt with collar
» warm hat, scarf and gloves in winter
» waterproof jacket
» waterproof pants

EQUIPMENT

» backpack with waterproof liner
» first-aid kit
» high-energy food and snacks and one day's emergency supplies
» insect repellent
» map, compass and guidebook
» map case or clip-seal plastic bags
» pocket knife
» sunglasses
» sunscreen and lip balm
» survival bag or blanket
» toilet paper and trowel
» flashlight or headlamp, spare batteries and bulb
» watch
» water container
» whistle

OVERNIGHT HIKES

» biodegradable soap
» cooking, eating and drinking utensils
» matches and lighter
» sewing/repair kit
» sleeping bag and/or liner
» sleeping pad/mat
» spare cord
» stove and fuel
» tent, tarp and rainfly
» toiletries
» towel
» water-purification tablets, iodine or filter

OPTIONAL ITEMS

» altimeter
» backpack cover (waterproof, slip-on)
» binoculars
» camera, film and batteries
» candle
» emergency distress beacon
» gaiters
» GPS receiver
» groundsheet
» hiking poles
» mobile phone
» mosquito net
» notebook and pen
» swimsuit

GPS receivers will only work properly in the open. The signals from a crucial satellite may be blocked (or bounce off rock or water) directly below high cliffs, near large bodies of water or in dense tree cover and give inaccurate readings.

GPS receivers are more vulnerable to breakdowns (including dead batteries) than the humble magnetic compass – a low-tech device that has served navigators faithfully for centuries – so don't rely on them entirely.

Equipment

It doesn't have to be fancy or from the highest-end manufacturer's New! Improved! collection, but making sure you have the basic equipment will contribute greatly to a safe and comfortable journey.

Backpacks & Daypacks

» A good backpack will have a robust, easily adjustable waist-belt that can comfortably support the entire weight carried, effectively transferring the load from your shoulders onto your hips. Shoulder straps should serve only to steady the backpack.

» Backpacks with a relatively large capacity (at least 5500 cubic inches) are best for overnight hiking in the back-country.

» Internal-frame backpacks fit snugly against your back, keeping the weight close to your center of gravity but trapping sweat. Newer, arched-back designs allow for better ventilation. External-frame backpacks have good ventilation and allow hikers to carry more weight, but are slightly cumbersome. Ultimately, choose what's most comfortable for you.

» Even if the manufacturer claims your pack is waterproof, use heavy-duty liners.

» For day hikes or side trips from camp, daypacks that double as hydration systems (like Camelbaks) eliminate the hassle of toting unwieldy water bottles and can carry all your necessities.

Tents

» A three-season tent will suffice for most backpacking expeditions. Winter overnight trips will necessitate a four-season tent for protection from the elements.

» The floor and the outer shell, or rainfly, should have taped or sealed seams and covered zips to stop leaks.

» Dome- and tunnel-shaped tents handle windy conditions better than flat-sided tents.

» Most hikers find tents of around 5lb or 6lb a comfortable carrying weight.

Sleeping Bag & Pad

» Three-season sleeping bags will serve the needs of most campers. Down fillings are warmer than synthetic for the same weight and bulk but, unlike synthetic fillings, do not retain warmth when wet.

» Mummy bags are the best shape for weight and warmth. Third-party European Norm (EN) temperature ratings (30°F, for instance) show the coldest temperatures at which a typical man or woman should feel comfortable in the bag.

» An inner liner helps keep your sleeping bag clean, as well as adding an insulating layer. Silk liners are lightest.

» During the summer, the canyon floor is usually sweltering enough to forego a sleeping bag altogether; backcountry campers might consider bringing just a sleeping-bag liner or a sheet. Some even soak a sheet in the river for the evaporative cooling effect.

» Cooler seasons, especially on the North Rim, call for both sleeping bag and sleeping pad for insulation from the cold ground. Self-inflating pads put an air cushion between you and the ground. Foam mats are a low-cost but less comfortable alternative.

Stoves & Fuel

The type of fuel you'll use most often will help determine what kind of camp stove is best for you. The following types of fuel can be found in the US, and local outdoors stores can help you choose an appropriate camp stove if you aren't traveling with your own.

White gas Inexpensive, efficient and readily available throughout the country, reliable in all temperatures and clean-burning. More volatile than other types of fuel.

Butane, propane and isobutane These clean-burning fuels come in nonrecyclable canisters and tend to be more expensive. Best for camping in warmer conditions, as their performance markedly decreases in below-freezing temperatures.

Denatured alcohol Renewable; the most sustainable alternative. Burns slowly but also extremely quietly.

Buying & Renting Locally

If you haven't arrived with all the equipment you need, it can actually be a boon to buy or rent locally, as you can take advantage of local expertise on what works best in the region. **Canyon Village Marketplace** (p84), the park's full-sized grocery on the South Rim, also sells and rents camping equipment, and cross-country skis in the winter. It offers the park's largest selection of gear and can even tackle simple repairs. **Desert View Marketplace** (p84) offers a few camping necessities like flashlights, water-purification tablets and thermal blankets.

Outdoor stores in Flagstaff (p108) sell and rent camping equipment.

On the North Rim, the North Rim General Store (p146) also sells a limited selection of camping gear, including fuel, sleeping bags and pads. Willow Canyon Outdoor Co (p156) in Kanab sells outdoor gear, books and maps.

behind the scenes

SEND US YOUR FEEDBACK

We love to hear from travelers – your comments keep us on our toes and help make our books better. Our well-traveled team reads every word on what you loved or loathed about this book. Although we cannot reply individually to postal submissions, we always guarantee that your feedback goes straight to the appropriate authors, in time for the next edition. Each person who sends us information is thanked in the next edition – and the most useful submissions are rewarded with a free book.

Visit **lonelyplanet.com/contact** to submit your updates and suggestions or to ask for help. Our award-winning website also features inspirational travel stories, news and discussions.

Note: We may edit, reproduce and incorporate your comments in Lonely Planet products such as guidebooks, websites and digital products, so let us know if you don't want your comments reproduced or your name acknowledged. For a copy of our privacy policy visit lonelyplanet.com/privacy.

AUTHOR THANKS

Wendy Yanagihara

Huge thanks to Jennifer for being such a pleasure to work with. For invaluable wisdom and generosity, thanks to Danna, Bill and lovely Estelle. Thanks to Shannon for Jasper care, Betty Upchurch and Rick Moore for fact checks, and the many locals who shared their expertise and smoothed the road. Most especially, thank you to my family, biological and surrogate, for always keeping me afloat. I dedicate this book to my dad, Harry Yanagihara (1938–2009), who took me on my first trip to the Grand Canyon and whom I miss daily.

Jennifer Denniston

Huge thanks to Kathleen, Alison and Wendy – you guys are amazing and fantastic to work with. Special thanks to my husband, Rhawn, and my daughters, Anna and Harper – without you, I couldn't do what I do. Thanks for always being game to hit the road, and for not only tolerating but encouraging my wanderlust. Thanks to Brian, Michelle, Eleanor and Henry for watching Chilton, to Marj Whitley for holding down the homefront, and to Suki Gear.

ACKNOWLEDGMENTS

Climate map data adapted from Peel MC, Finlayson BL & McMahon TA (2007) 'Updated World Map of the Köppen-Geiger Climate Classification', Hydrology and Earth System Sciences, 11, 163344.

Cover photograph: A condor soars over Grand Canyon National Park, Arizona. Gerilyn Attebery / Lonely Planet Images

Many of the images in this guide are available for licensing from Lonely Planet Images: www.lonelyplanetimages.com.

THIS BOOK

This 3rd edition of Lonely Planet's Grand Canyon National Park guidebook was researched and written by Wendy Yanagihara and Jennifer Denniston. Thanks also to Sarah Chandler, who provided the Las Vegas text. The previous edition was also written by Wendy Yanagihara and Jennifer Denniston, along with David Lukas. The 1st edition was written by Jennifer Denniston, Amy Marr, David Lukas and Kimberley O'Neil.

This guidebook was commissioned in Lonely Planet's Oakland office, and produced by the following:

Commissioning Editor Kathleen Munnelly

Coordinating Editors Kate James, Pat Kinsella

Coordinating Cartographer Andy Rojas

Coordinating Layout Designer Joseph Spanti

Managing Editor Kirsten Rawlings

Senior Editor Susan Paterson

Managing Cartographer Alison Lyall

Managing Layout Designers Jane Hart, Chris Girdler

Assisting Editor Andrew Bain

Cover Research Aude Vauconsant

Internal Image Research Sabrina Dalbesio

Thanks to Lucy Birchley, Helen Christinis, Ryan Evans, Heather Howard, Paul Iacono, Yvonne Kirk, Jenny Sachtjen, Angela Tinson, Gerard Walker

BEHIND THE SCENES

NOTES

NOTES

NOTES

index

000 Map pages
000 Photo pages

how to use this book

These symbols will help you find the listings you want:

🚗 Driving   🚶 Hiking   🚲 Biking

These symbols give you the vital information for each listing:

☎	Telephone Numbers	🛜	Wi-Fi Access	🚌	Bus
⏱	Opening Hours	🏊	Swimming Pool	⛴	Ferry
P	Parking	🥗	Vegetarian Selection	Ⓜ	Metro
⊖	Nonsmoking	📖	English-Language Menu	Ⓢ	Subway
✳	Air-Conditioning	👪	Family-Friendly	⊖	London Tube
@	Internet Access	🐾	Pet-Friendly	🚊	Tram
				Ⓡ	Train

Reviews are organised by author preference

Look out for these icons:

TOP CHOICE Our author's recommendation

FREE No payment required

🌿 A green or sustainable option

Our authors have nominated these places as demonstrating a strong commitment to sustainability – for example by supporting local communities and producers, operating in an environmentally friendly way, or supporting conservation projects.

Map Legend

Sights
- 🏖 Beach
- 🛕 Buddhist
- 🏰 Castle
- ✝ Christian
- 🕉 Hindu
- ☪ Islamic
- ✡ Jewish
- ❶ Monument
- 🏛 Museum/Gallery
- 🏚 Ruin
- 🍷 Winery/Vineyard
- 🐘 Zoo
- ⊙ Other Sight

Activities, Courses & Tours
- 🤿 Diving/Snorkelling
- 🛶 Canoeing/Kayaking
- ⛷ Skiing
- 🏄 Surfing
- 🏊 Swimming/Pool
- 🚶 Walking
- 🏄 Windsurfing
- ➕ Other Activity/Course/Tour

Sleeping
- 🛏 Sleeping
- ⛺ Camping

Eating
- 🍴 Eating

Drinking
- ☕ Drinking
- ☕ Cafe

Entertainment
- 🎭 Entertainment

Shopping
- 🛍 Shopping

Information
- ✉ Post Office
- ❶ Tourist Information

Transport
- ✈ Airport
- ⊗ Border Crossing
- 🚌 Bus
- ⊶⊕⊷ Cable Car/Funicular
- ⊙ Cycling
- ⊖ Ferry
- Ⓜ Metro
- ⊖ Monorail
- P Parking
- Ⓢ S-Bahn
- 🚕 Taxi
- ⊶⊕⊷ Train/Railway
- ⊶⊕⊷ Tram
- ⊖ Tube Station
- Ⓤ U-Bahn
- • Other Transport

Routes
- Tollway
- Freeway
- Primary
- Secondary
- Tertiary
- Lane
- Unsealed Road
- Plaza/Mall
- Steps
- Tunnel
- Pedestrian Overpass
- Walking Tour
- Walking Tour Detour
- Path

Boundaries
- International
- State/Province
- Disputed
- Regional/Suburb
- Marine Park
- Cliff
- Wall

Population
- ✪ Capital (National)
- ◉ Capital (State/Province)
- ● City/Large Town
- ○ Town/Village

Geographic
- 🛖 Hut/Shelter
- 🔦 Lighthouse
- 📷 Lookout
- ▲ Mountain/Volcano
- 🌴 Oasis
- 🌳 Park
-)(Pass
- 🌳 Picnic Area
- 💧 Waterfall

Hydrography
- River/Creek
- Intermittent River
- Swamp/Mangrove
- Reef
- Canal
- Water
- Dry/Salt/Intermittent Lake
- Glacier

Areas
- Beach/Desert
- + + + Cemetery (Christian)
- × × × Cemetery (Other)
- Park
- Forest
- Sportsground
- Sight (Building)
- Top Sight (Building)

OUR STORY

A beat-up old car, a few dollars in the pocket and a sense of adventure. In 1972 that's all Tony and Maureen Wheeler needed for the trip of a lifetime – across Europe and Asia overland to Australia. It took several months, and at the end – broke but inspired – they sat at their kitchen table writing and stapling together their first travel guide, *Across Asia on the Cheap*. Within a week they'd sold 1500 copies. Lonely Planet was born.

Today, Lonely Planet has offices in Melbourne, London and Oakland, with more than 600 staff and writers. We share Tony's belief that 'a great guidebook should do three things: inform, educate and amuse'.

OUR WRITERS

Wendy Yanagihara

Coordinating Author, South Rim On her first trip to the Grand Canyon at age 13, Wendy fell in love with the colors of the desert. Since returning over the years, she has gained a deep appreciation not only for the warm hues of globe mallow and Kaibab limestone, but also the richer spectrum of the canyon experience. Hiking the threshold trails is a walking meditation, sleeping on the Colorado's riverside beaches a profound privilege. Wendy has covered everything from the wilds of Papua, Indonesia to the urban jungle of Tokyo, Japan – and points beyond – for Lonely Planet. Rafting the Colorado ranks among her lifetime highlights.

Read more about Wendy at:
lonelyplanet.com/members/wendyyanagihara

Jennifer Denniston

North Rim, Travel with Children, Travel with Pets Jennifer caught the travel bug at age nine, when her parents took the family on a 10-week trip through Europe, and has since traveled independently across five continents. She and her husband, a geology professor, spend three or four months every year road-tripping with their daughters Anna (10) and Harper (8). They live in Iowa, where Jennifer earned her Masters degree in American Studies and taught writing at the University of Iowa.

Published by Lonely Planet Publications Pty Ltd
ABN 36 005 607 983
3rd edition – Feb 2012
ISBN 978 1 74179 404 5
© Lonely Planet 2012   Photographs © as indicated 2012
10 9 8 7 6 5 4 3 2 1
Printed in China

Although the authors and Lonely Planet have taken all reasonable care in preparing this book, we make no warranty about the accuracy or completeness of its content and, to the maximum extent permitted, disclaim all liability arising from its use.